DIPLOMATS AT WAR

Miller Center Studies on the Presidency

GUIAN A. MCKEE AND MARC J. SELVERSTONE, EDITORS

Diplomats at War

FRIENDSHIP AND BETRAYAL
ON THE BRINK OF THE VIETNAM CONFLICT

Charles Trueheart

UNIVERSITY OF VIRGINIA PRESS

Charlottesville and London

Published in association with the University of Virginia's
Miller Center of Public Affairs

University of Virginia Press
© 2024 by Charles Trueheart
All rights reserved
Printed in the United States of America on acid-free paper

First published 2024

1 3 5 7 9 8 6 4 2

LIBRARY OF CONGRESS CATALOGING-IN-PUBLICATION DATA

Names: Trueheart, Charles, author.
Title: Diplomats at war : friendship and betrayal on the brink of the Vietnam Conflict /
Charles Trueheart.
Other titles: Friendship and betrayal on the brink of the Vietnam Conflict
Description: Charlottesville : University of Virginia Press, 2024. | Series: Miller Center studies
on the presidency | Includes bibliographical references and index.
Identifiers: LCCN 2023043135 (print) | LCCN 2023043136 (ebook) | ISBN 9780813951287
(hardcover) | ISBN 9780813951294 (ebook)
Subjects: LCSH: United States—Foreign relations—Vietnam. | Vietnam—Foreign relations—
United States. | United States—Foreign relations—1961–1963. | Vietnam War, 1961–1975—
United States. | Trueheart, William C., 1918–1992. | Nolting, Frederick E., Jr., 1911–1989. |
Diplomatic and consular service—United States—History—20th century. |
United States. Foreign Service—Officials and employees—Biography. | Diplomats—
United States—Biography. | Trueheart, Charles, 1951–x Childhood and youth. |
Ngô, Đình Diệm, 1901–1963—Assassination.
Classification: LCC E183.8.V5 T78 2024 (print) | LCC E183.8.V5 (ebook) |
DDC 327.730597—dc23/eng/20230922
LC record available at https://lccn.loc.gov/2023043135
LC ebook record available at https://lccn.loc.gov/2023043136

Cover art: Image of monk, socrates471/shutterstock.com
Cover design: David Fassett

FOR ANNE,
sine qua non

CONTENTS

Illustration gallery follows page 162

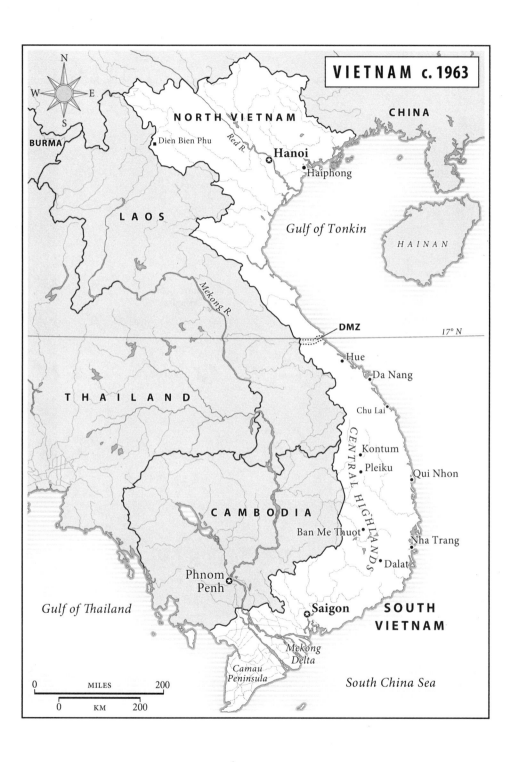

VIETNAM c. 1963

N
W   E
S

BURMA

NORTH VIETNAM

CHINA

Dien Bien Phu

Red R.

Hanoi

Haiphong

LAOS

Gulf of Tonkin

HAINAN

Mekong R.

DMZ

17° N

Hue

Da Nang

THAILAND

Chu Lai

Kontum

CENTRAL HIGHLANDS

Pleiku

Qui Nhon

CAMBODIA

Ban Me Thuot

Nha Trang

Dalat

Phnom Penh

Gulf of Thailand

Saigon

SOUTH VIETNAM

Mekong Delta

Camau Peninsula

South China Sea

0   MILES   200
0   KM   200

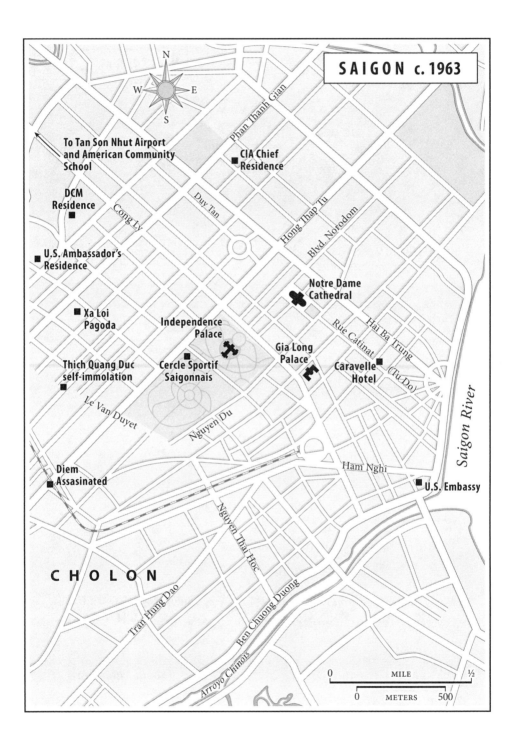

SAIGON c. 1963

N
W · E
S

To Tan Son Nhut Airport
and American Community
School

CIA Chief
Residence

DCM
Residence

Cong Ly

Duy Tan

Hong Thap Tu

Blvd. Norodom

U.S. Ambassador's
Residence

Notre Dame
Cathedral

Xa Loi
Pagoda

Independence
Palace

Hai Ba Trung

Rue Catinat

Gia Long
Palace

Thich Quang Duc
self-immolation

Cercle Sportif
Saigonnais

Caravelle
Hotel

(Tu Do)

Le Van Duyet

Nguyen Du

Saigon River

Ham Nghi

Diem
Assasinated

Nguyen Thai Hoc

U.S. Embassy

CHOLON

Tran Hung Dao

Ben Chuong Duong

Arroyo Chinois

Phan Thanh Gian

0   MILE   ½

0   METERS   500

Prologue

A DEATH IN THE FAMILY is not something you tend to learn about in a newspaper. But that's how I first got the news that Fritz Nolting had died. The item was buried deep in the pages of the *Washington Post* and the *New York Times*. If it had not been a Saturday morning, with more time to spare over breakfast, I might have missed the obituary altogether.

It could not have been otherwise. I had not heard anything about Fritz, let alone from him, in a very long time. Yet since my childhood, few days had passed when I hadn't thought of him, when I hadn't remembered especially those early years in Saigon, the last time our families were together. Now, abruptly, Fritz was gone, and with him one of two keys to a mystery.

The obituaries of Frederick E. Nolting Jr. noted his two years as ambassador to South Vietnam a quarter century before—the high point and low point of his life, about which I knew a good deal already. About the rest of his life, I knew precious little, as I could see from the obituaries. After his resignation from the Foreign Service, at only fifty-two, Nolting had worked for Morgan Guaranty Bank, in Paris and New York, for more years than he had spent as a diplomat. Then he settled in Charlottesville and returned to the bosom of his alma mater, the University of Virginia, to teach. The *Washington Post*'s obituary said a memorial service would take place at his church outside Charlottesville the following Monday morning.

Fritz Nolting was not a blood relative. He was my godfather. He and my father had been close friends since their prewar graduate school days in Charlottesville. They were serious, ambitious young Virginians pointed toward careers as university professors of philosophy. Instead, when the United States went to war in 1941, and like so many other young Americans, Fritz Nolting and Bill Trueheart put on uniforms and served their country. Afterward they were drawn into the burgeoning civil service in postwar Washington. They became diplomats at the dawn of the Cold War.

Their lives, our family lives, continued to intertwine. After Fritz and Bill joined the Foreign Service in the mid-1950s, their first assignments were to Paris, at the US delegation to NATO, where Bill became Fritz's deputy. Then, after John F. Kennedy became president of the United States in 1961, first Nolting and then Trueheart were dispatched to Saigon, Fritz as the US ambassador and Bill as his chosen deputy.

The two young Foreign Service Officers knew Vietnam was riven by a Communist insurgency that had already defeated the French and that their work would be followed at the highest levels in Washington. They were hungry for the challenge and the responsibility. They could not have reckoned that they were on the scene for the opening act of America's Vietnam War, the ten-year cataclysm that would define their generation and mine.

Their assignment in Saigon began in New Frontier optimism and a belief in new doctrines of counterinsurgency. It ended in the bitter demise of the South Vietnamese regime: the military coup d'état of November 1, 1963. That nearly bloodless revolt, sanctioned and encouraged by the Kennedy administration, overthrew the constitutional government of South Vietnam. But the blood that *was* spilled in the coup included that of the country's president and his brother, murdered by machete and machine gun, hands bound behind them, in an armored personnel carrier, by Vietnamese officers.

The November coup was a fateful step. Many historians believe it sealed America's commitment to a decade of war, concluding many years later in its first military defeat. As the coup loomed in the spring and summer and fall of 1963, the Kennedy administration agonized over the viability of the troubled regime in a deepening military stalemate. As it so often is, the debate in Washington and Saigon was about means and ends, principles and priorities and realities. Hindsight makes all this much clearer than it was.

Among many much graver consequences of those decisions, among deeper and broader tragedies that befell the United States, was a sadly private one. The way it all turned out abruptly ended the friendship between Nolting and Trueheart, indeed between the Noltings and the Truehearts. A matter of state had broken a personal bond.

After the summer of 1963, the two men never spoke to one another again. Such was the rupture between them that, for just as long, the matter was rarely mentioned in the Trueheart household. In the way a family carefully avoids referring to a bitter divorce, or a suicide, or a criminal conviction, mine avoided this subject.

At the time of Fritz's passing—on December 14, 1989—I was thirty-eight, living in Washington, working for the *Washington Post*. My first child, Louise, had been born two weeks earlier, a joyous time for her mother and me, and of course for her grandparents. Bill and Phoebe Trueheart, long since retired from the Foreign Service, didn't live far away. It wasn't unusual for me to drop by unannounced on weekends.

When I walked into the house on Hawthorne Place later that Saturday morning, I could see by the look in my mother's eyes that, unsurprisingly, they had read the news too. "You saw that Fritz died," I said, still standing in the front hall, taking off my coat and scarf. My father, standing to greet me in the living room, said they had. A leaden silence followed.

I then said, without preliminaries, what I must have been thinking, and perhaps for a very long time. I said I thought I would go down to Charlottesville to Fritz's memorial service Monday morning. "To represent the family."

My father may have hesitated, but not for more than a second. "Not if you care what *I* think you won't," he said, looking me in the eye. It seems to me he then walked away. I can hear Phoebe saying helplessly, sadly, in the background, "Oh, Bill . . ."

I may have remonstrated. I don't remember. It was a hot blur. I was stunned, even knowing what I knew, or thinking I knew what I knew. I felt embarrassment for my father, pitying him for being in the implacable grip of this wound. Just as keenly I felt my own anger and humiliation—and ignorance.

As I reconstruct it now, the prince (me) had stepped up to take from the old king the burden of the family, to seize the chance to extinguish old animosities. The king was putting the pretender in his place, on a point of honor and loyalty. No such hatchet would be buried until he would be.

Remarkably, maddeningly, my father never spoke a meaningful word to me about the summer of 1963, the most dramatic and painful transit in his life—as it was, and much more so, for Fritz Nolting. It's said that when men come home from military combat, often they don't want to talk about what they went through. That could be the case here. If the laconic Bill referred to the matter at all, which was seldom, he called it "the business with Fritz."

Not long ago I asked my brother, Josh, who was ten months old when we reached Saigon in 1961, what he knew of this breach between the Noltings and the Truehearts, and how he had first learned of it. Josh remembered right away that it was—how else, under the circumstances of an incommunicative father?—by reading a book. *What happened with Fritz?* the teenaged Josh had asked his father, in the 1970s. Bill had said something dismissive, but not entirely disinterested: "It's all in the Halberstam book."

The Best and the Brightest, that is, David Halberstam's sprawling and influential bestseller about the tumbling succession of misjudgments that led the United States into the morass of military conflict in Vietnam. *The Best and the Brightest* captured the war-exhausted zeitgeist of its day, put that phrase into the English language, and made Halberstam famous.

The book was published to considerable acclaim in the late fall of 1972, with conflict still raging in Vietnam and so too in the streets of America. As someone with an obvious interest from the young years I had lived there, and an even more active interest as a college journalist urging an end to the war, I bought the book. I read it avidly, not at first knowing (of course!) that Halberstam's dramatic account of his denouement with Nolting had my father's tacit imprimatur.

The details in the book—and the eerie sensation of seeing one's own surname and father in a work of history—were a revelation to me. They were a source of pride, yes. But also of sadness about the estrangement it chronicled, and the distance between what I read and how little I knew. People I ran into at Christmas in Washington, home from my senior year in college, seemed all to have read it; when I returned to Amherst in January, so had professors and the president of the college. They remembered the pages—not many in this decade-long saga—where my father makes, for Halberstam, a heroic appearance, and Nolting a tragic one.

Halberstam knew my father well, having been the pugnacious young *New York Times* correspondent in Saigon in the crucial years when Trueheart was the second in command at the US embassy, and during the frequent periods when he was in charge in Nolting's absences. Trueheart was among Halberstam's sources there—Nolting couldn't bear him, for one thing—but their relationship was often stormy. Bill suffered ungladly the young reporter's violent tempers over access and protection and admissions of inconvenient truths. There are places in the book where Bill doesn't shine either. But by the evidence of his endorsement to the family (and actual evidence too), Trueheart was a source for *The Best and the Brightest,* which, Bob Woodward–like, has no footnotes or citations.

The book portrays William Trueheart in 1963 as a young Foreign Service Officer "at the fulcrum" of the deepening policy debate in Washington over the course of the struggle against Communist guerrillas. His eyewitness to the chaotic deterioration of the government of President Ngo Dinh Diem led him to "dissent" from official policy. Trueheart, for Halberstam, was "not a likely candidate" for dissent: "Not only had he faithfully followed the official line from the start but he was a Nolting man, brought to Saigon at the ambassador's personal request; the two were old friends and had stayed in very close touch. Nolting was the godfather of both of Trueheart's sons, and Trueheart seemed, if anything, more Nolting than Nolting, a little stiffer at first glance, a product of the same Virginia gentleman school of the Foreign Service."[1] I know what Halberstam means by "stiffer" but would dispute the last phrase. There is no question that Fritz and Bill were Virginians, Foreign Service Officers, and gentlemen, but they were a school of two.

Those pages about the summer of 1963 conclude with a harrowing account of Nolting's ignominious sacking while he was gone from Saigon on a family vacation as the Diem regime began its last downward spiral and Trueheart was in charge at the embassy. When the cashiered ambassador came back to Saigon to pick up the pieces and pack his bags, in Halberstam's telling, Nolting vented his "fury" at Trueheart and retaliated with "a rank charge of disloyalty." Disloyalty was a fighting word for the generation of American diplomats who had survived McCarthyism, as it is for anyone who takes honor seriously. "It almost destroyed Trueheart's career."

My father died in 1992, three years after Fritz. When Neil Sheehan, one of the other American reporters who made his mark in Saigon in 1963, greeted my brother in the receiving line at Bill's memorial service, he told Josh our father "was the bravest Foreign Service Officer I ever knew." One of the two CIA station chiefs in Saigon at the time, John Richardson, said Trueheart was "one of the few high-ranking Americans to leave Vietnam with his integrity intact."[2]

The CIA officer who had preceded Richardson, William Colby, saw it exactly the opposite way. Nolting was the hero: "In the end he lost the battle, but his story is among the more useful, prescient, and honorable of the American role in the Second Indochinese War."[3] In a testimonial to Nolting at the University of Virginia after he died, one of his former colleagues related the matter as Fritz must have framed it for his colleagues: "A longtime friend who was left in charge when he took leave from his post in Vietnam sold their friendship for a bowl of pottage and increased portion of prestige."[4]

The business with Fritz was all about betrayal, and betrayal on multiple levels. Nolting's Vietnam memoir, published the year before he died, is entitled *From Trust to Tragedy,* an allusion to its recounting of the US betrayal of its ally. In Halberstam's ventriloquism of the two men—and in every account Nolting ever gave of this moment—you can hear Nolting's preoccupation with matters of trust and honor, and of his sense of betrayal by his government and, along the way, by his old friend. Nolting spent the rest of his life after Saigon worrying the bone of this disaster and sticking up for principles: We don't overthrow governments. We keep our word to our allies. We are loyal to our friends.

Somewhere lurking behind my father's warning to me about going to Charlottesville for Fritz's memorial service was an analogously principled thing: We don't confuse professionalism with loyalty. We don't repay conscience and duty, and the exigencies of statecraft, with character assassination. *That* is betrayal.

In any case, the enmity still burned in the closing years of my father's own life. The symbolism of his son at his former friend's graveside was intolerable.

I did not go to Charlottesville, not then.

The origin of a war, like the origin of a personal conflict, is almost always murky. Motive and happenstance, memory and ambition, uncertainty and posturing, all curl around one another to create unexpected and uncontrolled outcomes. Looking back, the historian or journalist or memoirist looks for turning points, even if they are nearly infinite and more fluid than any inflection. Yet the summer of 1963, in Washington and Saigon, was one such moment of calculation and hubris that, in hindsight, condemned the United States to a catastrophic ten-year war that cost fifty-eight thousand American lives and more than a million Vietnamese ones, and wrecked, temporarily, both countries. If that's not how it had turned out, the events of 1963 would be less poignant, less pregnant.

The war itself is fifty years gone, but its lessons, especially the lessons of good intentions gone spectacularly awry, persist. When we hear about nation-building today, at least some of us of an age can't *not* think about the consequences of our embrace of Ngo Dinh Diem. When we think about the high price we pay for strategic alliances with distasteful (or even murderous) partners—in Chile, Nicaragua, Afghanistan, Pakistan, Saudi Arabia, Turkey—the case of Diem is a compellingly cautionary tale. When we consider what it takes to make another country do our bidding, we might look at what happened in Saigon in 1963.

Many historians have done so, and with succeeding generations of scholarship and revisionist thinking, the overthrow of the Diem regime in November of that year is regularly cited as a point of no return for the United States as it lurched toward war—a last chance forsaken. A younger generation of American scholars of Vietnam has made the case—the one Nolting made in 1963 and continued to make for the rest of his life—that the US government's dispatch of Ngo Dinh Diem meant there would be no turning back from a deeper involvement in an intractable struggle.

One cannot say for sure. It's possible that had he lived, John F. Kennedy might have withdrawn from Vietnam many years and lives earlier than his successors did. Only—"only"—120 Americans were killed in combat there during the Kennedy years. In his last months of life Kennedy said as much to some associates, wanting, they reported, only a reelection victory behind him to take the politically risky but necessary step. But even Kennedy could not have predicted the political and military quagmire that Vietnam became in 1964 and 1965. Who can know whether his options would have been any more numerous or palatable than those of his two successors?

What is undeniable is that the removal of Ngo Dinh Diem in 1963 constituted what had not been intended but could rather easily have been foreseen. The US instrumentation of the coup, and the installation of a supposedly more compliant client government, constituted explicit and incontrovertible American ownership of the Vietnam conflict. The antique shop warning that if you break it, you bought it, is pertinent here. For reasons not unlike Fritz Nolting's, Vice President Lyndon Johnson had opposed the coup and had been powerless to stop it. Yet it was he who, three weeks later, with Kennedy's murder, became the proprietor—and quickly the prisoner—of its consequences.

Nothing about Vietnam in those days happened in a vacuum. That is worth remembering in this worm's-eye view of a looming catastrophe. The Kennedy administration got off to a terrible start in 1961 with the botched liberation attack on Cuba known as the Bay of Pigs, and then with the young American president's humiliating standoff over Berlin with the Soviet leader, Nikita Khrushchev, in Vienna a few months later. Laos, Vietnam's Communist-prone neighbor, was a constant early strain too. No understanding of Vietnam in the early 1960s is coherent outside this Cold War context in the emerging postcolonial world.

The domestic context is just as powerful. During the climactic months of this Vietnam narrative the American civil rights movement was undergoing its most convulsive moments to date, including the murder of Medgar Evers and the church bombing in Birmingham. While Kennedy and his men were having their most consequential conversations about the fate of Ngo Dinh Diem, outside the windows of the White House immense crowds were marching, and the Reverend Martin Luther King Jr. was delivering his "I Have a Dream" speech.

Irritated by a question about Vietnam during this period, Attorney General Robert Kennedy, the president's brother, snapped, "We've got twenty Vietnams."

Like presidents before and after, John F. Kennedy mistrusted the diplomatic bureaucracy. He chuckled with John Kenneth Galbraith, whom he sent to India as ambassador, over the "elephantiasis" of the State Department.[5] To compensate, the president sought broad and eclectic counsel about thorny problems in ways that have largely disappeared in the twenty-first-century White House. Such missions had the advantage, too, of being good theater, at a minimum conveying a sense that the problem was being studied on the ground, at the highest levels, and very carefully.

To find his way through to wisdom under these pressures, Kennedy turned to a remarkable array of people—all men, as was common enough—whose advice he sought and trusted, even if it was predictably, intentionally, mixed: A former automobile executive, Robert S. McNamara. A swashbuckling former adman and spy, Edward Lansdale. A Canadian-born economist, John Kenneth Galbraith. A maverick general, Maxwell Taylor. An aging Democratic warhorse, Averell Harriman. A Montana professor-politician, Mike Mansfield. A former British colonial adminis-trator, Sir Robert G. K. Thompson. An enigmatic French-born CIA agent, Lucien Conein. A young Wall Street lawyer, Michael V. Forrestal. The president's brother, Robert F. Kennedy. The vice president, Lyndon Johnson. And ultimately the vice-presidential candidate of the Republican Party in 1960, Henry Cabot Lodge. Those are but a few.

In the period leading up to the coup of 1963, all of the above were in Vietnam at least once (and some throughout) to take their own measure of the problem. If the story that follows tracks their visits and insights and reports to the president, it is just as much an account of what it meant to be an American diplomat such as Nolting or Trueheart in a critical posting in late midcentury. This was a time when slow and primitive (to us today) communications and ingrained habits of official confidence guaranteed American diplomats a certain level of autonomy and discretion in exe-cuting US policy in a distant capital. Yet the advice and information that President Kennedy was getting at the source, from Saigon, was no less conflicted than what he was getting from his cabinet and special emissar-ies. But it was coming from men who were strangers to him.

Nolting and Trueheart were nobodies, really. Not yet fifty and some-what randomly selected for their jobs in 1961, they were among the most promising of a cohort of Foreign Service Officers, World War II veterans turned credentialed diplomats. Their perspective was resolutely Euro-centric after years working in Paris, and reflexively anti-Communist. But they were no ideologues. Their view of the world was little different from Kennedy's, for whom they had voted with enthusiasm. Their understand-ing of wars of national liberation and counterinsurgency in postcolonial societies was rudimentary, their familiarity with Asia thin. But they were smart and able, and they spoke French, as did the Vietnamese ruling class after a hundred years of French domination.

Vietnam in 1963 was the dark side of the moon in another way. In those days, two Vietnamese nationalists bestrode the stage. Today, only one is remembered: Ho Chi Minh, the father of his country no less than George Washington, as genuine a twentieth-century nationalist as can be found, and the first leader from anywhere to defeat the greatest military power in the world. Today the city where I lived as a preadolescent bears his name.

But in the 1950s and early 1960s, the leadership of modern Vietnam was still very much a contest. Ho Chi Minh was the doughty challenger, waging a war of attrition through surrogates in the South in a test of wills with another formidable Vietnamese nationalist, Ngo Dinh Diem. Of the two, it's the loser, not the victor, who's at the formal center of this story.

In the generalized haze of memory and received wisdom about what the Vietnam War was "about," there's a tendency to remember mainly what came well after 1963: the long and agonized national debate in America between those who wanted to prosecute the war more aggressively or shrewdly and those who wanted to cut US losses and withdraw with a peace deal. In the mid- and late 1960s, they were called hawks and doves, understood to mean militarists versus peaceniks, or patriots versus apostates.

Hawks and doves were *not* terms of reference in Saigon in 1963. Everyone was a "hawk." Few questioned the threat—Communist subversion abetted by Moscow and Peking—and almost no one questioned the implications of defeat in Vietnam, the serial tumbling of dominoes in the newest theater of the Cold War. Nolting, Trueheart, Halberstam, Sheehan, all of them—at the beginning of 1963 they believed, as Kennedy and most everyone else in Washington did, that the war was worth fighting, a grim necessity, a policy without plausible alternatives. Vietnam furthermore was materializing as Kennedy's chance to put right the blunders of the Bay of Pigs and Vienna, to appear resolute to the Soviet Union and Communist China, and to win reelection to the presidency in 1964.

The real source of friction was not nearly so basic as the wisdom of the objective. Instead, as matters of state so often are, the arguing was about the available means at hand: whether Ngo Dinh Diem, Washington's fulsomely embraced leader, really had the mettle to wage a war against a popular and determined insurgency of fellow Vietnamese; indeed, whether he had the skills and instincts—and the popular support—to lead the country at all. The United States would provide the arms and the economic assistance and then the military personnel in a struggle against North Vietnam's proxy guerrilla forces, backed by Chinese and Russian assistance. What would Diem offer in return? How could he put his house in order by responding to American demands for reform? How could he be made to focus on waging a war that mattered so much to the United States without looking like a lackey of a foreign power, like a hundred generations of Vietnamese leaders before him?

These very questions had frustrated US ambassadors and vexed the

State Department for eight years already. It fell to a couple of Virginians, feeling the hot breath of an anxious president of the United States, to wade into what either Fritz or Bill could have called, in the authentic idiom of their time and heritage, a tar baby.

This is a work of memory hiding inside a work of history. The prelude to the coup of 1963 alone has inspired more than a hundred books and mountains of documents and recordings that scholars have plumbed and enriched with their own discoveries. Nolting, and less often Trueheart, appear in many of them. Today one can even listen to Kennedy and his cabinet discussing events in Vietnam day to day. Nolting speaks there in crucial meetings.

For documentation on Nolting and Trueheart, I faced a peculiar, even paradoxical, problem.[6] My most obvious source had been reticent and self-effacing; I had asked no questions, a psychological point in itself; and since 1992 Bill was no longer with us. But for his part Nolting spoke and wrote often, with the passion of an angry victim and an unsung prophet, about the events here. Nolting's papers are at the University of Virginia, and his writings, speeches, and interviews about all of this are numerous. His widow survives into her second century. For Trueheart, none of this is so. He dismissed his wife's urgings to write it all down.

But there does remain, somewhat miraculously, a priceless personal archive: handwritten letters William Trueheart wrote to his mother in Richmond, Virginia, two or three times *a week* for *forty* years, from the day he left home in 1934 until the day she died in 1976, long after the events covered here. My grandmother saved every letter, in its envelope, in sequence—interspersed by many from Phoebe as well, and from me— in a Miller & Rhoads department store dress box. I regret that in the letters from 1963 Bill says virtually nothing to his mother about the greatest drama of his life, involving a best friend she knew and adored, and precious little else about policy at all. My mother's letters, channeling her husband and recording history in the summer and fall of 1963, are another matter.

Not all of Nolting's papers at the University of Virginia are of an official nature, thank goodness. There is no classified material; that's elsewhere and richly available. The Nolting papers have been pruned, judging by the archivists' dutiful noting of items deleted at the request of the family.

Fritz Nolting was a prodigious and enthusiastic correspondent as a diplomat in Paris. His files are full of dictated letters to his family and friends, many of them about family or financial matters.

I can't fail to mention the eerie sensation I had, in 2017, when I sat down for the first time to go through the Frederick E. Nolting, Jr., Papers at the University of Virginia's Albert and Shirley Small Library. When I opened the first folder in the first document box I happened to request—*Personal Correspondence, 1960*—the top letter on the stack in the folder was from one Charles Trueheart. It was a January 3, 1960, post-Christmas thank-you note that was an unquestioned obligation in my upbringing. Written on teal-blue stationery from the house where we lived then, at 38, Cadogan Place, London, it read in full:

> Dear Mr. Nolting
> Thank you so much for the French books. I hope you have a happy new year.
> Love Charlie.

Pinned to the letter was a carbon of the typed reply from my godfather, a man so thoughtful he replies to a child's thank-you letter:

> Dear Charlie, I enjoyed getting your very nice note. It was very well written and very much to the point. I hope you can still read French books. We had snow here yesterday, and last night the girls and I went sleigh riding. Give my love to your father and mother.[7]

Bill Trueheart was just seventy-four when he died in 1992. Seventeen years later, in 2009, when Phoebe Trueheart joined him, that long-ago impasse over Fritz's memorial service still festered. I felt freed to track down Bittie Nolting's address in Charlottesville, dusting off a friendship that had lain dormant for a half century. I wrote her a note to tell her about my mother's passing, only to discover that Phoebe had corresponded with Bittie shortly before she died.

Some months later, following a warm note back from Bittie, I heard from her youngest daughter, Jane. She was the one closest to me in age, a dear friend from our early days in Paris and then Saigon, where we shared a passion for stamp collecting. I had not seen or heard from Jane in forty years. Until her death in March 2023, she lived alone not far from her mother in Charlottesville. Jane's letter to me in 2010 was long and rambling and anecdotal, nine handwritten pages covering an odyssey of travel in Europe with her daughter more than a decade earlier. But the very first words of her letter were, as her father put it, very much to the point.

> It was good of you to communicate. I was sorry to hear of Phoebe's depar-
> ture from this world but had felt touched by the fact that she had taken the
> trouble the previous Christmas to re-open communications with mama. I
> wish you had communicated with Daddy over all those years. It was your
> father he could not forgive, not you. He could have used an active Godson,
> especially in his later years. Everything was so much harder for him after
> his failure to deter the murder of Diem, but he valiantly continued to do the
> right thing and never quit being the best, not in a self-aggrandizing way,
> but just carrying onward with a very heavy weight as more and more of
> the things he held dear just fell away from him. *En meme temps il est devenu
> de plus en plus mal-chanceux* [At the same time he became more and more
> unlucky], which didn't help much either. It was hard to witness.[8]

Thus began my own modest reconciliation with the surviving members of the Nolting family. Presumably this is in contravention of my father's wishes. I would imagine this book is too.

1

★ ★ ★

Legends of the Fall

VIETNAM WOULD GROW TO command most of America's attention and resources and passions in the decade to come. But its
weight on the foreign policy agenda in January 1961 was surpassingly light. President Dwight D. Eisenhower, in his handoff conversation
with President-elect John F. Kennedy, had not even brought up the subject. Eisenhower focused on hotter issues, Cuba and Berlin and the Soviet
Union; the Cold War was on. He did touch briefly on Laos, which was
descending into political and military chaos along the Vietnamese border.

Vietnam came up immediately anyway. When Walt Rostow, the new
president's deputy national security adviser, brought Kennedy the latest
report on the situation, the president was impatient: "I've only got half
an hour today." Rostow told him he had to read it. "All of it?" By Rostow's
account, Kennedy proceeded to read the document in his presence, taking
his time. At the end, he looked up and said, "This is the worst one we've
got, isn't it?"[1]

John F. Kennedy—providentially, perhaps—needed no general briefing on Vietnam. On Capitol Hill he was what passed for an expert and a
quotable champion of the cause: that is, American support for an independent, democratic, non-Communist bastion to thwart a revolutionary
insurrection fueled by Communists. Kennedy had visited Vietnam as a
thirty-four-year-old congressman in 1951, with his brother Bobby and
sister Jean along. Such was his prominence even then that Kennedy was
greeted at the airport by Bao Dai, the puppet emperor, himself. Keenly
interested in France's protracted struggle with the Communist Viet Minh,
Kennedy spent time with a French general, who flew the Kennedys north
to witness the battlefield action and who was confident about prospects
for victory. Kennedy was dubious, especially after spending time with the

Associated Press's Seymour Topping, a budding expert on Asia, and with Foreign Service Officer Edmund Gullion at the US embassy, both bearish observers of the impending deluge.[2]

As a senator not long afterward, Kennedy spoke stoutly—presciently, in some respects—about the perils of American military intervention to rescue the French from defeat. Kennedy had the struggle about right, long before he became president and had to deal with it: "No amount of American military assistance in Indo-China can conquer an enemy which is everywhere, and at the same time nowhere, 'an enemy of the people' which has the sympathy and covert support of the people."[3]

Against Franklin Roosevelt's hopes and private commitments, the United States had acquiesced to the return of French rule in Indochina at the end of World War II. France's economic stability, and its political cooperation with Washington in the new mutual security arrangements in Europe, were pressing priorities. With the same wariness that Kennedy would feel throughout his presidency, President Eisenhower with bipartisan support had financed the French war effort against the Viet Minh until the bitter end. But he had refused to step in at the critical moment, just before the humiliating French defeat by the Viet Minh at Dien Bien Phu in May 1954.

Yet two months later, after the Geneva Accords that ended the First Indochina War, the United States inherited the struggle, lifted by America's patronizing sense of superiority over the French, who warned the Americans of the quagmire they were wading into. Senator Kennedy, too, had come around to embrace the "theory" that would dominate all the decisions to come: if the first domino fell, it would topple the neighboring ones. In 1956, unblocking a string of metaphors, he said Vietnam was not just "a proving ground for democracy in Asia" but, rather, "the keystone of the arch, the finger in the dike. Burma, Thailand, India, Japan, the Philippines and obviously Laos and Cambodia are among those whose security will be threatened if the red tide of Communism overflowed into Vietnam." Then Kennedy added the notion of geopolitical paternity: "If we are not the parents of little Vietnam, then surely we are the godparents. We presided at its birth, we gave assistance to its life, we helped to shape its future."[4]

The Geneva Accords divided Vietnam according to the reality on the ground, the north dominated by Ho Chi Minh's victorious Viet Minh forces, the south headed by a quasi-monarch, Emperor Bao Dai, a quis-ling of long standing who spent much of his life in dissolution on the Cote d'Azur. The real new power in the south lay—prospectively—with the appointed prime minister, a long-ago civil servant from a well-to-do Catholic family near Hue, in the central highlands.

A Messiah without a Message

Stately, plump Ngo Dinh Diem was a most peculiar American client, the kind of local eccentric who springs seemingly from nowhere to vex the great powers.

When he stepped off the plane in Saigon in June 1954 to assume his new duties, he had been in exile for four years and out of political of-fice for twenty. In younger years, Diem—pronounced *Ziem*—had held important positions as a promising member of the mandarinate, a corps of high-end civil servants who ran the machinery of Vietnam on behalf of the Paris-based factory owners. He became the colony's interior minister at thirty-two but was stunned to discover that the French had no inten-tion of ceding real power or opening the way to Vietnamese autonomy. In an act of principle that became part of his early identity, Diem withdrew from public life. He rejected offers to be prime minister twice, once by the French and once by the Japanese, who had occupied Vietnam with Vichy connivance during World War II. The third time Diem found it propitious to accept. He always believed that he had the "mandate of heaven" to lead his country—a Confucian concept.

Diem's ambitions—his calling, as he saw it—to return as the providen-tial leader of an independent Vietnam had been undisguised during his years in self-imposed exile. The United States, for its part, was drawn not just to his anti-Communist credentials and plausible political credibility but to his religious faith. Diem was a Roman Catholic from a long line of prominent Vietnamese Catholics and was himself a onetime seminarian with a monastic bent. Two of his years of exile had been at Maryknoll Seminaries in New Jersey and New York, where he joined the other adepts in prayer, and in such menial tasks as washing floors and taking out the garbage.[5] Only months before he returned to lead Vietnam, Diem took steps to enter a Benedictine monastery in Belgium, more evidence to his acolytes of his self-abnegation and humility. There was an otherworldly quality to Ngo Dinh Diem. For a nationalist, he was a singular figure. "Of his own choice he had denied himself a normal family life, seeking emotional satisfaction instead in an extreme form of religious contemplation which . . . isolated him from the world," said an American who first met him in the mid-1950s. "He had never fired a rifle in anger, never fought with his hands for anything, however strong his principles, yet he came to a country torn by war. He had no organized popular support. A vast majority of his countrymen had never heard of him."[6]

Diem was highly educated, strictly principled, personally ascetic, divinely inspired, pseudodemocratic. Strange as he was, and there being no viable alternatives who could be agreed upon, Diem was anointed the man destined to lead postcolonial Vietnam into self-sufficiency and self-government and, for good measure, military victory against the latent Communist insurgency.

With significant American help, Diem established power in the supposedly temporary southern zone, quickly orchestrating a plebiscite to replace the feckless emperor. He garnered 98 percent of the vote, including two hundred thousand more votes in Saigon than there were registered voters. More boldly yet, he set about crushing religious sects and gangsters that had flourished in the fading years of the French presence. He surprised even his detractors, who were numerous, and who had included the US secretary of state, John Foster Dulles. Shortly thereafter Diem abrogated the Accords to hold elections throughout Vietnam in 1956, knowing he would lose them to Ho Chi Minh's Viet Minh by hook or crook. Washington, all realpolitik, didn't see things differently and looked the other way.

Diem had guts and wile, it seemed, but to an American journalist in Saigon at the time, and to many more later, "he revealed himself quickly as a humorless, egotistical, incredibly stubborn perfectionist, who refused to act on any question, however trivial, without exhaustive meditation and ideal conditions. He was neurotically suspicious of everyone except his family, refused advice, refused to delegate power. He was a messiah with a persecution complex."[7] The deputy chief of the US mission in Saigon in 1954, Robert McClintock, put it slightly differently. He called him "a messiah without a message."[8]

Among the journalists and writers who flocked to Saigon to learn more about this postcolonial struggle was the novelist Graham Greene. One of the articles he published about his 1955 visit painted this indelible and prescient portrait of the new leader:

> Diem is separated from the people by cardinals and police cars with wailing sirens and foreign advisers when he should be walking in the rice fields unprotected learning the hard way how to be loved and obeyed—the two cannot be separated. One pictured him sitting there in the Norodom Palace, sitting with his blank, brown gaze, incorruptible, obstinate, ill-advised, going to his weekly confession, bolstered up by his belief that God is always on the Catholic side, waiting for a miracle. The name I would write under his portrait is Patriot Ruined by the West.[9]

John F. Kennedy was not alone among American politicians, and leading Catholics, who were well acquainted with Diem and became his influential champions. Those drawn with Kennedy into the influential domestic lobby called American Friends of Vietnam included Supreme Court Justice William O. Douglas; Francis Cardinal Spellman, archbishop of New York; historian Samuel Eliot Morison; publishing moguls Henry Luce and Whitelaw Reid; and a bipartisan host of prominent US politicians.

Diem was that rare chief of state, especially from an undeveloped country of just fourteen million people, accorded full honors on a visit to the United States, in May 1957. President Eisenhower met him at the airport, an exceptional honor, and rode into Washington with him in an open car as crowds cheered the motorcade. Diem spoke (in his imperfect English) before a joint session of Congress. A ticker-tape parade in New York drew 250,000 spectators. The *Saturday Evening Post* dubbed him the "mandarin in a sharkskin suit who's upsetting the Reds' timetable." *Life* magazine captured the moment, and America's eternally rosy optimism, with a long and admiring feature that proclaimed Diem "The Tough Miracle Man of Vietnam"—just the encomium President Eisenhower had bestowed.[10]

Through this visit Diem was anointed as a symbol of the new battlefields in the Cold War, the conjunction of postcolonial independence movements and strategic alliances in zones of revolutionary conflict.[11] American support for the Diem regime was not merely rhetorical and symbolic. By 1957, the United States was shouldering the entire cost of the South Vietnamese armed forces, most other government spending, and nearly 90 percent of all imports. This led one group of analysts to the grim conclusion that South Vietnam was becoming "a permanent mendicant" wholly dependent on foreign assistance rather than popular support: "American aid had built a castle on sand."[12]

Ugly Americans

Notwithstanding the official fanfare and accolades for Diem, Vietnam was little known to most Americans in those days. Yet as flyspecks go, the country was not entirely obscure. By the time Kennedy became president, two significant personal American legends had sprung from the looming Vietnam saga already. These two were legends with whom Fritz Nolting and Bill Trueheart were quite familiar, and into whose train they were swept. One legend was like fireworks, dazzling and evanescent. The other was more like an orbiting planet, often out of sight, never gone.

The first and ultimately the lesser of the legends was Tom Dooley. He was not the same Tom Dooley of song, who hung down his head in shame. Dr. Thomas Dooley was a young American physician who was dispatched to Vietnam in 1954 to help with one of the most significant humanitarian movements of the decade.

The Geneva Accords, dividing Vietnam "temporarily" at the 17th parallel, permitted a grace period to allow the free flow of people from north to south, or south to north, pending the elections that never came. Refugees moved much more numerously from north to south. The consequences of this dual migration were momentous. On one side, it bolstered the Catholic population in the south, where their fortunes were ostensibly protected and improved under a new government dominated by Catholics. On the other, it afforded Ho Chi Minh's government a perfect opportunity to organize a sleeper infrastructure of eight thousand to ten thousand sympathetic cadres who stayed behind. The migration also repatriated to the north Viet Minh cadres intimately familiar with the south and tied to its family networks.

This massive resettlement of nearly a million Vietnamese—the southbound one was called, by Americans, Passage to Freedom—was orchestrated with the kind of assistance that only the United States could muster and had an interest in assuring. American (and French and British) ships and aircraft were pressed into service, and American personnel dispatched to oversee the transshipment and resettlement of refugees. A twenty-six-year-old US Navy lieutenant and physician, Tom Dooley was among them. His best-selling 1956 book about his experiences, *Deliver Us from Evil,* ghosted by a journalist named William Lederer, was the introduction to Vietnam for millions of Americans who read it first in abridged form in *Reader's Digest,* then the biggest-circulating publication in the world.

With his stirring tales of humanitarian rescue and the flight of the refugees from Communist oppression, and his terrifying portrait of the bestial and bloodthirsty Viet Minh guerrillas, Dooley helped to frame Vietnam in Manichean terms that would dominate the discourse to come. Dooley's horror stories only confirmed the widespread perception, memorably articulated by evangelist Billy Graham, that communism was "inspired, directed, and motivated by the devil himself, who has declared war on Almighty God."[13]

While there is little doubt of Dooley's convictions and patriotism, it transpired later (not much later, internally) that much of what Dooley wrote about his own exploits was invented or exaggerated, and what he said of the Viet Minh's torture techniques preposterous. That's for one. For another, from the day he arrived he was serving not just as a humanitarian doctor outside his borders but sub rosa as a US intelligence asset, reporting on the people he was resettling.[14]

Dooley's story, which captivated so many, allowed Vietnam to shimmer into American consciousness in the 1950s and to take the form it would hold until it didn't: a doughty anti-Communist nation forging its independence against another "red" Asian menace. It was Korea all over again, the Asian land war just ended, with the bad guys in the north and the good guys in the south.

Though lesser known to the public, an even more important Vietnam legend of the 1950s was Edward G. Lansdale, an undercover intelligence officer. Recruited from the US Air Force after World War II, the former public relations executive from Southern California joined the precursor to the CIA and began to implement his skills, and the agency's, at psychological warfare, or psyops. These were new tools and theories of bending susceptible adversaries (and allies) to the dictates of US national security interests, and they presupposed something high-minded: a deep cultural understanding of non-European societies theretofore unfamiliar to the United States.

Lansdale was a quick study and always full of clever ideas. He was assigned first to the Philippines to deal with an insurrection of Communist Huks that threatened the stability of the elected government. Lansdale befriended a charismatic Filipino leader named Raymond Magsaysay and, using courtship and spycraft, helped the government succeed in crushing the Huks, shortly thereafter installing Magsaysay in power in a well-oiled election. Such were Lansdale's successes in delivering overwhelming majorities to his Southeast Asian clients that he was known as "Colonel Landslide."

Lansdale's next assignment was Vietnam, where it was expected he would work his magic on America's reluctant choice to lead the new nation. Lansdale was there, undercover in the first US military mission to Vietnam, when Ngo Dinh Diem returned from exile in 1954, summoned by Bao Dai to become prime minister. Lansdale noted in a report home that Diem left a deflated impression on the crowds who thronged to watch him pass on the way into town from the airport, riding invisibly in a car with darkened windows.[15] Yet Lansdale was a committed Diemist. He was at Diem's side throughout the difficult first two years as the novice president worked to establish power in the vacuum of leadership bequeathed by the French after their exodus.

Lansdale also was a driving force in the refugee exodus of 1954, when Dr. Dooley found his fame. While the US Navy assembled the sealift, Lansdale worked with the French on an airlift and pushed for the newcomers to be integrated into village life rather than held in resettlement camps. He also did psyops, including feeding Dr. Dooley some of the anti-Communist nonsense—chopsticks stuck in the ears of children—that he put in his book.

The US Air Force colonel, his cover ever since he had left ordinary service, had a personal hand in rescuing Diem when Secretary of State Dulles, in 1955, egged on by the US special envoy in Saigon, General J. Lawton Collins, began to entertain the first serious doubts about whether the United States had chosen the right leader for South Vietnam. Lansdale had practically moved into the presidential palace and was at Diem's side when he crushed the sects and the gangsters who ruled in Saigon, forcing Dulles to retract an order to let Diem go.

Lansdale was a facile writer, and all of his ingenuity was couched in a homespun philosophy of American can-doism and a respect for humankind. "We don't want to be like the French . . . brave men whose heroism and weapons and numbers were not enough—licked by a local army wearing tennis shoes and pajamas," Lansdale said. He eagerly professed his "strong feelings about how to fight Communism: by giving the guy in the street or the rice paddy something he can believe in so strongly that he will defend it with everything he has. . . . It's old-fashioned Americanism, representative government, an armed force which protects the people as brothers, all men created equal."[16]

In those late Eisenhower years, Ed Lansdale received the official accolade of a legend: reincarnation as a fictional character. He was the model for one of the principal figures in a famous Vietnam novel of the 1950s.

That book is *not* Graham Greene's superb *The Quiet American,* as is sometimes supposed. Greene himself, though in Saigon during Lansdale's first days there, claimed never to have heard of him when he wrote the book. Still, Greene's naïve American do-gooder, Alden Pyle, uncannily captures something of Lansdale's sunny disposition and misguided good intentions. (In a twist, when *The Quiet American* was turned into a movie in 1958, it was Lansdale who helped persuade its prominent director, Joseph L. Mankiewicz, to rewrite the story to pro-American specifications and outcomes, unashamedly twisting Greene's cynical story to the rosy political messaging of the Department of State and the American Friends of Vietnam. Greene abhorred the movie.)

Rather, the best-selling novel in question is *The Ugly American.* One of its authors was Eugene Burdick, who would go on to co-write the nuclear-age yarn *Fail-Safe;* the other was William Lederer, the journalist who had ghosted Tom Dooley's hyped-up account of Viet Minh atrocities.

The Ugly American is a series of loosely connected fictional vignettes set in and around a Southeast Asian country called Sarkhan. The book developed the idea of an American foreign policy and anti-Communist strategy based not on military might but democratic values, not on the American way but on indigenous sensitivity. It captured the new idea of "winning hearts and minds" to defeat Communist insurgencies and build free nations. This was the cartoon version of a serious new line of thought in strategic thinking about unconventional warfare that would see its modern apotheosis in the long struggle ahead.

Lansdale materialized in *The Ugly American* as "Colonel Edwin Barnum Hillandale." But Lansdale's ideas more closely resonate with the Ugly American of the title: Homer Atkins is a selfless retired engineer from the

American heartland who lives humbly with his wife among Sarkhanese peasants and teaches them the arts of self-sufficiency, notably how to turn a bicycle into a water pump.

Homer's physical ugliness was meant to be ironic, as he was actually the virtuous figure in the book. With the cussedness of popular misapprehensions, the term *Ugly American* promptly entered the lexicon to mean precisely the opposite of the authors' ironic meaning,[17] to mean instead the overweening know-it-all of anti-American caricature. Even Fritz Nolting, who knew better, worried jokily to a colleague in the State Department before heading to Saigon that he didn't want to come off sounding to the Vietnamese like an "Ugly American."[18]

The Ugly American, a bestseller for seventy-eight weeks, was praised for its fresh insights and sharp portraits of the challenges facing the postcolonial world, and the interplay between economic development and political struggle. The book "was accepted well into the 1960s as an example of serious political thought," observed Neil Sheehan.[19] John F. Kennedy was so seized with its importance that he ordered copies for each of his ninety-five Senate colleagues, once again staking out his own expertise and concern about Vietnam. The book was said to have inspired Kennedy to create the Peace Corps.

It can't have escaped anyone reading the book in the late 1950s—it was on Bill and Phoebe's night tables—that the principal objects of derision and ridicule are the American diplomats in Sarkhan, clueless in their arrogance and insularity, blind to the new world around them, and doomed to fail.

The Mandarin Monarchy

The sobering Vietnam report Walt Rostow had made Kennedy read in the first days of his presidency was written by . . . Edward G. Lansdale. Through the late 1950s, back in Washington, Colonel Lansdale had stayed in touch with his friend Ngo Dinh Diem. He watched with alarm as neither US persuasiveness nor his executive skills had proved fruitful in reversing the guerrilla insurgency supported by North Vietnam, which had intensified significantly in 1959. In an attack on a remote military camp in July, two American military advisers were killed, the first US casualties of the Second Indochina War.

After a period of retrenchment following Diem's accession to power, and goaded by impatient younger leaders, Ho Chi Minh now made explicit his intention to bring down the Saigon regime by military force ("to end the plight of the poor and miserable people in the South" and "defeat the wicked policy of American imperalists and their puppets").[20] Ngo Dinh Diem was dubbed "My-Diem," which means "American Diem." Emboldened and shrewdly led, well-supplied with captured French and American weaponry, guerrilla forces escalated their attacks on South Vietnamese military installations, terrorizing the populace by executing Diem's agents in the villages. In the closing days of 1960, Hanoi proclaimed its new organization in the south, the National Liberation Front. Its armed forces were known from then on as the Viet Cong.

With Kennedy not yet inaugurated, in the first days of January 1961, Lansdale had undertaken another trip to Vietnam. He called on President Diem and helped him pick up the pieces from a very bad year. Eversolicitous, he brought the mandarin president a hand-carved mahogany desk from a Washington department store into which had been screwed a brass plaque reading, "To the Father of His Country, Ngo Dinh Diem."

Lansdale listened sympathetically as Diem talked about, or around, two developments that had shaken his government, one peaceful, one violent, in the year just concluding. Together these events had deepened the mistrust between the United States and its embattled client. The icy relationship that ensued was the immediate foreground to the mission Nolting and Trueheart took on.

In April 1960, outraged by sham legislative elections the summer before, and the arrest of the lone candidate to have defeated a government-backed candidate, a group of eighteen Vietnamese intellectuals unaffiliated with the Diem regime (and not yet in jail) issued a blistering manifesto. It decried all the ills that beset Vietnam, from arbitrary arrests to economic stagnation, from bureaucratic paralysis to a muzzled press, from a toothless legislature to an anemic military. The manifesto also alluded to the most sensitive issue of all: the concentration of authority and decision-making in the Ngo family.

The dissidents became known as the Caravelle Group, named for the site of their press conference at Saigon's newest and tallest hotel. The world was able to read about the demands, but not a word of it was disseminated in Vietnam. Diem pretended to ignore the manifesto, but the United States took notice. American diplomats in Saigon had been reporting the same grievances. It was obvious that support for the Diem government, at least among the middle class and the urban populations, was eroding. In the southern Delta and elsewhere in the Vietnamese hinterland, the government was hemorrhaging control to the Viet Cong, who were believed to control most of the countryside outside the cities. The long-simmering concerns about the regime's capacity to win the armed struggle began to spread more generally to its capacity to govern. The former would depend on the latter.[21]

The second shock of 1960 came on November 11, 1960, when two decorated Vietnamese paratroopers, army colonels who were close to Diem, launched a misbegotten coup d'état. Five paratroop battalions succeeded in taking Saigon's airport, the military headquarters, and the radio station, before surrounding the presidential palace, where Diem's security forces held their ground. Diem called the American ambassador, Elbridge Durbrow, and asked for help. Durbrow turned him down. There ensued a standoff, as Diem and his brother Ngo Dinh Nhu stalled for time in a subterranean bunker and called in loyal battalions from the field.

There's some evidence that the timing of the coup attempt anticipated the new administration in Washington; if successful, it would have offered President Kennedy a clean slate in Vietnam. But the plotters had not thought things through. Cowed by President Diem's personal stature, whatever his shortcomings, in tense negotiations they were willing to let him stay in power under certain conditions. Diem put his prowess as a talker to lifesaving use. He readily promised reforms and free elections, vowed to free the press and the prisoners, and haggled over cabinet choices with the "revolutionary council." He taped a personal vow of his extraordinary concessions for national broadcast.

But by the second day of the revolt, the tide turned. Reinforcements including troops led by another colonel, Nguyen Van Thieu, much later president of South Vietnam, repulsed the paratroop battalions and rescued the president, and the coup collapsed. When they met in January, Diem showed Lansdale the damage inflicted by paratrooper fire on his private quarters in the palace.

Ngo Dinh Diem had proved a shrewd adversary and brought off another of his miracles, but no one was reassured. He had been betrayed by the elite of his armed forces—and, he believed, by the United States as well. America's reluctance to enter the fray in November was read at the palace as US support for the coup. Indeed, its success would not have displeased some in the embassy who had already lost patience.

The abrasive Durbrow—on instructions from Washington, needless to point out—had been putting pressure on Diem to carry out the very reforms embodied in the Caravelle manifesto. This was the very wish list that had been part of US policy in Vietnam to one degree or another from the outset. It would continue to be until—and indeed well after—the end of the Diem regime.

One of the sharpest demands of the Caravelle Group and the coup-minded colonels was at the heart of public antagonism toward the regime in Saigon. From a distance the American demand seems audacious if not outrageous, and it was no less so when it came from the unloved Ambassador Durbrow himself in his last approaches to President Diem. His "suggestion" was both simple and radioactive: that the president find a way to remove Ngo Dinh Nhu, his most influential adviser and closest brother. Speaking to Diem "as a straight Dutch uncle," as Durbrow put it, in September 1960 the ambassador proposed that a suitable diplomatic posting or academic fellowship abroad be found for Nhu.[22] President Diem was more than irritated and dismissed the idea. The aborted coup against his regime followed by just a few weeks. Diem and Nhu couldn't help making the connection.

For the United States, there was no treating with Diem without appreciating the spell his brother cast. Brother Nhu, as the Americans called him, had been at Diem's side during the wilderness years, and then in the passage to power, as his political fixer, his house theoretician, his spine-stiffener, his Rasputin. A French-trained intellectual and former archivist at the Central Library in Hanoi, over the years he had developed grandiose ideas and a governing philosophy, "personalism," adapted from French antecedents to Vietnamese purposes, that sought to reconcile the tension between collective action and individual autonomy. No one quite understood personalism, though many serious people have tried.[23]

To go with his ineffable construct, Nhu accumulated and wielded real power, the kind for which Diem had no time, taste, or skill. Nhu was a supple political operator with working ties to the CIA dating from the 1940s.[24] Under Diem he ran Vietnam's Republican Youth, the Blue Shirts, modeled on Hitler's Brown Shirts, who could be used as spies and enforcers. He ran the president's political party, Can Lao, where initiation ceremonies included kneeling and kissing a portrait of Diem. Most significantly for the events to follow, Nhu closely oversaw the CIA-funded secret police. Though he had no title other than "Counselor to the President," at one time Nhu commanded thirteen different security agencies with extrajudicial powers to arrest, imprison, or execute, and a record of repression that included secret gulags and the torture and elimination of political opponents.[25]

The Americans had reason to believe Brother Nhu was also mixed up in criminal syndicates, and probably addicted to opium too. By his proximity to Diem and his exercise of power behind the curtain, Nhu could not be ignored. His weekly séances with the US CIA station chief were a mutually useful arrangement, though the exclusive channel was a sensitive one for an ambassador, and the station chief, to manage.

For the broader public, however, and the US government, Ngo Dinh Nhu crystallized the uncomfortable fact that President Diem headed a family clan with virtually autocratic powers in a newly, and still ostensibly, democratic Republic of Vietnam. The clan's alienation from the population was underscored by its adhesion to Catholicism, a religious minority predating the French colonial era in Indochina but much enhanced by it. Another Ngo brother was Archbishop of Hue. Yet another brother was the political capo of central Vietnam. A fourth one was Vietnam's ambassador in London.

Finally, Ngo Dinh Nhu had married Tran Le Xuan (Tears of Spring), a high-born northern Buddhist who had once been imprisoned by the Viet Minh, and who converted to Catholicism upon her marriage into the Ngo family. Now, as the bachelor president's sister-in-law, Madame Nhu served as the First Lady of South Vietnam. She, her husband, and their four young children lived with Diem in the vast presidential palace that once housed French governors-general. There they took their meals together, and Madame Nhu served as the hostess at official functions. She cultivated a political identity of her own as a member of parliament and head of the Women's Solidarity Movement (to go with her husband's Republican Youth movement of male Diem devotees and thugs). Extending the reach of the extended royal family, Madame Nhu's father and mother were, respectively, the South Vietnamese envoys in Washington and at the United Nations.

By 1960 Madame Nhu had become notorious in Saigon for blue laws she championed and browbeat her brother-in-law into promulgating. Like the convert of caricature, she was determined to be more "Catholic" than anyone. Her decrees prohibited such familiar bêtes noires as prostitution and gambling, contraception and divorce. But also cockfights, fortune-telling, fighting fish, underwire bras, dancing, "sentimental" songs, and "fraternizing" (it was Americans she had in mind). These statutes also proscribed polygamy in a country where it was common, and "spiritual-ism and occultism" in a country where religious sects and practices pro-liferated. Saigon, a cosmopolitan city ruled and made laissez-faire by the French for a century, was unaccustomed to such official standards of prudence.

Madame Nhu, aka the "Dragon Lady," kept a high profile with her public screeds and harangues, and American correspondents found her reliably quotable and vicious, to say nothing of photogenic. Her gender in a day when women were still a novelty in the circles of statecraft—Eva Perón had only just preceded her on the stage—also made her irresistible copy. In the peculiar context of Ngo Dinh Diem, who had taken a vow of chastity and was said never to have had sexual relations with anyone, Madame Nhu's intimacy with the chief of state, and power over him, was all the more absorbing.

Many Westerners in Saigon were struck by the ruling family's Shake-spearean vibe: the self-righteous, ascetic, roly-poly king; the gaunt, sinis-ter, scheming brother behind the throne; and beguiling them, prodding them, shaming them, the tiny, sylphlike, stiletto-heeled Madame Nhu. A Buddhist leader once described her as the "Vietnamese Lady Macbeth. She and her husband want to kill the King."[26]

Feeling embattled and more suspicious than ever, the Ngo brothers were in no mood to be acquiescent when Ambassador Durbrow returned to the palace in late 1960 to ask agreement on a new counterinsurgency plan worked out by the US embassy in Saigon. Written by the tough-minded embassy political counselor Joseph Mendenhall, the plan recommended changes in the command structure of the Vietnamese armed forces and intelligence agencies, and a consequent dilution of the authority Diem and Nhu wielded. Diem was infamous for his micromanagement of—well, everything, including military deployments, down to the battlefield level. Diem hated casualties because they made him lose face, so it is little wonder that officers in the field did everything to avoid military engagement with the Viet Cong.

To win Diem's favor for reforms, Durbrow endured the president's monologues during three or four meetings of four to six hours each. The president offered only stiff promises to think matters over. "He didn't agree with any of it, basically, but he didn't throw me out or didn't try to change the subject," Durbrow recalled.[27] Mendenhall put matters more bluntly: "It showed that he had learned nothing . . . and it became increasingly obvious to me that Diem himself would have to go if we had any hope of winning the war."[28]

Diem in any case was waiting Durbrow out, as were the ambassador's new Washington overseers. "Durbrow should relax with Diem from here on out and leave the arm-twisting to men with fresh capital," Walt Rostow told President Kennedy. Diem for his part hoped the new administration in Washington would send a more positive US interlocutor to take over following his reelection in April for a second term as president of South Vietnam.

2

★ ★ ★

Assignment Saigon

E DWARD LANSDALE'S BRACING REPORT to President Kennedy in January 1961 challenged him to treat Vietnam "as a combat area of the Cold War." The picture it painted was alarming: "The Viet Cong have the initiative and most of the control over the region from the jungled foothills of the High Plateau north of Saigon all the way south down to the Gulf of Siam, excluding the big-city area of Saigon-Cholon." As for Ngo Dinh Diem, his old friend reported, unsurprisingly, that he was "still the only Vietnamese with executive ability and the required determination to be an effective president. If the next American to talk to President Diem would have the good sense to see him as a human being who has been through a lot of hell for years—and not as an opponent to be beaten to his knees—we would start regaining our influence with him in a healthy way." The negative reference was to the "tired" ambassador, Elbridge Durbrow. He should be replaced, Lansdale advised, with someone who displayed "marked leadership talents, who can make the Country Team function harmoniously and spiritually, who can influence Asians through understanding them sympathetically, who is alert to the power of Mao Tse Tung tactics now being employed to capture Vietnam, and who is dedicated to feasible and practical means to defeat those Communist tactics."[1]

The man Lansdale had in mind for the job, it was obvious to many who read the report, was himself. He was a Kennedy kind of guy. The new president was an avid reader of Ian Fleming, the creator of James Bond, and had developed a natural affinity for the flair and derring-do exhibited by Lansdale in the gray 1950s. Kennedy also was enamored of the new "science" of counterinsurgency. Before the term *asymmetrical war* was coined, President Kennedy understood that that's what he was facing in Vietnam and that Lansdale seemed to have a handle on it.

Colonel Lansdale was invited by Secretary of Defense Robert McNamara to join a high-level White House meeting on January 28, 1961. Kennedy invited Lansdale to share the essentials of his written report with the august men who would be dealing with the Vietnam problem for the next thirty months, and some—Vice President Johnson, Secretary of State Rusk, and McNamara—for much, much longer.

What about Durbrow, Kennedy asked Lansdale when he finished his report. "You're the president and you need the truth," Lansdale responded. "He's a very ill man. His judgment's impaired by his very frail condition." Durbrow had developed impetigo, leaving his mouth covered in scabs, which he attempted to disguise with a moustache he himself called "ugly." Back in 1954, Lansdale had successfully engineered the removal of Donald Heath as the US ambassador, so this flick at the incumbent was a practiced tactic.[2]

Kennedy surprised Lansdale by popping another question: "Did Dean Rusk tell you I want you to be ambassador to Vietnam?" Lansdale was silent at first. "It would be a great honor," he recalled answering in two oral histories.[3] Secretary of State Rusk was more than just surprised by Kennedy's sally. Usually a guarded, patient man, Rusk was furious. Lansdale was not just—or very simply not—a "regular military officer." He was a spy, and more than that, infamous for being a non–team player, singing his own tune, "a lone wolf and operator . . . flamboyant" in the words of another senior official at State.[4] Lansdale's closeness to Diem, paradoxically, could easily be a handicap, not just an entrée if the situation turned worse. The idea was dropped, even as Lansdale hovered over Vietnam like a ghost for years to come.

As Kennedy's breezy improvisation might suggest, the matter of selecting an ambassador to South Vietnam had been given scant thought in the young days of the Kennedy administration. More senior appointments had priority, as apparently did launching fantastical Cuban invasions. Such focus as could be mustered concerned what the Vietnam policy would *be* and thus what instructions the new ambassador would follow.

The diplomatic players were fungible, certainly in the eyes of the president. An ambassador anywhere is the president's personal representative and serves at the president's pleasure; American diplomats are instruments of policy set in Washington. They are also reporters and analysts, offering a privileged picture of the reality that surrounds them. And they are, perhaps most importantly, messengers: they relay messages from one government to the other. But they aren't calling the shots. This would be a theme. So would the often-random nature of assignments.

The field of plausible American ambassadors to South Vietnam in 1961 was not large. The US anti-Communist purges and show trials of the early and mid-1950s had decimated the ranks of Asia experts in government service and traumatized those who remained. Purportedly these able Foreign Service Officers (FSOs) were responsible for the "loss" of China to communism, which gave the generation of diplomats who survived, or who were recruited from elsewhere in the civil service—like Fritz Nolting and Bill Trueheart—few incentives to specialize in Asia.

One obvious choice for Saigon was Kenneth Todd Young, a well-connected former FSO who had moved to the private sector, working for Standard Oil in Southeast Asia and staying in close touch with the region. Young knew Diem. But Kennedy tapped Young to be ambassador to Thailand instead. In his memoir, Nolting recalls that on the very *day* he was to be sworn in as ambassador to South Vietnam at the State Department, word came from the White House that under pressure from the new under secretary of state, Chester Bowles, there might be a last-minute switch. Young would go to Saigon after all, and Nolting to Bangkok. Were they OK with this? The two men gamely agreed, per Nolting's memoir, a picture of grim professionalism.[5]

In Halberstam's book, the matter is stormier: Young didn't want to undercut Nolting, his former colleague, and was doubtful he could make any headway with Diem; Nolting seethed *about* being undercut and wanted the Vietnam assignment at all costs. In any case, this idea was quashed at the last minute. John Anspacher, Nolting's first press officer in Saigon, maintained that if the names had not been "switched," as he put it, "the course of events in Southeast Asia might have been changed. Kenneth Young was a completely different person. He would not for a moment have taken a lot of the guff that Diem handed Nolting and which Nolting swallowed hook, line and sinker, I'm afraid."[6]

"Fritz Was a Comer"

"Why I was selected for that post I do not know," Nolting said much later.[7] He surmised that Dean Rusk had had something to do with it and that he must have been a compromise choice. They had worked together at the State Department during Rusk's years as an assistant secretary of state in the Truman administration.

Frederick E. Nolting Jr., a forty-nine-year-old Virginian often described as genial and scholarly, was ending a six-year tour in Paris as the number-two American diplomat at NATO. He was no expert in Asian affairs, but, again, there weren't many available. He was senior enough to be noticed and capable enough to be seen as ambassadorial. "Fritz was a comer," recalled his colleague and contemporary William Sullivan. "He'd been a bright shining star in Paris. . . . When he was chosen, I think everyone felt that this promised very fine things."[8]

Apart from his obvious skills and political sophistication, Nolting spoke French. One of the legacies of the French period in Indochina just shuddering to a conclusion was the prevailing use of French as the diplomatic lingua franca in Vietnam, among many other places. And Saigon had good French schools. And was a very important embassy.

A year earlier, in fact, Nolting had been offered the ambassadorship to neighboring Laos and had done the professionally hazardous by turning it down. Vientiane, the Lao capital, was unsuitable for the education of his daughters, then eighteen, sixteen, fourteen, and eleven, and a backwater by any measure. Rather than decline it outright, Nolting persuaded his influential superior in Paris, Ambassador Randolph Burgess, to insist to the State Department that Nolting could not be spared there.[9] This is a telling glimpse of three things: of the importance Nolting attached to his family, of his willingness to go by his own lights, and of his bureaucratic savoir-faire.

When Nolting met with Rusk to discuss the Vietnam appointment in early 1961, he brought up his family again. Nolting told the secretary of state (this conversation would be a matter of bitter recriminations) that he could only commit to two years in Saigon because of his daughters' schooling—that is, until the summer of 1963. Rusk brushed it off with a mordant remark: "You don't have to worry about the length of your stay. The way things are going out there, we'll be lucky if we still *have* a mission in Saigon six months from now."[10] Nolting observed in his memoir: "His remark was not encouraging, but at least it gave me reason to think that he would recall our conversation at a later date."

President Kennedy signed off on the idea without meeting Nolting, although they would meet twice in the weeks to come. Walt Rostow reassured the president that Landsale might have been good, "but Diem never had to deal with him when he bore the full burden of an Ambassador, with all the awkward inevitable problems of negotiation. I think we must go with Nolting, whom I know well personally. You will find him a man of rare strength and character."[11]

Nolting's appointment was confirmed by the Senate Foreign Relations Committee on March 14—as it happened, just as Fritz and Bittie were visiting the Truehearts in London. The ambassador-designate returned to Washington for briefings. He sat in on the interagency task force studying Vietnam for a few sessions. Nolting was struck that it met at the Pentagon and was chaired by the deputy secretary of defense, suggesting an approach Nolting thought misplaced—military management of a fundamentally political challenge.[12] This would come up not just again but regularly. A big part of the problem was that Dean Rusk—surprisingly, as an old Asia hand, but unsurprisingly, as a seasoned government operator— saw Vietnam as a military problem, too. Rusk had quickly outsourced the dossier to Robert McNamara.

"They have really chosen a neophyte to succeed you," Nolting wrote to Durbrow in Saigon. "As you can imagine, I have a helluva lot to learn."[13] In the customary exchange of personal letters about the changing of the guard, rinsed of any classified information or policy substance, Durbrow wrote his friend Nolting—they all knew each other in those days in the Foreign Service—that he looked forward to a "a good bull session." They would have several.

At the Saigon embassy, "while we have our family squabbles, we iron them out *in camera* and whip up a solid front in the process," Durbrow told Nolting. With the second-largest US economic assistance program in the world and a significant military contingent, "plus the stepped-up Commie guerrilla activities, you will never have a dull moment and will find you have, as usual, too many papers to push."[14]

The preoccupations of diplomats in transition to new places in the world were and doubtless still are centered on creature comforts and cultural vagaries, practical family matters and social advice. In the context of the quagmire and death spiral looming ahead, Durbrow's handoff to Nolting rings with innocence.

Durbrow described the "not too large" official residence at 234 Hien Vuong where the Noltings would live, with window air conditioners in the home office, the principal bedroom, and a sitting room. He stressed the need to enlarge the dining room to seat twenty-four and said the work could be completed by their arrival. Answering a specific question from Nolting, he said the residence had a new piano. As for the household staff, Durbrow said Chinese would be more reliable servants but it was impolitic to hire them. With the bull session ahead of them, Durbrow said only that Nolting should read the counterintelligence report and recommendations Mendenhall had prepared the prior December: "As the plan is very fundamental to all our operations here I suggest that you read it fairly carefully."[15]

The ambassadors crossed one another in Honolulu in May, as one headed to Vietnam and the other headed home. The cantankerous Durbrow, an old Soviet bloc hand, told Nolting that Diem's regime "wasn't Stalin. I had the dubious pleasure of spending all my six years in Moscow under Stalin, so I know what a real son-of-a-bitch can be and how he operates, with real secret police and no opposition whatsoever. [The Diem regime] is authoritarian. It has to be. They have not had a government of their own for two or three centuries." This is a curious and telling comparison to be making about a non-Communist ally professing to be a democracy. But Durbrow wasn't wrong. He was archly frank with Nolting about the prospects for success in getting Diem to reform his government, or even the point of trying: "We are completely wonderful in our thoughts about everybody having all the Four Freedoms, all the civil rights and the ten commandments and the original [Bill of Rights]. I hope it works in every country, but it can't."[16]

Fritz Nolting, a sunnier person than the one he was replacing, believed he might be able to make headway nonetheless. The "bible" for his assignment to Vietnam, Nolting said, was straight out of the forward-thinking counterinsurgency handbook of the era: "to get a rapport between the two partners, to create confidence in each other's motives, and to use that confidence to build real advances in social, economic and political matters, as well as in the military part of the anti-subversion campaign. . . . This was all of a piece. You couldn't put down the Viet Cong or pacify the country without a very broad and deep program of winning the people. And winning the people involved education, health, government services . . . to build the basis for a more democratic system."[17]

Nolting was careful to see the sensitivity of the US position: "We would not use our new relationship, our new influence, and our aid leverage to pressure the government on internal matters." The United States expected to have influence, but it could not be seen to be exerting it. "By giving the impression of twisting the arm of a government which was itself quite willing and anxious to bring these things about would have only played into the hands of the Viet Cong. . . . It couldn't afford to be submerged by the colossus of the United States coming in as its teacher and adviser and helper."[18]

He stuck to this guidance until the end, until well after it had ceased to be US policy.

The Noltings had planned to reach their new post by ocean voyage across the Pacific, just as they and their Foreign Service colleagues had always sailed back and forth to France during the 1950s. Fritz had told the assistant secretary of state, Jeff Parsons, of his desire for a more leisurely and considered approach to his destination, "to get a little relaxation, and to acquire, by reading, some background in the culture and history of the new post as distinguished from current matters covered in the briefing. Perhaps even to learn a few phrases in Vietnamese."[19]

But as the Noltings were preparing the voyage, there came a flash message from the State Department: Vice President Johnson, accompanied by his wife and President Kennedy's sister, Jean Kennedy Smith, among others, were heading to Vietnam. The visit was only a few *days* away. The Noltings had to scrap the cruise and rush to Saigon by air. They arrived to the mess of scheduled renovations—an expanded dining room, a fourth bedroom—at the ambassador's residence on Hien Vuong. Nolting was fitted overnight with a white sharkskin suit, the male dress of choice for official Saigon. The next day he presented his credentials at Independence Palace to another man in a white sharkskin suit, "a stout, short man in his late fifties, with coal-black hair,"[20] Ngo Dinh Diem. The next morning Lyndon Johnson arrived.

No American visitor of comparable importance had been in Saigon since 1957, when then vice president Richard Nixon had come through. His successor's visit was meant to put flesh on the importance of Vietnam to the new administration, as well as to give Lyndon Johnson something to do. He had an explicit mandate to give Ngo Dinh Diem a diplomatic bear-hug and assure him of Washington's unwavering support, to dispel the ghosts of 1960—and Elbridge Durbrow—and set a key relationship on a new path. Johnson was, however, also there to test his acquiescence to an intensified US military presence.

As Johnson's motorcade rolled into Saigon from the airport, Vietnamese citizens encouraged to turn up by Ngo Dinh Nhu's squads cried *"Van tue!* Long life!" along the roadway, waving American and Vietnamese flags. He went to the presidential guest house and then off to a six-course dinner in his honor the Noltings hosted on the roof of the Caravelle Hotel. The next morning, the American vice president met Ngo Dinh Diem and presented him with a set of American Heritage books.

He also carried a letter from President Kennedy, which Diem read in his presence. Essentially it "thanked Diem for allowing the United States to underwrite his government," in the plainspoken interpretation of A. J. Langguth.[21] Diem put a price on his cooperation—another $30 million above the current contributions. He wanted to add one hundred thousand men to his army. Johnson seemed to agree on the spot. The vice president's interpreter at breakfast that morning, Thomas Conlon of the US embassy, had been summoned the night before without preparation but knew the general outlines of US policy—that there was conditionality to aid requests, the institution of reforms for military assistance. Conlon "was astonished to hear Vice President Johnson simply giving assurances of increased military and economic assistance without insisting on anything in return at all."[22]

Bittie Nolting showed Lady Bird Johnson and Jean Smith around a city she was seeing for the first time herself. The tour included a rare visit to Madame Nhu's bedroom, where she showed off a dozen tiger skins, heads attached, lined up on the floor. They had been hunted and shot by her husband. "He killed the most beautiful beasts," she said.

As Vice President Johnson drove around Saigon, he leapt from his car to do some Texas-style handshaking with bewildered Vietnamese, who were accustomed to greeting strangers and the eminent with palms pressed together and a bow. "VEEP WOWS 'EM IN SAIGON," ran the *New York Daily News* banner headline. Lyndon Johnson sweated profusely through his campaigning, changing his shirt repeatedly in the back of Nolting's car. His motorcade crossed an unlikely sight in a Saigon suburb—a herd of cattle bred on the King ranch in Texas! The vice president chased the cows around a pasture for the benefit of photographers. In the presence of reporters back in his hotel room, "he disrobed, toweled himself off, and climbed into fresh clothes."[23]

Joe Mendenhall, the acting *chargé,* was impressed: "This was a man who six years earlier had had a severe heart attack. . . . He slept one hour of that first night. I was in his room with Lady Bird Johnson sleeping in bed, Johnson on the phone to Washington at 2 or 3 in the morning. He slept one hour and had four more countries to go."[24] Anspacher, the press officer, recalls the same scene in the bedroom, only Johnson was wearing just the *tops* of his pajamas. Anspacher stood slack-jawed as the vice president bellowed into a static-prone radio telephone, "Jack! Jack! Jack, this is Lyndon!" The next thing the diplomat heard was, "Lyndon *Johnson!* Who do you *think!*"[25]

There was a moment of low comedy for Nolting, too, just two days on the job, after a long night at the embassy negotiating guidance with the State Department on Johnson's final communiqué before leaving Saigon. At 4:00 a.m., Nolting picked up the phone in his office and asked to be put through to the vice president. A few moments later he had awakened the vice president . . . of *South Vietnam,* Nguyen Ngoc Tho.[26]

At a steamy farewell dinner, Johnson notoriously declared his country's unwavering support for Diem, speaking politician to politician when he complimented Diem's recent reelection victory. "Some are content with 55 percent of the vote," he said, but "your people, Mr. President, returned you to office for a second term with 91 percent of the votes. You are not only the George Washington of your country, but the Franklin Roosevelt as well."[27]

It was not George Washington—or Franklin Roosevelt or Andrew Jackson or Woodrow Wilson—who is best remembered from the list of Johnson's reckless comparisons (which amused even Ngo Dinh Diem). As the dignitaries toasted Diem with warm champagne, Johnson called him the "Winston Churchill of Asia." On the way back to Washington, Stanley Karnow of the *Saturday Evening Post* took him aside and asked him if he really meant that. "Shit," said Lyndon Johnson, "he's the only boy we got out there."[28]

To President Kennedy, when he got back to Washington, Johnson proposed the military "get out of their dress uniforms and into their fatigues more often and out of the cities and into the jungles." He said "handshakes on the streets [and] shirtsleeves must be the hallmark of Americans." As for Diem, he wrote, "The ordinary people of the cities and probably even more of the rural areas are starved for leadership with understanding and warmth. . . . But it cannot be evoked by men in white linen suits whose contact with the ordinary people is largely through the rolled-up windows of a Mercedes-Benz."[29]

"The Person I Would Most Want"

After the vice president's whirlwind visit, the Noltings settled into Saigon life with three of their daughters. The eldest, Molly, had enrolled in Wellesley, and the next, Lindsay, would follow her there soon. Frances and Jane, their French perfected after six years in Paris, went to a French Catholic school, Les Oiseaux, in Saigon.

Two weeks after their arrival, President Diem invited the Nolting family to Dalat, a cool mountaintop resort in the central highlands where poinsettias were in bloom and logs crackled in the hearth, as sharp a contrast to Saigon's oppressive heat as Vietnam offered. The Noltings were quartered in a guest house known as "Bao Dai's Second Concubine's Villa," a reference to the randy former emperor.

Nolting spent the first afternoon alone with Diem, their first private meeting. He found Diem "dedicated, courteous, sincere, proud, suspicious, stubborn (and) above all passionate in his conviction that the cause of a free Vietnam was worth any price, to himself and to all of his countrymen."[30] He also learned more about Vietnamese history in one sitting than he ever imagined, "from the ancient past, through the Chinese wars, the French occupation, the Japanese conquest, and the confused aftermath of World War II, . . . the Vietnamese people, their origins, their culture, and their destiny that started before the Christian era and ended, not in the present, but several centuries into the future."[31]

The ambassador may have been wondering if access to the chief of state could be double-edged. "Between us, we must have smoked several packs of Vietnamese cigarettes and drunk dozens of cups of pale, lukewarm Vietnamese tea." Unfailingly polite about Diem's logorrhea, Nolting noted transitionally, "When I left six hours later to join my wife and children before dinner . . ."

The Noltings and President Diem dined that night at Ngo Dinh Nhu's Dalat retreat. Nhu himself was away—tiger-hunting again—but Madame

Nhu and her children were there. A sharp-eyed Frances Nolting, fifteen, noted in her new Saigon diary that Madame Nhu "talked with her finger-nails and eyelashes."[32] Frances and her sisters began a close friendship with the Nhus' eldest daughter, Le Thuy.[33]

Two months in, Ambassador Nolting had traveled extensively around South Vietnam, learning his brief, often in Diem's company. "I like and admire him as a person," he said in a telegram on July 14. "I am convinced he is no dictator, in the sense of relishing power for its own sake." Diem "does not fundamentally enjoy power or the exercise of it. He is, never-theless, an egoist in the sense that he believes (in my judgment, with some justification) that he can govern in South Vietnam in general and in detail, better than anyone else now available."[34]

At the White House, there was a trace of impatience for this approach. "We must somehow impress Diem with a sufficient sense of crisis to move faster than he is," wrote Robert Komer of the National Security Council staff after reading Nolting's cable. Diem was "caught up in a desperate cri-sis in which his very survival is at stake" and must "undertake the massive and dynamic reform program without which the countryside cannot be won. After Laos, and with Berlin on the horizon, we cannot afford to go less than all-out in cleaning up South Vietnam."[35]

The stated policy and Nolting's mandate notwithstanding, doubts about the Diem government's ability to survive were very much on the table in Washington. The day Nolting arrived in Saigon with orders to save Diem, Rostow sounded sanguine in a note to the president: "Although we have no alternative but to support Diem now, he may be overthrown. . . . If so, we should be prepared to move fast with the younger army types who may then emerge."

Rostow spoke bluntly about the frustrations Nolting's predecessors had endured in pressing Diem for reforms "without notable success." He wondered aloud about how to bring "our great bargaining power to bear on leaders of client states to do things they ought to do but don't want to do."[36]

Even during the swirl of the Johnson visit, Nolting turned immediately to the choice of a new deputy chief of mission, called the DCM. It was the first move in what would constitute, by the following summer, a complete overhaul of personnel in the US diplomatic and military establishment in Saigon. The new ambassador seemed in a hurry. The DCM he had inher-ited was not yet due to rotate out, but Nolting wanted to populate his embassy with his own people.

Ostensibly without any prior consultation between friends of very long standing, Nolting worked his channels in the State Department and within a matter of three weeks secured Bill Trueheart's appointment. It is hard (for me) to fathom they would not have discussed this privately, speculatively, but it's entirely possible Nolting wanted to spare his old friend the possibility the idea might fall through. As we shall see, there is a great deal they never said to each other.

"You will be amused to hear that the big news reached me in Paris, of all places," Bill wrote Fritz on June 17, 1961.[37] He'd gone over from London, where we lived, for NATO meetings. He was meeting Nolting's successor in Paris, Raymond Thurston, who told the story to Fritz later:

> We were riding home from my office to have lunch together there, and Bill asked if I had had any news from you since your arrival in Saigon. I said no. . . . Bill then went on at some length to express his view that you had a very difficult assignment, etc. etc. We had been in my house only two or three minutes when a telephone call came from London telling him he had been assigned to Saigon as your deputy. He immediately began to take a more constructive point of view on Saigon as a post![38]

That unexpected phone call actually had been from Phoebe Trueheart, "having gotten the word from an unauthorized source in the Embassy," Bill wrote Fritz. (So much for official channels.) "All this had the effect of enhancing my pleasure considerably: to my satisfaction over the assignment was added relief that Charlie had not been run over by the Underground or Josh eaten by the dog, which is what I usually expect when Phoebe telephones."[39]

Bill's letter to his old friend went on, speaking in humor and gratitude: "The Department's telegram was sobering as well as flattering. It also appears to fix squarely on you in advance the blame for any shortcomings in my performance. You can count on it that I will make my maximum effort to see that there are none. You should also know that I regard the assignment as the break of a lifetime in a professional way and am deeply grateful for your confidence." He said he would get to work brushing up his French, rusty after three years away from Paris, and his calendar that summer showed French lessons three times a week.

Trueheart wrote his mother in Richmond the same day: "Today I have big news for you. I am to be transferred . . .—a big job in a crucial area of the world with responsibilities for supervising major diplomatic, economic, and military operations involving many hundreds of Americans. When Fritz is away, I shall be in full charge of American interests in Viet-Nam."[40]

Nolting, for his part, wrote his old friend a personal letter with encouraging words about their upcoming collaboration in Saigon. "After a month here, I can say with considerable assurance that you would like it—both the work and the country. It is hard, hot, fundamental, vigorous, vital, viable, satisfying, and tough. . . . Work requires skillful coordination of a helluva lot of do-it-now Americans, sometimes running off in different directions—that's where you'll be the most needed. We've also, I think, got to get some realism into the heads of some over-idealistic Americans who seem to think the Communists won't swallow up an infant democracy tenderized a la Rousseau." Nolting told Trueheart he was filling the DCM job with "the person I would most want to have—you."[41]

Preparing for Saigon

Although I was only nine, I had actually heard of Saigon. I liked cinnamon toast. The McCormick cinnamon jars, which we got from the commissary in London, described the contents as "Saigon Cinnamon"—still do, sometimes. I was very happy, I think, to be going to a new and exotic place with a war on. But the record also suggests some larger disappointment that I was not returning to the United States after what seemed to me a long wait—seven years, most of my sentient life, with most of my acculturation in France and Britain.

On July 11, 1961, Bill gave his mother, who was about to have me as her guest in Richmond for a week, some guidance: "Charlie is almost pathetically eager to get back to America and to be an American boy in every way. The greatest thing you can do is make him feel that he is. The less said about his French education and foreign travels the better—unless he brings them up."[42]

Bill also added this to the letter: "We were all overjoyed that Fritz had his rabbit's foot with him last weekend." As Ambassador Nolting was driving back to the embassy in Saigon after lunch on July 8, two Vietnamese on a motorcycle had pulled abreast of the ambassador's chauffeured Mercury sedan at a busy downtown intersection and tossed a homemade bomb through the open windows into the back seat. "I threw it out while it was still sputtering," Nolting later recalled the event, and it never went off. "The damn-fool bodyguard was shooting at the guy who threw it." Fritz jumped out of the car shouting at schoolchildren to clear out of the way. Then he ran across the street and picked the bomb up again and tossed it away. "I was shaking like a leaf." He told the bodyguard to stand down.

Showing admirable sangfroid, Nolting went on to work a normal afternoon. Later he did what he could to not press charges against the assailants (who were caught and tried anyway) or to do anything to draw attention to the incident. Bill too. "This kind of thing happens from time to time, and in much quieter places," my father calmly wrote his mother.[43] This incident only whetted my appetite for the drama I supposed was ahead.

My parents sent me to the United States at the end of the school year in London. It was my first transatlantic plane flight, and I flew alone. I visited Richmond to see my grandmother Sallie and her second husband, Peter Williams, known as "Peto," an electric garage-door salesman who drove only Nashes, a new one every year. The Civil War centennial was afoot, and he drove me to many a battlefield. For the first time in their company I understood that Sallie was at the least a heavy drinker, and probably an alcoholic. Their little apartment in Richmond's Fan District, on Grove Avenue, smelled of rancid age marked by the ticking and chiming of several clocks. My grandmother put me on the train for an awkward Sunday lunch with my grandfather, who still lived in Chester, well outside Richmond.

A happier time for me was my next stop, Maysville, Kentucky, my mother's hometown, staying with her mother, Thelma Everett. Thelma was a feisty, fun, irritable woman widowed early, and from just the wrong side of the tracks, I gathered; the social distinctions in Maysville were byzantine and closely parsed. Thelma bought me a used bike for five dollars and sent me off down the road to be with my second and third cousins and their friends every day, mostly poolside behind one of the imposing mansions on Edgemont Road or at the Maysville Country Club. These visits, like others we made on home leave over the years, made big impressions on me—my first and earliest and only passing glimpses of American culture, a vast and intimidating world I felt I could never fully master or understand, and of my American contemporaries leading normal lives I feared I could never catch up with.

Bill Trueheart got his orders to Saigon only on July 27. He left London and headed to Washington two weeks later for some general orientation about Southeast Asia, and meetings with State Department, CIA, and Pentagon people who oversaw the region. He also had an audience with a "noncommittal" Colonel Lansdale, who "didn't tell me much of anything," Trueheart told an oral historian with a smile. When asked why the smile, he said that nothing in their conversation indicated the serious concerns Lansdale had about the Vietnam enterprise that he had shared with Kennedy seven months before.[44]

During those weeks in Washington, Lyndon Johnson materialized for the first and only time in Bill Trueheart's life. Under Secretary Chester Bowles had decided that Vice President Johnson needed a foreign affairs adviser from the State Department on his staff—a State Department handler and "spy," in other words. Trueheart couldn't say no to this chance, even though a big DCM job was his preference. He went over to be interviewed by Lyndon Johnson at his office on Capitol Hill. After waiting forty-five minutes, he was ushered into the vice president's inner sanctum. Choosing his words carefully in an LBJ Library oral history interview years later, Trueheart says he was surprised to find the only other person in the room with the vice president was his secretary, "and not too far away. It was a very dark room."

Although he'd been told by those who knew Johnson that he was "a man of enormous mental capacity, a brilliant man," Bill Trueheart found Johnson that day "in his country boy mood. He said he was having to go to all these NSC meetings and read all these papers about foreign affairs and things and he really couldn't follow them. He needed somebody who could help him to understand that these were all about." When Johnson asked if he were interested in the position, Trueheart said he was "torn" and headed for "a job that I was very keen to do," but working for the vice president was a compelling alternative. Johnson told him that "he didn't want to do anything to disadvantage the mission in Vietnam, which he thought was so important."

When he left Johnson and the silent secretary after about twenty minutes, Johnson's aides outside told him, "don't call us, we'll call you," as Trueheart put it, and that seemed to be that, a relief. "But unfortunately they *didn't* call me, and I was supposed to leave momentarily for Saigon, but until this matter had been resolved the State Department was not going to let me go. So I sat around for about ten days waiting to hear what the vice president wanted, and he said neither yea nor nay."[45]

Finally someone from the State Department intervened, and Trueheart was free to go. I can think of few less naturally congenial men than Lyndon Johnson and Bill Trueheart.

Bill and Phoebe made farewell trips to see family in Kentucky and Virginia. The *Richmond News Leader* ran an "Area News" story headlined "2nd Virginian Goes to South Viet Nam." Bill was pictured and quoted as saying "Before you know it we'll have an all-Virginia team out there." His long friendship with Fritz was highlighted. "It's quite a chance for me. It's an executive-type job I've always wanted to get," said the "quiet-spoken, mild-mannered Trueheart."[46] He was also described as "youthful-looking," which I found amusing.

Our family set out from Washington in early October, flying to San Francisco and then Honolulu and then Hong Kong, a leisurely series of hops that lasted about two weeks. It was the first time my father, or any of us, had been west of Chicago, as he always liked to say (although he had done basic training at Fort Sill, Oklahoma). My parents, between full-time nannies behind them and ahead of them, strained to contain a rambunctious ten-month-old Josh. I was allowed to drive an open-air pink Jeep around a parking lot near Waikiki Beach. When Josh threw up Pan American's lobster thermidor in the Tokyo airport, reportedly my father and I wandered off to buy me a transistor radio and let Phoebe handle the disaster. By way of a stop in Hong Kong, we arrived in Saigon at noon on October 20, 1961.

Every visitor to Saigon in those days first remarked, as I did, on the engulfing heat at the top of the airplane stairs; the wet smell, once clear of jet fuel fumes, of the thick tropical vegetation; crossing a tarmac so molten your shoes sunk into it. This was Tan Son Nhut airport.[47] Military aircraft and vehicles were everywhere. We were met by people from the embassy—my father reported fifty or more to his mother.[48]

I'm not sure I even noticed that the Noltings were not among them. But by the time we had been whisked through the sweltering VIP terminal, without formalities, far across the parking lot at the gates to the airport came the stirring sight of the ambassador's car, flags flying, roaring toward us and halting in a flurry of uniformed people to open the car doors. There sprung from the black Mercury the imposing Fritz Nolting, flushed red with the heat and the haste of a late arrival and apology, rushing to embrace us. Bittie Nolting materialized behind him for the reunion, accompanied by the new amah Phoebe had asked her to hire for Josh.

What impressed me most about that arrival was the car and the flags. Cars were an obsession for me. On the rear passenger doors, the size of a big coaster, was the Great Seal of the United States. The American flag on a slender pole attached to the bumper was twinned, on the left side, with the navy-blue ambassadorial standard, not unlike the presidential one. This turned out to have been a special occasion, though, perhaps a way to cut through noonday traffic from a long-running Diem meeting; as a matter of daily course, and appropriate discretion for the elephant in the diplomatic corps, the flags were furled and tucked into leatherette sheaths.

On the way into Saigon I sat in the front seat of our 1959 Ford Fairlane—no bodyguard for the DCM—next to the driver. His name was Nguyen Van Sinh. He would become my closest Vietnamese friend. Saigon was surpassingly strange for a boy raised in Europe. The crush of traffic, most of it two-wheeled. The hum of humanity in the streets, quite unlike anything I knew. The rank smells of cooking and outdoor smoke, and always a cloying vegetal assault on the nostrils.

All along the honking boulevard leading into the city, Vietnamese flags hung in abandon. Intermittently, from a garish display on a building or a lamppost, I glimpsed the face of Ngo Dinh Diem. Vietnam's national day was coming up six days later. I would ask for such a flag—to plant in my new terrain, as it were—as soon as I got settled: a saffron field with three red stripes signifying the three historical zones of Vietnam: Tonkin, Annam, Cochinchina. I was ten. This was going to be fun.

A Flood of Advice

Despite the new American ambassador's optimistic reports during the summer, vigorous Viet Cong offensives in September were difficult to ignore. Mustering thousands of irregulars, the Viet Cong launched more than four hundred attacks on South Vietnamese military outposts that month. After capturing Phuoc Vinh, a provincial capital fifty miles from Saigon, the Viet Cong disemboweled the provincial chief in the public square.

To assess the new challenges on the ground, President Kennedy sent two of the young administration's leading hawks for an inspection: General Maxwell Taylor, the president's military adviser and soon to be his new chairman of the Joint Chiefs of Staff, and Walt Rostow, his deputy national security adviser.

Taylor and Rostow were accompanied on the October mission by, among others, Edward Lansdale, whose reputation followed him everywhere. On General Taylor's orders, Lansdale was shut out of the official delegations that were to call on President Diem. Lansdale had to point out that Diem himself had asked to see him—alone, before he saw anyone else—an invitation Taylor irritably had to approve. That evening, Lansdale found Diem looking "down in the dumps—so I told him to go to bed instead of talking to me." A few days later, under Lansdale's ministrations, he became "the fighter we knew of yore."[49]

Unsurprisingly, when they said goodbye Diem asked Taylor to recommend to President Kennedy that Lansdale be sent to Saigon as his personal American adviser. The idea could only have met with an icy reception from Nolting and Trueheart, as it did with the State Department. Scrawled in the margin of the cable carrying this request after it arrived in Washington, someone unnamed scribbled, "No. No. NO!"[50]

President Kennedy had another job for Lansdale: he wanted him to run Operation Mongoose, the post–Bay of Pigs scheme to undermine and overthrow the government of Fidel Castro by other than military means—psyops, a Lansdale specialty. This sorry chapter in his and the Kennedy administration's life would keep Lansdale out of everyone's hair, at least for a while. But Vietnam was never far from his thoughts.

One new scheme rattling around Washington that Taylor and Rostow pursued in Saigon had been inspired by the news of dramatic floods that ravaged South Vietnam during October. The lower reaches of the Mekong River, which passes through Saigon and winds through the Delta to the sea, had inundated the region. Thirty percent of the cultivated areas had been lost, and two hundred thousand people were homeless. Nolting reported to Washington that the situation was "catastrophic," but the presidential palace in Saigon, always touchy about bad news and its ability to cope, didn't want to say much about it.[51]

The State Department replied to Nolting in telegramese that "flood area will doubtless absorb its losses and recover in time, but chance for major psychological victory will have been lost. Recommend Embassy urge Diem declare a disaster area, request assistance friendly nations, perhaps make radio appeal to nation, mobilize resources government bureaucracy and military on a crash basis."[52]

These were the kinds of things that Diem was congenitally unwilling to do, but they made sense in Washington. US flood relief assistance was "a subterfuge," Trueheart recalled, an excuse for inserting military personnel "without announcing exactly what the ultimate objective was." And "it didn't make any engineering or military sense to do it."[53]

What the Taylor-Rostow mission wound up recommending upon its return was the introduction of eight thousand US combat personnel to bolster South Vietnamese forces, an idea Kennedy was inclined to reject. He famously told his house historian, Arthur Schlesinger Jr., that sending in troops would be "just like Berlin. The troops will march in; the bands will play; the crowds will cheer; and in four days everyone will have forgotten. Then we will be told we have to send in more troops. It's like taking a drink. The effect wears off, and you have to take another."[54]

One day at the White House swimming pool, President Kennedy asked McGeorge Bundy, the national security adviser, to set down on paper what he thought before a crucial meeting on November 15. Bundy tried to draw it down the middle, urging "*limited* US combat units if necessary for *military* purposes (not for morale) to help save South Vietnam." Having waffled, he then confronted Kennedy about *his* indecision: "I am troubled by your most natural desire to act on other items now, without taking the troop decision. Whatever the reason, this has now become a sort of touchstone of our will."[55]

When the National Security Council met that morning, Kennedy's apprehensions were evident. He rejected comparisons to Korea and Berlin. He said he could make a strong case against intervening, on domestic political grounds and world opinion alike, to say nothing of the recent disastrous experience of the French against the same enemy.

On everyone's mind were the seven-year-old Geneva Accords, which set limits on how many US military personnel could be in Vietnam—685 precisely. Kennedy wondered how to finesse the prospective (and in fact ongoing) violation of those limits and how to charge the other side with egregious violations of their own.[56] To that end, the State Department had commissioned a thoroughgoing report, *A Threat to Peace,* by a former *New York Times* reporter, William Jorden. Beyond its analysis about the nature of the insurgency and the enemy, the report served as documentation to support the case that the North had been violating the Accords all along.

Kennedy's rejection of the troop proposal was not explicit, thus not irrevocable. And it didn't seem to matter. American soldiers started heading to Vietnam anyway, under ingenious workarounds and euphemistic feints. They were sent as "advisers," part of a vast and sensitive counterpart system designed to take the Vietnamese by the hand without appearing to do so. Within a year, the US military deployment in Vietnam would grow tenfold, to nine thousand, roughly what Taylor had proposed.

Ambassador Nolting was not informed of these recommendations nor of any presidential decisions from Washington. He learned of them from Bill Trueheart. In the course of a new-DCM courtesy call on the British ambassador in Saigon, Sir Harry Hohler read Trueheart a message from Her Majesty's embassy in Washington with all the inside details about the report. Nolting was unhappy at his treatment. "You can imagine," he cabled the Department of State, that after waiting to hear the results "anxiously and impatiently," how "embarrassing and discouraging" it was to learn of them from the British.[57]

Once briefed, the ambassador sat down for two and a half hours with Ngo Dinh Diem to lay out the recommendations about a "new partnership" with the United States. He fielded the president's questions about the quid pro quos for military and economic assistance—broadening his government, depersonalizing the chain of command, and the like. Diem's chief concern was what it would always be. He feared that the greater the American presence, the greater the threat to Vietnamese sovereignty: "Vietnam, he said, does not want to be a protectorate." Nolting went back several times to reassure a "brooding" and "disappointed" Diem.[58]

There was a deep contradiction in President Diem's worries—both that the United States was getting in too deep and that, as he saw it in Laos, it was getting ready to abandon Vietnam. Diem told Nolting that he found the American demands so disturbing that he had not even shared them with his cabinet—only with his brother Nhu; his closest nonfamily counselor, Nguyen Dinh Thuan, the secretary of state; and the foreign minister, Vu Van Mau. Diem told Nolting the plan "played right into the hands of the Communists" and that "we are pressing him to give a monopoly on nationalism to the Communists." Nolting insisted the opposite was the case, that "we were not seeking a quid pro quo as such" but "a structure of government in Vietnam, under his leadership, which could bear the weight of increased US assistance."[59]

After many more such meetings, and more pressure from Washington, Nolting eventually prevailed upon Diem to accept the new deal. But even as he poured on the honey, back in Washington, through the looking glass, the need to remove the Ngo family was under active consideration two years before the fact. Diem's rejection of the deal was imminent, officials believed, and their planning for the US response went down to such hair-brained moves as "pull[ing] our ambassador out and put[ting] Lansdale in Saigon if Diem refuses to sign on the dotted line." Lansdale aside (as he never seemed to be), some believed it was better that Nolting not leave the country in the event of a coup: "Unfortunately the DCM is so new to that part of the world that he would be in great difficulty."[60]

Walt Rostow was blunt with the president about Diem's four principal weaknesses: "He cannot protect his peasants"; "the intellectuals are affronted by his dictatorial political style"; "the army, the civil servants, and even his ministers are frustrated by his administrative style"; and "he lacks the ability to communicate and identify with the mass of his people."[61] Rostow summoned some hope that the new partnership being launched would shore up those weaknesses that were undermining the war effort. He told Kennedy that he "wished it were not so, but the New Frontier will be measured in history in part on how that challenge was met."[62]

In late November, President Kennedy shook up the State Department hierarchy in what was called thereafter the "Thanksgiving Day Massacre." Chester Bowles was removed as under secretary of state and George Ball promoted to succeed him. Averell Harriman, the lead negotiator on the Laos settlement, was elevated to assistant secretary of state for Far Eastern affairs, becoming Nolting's boss.[63]

An old Washington hand, Ball was an experienced international lawyer long associated with the presidential campaigns of Adlai Stevenson. Just before Thanksgiving, Ball gave President Kennedy an earful about the slippery slope of committing ground forces to Vietnam in any guise: "Within five years we'll have three hundred thousand men in the paddies and jungles and never find them again. That was the French experience. Vietnam is the worst possible terrain both from a physical and political point of view." Ball was surprised at the president's reaction, delivered with "an overtone of asperity": "George, you're just crazier than hell. That isn't going to happen."[64]

Ball found Kennedy's riposte ambiguous: "Either he was convinced that events would so evolve as not to require escalation, or he was determined not to permit such escalation to occur." Ball wondered whether, in fact, Kennedy had been abrupt and dismissive precisely because "he hated to admit, even to himself, that he shared some of my apprehensions."[65] This was a perceptive observation about the young president, and the beginning of Ball's role as a persistent skeptic of America's course in Vietnam.

Rue d'Arfeuilles

The DCM's house at 107 Nguyen dinh Chieu, formerly but still familiarly rue d'Arfeuilles, was a low-slung villa built in the Saigon colonial style of 1940: stucco exterior, red tile roof, surrounded by a high wall topped with spiky shards of broken bottles pressed into cement. Vietnamese policemen in white uniforms—expats called them "white mice"—guarded the front gate from a battered sentry box.

Inside upstairs and down were cool tile floors and lazy ceiling fans. Geckos slithered freely on the interior walls. There were two seating areas in the living room, and a dining room, one step up, open to the rest. A wicker-furnished veranda and semicircular terrace stretched beyond screened windows. In one corner of the living room behind a door was a den, decorated in blue, lamplit and cool. This was what we called the Blue Room, where cocktails happened before dinner, and my father's one martini before lunch. The Blue Room was the family place in the house, intimate and private, air-conditioned, the place for the books and the Victrola, the desk with correspondence and stationery, the place where confidential conversations took place in the middle of the night.

In Saigon we outlanders could not drink the water from the tap, although somehow brushing one's teeth in it was fine. In each bedroom was a tall thermos of filtered ice water, replenished twice a day, at the bedside. Each room had an electric bell by the door to summon a servant, the summoner's location displayed on a wall-mounted device in the pantry. I had only to avail myself of this service once or twice, for refreshments with friends in my room, to be called on the carpet by my mother.[66]

It may have been a day or two after we arrived in Saigon that I looked out my bedroom window to the area just below, a kind of sheltered passageway between the house and the detached kitchen and servants' living quarters, creating a grassless yard in between. There I saw the cook, Rong, walk into the yard with a cleaver in one hand, a chicken by the neck in the other one, and half a smoke clenched in his lips. He set the neck down on a well-worn stump and whacked the chicken's head off. I ran to my mother for consolation and shortly thereafter had chicken for lunch.

I was first enrolled in a French school, having spent all but one year of my schooling in French already. I recall objecting strongly to this and hating what I found: a crowded classroom of Vietnamese boys furiously taking notes as the middle-aged French professor barked his lecture, pacing back and forth and gesturing with a cigarette. My parents, both heavy smokers, found this detail particularly objectionable. My father sanitized the crisis by writing his mother "the French schools are terribly overcrowded . . . so it seemed better to let him do what he wanted to do anyway."[67] Which was to attend the American Community School and attempt to play catch-up in learning the American way. I enrolled in fifth grade and loved it right away.

My infant brother was absorbed into the bosom of the Vietnamese staff. "The amah is spoiling him to death, but it can't be helped. All the servants adore him," Phoebe wrote her mother-in-law. "The Vietnamese neighbors thought he was a girl until I met them and straightened them out. They can't understand why I don't cut his curls off. The humidity has made his hair very curly—and lovely. Like C's at that age."[68] I can remember coming into the pantry and seeing Josh sitting on the countertop with Thi Lan and the upstairs maids, Thi Ba and Thi Hoi, clapping and cheering him on with his first words of Vietnamese. As well as a one-year-old can do, within a few months he would be speaking Vietnamese and French and English.

The letters home for the next two years spoke of a social schedule of frightening constancy, beginning with Bill's calls on the ambassadors and deputies of the major countries—in two days in November, Japan, Italy, West Germany, France, and the United Kingdom. The Joey Adams variety show, on a regional tour, gave a performance on November 2. There was a Marine Corps ball on November 10, a regular event at embassies around the world, where US Marine contingents provided local security inside the often-permeable shell of police from the host country. The Noltings had a black-tie dinner on November 13. The Truehearts gave a cocktail party with 120 guests for a visiting congressional delegation on November 17, well before our personal effects, including our dachshund, Edward, and our green Mercedes 220S, had arrived from London by ship. "I hope they will be impressed by the austerity of our household," my father wrote his mother.[69]

Socially, it went on like this, more or less, every week for the next twenty-seven months.[70]

On Christmas Eve, his calendar shows, Bill Trueheart ushered at St. Christopher's Church, an Anglican-Episcopal hybrid parish with a small sanctuary on the boulevard Norodom, a few blocks from the presidential palace. It sat next door to a compound of grim prefab American housing for junior embassy officers, where I often had play dates. St. Christopher's quietly followed a diplomatic practice of according the front pew to the ambassadors of the United States (left) and the United Kingdom (right). Their number twos sat in the second pews, and so forth. It never occurred to me that these two nations would be represented by anyone but Episcopalians and Anglicans.

We attended St. Christopher's regularly. The heat in church was stifling: the ceiling fans were kept off so as not to blow out the candles. The younger Nolting girls, Frances and Jane, sang in the tiny choir. Lindsay Nolting, the second born, remembers being recruited to play the 1855 pump organ, a challenging syncopation of feet and hands: "Do you remember a few days after you got to Saigon you were put on stage. It was a great big hoopla of all religions and cultures of Vietnam and we were to stand up and sing our folk songs. You were *braaave!* You were *singin'.* We chose a Mozart alleluia. You were *staunch.*"[71]

The correspondence in those first weeks in Saigon includes Phoebe fretting over my making new friends in Saigon—but really Phoebe's own preoccupations: "It is slim pickins, I'm afraid. He is with a boy this afternoon I can't bear. So rude and unmannerly, never says thank you for lunch and has horrible table manners . . . even Charlie was embarrassed."[72]

And Bill about my making new friends in Saigon, but really Bill bragging about his son: "His principal problem is that all the girls have a crush on him and don't try to hide it. He is constantly receiving telephone calls from one or another of them. He displays great irritation at their attentions, but I suspect that secretly he rather likes it."[73]

At the end of November, under parental duress, I started judo lessons at the Cercle Sportif. My father explained to his mother that judo "is the proper name for what we call ju-jitsu, a scheme whereby the small and weak can overpower the large and strong. I am sometimes sorry I didn't study it myself."[74] He was not, I don't believe, thinking of the asymmetrical war the United States was facing.

Only two weeks later, Bill wrote her that Fritz was away in Honolulu for the weekend—the first of many times, for that is where all the big Vietnam powwows were held, equidistant from Washington and Saigon. "Meanwhile I am in charge and all the messages and telegrams going out of here are signed TRUEHEART. I confess that I get a kick out of this!"[75]

An Alliance with Incompetence

President Kennedy's thinking about Vietnam was always stimulated by John Kenneth Galbraith, whom he had sent to New Delhi as ambassador in May. Galbraith wrote Kennedy a steady stream of personal letters of advice about many matters, especially Vietnam. Kennedy encouraged this, even delighted in it, though he sometimes found Galbraith to be "full of shit."[76]

Trained neither as a diplomat nor an Asia specialist but as an economist, Galbraith had no shortage of opinions. Nonetheless, for all his pomposity, what Galbraith was telling the president was uncomfortably closer to the bald truth, and certainly more far-seeing, than Kennedy was hearing from almost anyone else.

"These jungle regimes," the Canadian-born don opined to the president, "where the writ of government runs only as far as the airport, are going to be a hideous problem for us in the months ahead. . . . The rulers do not control or particularly influence their own people; and they neither have nor warrant their people's support."[77] His common sense was prophecy: "We cannot always back winners and we cannot be sure that the winners we back will stay on our side."

In July 1961, Galbraith wrote the president that in his view the situation in South Vietnam is "exceedingly bad." He said, "Diem has alienated his people to a far greater extent than we allow ourselves to know. This is our old mistake. We take the ruler's word and that of our own people who have become committed to him."[78]

Although Ambassador Nolting had barely arrived and they had never met, Galbraith had already taken a dim view of him. He would press the point again in October, in a diary entry. Nolting, he said, "seems to be lacking in independent judgment or capacity to see the consequences (in the United States) of another Korea. Nor does he appear to put any real pressure on Diem. I worry more about South Vietnam than Berlin." In a footnote to his diary, published eight years later, Galbraith observed: "This judgment is not entirely fair. Though I disagreed with him, Nolting was a brave man of strongly held views."

It was not until November 17 that Galbraith visited Saigon and met the ambassador for the first time. He and his wife, Kitty, were houseguests of the Noltings in their "spacious house with high ceilings and an incredible traffic noise pounding by outside." Galbraith naturally spent time at the

US embassy, "a shabby six-story building near the Saigon River"—a former bank building, in fact, built by the Chinese. He compared Saigon to a "shabby" (again) French provincial city, suggesting Toulouse. Galbraith also found Saigon a city "in a modified state of siege. The Ambassador and senior officials are followed everywhere by a car filled with gun-bearers."[79] When he left on November 20, in a US air attaché's plane heading for Bangkok, "We took off steeply" to avoid Viet Cong snipers by the airport. He surveyed the flooding in the Delta, and the onetime agronomist judged it not as bad as advertised—"the rice grows better than ever" after the floodwaters recede.

Back in New Delhi, Galbraith ruminated to Kennedy on his visit and the stakes in Vietnam: "We are increasingly replacing the French as the colonial military force and will increasingly arouse the resentments associated therewith." He thought the United States was playing the Russians' game: "They couldn't be more pleased than to have us spend our billions in these distant jungles where it does us no good and them no harm."

Challenging the president directly, if jocularly, he later asked: "Incidentally, who is the man in your administration who decides what countries are strategic? I would like to have his name and address and ask him what is so important about this real estate in the space age. What strength do we gain from alliance with an incompetent government and a people who are so largely indifferent to their own salvation?"[80]

The Noltings' hospitality notwithstanding, and his view that Nolting had been "treated abominably by the State Department" (in keeping him out of the loop about the Taylor-Rostow recommendations), Galbraith also told Kennedy he needed a new ambassador in Saigon. The incumbent had been there only six months. Nolting would hear of many such moves to replace him during his brief time in Saigon, yet the one that actually happened blindsided him.

Galbraith was scarcely more charitable about Bill Trueheart. He wrote Harriman about Trueheart's views as he encountered them in late 1961, when Trueheart was very much on the Diem program: "He impressed me very unfavorably . . . as a young and belligerent character with strong pro-Dulles convictions. Indeed, I would regard him . . . as a menace."[81] Notwithstanding this first assessment, their views about the Diem regime would soon converge.

3

★ ★ ★

Two Gentlemen of Virginia

THE *NEW YORK TIMES* chose Frederick E. Nolting Jr. as its "Man in the News" on January 13, 1962, under the headline "Therapeutic Envoy." The writer appreciated Nolting's "country-doctor manner . . . gentle but firm, a bit of old Virginia . . . lyrical and hard-headed." In this portrait Nolting sounds winningly homespun, a man of wit and sympathy. Pressuring President Diem to undertake political and economic reforms in wartime, he told the *Times,* "was like trying to perform an appendectomy on a man who was carrying a trunk up a flight of stairs." Who would want such an assignment?

Of the two Virginians heading the embassy in Saigon, Fritz Nolting was the extrovert, warmer and more garrulous than his younger friend Bill Trueheart, though both were understated men. To me as a ten-year-old, and even before, my godfather was a magnetic figure: tall, big-boned, stout-headed, with a ready smile and a gravelly voice that I can still summon. Fritz always seemed delighted to see me. Inferring from what two of his four daughters have said to me, I wonder if Fritz was curious about what it might have been like to have had a son.

Fritz had the kind of baby face ("almost cherubic," said the *Times*) that some men keep in vestigial form all their lives—think of Leonardo DiCaprio, whom Fritz distantly resembled as a youth and as a middle-aged man. Indeed, all the Noltings were glamorous. When we were all in Paris, the four confident girls, shimmering in their summer dresses and flat shoes, were a palpable and charged presence to a sisterless boy. Their mother, Bittie, was a tiny golden beauty with a tinkling laugh, a forgiving smile, and a clever tongue. I had long since stopped hearing my own parents' lingering southern accents and colloquialisms, as one does, but all the Noltings spoke an unapologetic and melodious Virginian that went with their personae. It sounded high-born and Old World to me.

I had known them all my short life, but in Saigon, now they were not just godparents and family friends. Fritz was the local potentate, the Noltings the first family of the American colony. The ambassador represented power—American power specifically—with a formal title ("extraordinary and plenipotentiary") and honorifics and protocols. In Vietnam, as I nibbled at understanding it all, the exercise of power was far from abstract.

I knew Bill Trueheart only as a son knows a father—that is, intimately, but not all that well. Bill's imprint—the sound of his voice, the way he gestured—is dimmed, frustratingly for me now, by the passing of thirty years since his death. I never knew him as Fritz did, or as a colleague or friend might, let alone a Vietnamese mandarin, a newspaper reporter, or a four-star general.

Bill was five foot eleven, just two inches shorter than Fritz but seemingly a bit more so. Nolting's luxuriant gray hair was swept back on his prominent head like a matinee idol's. Trueheart's hairline had been receding since he was about twenty. Unlike his friend, all his life Bill wore thick corrective lenses, since the war in heavy, dark frames. My childhood drawings of Daddy always emphasized the narrowness of his cranium and the height of his dome.

My father did not come across as someone always at ease with himself. He was certainly correct in his behavior, to a fault, but always a bit stiff, as Josh Trueheart *and* David Halberstam have pointed out. Strange for a diplomat, he was awkward at ceremonial gestures, even domestic ones. To command the floor ("What can I get you to drink?") he would hold his hands together in an angled clasp before his midsection. He was an uncertain public speaker. The only recording I have heard of him speaking in an official capacity—brief thanks after being sworn in as an ambassador in 1969—is sweetly painful to hear, an occasion unrisen to.

One very young Foreign Service Officer, arriving in Saigon for his first posting at the age of twenty-four, recalled Bill more flatteringly than I do. "He was God. He was the ultimate Foreign Service Officer. Always well turned out. Always crisp."[1] My father had a deep and keen intelligence, opinions plainly expressed, and an evident seriousness. So serious did I find him as a child, at least in contrast to my gregarious and eccentric mother, that I once remarked to her that it was too bad Daddy wasn't funny. With heat she corrected me: "Your *father* is one of the funniest people alive." (What I must have meant was "fun," or perhaps I hadn't picked up on his humor, or I was flattering my mother.)

Indeed, the Bill I came to know as an adult was a drily witty man, mordant, caustic, skeptical, spontaneous, unafraid to respond in contempt or disgust. "Oh, balls!" was his favorite dismissal. He may have been an unsmoothed stone, but—perhaps for that reason—I'd say his ego was well in check.

Back then, as indeed we all did, I took the friendship of Bill and Fritz for granted. I assumed from their Virginia days, their academic interests, their career crossings, their chain-smoking and liberal drinking, and of course their common mission in the service of the United States, that they were peas in a pod. They must have thought so too.

The friendship between Fritz Nolting and Bill Trueheart dates to Charlottesville in the autumn of 1939. That September Nazi Germany invaded Poland and the war in Europe began in earnest, with all it would soon portend in their own lives. They were beginning their graduate studies in philosophy at the University of Virginia. They intended to be philosophy professors.

Fritz had gotten his bachelor's degree from the university long before, in 1932. But there had been a significant interruption in his studies and plans: the Stock Market Crash of 1929 and ensuing Depression had wrecked his family fortunes; young Fritz had been drawn in to help salvage his father's business. Now he was picking up where he left off. That meant that in the fall of 1939, at the same juncture in their postgraduate lives, precocious Bill was all of twenty, while Fritz was twenty-eight, and already betrothed.

Fritz must have felt the forfeited years intensely: He collected three advanced degrees swiftly. His 1940 master's thesis was titled "Time and Duration in Descartes' Philosophy." He then went to Harvard for a year, studied under Bertrand Russell, and in Cambridge got another master's degree along with a first daughter, Molly. Back at the University of Virginia, he earned his PhD in 1942 with the dissertation "Certainty, Truth, and Probability: A Study in Epistemology." Bill's 1941 master's thesis, his highest degree, was titled "The Eros Doctrine in the Philosophy of Plato."

It is hard to think of these two sitting around in their Charlottesville rooms discussing such abstruse matters, let alone spending the rest of their lives considering and teaching them. They seemed to me, and they were, very much men of action and of the world. But in their youth they bonded over great minds and myriad philosophies and deep (or at least imponderable) moral questions.

Yet they were hardly humorless brainiacs or donnish aesthetes. Fritz Nolting was famous in his circles, and in the life of our two families, for singing and playing the piano, and getting everyone else to sing along. Bill Trueheart and another UVa classmate once made recordings on primitive wax discs in which they improvised two heavily accented German gynecologists discussing the fine points of feminine sexual response. The recordings, alas, are lost to time.

The Families Intertwine

William Clyde Trueheart was born on December 18, 1918, in Chester, Virginia, a crossroads farm town south of Richmond. The global influenza epidemic was at its most devastating, and the baby was born "all black and blue," or so went the family story; he was not expected to survive. The baby's mother, Sallie Leftwich Shepherd, was a teenaged beauty who had caught the eye of the widowed forty-two-year-old local banker, also William C. Trueheart, but known to his friends as "Heart." Their age difference (twenty-five years), and surely other factors lost to memory, made the marriage impossible. They separated when my father was a child. My father wrote in a 1985 family genealogy that his parents were divorced in 1927; the public record indicates the divorce was not until 1931, that my grandfather was the plaintiff, and the grounds "desertion."

Given how close mother and son were, and the usual legal customs, whatever was behind that judgment may explain why young William (his mother eschewed *Bill*) was raised in Chester and lived with his father. Sallie moved to Richmond, twenty-one minutes away on the train.[2] That arrangement may have been the price of her ex-husband's financial support for their son. But my grandfather was never a wealthy man, and there's evidence the Depression hit his household hard. The 1920 census, for example, shows the new Trueheart couple living together in their own house with their new son William; his older half sister from the first marriage, Rose; and two black servants, aged thirty-four and fourteen. The census a decade later, just after the Crash, lists the Trueheart family as boarders in someone else's house, with Sallie *and* the servants gone.

My father's letters to his mother during this time, the beginning of the remarkable archive of reading between the lines, speak only obliquely of the divorce. After spending the summer with his mother on West Franklin Avenue in Richmond, where she was living with her sister, he said, "I hated to leave but we must not worry about something that can't be helped." That winter he apologized for his Christmas presents to her when what she really needed was more basic: "I certainly will be glad when I can make enough money to send you all you want. That is my ambition, to repay you for all that you have done for me but I'm afraid that it is not humanly possible to do so."[3] He was fourteen.

In an oral history interview for the Lyndon B. Johnson Presidential Library, one of the first questions my father was asked (leadingly) about his assignment to Saigon in 1961 was whether, at the time, he had known Fritz Nolting long. Bill replied, "I'd known him all my life, just about. Fritz's father started my father in the banking business."[4]

This was news to me. When I asked, Bittie Nolting remembered nothing of this either. Eventually I found a version of the colorful tale in the *Richmond Times-Dispatch,* in a feature on my grandfather's retirement after fifty years at the Chesterfield County Bank. The priceless headline might well have gone on his obituary: "Chesterfield Banker, 80, Moves Upstairs."

According to this account, my grandfather decided when he was thirty that he wanted to learn something about banking. Born in 1875, the fifth of seven children, Heart had been working as a substitute telegrapher on the Seaboard Air Line railroad in Virginia and North Carolina. During the summer of 1905, he called on the Bank of Richmond, where he met two of its directors, Tucker Sands and Frederick E. Nolting, Fritz's future father. He asked for a job. In old Heart's retelling in the newspaper, the two bankers responded, "Any boy who wants to learn about banking on a hot July day like this can start tomorrow."[5]

Heart had scarcely started work in Richmond when he began hounding the two bankers about starting a bank in Chester. Nolting and Sands were dubious but realized, "we've got to start a bank in Chester or he'll worry us to death." The Bank of Chesterfield County opened on July 12, 1906. William C. Trueheart was cashier, director, stenographer, and janitor—

the only employee. Sands and Nolting were president and vice president, respectively, of the bank; *sous-entendu,* I suppose, they were overseeing their investment in Chester and my grandfather's debt to them. Being a self-made banker, the senior William C. Trueheart never used his middle name: Cheatham.

The retirement feature reports that Heart never missed a day of work for illness in fifty years. Another article, about my grandfather taking his very first airplane trip to visit his three-year-old grandson in Paris, quotes Heart claiming to have never smoked or taken a drink, even a *soft* drink.[6] His abstemiousness was a subject of much merriment when I was growing up.

My grandfather's formality was not genteel but something like its opposite, a compensation for awkwardness that to some degree my father inherited, for all his later sophistication. For example, my mother never addressed her father-in-law as anything but Mr. Trueheart. His third wife, Mabel, didn't either, at least in company.

From these circumstances of his upbringing one can imagine the desire to leave them behind. Bill was evidently a bright and hardworking boy. He graduated at the top of his class at Chester High School in 1934, its fifteen-year-old valedictorian. Sallie may have been protective and even smothering—she seemed that way to me—but she was also realistic and had aspirations for her only child.

She had read in *Saturday Review,* the leading middlebrow magazine of the day, about a place called Phillips Exeter Academy in New Hampshire. She wrote away for the materials and enrolled William by mail. At Exeter, even then, they were searching for what passed for diversity; my father constituted a good candidate for the school's serious ambitions to be a "national high school." William enrolled as a postgraduate scholarship student, a one-year status normally reserved for exceptional athletes, which my father was far from. Exeter changed his life, he said.

Bill matriculated at Yale in the fall of 1935, soaking up his new circumstances. Judging from his correspondence with his mother, he was having a glorious time, cheering the Elis at football games (he brought home part of a goalpost from the Yale-Harvard game), rushing for the *Yale Daily News,* listening to the Joe Louis–Max Baer boxing match, dating girls from Vassar and Barnard, taking them to hear Louis Armstrong and "a colored floor show" or dinner and dancing in Manhattan. "I hardly know how to tell you how much I like it here," he gushed to Sallie. "I'm still sticking to my old plan, however, of work first and then play."[7]

Yet, by the spring of his sophomore year, he was telling his mother he was considering transferring to the University of Virginia. He complained of the weather in Connecticut. He said he worried about losing his connections to home. "I shall be virtually a man without a country," he declared; he said a Yale degree was "merely a sheet of paper certifying that I have lived in New Haven for four years. . . . Did you ever consider whether it was worth eight thousand dollars?" Always sounding wise, or wanting to sound so: "Schools are mostly what the student wants to make out of them."[8]

The real reason, he told me much later, was straightforward. He couldn't keep up with his friends at Yale, or maybe most students at Yale, who came from families with money. "You can't get along very well without tails here," he had confided to his mother, after his father refused to pay for them.[9] That was probably the least of it. It's possible Heart made the decision to transfer out of Yale for him, but William left his father out of the equation when he shared the news with his mother.

When Bill settled in Charlottesville, as a Virginian he paid only modest tuition. He earned money working as a bookkeeper for the university dining hall system, and still more delivering ice to the private rooms on the Range, where the luckiest students lived at the university Thomas Jefferson designed. The only time we visited the university together, Bill showed me the backs of the rooms, accessible by alleys inside the famous serpentine walls, from which the iceboxes projected and into which he would deliver his freezing cargo at dawn, invisible to the occupant.

The Depression Hits Home

Fritz Nolting was cut from finer cloth. The first American Noltings had come to the United States, from Germany, a hundred years later than the Truehearts came from England (not that anyone's counting). But they had arrived from the Old World with important connections.

Fritz's great-grandfather had distinguished himself as an officer in the Hanoverian army, which fought alongside the British in all the Napoleonic campaigns, even mimicking their uniforms. The Hanoverians were in fact rallying to their own king, the Elector of Hanover, who was also King George III of England. That Nolting ancestor served through the

Peninsula campaign under Wellington and fought under his command in the Battle of Waterloo.[10] His son, Emil Otto Nolting, was born in 1824 on the family estate in Prussia and orphaned at fourteen. After an education in Bremen, he emigrated as a young man to Richmond and joined his uncle's tobacco export company, already well established. After 1850 he started his own tobacco business. All the great fortunes of Virginia, and many thousands of small ones, were in tobacco.

E. O. Nolting also was president of two banks, and of the tobacco exchange and chamber of commerce. In 1873 he bought a magnificent Greek revival mansion on Main Street in Richmond's Fan District.[11] Peculiarly, he became Belgium's consul in Richmond and received the Order of Leopold—an honor he had inherited, as it were, from his uncle and passed on to his son, who passed it on to Fritz's older brother, Buford Nolting. During the Civil War, the story goes, the Belgian flag flew from the house in Richmond, and Nolting's friends surreptitiously hid their silver and jewelry from predatory Union forces within its diplomatic immunity.[12]

E. O.'s second son was Frederick Ernst Nolting, the banker who launched my grandfather on his banking career in 1906. Fritz, who bore his father's name at birth, would add the second *e* in Ernest, an assimilative step in a century when Germany was twice at war with the United States. The patriarch liked to joke that the umlaut over their surname had been shot off in World War I.

So it was that Frederick E. Nolting Jr. was born, on August 24, 1911, into more than comfortable circumstances. He attended Richmond's school of choice for the ruling class, St. Christopher's, and in 1929 went on to the University of Virginia, where he excelled in the classroom and the playing field. Virginius Dabney, the eminent editor of the *Richmond Times-Dispatch,* and a mentor, later recommended Nolting as "not only prominent and popular at the University but a star student as well."[13]

The piano-playing bon vivant was already thriving. As an undergraduate in Charlottesville, Fritz was selected for the ultimate and quasi-secret distinction, the Z Society, whose members are anonymous. (In Saigon, I noticed his black and silver Z signet ring and asked him what it was about; he smiled and genially told me he couldn't tell me. Odd that you would advertise on your person what you couldn't discuss, or so it seemed to me, and still does.)

The Nolting family was worldly and prosperous enough in 1928 to have sent Fritz for a semester to Vienna, to study piano, accompanied by a tour of the European capitals, including Paris. He wasn't just privileged; he was adventurous. Fritz and a friend went on a bicycle trip to China and Japan in the summer of 1931. His friend's parents were missionaries in Japan, and as such had a chance to introduce the young men to a world-touring Charles Lindbergh.

But the Nolting family fortune had just swung the other way, sharply. Fritz and his friend had had to work their way to Shanghai on a merchant vessel when discretionary money evaporated after the financial crash. In 1932, as the Great Depression squeezed or eliminated fortunes, the senior Nolting's brokerage collapsed. Fritz, with enough credit for a bachelor's degree after only three years in Charlottesville, set aside his academic plans. For five years he joined his father in the office every day—as "general factotum," he later said—and studied economics in night school.

"You didn't take bankruptcy in those days, and he was just paying off the debts," as his widow put it eighty years later. The business never recovered. "They lost everything. They had to sell the house," Bittie told me.[14] Her daughter Lindsay acknowledged that Faderley, as her grandfather was called by his family, felt hugely responsible for losing his clients' money; she said he eventually "repaid" 90 percent of it.[15]

On a holiday strolling down the strand in Virginia Beach, in 1935, Fritz had come across Olivia Lindsay Crumpler, a belle from a good family in Danville, and her mother; he hit it off with both of them. He was twenty-four, and Bittie was fourteen. These were different times; the relationship was allowed to incubate. The couple was known to their set as Lil' Abner and Daisy Mae—he big and strapping, she tiny and fair.[16] They married in 1940; Bill Trueheart was among the groomsmen. The first of their daughters was born in 1941. By 1948 they had four.

Intelligence in Wartime

In the fall of 1941, while Fritz began a year at Harvard getting his second master's degree, in Charlottesville Bill accelerated work on his (never completed) PhD dissertation and "graded papers" as a philosophy department teaching assistant. By now Germany had invaded western Europe, and Britain, battered by the Blitz, was in its most perilous hours. No male American of draftable age doubted he might be called to service, and many sought it.

A professor at the university—William Weedon, Trueheart's philosophy thesis adviser, and Nolting's too—suggested that some of the brighter y oung men could make themselves highly employable in the impending war by taking a US Navy correspondence course in cryptanalysis. After Pearl Harbor that December, Trueheart and the others who had completed the course were promptly offered jobs in Washington, as civilian employees of the navy, reading and analyzing Japanese code, with a full commission promised. Thus began my father's reluctant thirteen-year dance in an area—intelligence—he professed to disdain.

When Bill's myopia turned out to disqualify him for the navy job, he was just as glad, he said. He found cryptanalysis "cloying" and said "it drove me crazy." He then joined the US Army—and "the first thing the Army did was to identify me as a cryptanalyst," he recalled.[17] He tried to escape his fate again by going to Officer Candidate School, spent much of a year in Fort Bragg, North Carolina, and Fort Sill, Oklahoma, mastering field artillery, only to be assigned at the end, as a newly minted lieutenant, to the "Special Branch" in Washington: cryptanalysis for the army. This led to a job as editor of the daily diplomatic summary of the latest Japanese intelligence. At the end of the war, he continued to edit such summaries as a civilian in a succession of agencies. His immersion in intelligence matters in these formative years can only lead one to wonder why he did not find his way into the CIA.

The end of the war gave Trueheart and Nolting and countless others unexpected opportunities for service in the new national security state under construction. It was a heady time. These were the years that gave birth to the Marshall Plan, the US Information Agency (USIA), the Central Intelligence Agency (CIA), the Arms Control and Disarmament Agency (ACDA), the World Bank, the International Monetary Fund (IMF), and, of course, the North Atlantic Treaty Organization (NATO)—"an 'entangling alliance' in peacetime," as one of their colleagues described it, where Fritz and Bill would begin their foreign service.[18]

Bill's earliest work as a postwar civil servant was serving as a rapporteur at the Paris Peace Conference in 1946, where the first deals about postwar reconstruction and security in Europe were hammered out. It gave him his first transformative taste of Paris—three months—and allowed him to travel to devastated zones in Germany and Austria.

When the Atomic Energy Commission was established in 1947, he was brought in to set up its intelligence unit. In that capacity, deep in a metastasizing bureaucracy, he participated in drafting National Security Council directives that governed the new federal intelligence agencies. His personnel records from these years are uniformly outstanding if colorless records of an able achiever. Under Trueheart's "Principal Shortcomings," wrote the first head of the Atomic Energy Commission, Lewis Strauss, "None observed other than shyness."

In 1947 he met my mother, Phoebe Anna Everett, through their expanding circle of friends in Washington, and they married in Maysville, Kentucky, in August 1948. Phoebe was born there in 1923, the eldest of three, and raised on the old river town's choicest street overlooking the Ohio River. Her grandfather's obituary describes the family as "pioneer stock," having settled and cultivated this land since the late eighteenth century. The J. C. Everett Company, established in 1886, supplied the surrounding tobacco country with its grain, feed, and farming equipment; her father, John Chenoweth Everett, ran the business and was a leading citizen of Maysville, a town not much bigger than Chester, but with more charm and more airs.

Thanks to a rich, Princeton-educated uncle who underwrote her tuition, Phoebe went to Bennett College in Millbrook, New York, a combination finishing school and junior college. She got a degree that helped her become a commercial artist, drawing fashion illustrations for Pogue's, a department store in Cincinnati, the biggest city in the vicinity of Maysville. Eager to add distance from her own upbringing, I surmise, she moved to Washington to do the same commercial art for Garfinkel's and Janney's, among other bygone emporia. She lived near Dupont Circle in the Fairfax Hotel, then a kind of dormitory for single working women. That's when she met Bill Trueheart, who lived a few blocks away at 2222 I Street, NW, now deep in the heart of George Washington University.

In 1949 a friend from Special Branch hired Trueheart to work in the "R" area at the State Department—intelligence, of course. His work was not collection but liaison with all the other intel agencies in Washington. They worked on debriefing and settling Soviet defectors and monitoring Soviet nuclear testing. He worked on these matters for five years, through the Korean War and the election of a Republican president.

In Marshall Plan–era Paris, meanwhile, there had mushroomed a US presence of organizations—NATO and the Organisation for Economic Co-operation and Development (OECD)—and a crowd of American ambassadors. One of them, William Draper, a would-be proconsul "with a very grandiose idea of what his mission was," per Trueheart, decided he wanted a special assistant for intelligence so he could have access to all of it. A friend of Bill's had had the job first; on his recommendation my father was chosen to succeed him in 1954, almost simultaneously joining the Foreign Service as a class 2 officer.

Once in Paris, he had an office next to the ambassador and DCM and every day briefed them on intelligence material that "only the three of us were cleared for." But within months he realized that "this was not much of a job, frankly. I asked if we couldn't abolish it and let me go into the political section and do ordinary political work."[19] After thirteen years as a soldier and civil servant, he had finally unshackled himself from an intelligence portfolio.

Reunion in Paris

Nolting also left Charlottesville after Pearl Harbor. He spent four years in the navy as a gunnery officer in North Africa, Italy, and France, overseas service interspersed with procreational leaves. In 1946, long proficient in German, he joined the State Department as a civil servant. There's no record of how this coincidence in the two friends' careers came to pass, or whether they worked together on anything.

Nolting's first line job in the State Department was on the Netherlands desk, where the main issue was an Asian one: the fate of Indonesia, then a Dutch colony, facing its own restive postwar independence movement. (The rap that Nolting knew zero about Asia before Vietnam is belied by this, not to mention his bicycle trip in China and Japan.) Nolting's next job was running the Swiss/Benelux bureau. By 1953, he had risen to become a special assistant to first Dean Acheson and then John Foster Dulles, two formidable secretaries of state, in charge of "mutual security affairs," then the term of art for military alliances, notably NATO.

Being thus well placed, in early 1955, Fritz had a shot at a top job in the US mission to NATO in Paris, and with it the chance (or the obligation) to formally join the Foreign Service. A March 1 deadline for lateral entry loomed: the so-called "Wristonization" program, named for Henry M. Wriston, the president of Brown University, who had been brought in to devise such a scheme for a burgeoning diplomatic service that was suddenly short-handed at senior levels. It brought Nolting (and Trueheart) and scores of others into the Foreign Service from the civil service across the federal government. Wristonization was a kind of fast track that waived the competitive written and oral examinations for entry, a bitter pill for the old guard.[20]

Fritz was initially more undecided than Bill about the Foreign Service, having planned to work in government only two years and then return to teaching. Eight years later he was still at it. Two days before the March 1 deadline, he wrote a friend of his indecision.[21] He was torn by the need to find more lucrative work to put his four daughters through Potomac School, where he drove them every morning from their Virginia farm on his way to Foggy Bottom. Nonetheless he bit the bullet. (Halberstam says Trueheart "talked Nolting into joining the Foreign Service," on what evidence I don't know.) By August 1955 Nolting had become a class 1 officer, FSO-1, from the outset, the equivalent of joining the army as a major general. In September Fritz sailed with his family on the SS *United States* for the six-day crossing to his new posting in Paris, his first diplomatic assignment overseas. He was forty-four.

I had turned three aboard the same vessel on the same crossing the prior September. Of course I remember almost nothing about this period of my life, even though the sensations of Paris that I first experienced inform the ones I have today. But at that age I did understand readily (and have confirmed in rather fulsome detail in the letters) that we were living in a country not our own, and I was conscious, even self-conscious, about it, and also about living in two languages. My parents had decided to educate me in French kindergarten, which I endured in near silence. I remember watching, from open office windows on Place de la Concorde, all the music and parades for the July 14 celebrations ("Bastille Day," as they never say in France). This perch was where Fritz and Bill worked: the Hotel Talleyrand, an eighteenth-century palace once occupied by the selfsame statesman. US property since the end of World War II, the Talleyrand was where the Marshall Plan had been hammered out, and later served as an annex to the embassy nearby.[22]

The job Bill Trueheart had landed, after bailing out of the initial intelligence slot, was as political counselor at the US delegation to NATO. The delegation was a mini-embassy to the new Atlantic alliance, which was headquartered, until Charles de Gaulle requested its removal in 1967, in Paris. USRO, in the parlance, was a small but important shop. My father was thirty-six. When we returned from a family trip to Spain, Bill had news that his new boss in Paris would be his old friend Fritz Nolting. "You can imagine how pleased we are," he wrote his mother.[23]

His letters to her in the ensuing Paris years, and Phoebe's too, speak frequently of Fritz and Bittie and their four girls, who settled in Auteuil. We dined frequently *en famille*, went to church together, often heading to lunch and the races at Longchamp after the service. On pleasant weekdays Bittie and Phoebe would drive out to paint in the French countryside and bring a picnic lunch. Fritz's absences from the office on official business (when Bill would act on his behalf) were always noted in letters to Sallie.

When Fritz was in Washington, he would check in with his own family on Park Avenue in Richmond and seemed never to fail to call on, or at least call, Bill's mother, whom he had known already for fifteen years. Fritz was that kind of man, and it was that kind of friendship. In May 1957 I was baptized—late in life by almost any standard—at the American Cathedral in Paris. My parents asked Fritz to be one of my godfathers. Fritz was born an Episcopalian; my parents had joined the church only in Paris and there became lifelong Episcopalians.[24]

Ankara and London

In 1958, after four years in Paris, in four dwellings, Bill Trueheart was posted to Baghdad. He had wished to return to Washington to a job at the State Department related to NATO affairs, as might have been logical. Robert H. Miller, Bill's colleague in Paris and Saigon, could have been describing the lives of many American diplomats in an era when specialization was not yet de rigueur; he called his own career "an odyssey without any apparent logic or central theme or purpose . . . a seemingly disconnected journey for nearly forty years."[25]

My father's new job was to be political adviser to the secretary general of the Baghdad Pact, a new Middle East version of NATO, called in other iterations CENTO, or Central Treaty Organization. The POLAD—political adviser—was an American slot, by treaty; he was not technically part of the US embassy but on loan to an international organization. Though Bill had never been in that part of the world and knew nothing of it, his expertise from NATO was seen to be a help to a similar mutual security organization just getting organized. "There was no comparison in any way," he said later. "It was a rather silly idea which wasn't going to accomplish anything, and I wasn't keen to get involved with it."[26]

That July, as our family packed to leave Paris for our next life in Baghdad, the government of Iraq, a Hashemite kingdom at the time presiding over the Sykes-Picot state, was overthrown in a military coup (by precursors to Saddam Hussein's Baath Party). As it happens, my father had flown across the English Channel on July 14, 1958, to meet his prospective new boss, an Iraqi diplomat, in London. The morning he arrived to meet the new secretary general, the news broke about the coup at home, in which the Iraqi king and his family had been slaughtered. "I found the Secretary General in a state of shock," Bill recalled.[27]

The coup made Baghdad no longer the ideal location for the headquarters of the US-backed security alliance. The Pact headquarters was shifted quickly to Ankara, Turkey, a new secretary general was found, and we changed our travel plans, too late to save a brand-new two-tone Plymouth on its way to Iraq and never heard from again.

I attended my first American school in Ankara, aged seven. It was run by the US Air Force for dependents of personnel at the nearby American airbase; its shuttering not long after was part of the trade President Kennedy made, under the table, in exchange for Nikita Khrushchev's removal of intercontinental ballistic missiles from Cuba in 1962. I do not recall having much fun at this school. I was an odd duck—essentially a little Parisian in short pants whose command of English may have been imperfect. My mother wrote that I was "always cheerful and philosophical about our gypsy life."

We left Ankara, I sensed rather abruptly, in the late summer of 1959, only eleven months in. I know now from the archives why this was, and it's a rare glimpse of Bill Trueheart caught in an awkward diplomatic quandary. As I discovered, he also chose to airbrush what happened. The incident, I think, resonates with what he confronted in Saigon in the summer of 1963.

As he later told the story, veering into detail for an oral historian who knew nothing of it, Bill Trueheart had bonded in Ankara with the organization's new secretary general, M. O. A. Baig by name, an accomplished Pakistani diplomat and brother of the sitting foreign minister. "I was very fond of him," Trueheart said. "Of course, I was reporting to him, and it was understood that he was my boss. On the other hand, there was a tacit understanding that I was supposed to be keeping the [US] Embassy [in Ankara] informed about what was going on in the secretariat. I didn't find this a difficult thing to do. I went to the staff meetings at the embassy."

One day in 1959 Baig came up with a plan to reorganize the secretariat, the Baghdad Pact's executive. Trueheart thought it was a poor idea and told him so frankly, "which Baig took without rancor," he told his interviewer forty years later. Following practice, Trueheart reported confidentially on Baig's idea to a US embassy staff meeting and said he didn't think much of it. The American DCM at the embassy in Ankara, newly arrived from Mexico, unfortunately remembered this fact when he was introduced to Baig at a cocktail party soon after—and "volunteered that he understood Trueheart didn't think much of his plan."

Trueheart laughed in telling the story to the interviewer: "Baig confronted me with this, quite rightly. I was about to go on home leave, so I said I really thought this was a serious matter, and I was sorry about it, but I thought the simplest thing would be . . . that I simply wouldn't return. He agreed with this."[28] But Bill was misremembering what happened.

In the immediate aftermath, he wrote—and, exceptionally and tellingly, saved—a contemporaneous formal report about the contretemps, a detailed, self-typed defense of his behavior. As my father related the Baig conversation to Fletcher Warren, the US ambassador to Turkey, the secretary general confronted Trueheart about the breach of confidence. Bill at first replied "non-committally" about any discussions he might have had at the US embassy—until Baig "made it clear that he did in fact know that I had expressed an opinion to the Embassy on the matter, and I admitted that I had."

Baig gave Trueheart a tongue-lashing. He said "I was responsible to him alone," and "I had not the right either to offer my personal views to the Embassy or to give them if requested to do so. My action amounted to 'disloyalty' and 'treachery,' to cite the most extreme adjectives that I recall being employed."

Disloyalty and treachery. Responding to Baig, Trueheart "felt bound to say that it was not realistic to suppose that officers seconded to an international organization would henceforth ignore what they regarded as the interests of their own country. He did not appear to be impressed with this line of argument."

Far from the suggestion coming from Trueheart, it was Baig who said "that when I went on home leave this summer, I should not return." Baig also threatened to register a protest about what happened to Washington and all the other government members of the Baghdad Pact. "His anger may subside, and quite possibly will, but it is difficult to see how any confidential relationship can be restored."[29]

This had not been a successful assignment for Trueheart, who had just turned forty.

Writing Ambassador Warren a personal letter that summer after he left Ankara, Trueheart thanked him for his support "in the unfortunate incident which arose." He'd just spent a week in Washington explaining himself and making amends in the State Department, feeling in the doghouse. During this time Fritz Nolting wrote him from Paris to report that he'd gotten a call from Robert Murphy, the under secretary of state, who was looking for a special assistant and was asking about Trueheart. "I gave him the 'woiks,'" Fritz wrote Bill.[30]

But Nolting didn't know what Trueheart had just found out: he was "absolutely flabbergasted" to learn he had been assigned to the US embassy in London, he told Warren. "I'm afraid I shall be a long time in living down this piece of good fortune among my friends! It was, of course, pure chance."

We were there by October 1959, and I was returned to schooling in French, at the Lycée de Londres, later renamed for Charles de Gaulle, who as president spoke to a school convocation I attended. I was given free rein in London almost immediately, as I was in Saigon later. At age eight, I rode the Underground alone to school, just a few stops away in Kensington, and until I made friends I went to the movies alone. I went to the movies with the child star Hayley Mills—with a group of other young people. Hers was the first signature I got in a new autograph book I had been given and would fill in Saigon. The Noltings, still in Paris, were again in our orbit and we in theirs, the couples hopping frequently back and forth to Paris and London.

Beginning to get a grip on the wider world, I began to read the evening newspaper—the *Daily Express*, tamer than today but still accessible. Well-mannered "Ban the Bomb" demonstrators sometimes marched on a Sunday down Sloane Street, across the park from our house on Cadogan Place. Yet I don't recall ever putting their agitation together with my father's responsibilities at the American embassy: "politico-military" affairs, and specifically managing at the bilateral level the US nuclear relationship with the United Kingdom. These peaceful marches were my first glimpse of political action in the streets, too, even though I had lived in Paris during the Algeria-related violence of those years, blissfully unaware.

Now I was becoming aware. A family letter reports a remark I made to a US Air Force general who was visiting us at home in London. When my father explained on introductions that the general was in charge of all US Air Force operations in the United Kingdom, supposedly I asked, "Including the U-2?"[31] This was the top-secret surveillance plane, based in Britain, that had just been shot down over the Soviet Union, causing deep embarrassment to the United States.

As I had two years before, I went to summer camp in France, in Talloires on Lac d'Annecy, in 1960. When my parents came to pick me up that August, they had news. Soon I would have a sibling. To cushion the blow, as they imagined it would be, when we got back to London I was presented with a dachshund, Edward. There then arrived, on December 23, 1960, Bill and Phoebe's long-awaited second child, Joshua Trueheart. We moved to Saigon, Edward too, the following autumn.

Sully

Fritz Nolting's correspondence, personal and professional, collected at the University of Virginia, is often touching in its overt concern for his family, especially his daughters. He doesn't hide his anxieties about his personal solvency and the weight of educating four teenagers at the same time. There is also in these letters here and there, and then more frequently, a tone of grievance about one slight or another from his masters in Washington. Sometimes the grievance is about a great deal more than a slight—for example, the expropriation of his property.

In 1946, the Noltings bought a seventy-one-acre farm on the outer edges of Fairfax County west of Washington, an area then largely undeveloped, for thirty thousand dollars. It was an eighteenth-century (1794) homestead with a name (Sully) and a pedigree (it had been owned by a prominent relative of Robert E. Lee, Richard Bland Lee). Sully is where the Nolting girls grew up before moving to Paris. It was where the family planned to live when they settled down in Washington, after or between overseas tours in the Foreign Service life stretching ahead of them. Sully may have been the kind of homeplace that could offer the security and permanence that the Depression had stolen from his parents, and that life in the diplomatic service would nourish a longing for. My mother remembered going to wonderful Sunday lunches at Sully when she and my father were courting, and then when I was an infant. Sully—"*Sulleh*"—always figured during the Paris years in the Noltings' banter about home.

In 1957, in Paris, Fritz Nolting heard devastating news. He learned from letters and news clippings sent from his Fairfax County neighbors and local lawyers that the new international airport being planned for Washington would be sited across the road from Sully. The Noltings' cherished property, their only real asset, would be expropriated by the US government for that purpose. There was nothing he could do about it. Being a civil servant with high career aspirations in the Foreign Service didn't expand Nolting's options. On December 2, 1957, Fritz wrote plaintively to General Elwood Quesada, the head of the Federal Aviation Agency, whom he may have known: "It does seem to me unwise and unnecessary to acquire new land and dispossess many happy people when Friendship Airport is available and crying for business, as I have heard."[32]

The Noltings went on home leave from Paris that winter via the SS *America* to deal with this financial setback. Nolting had had to borrow $4,500, representing about a quarter of his annual salary, to pay for housing in Paris because the government allowance was insufficient. He wrote his lawyer, James Keith: "I can say to you as a friend I am getting tired of being squeezed by the government at both ends. . . . You know our financial situation, which is strictly hand-to-mouth on current accounts."[33]

The title for Sully passed to the US government on July 1, 1958, for which the Noltings received $77,600 in exchange. A truncated version of the farm, with buildings open to visitors, remains open today on the saturated eight-lane commuter corridor that is Route 28. It's a charming place, vernacular and homespun, that once must have been quite lovely. Now it is a good spot to watch jumbo jets groan through the sky before touching down at the airport named for Nolting's old boss, John Foster Dulles.

The Families Intertwine (Bis)

David Halberstam, a New Yorker who had reporting jobs in Mississippi and Tennessee before joining the *New York Times,* developed certain ideas about southerners that he brought to the table in Saigon. One of them was the caricature of the Virginia gentleman Foreign Service Officer.

In *The Best and the Brightest,* he developed the character into an entire school, a shadowy force. In his character sketch of Nolting, he calls him a "hard-working, straight, somewhat unquestioning man . . . part of that special group of relatively conservative Democrats from Virginia who play a major role in the Foreign Service and control much of its apparatus from the inside, who regard the Foreign Service as a gentleman's calling, and feel they produce a particularly fine brand of gentleman."[34]

There is no evidence for this assertion. A caricature of the more common truth in those days would have been a clubbable tennis player from St. Paul's, Yale, and money. But there were plenty of exceptions, bright men from the boonies, and not just Virginians. The only other US ambassador of their generation who was a Virginian (and a friend) was Murat Williams, to El Salvador. The only other senior Virginian in Saigon at that time, besides Fritz and Bill, was Rufus Phillips, who had never met them before when he arrived in 1962. And he had gone to Yale and wasn't in the Foreign Service.

But Halberstam's trope was infectious. The late William Prochnau, in his 1995 book about Halberstam and the other Saigon reporters, *Once upon a Distant War*, takes Halberstam's caricature and runs with it. Twice in sketches of the two Virginians in Saigon, hilariously if you know the difference, he locates Nolting's upbringing in *Trueheart*'s home town. "A man of small-town nobility, [Nolting's] background read Faulknerian: at times a peanut farmer, at times a teacher of philosophy, and then an investment banker whose family, in the southern manner, ran the little Virginia tobacco-country town of Chester."[35] Notes and facts do get mixed up, or perhaps one Virginia gentleman is the same as another.

4

★ ★ ★

Sink or Swim

T HE COURSE PRESIDENT KENNEDY chose to follow in Vietnam at the end of 1961 would characterize his approach to the most important foreign policy issue that would outlive him. He would avoid hard decisions as long as possible, including the deployment of US combat forces. The courtship of the Diem regime would intensify, and the US military presence in Vietnam would grow, but it would be ostensibly advisory.

An immediate consequence was the transformation of the US mission in Saigon into something resembling a proconsular state. Saigon was already one of the biggest US diplomatic missions in the world, thanks in large part to its economic assistance program to the Republic of Vietnam, at $300 million a year. The resident American community in Vietnam was about 2,400 strong, including representatives of a dozen US government agencies—CIA, USIA, AID, and many more—and their families. Alongside the civilians, a dozen generals and admirals and their staffs oversaw a growing contingent of noncombatant (training, supplying, advising) US military personnel—well under 1,000 when Kennedy took office, approaching twice that number by the end of 1961.

A senior American official who joined the mission in the spring of 1962 captured the heady, frantic atmosphere. "Overnight in Washington, Vietnam became fashionable, a priority country, and everyone . . . scrambled to share in the resulting top-level attention. Since there was no precedent, there were no rules, no inter-agency jurisdictional limitations," wrote John Mecklin, a former reporter who had covered Vietnam in the 1950s and had been recruited as the embassy's public affairs officer. "It was like a contest among a dozen teams of carpenters to see who could build the house fastest, simultaneously, on the same lot." And money was no object. Secretary McNamara was dismissive about costs when a gene-ral in the field expressed concern: "We have a fifty-billion-dollar budget and this is our only war. Don't worry about money."[1]

Coordinating the many-headed American presence in Vietnam on the ambassador's behalf was the "management job" Bill Trueheart had dreamed of: running the "Country Team." I first came across that term while inspecting my father's red leatherette-bound "diary," as he called it, carrying over the affectation from his London days. He ordered this date-book every year of his life thereafter from the *Economist*. Every Wednesday, I observed, and sometimes other days too, he had something scheduled at nine in the morning, or sometimes five in the afternoon, called "CT." I could only imagine this referred to me. But I was in school every morning, and of course my father and I never made appointments. So I asked. He set me straight about what the Country Team was. He also said he thought of me every time he saw the initials on his calendar. Then he suggested in a not unfriendly way that his diary was really none of my business.

As a term, Country Team was in its bureaucratic infancy. It meant more than just an embassy; it meant the sprawl of US agencies and interests planted in Saigon and throughout South Vietnam. In bureaucratic prac-tice the group represented the heads of all the agencies, or their deputies: the embassy equivalent of a principals' meeting in Washington.

The Country Team also existed in subtly different iterations as the so-called Country Task Force, whose job was to work with its Washing-ton counterpart, the Vietnam Task Force (not to be confused with the Southeast Asia Task Force), still later known, as Washington bureaucrats doodled, as the Vietnam Working Group, the Vietnam Coordinating Com-mittee, and by other names too.

Finally at the embassy in Saigon in those days there was something called, perhaps because it was simpler, the Trueheart Committee. This committee oversaw the hearts-and-minds side of things: rural pacifi-cation and development and security, embodied in the new panacea of "strategic hamlets," a scheme to gather, resettle, organize, protect, and mobilize Vietnamese villagers to defend themselves against Viet Cong predation. The Trueheart Committee ran in parallel to, and in ostensible coordination with, a Vietnamese government committee with the same brief, chaired by Ngo Dinh Nhu. "The connection between these two com-mittees was tenuous, if it existed at all," Trueheart said later, but it put him in regular, vexing contact with the all-powerful éminence grise of the president, Brother Nhu, who had adopted the strategic hamlet program as his own.[2]

These high-level committees with their Vietnamese counterparts represented the top layer of a structure that went deep, burrowing American advisers and experts, and American pressure and expectations, into the fabric of Vietnamese society. What the United States had created in Saigon, almost overnight, as Mecklin saw it, was a kind of "shadow government," an unwieldly role for the United States and its diplomatic corps.

Its function, simply put, was "to figure out what needed to be done and then to try to persuade the government of Vietnam to do it." United States personnel were deployed to work with their Vietnamese counterparts on a list of administrative responsibilities that sounds for all the world like formal occupation: "police, intelligence, harbor maintenance, airport control towers, radio broadcasting, motion picture production, printing, traffic engineering, highway construction, railroad maintenance, education, health and medical training, industrial development, banking, taxation, rural development, pig raising, monetary controls, and, of course, at every level down to the company or equivalent of the Vietnamese Army, Navy, and Air Force."[3] The latter was the most sensitive, and the one best remembered even today as one of the first lies to be spoken unashamedly by the US government about what was going on in Vietnam. After the Taylor-Rostow visit (and well before in clandestine fashion), military arrangements allowed US officers to fly on combat missions as "advisers" on operations purportedly designed and executed by Vietnamese counterparts. In 1962 it took the form of a secret plan code-named Farmgate.

"I Don't See Nothing"

Farmgate announced itself immediately in the form of equipment—including T-28 fighter-bombers, so-called "reconnaissance" bombers, and helicopters—arriving in Vietnam on US aircraft carriers. They docked at the foot of rue Catinat, Saigon's principal commercial street. But officially they didn't exist. Stanley Karnow, another journalist later famous for his work in and about Vietnam, was sitting on the terrace of the Majestic Hotel on the Saigon riverfront early in 1962, having coffee with a US military press officer. As one of these naval behemoths approached in the distance, towering over the marshland, Karnow exclaimed, "Look at that carrier!"

"I don't see nothing," the officer replied.[4]

Washington instructed the embassy not to confirm what was visible to the naked eye. Why? Because "in carrying out the Taylor-Rostow recommendations and bringing in this new equipment and additional people we were clearly exceeding the limits agreed-upon in the Geneva Accords," Trueheart recalled. The 1954 Accords specified a maximum of 685 American military personnel. It was a laughably specific and shifting limit, but one that had to be taken seriously, on paper, even if the other side was violating the Accords just as outrageously. "It was the position of the US government that we were not going to be convicted out of our own mouth of having violated this agreement. We were going to violate it and not make any bones about it, but we were not going to confirm this so that we could later be in effect convicted in the United Nations," Trueheart told an oral history interviewer.

Trueheart was disgusted by the hypocrisy, the bald-faced lies about American "advisers" as "passengers" on air sorties against the Viet Cong. *Americans* were flying the planes and doing the strafing and bombing, with their Vietnamese counterparts as no more than passengers. "There were many questions about whether there was always a Vietnamese in the back seat, or the front seat, or whichever seat he was supposed to be in," as Trueheart sardonically recalled it. "There were claims that the Vietnamese co-pilot often had never been off the ground before."[5]

President Kennedy declared at a news conference on February 14, 1962, that "we have not sent combat troops in the generally understood sense of the word."[6] Ambassador Nolting had testified to the Senate Foreign Relations Committee on a January visit that no Americans were in combat "as of now," but he did not say the first Farmgate missions were due to start the next day.[7]

Kennedy's brother Robert, the US attorney general, stopped in Saigon in late February, his first trip to Vietnam since he had accompanied then congressman Kennedy in 1951. Kennedy was there for just four hours late one night, in the VIP terminal at Tan Son Nhut airport, holding meetings with military and embassy people (while Ethel Kennedy put her feet up with Bittie Nolting and the girls at the residence). Robert Kennedy also conferred with the other presidential brother in this story, Ngo Dinh Nhu, whom some Americans liked to call "Bobby Nhu."

At a postmidnight press conference concluding the visit, flanked by

Nhu and Trueheart, *chargé* again, Robert Kennedy was asked for a clarification about something he had just said: "What is the semantics of 'war'
and 'struggle'?" Kennedy's reply: "It is a legal difference. Perhaps it adds
up to the same thing. It is a struggle short of war."[8] Robert Kennedy would
be among the uneasiest of the president's confidants about the course of
events that followed.

Late on the evening of March 7, 1962, two American reporters came to see
the American *chargé* at home. (Lying in bed, I could often hear car doors
slamming, the scurry of activity to open the front door, the murmur of
greetings as my father led visitors into the Blue Room.) On that night
Ambassador Nolting was in Baguio, a resort in the Philippine highlands
favored for R&R throughout the region, meeting with the new assistant secretary of state for Far Eastern affairs, the redoubtable Averell
Harriman, and all the US ambassadors in the region.

Sitting in the Blue Room, David Hudson of NBC and Jerry Rose of
Time laid out before Trueheart evidence they had that was "in conflict
with their understanding of official statements," as Trueheart put it to
the State Department in the hours that followed. Using the classified
term *Farmgate* throughout, the two reporters laid out information they
said was widely known to foreign correspondents in Vietnam. US pilots
were spearheading ground support and bombing missions against the
Viet Cong, and there were essentially "two air forces" waging the war,
one Vietnamese and one American. The official line, of course, was that
US forces were merely advising and training and "supporting," which
Trueheart told them, denying they were "spearheading" anything.

Amazingly, by Trueheart's account, the reporters "accepted this explanation and would file their stories accordingly." But his final thought to the
State Department left no room for illusion. He said it was inevitable that
US control of and participation in air combat operations would become
known, and urged that the "inadequate" official guidance be revised "in
light these insistent inquiries."[9]

In Washington, Roger Hilsman was already persuaded that trying to
cover up Farmgate was not just a mistake. "It is an impossibility," he told his
colleagues at INR, the intelligence shop he ran at the State Department.[10]

Sometimes the bureaucratic record is inadvertently frank, even when it is
counseling the opposite. On March 1, 1962, Secretary of State Dean Rusk

sent "Task Force Saigon" the following press guidance on Vietnam, enumerating five statements about US policy that were "incorrect":

1. That the US is in support of the Diem regime rather than the people of Vietnam.
2. That we are in a partnership in a common effort rather than in support of a GVN [Government of Vietnam] effort.
3. That the situation is rapidly turning into a US war rather than a war controlled and directed by the GVN.
4. That US military personnel are in combat status on offensive operations rather than in training, logistics, transportation, support, and advisory capacity, defending themselves when attacked.
5. That the US is violating the Geneva accords . . . 1962.[11]

This is, in fact, a correct checklist of exactly what was going on in Vietnam. James Reston, in his *New York Times* column, spoke it plainly: "The United States is now in an undeclared war in Vietnam. This is well known to the Russians, the Chinese Communists, and everyone else concerned except the American people."[12]

Roaming a Capital at War

In London and Paris we as Americans had blended in and adopted the local folkways; in Vietnam in the early 1960s we were a visible minority. We were an enclave—not literally, but figuratively. We mixed largely with one another, and other diplomatic families. We kids wore chinos and madras shirts and Weejuns, hoping to emulate our contemporaries at home. We traveled to the American Community School on a khaki school bus fitted with antigrenade grilles and carrying US military police officers. We could occasionally hear the boom-boom in the distance at night. We knew that Americans and Vietnamese were dying in conflict not very far away, and occasionally in our midst. Probably half the Americans we ran into, and many more as time went on, were in uniform. It was hard not to appreciate, on some level, that we Americans were conspicuous visitors at best and an uneasily occupying power at worst.

New personnel at the embassy, I learn now, were briefed on personal security thoroughly and repeatedly—to establish irregular patterns in their schedules and movements and around the city, for example. The fear of grenades and attacks like the one on Fritz Nolting the previous summer was ever-present. One embassy officer recalled internal reports of poison-tipped needles carried by Vietnamese children sent into crowds to jab Americans. There was always the fear that a taxi driver would whisk you away and deliver you into the hands of the Viet Cong; another American memoirist of this period, younger than me at the time, remembers his amah foiling such an attempt in the cab they were riding by beating the driver with her umbrella.[13]

To the best of my recollection Phoebe and Bill did not take this very seriously, or they hid their worries masterfully. "Don't believe 90 percent of what you read in the papers about this place," Bill wrote his mother. "Above all don't worry about us. I am busy, but not busy dodging bullets. Saigon is very peaceful indeed, much more so than Paris or Algiers."[14] But that was not so. The following month two American prisoners were executed for not keeping up with their Viet Cong captors, and two French civilians were shot dead by the Viet Cong while boating near Saigon.

For all that tension and latent danger—remarkable for me to reckon now, postparenthood—my mother and father gave me permission to roam the capital of a country at war. My fifth-grade pals had the same freedom. I remember no admonitions, no fretting, no restrictions that wouldn't apply to any ten-year-old in America. I rode my bike where I wanted, usually to see friends or go to the colonial-era Cercle Sportif, the equivalent of a country club with tennis courts and an Olympic-size pool a few blocks away from home. There, according to Frances Nolting, "the French sunbathe(d) on one side of the pool, the Americans on the other, the Vietnamese on the ends."[15] At the poolside bar we ordered endless Cokes and *limonades* (like 7UP). I also joined Troop 1 Saigon of the Boy Scouts of America. I am not sure this consisted of more than a camping trip or two—to a secure field near the airport next to the golf course.

We American boys and girls were "other," but we intermixed unselfconsciously with the people of Saigon. We learned some basic phrases, as well as expressions sprinkled with French and English. *Bookoo* was beaucoup. Very good and very bad were *numbah one* and *numbah ten. Di mau* meant go fast, "*Di, di, mau, mau,*" we would cry to the *cyclopousse* (bicycle pedicab) driver to get us somewhere in a hurry. Vietnamese language courses were a token weekly hour in our school curriculum, but we learned from one another how to swear in Vietnamese, including *di mao,* fuck your mother.

The local currency in soiled piaster notes bore the portrait, inevitably, of Ngo Dinh Diem. Vietnamese slang for a piaster, the way we say *bucks* for dollars, was *dong*. They and we also called the piasters by their initial letter, *pee*. So it cost ten piasters, *ten pee, muoi dong*, to have a bicycle tire repaired—about thirteen cents. We watched in fascination as an old man squatted on his haunches and went to work, soaking the inner tube in the gray water to watch for the bubbles, finding the puncture, then cutting a perfect oval from a scrap of a discarded rubber to make the patch.

The bicycle man, and many more vendors, could be found at the central market downtown, which as we grew older and freer became a regular destination. It was like a souk in any other part of the word, physically close, full of smells of *nuoc mam* and incense and every beast and bird and creature of the sea. We boys were exotic and fair and drew appreciative onlookers, especially women who giggled and touched our hair and smiled at us with teeth blackened by the betel nut they chewed for relaxation. There was an open space where ancient codgers clustered; their single two-inch-long fingernails signified they didn't do manual work, their facial molehairs a foot long signified good luck. And everywhere we saw amputees or otherwise legless men, and wretched mothers holding sickly babies swathed in dingy rags; some of the babies, it was said, were dead, but still useful.[16]

By mid-1962, American servicemen were everywhere that American kids hung out—the bowling alley, the PX, the Capital Kinh Do movie theater, the baseball games at Pershing Field. The opening of the American bowling alley, across the street from the Cercle Sportif, was my first exposure to the "sport." The lanes were equipped with AMC pin-setting machinery, some of it not fully functioning, such that faceless Vietnamese worked in the darkness behind the clanking machinery, collecting the pins and setting them in place by hand after each turn. American GIs were invariably in the next lanes and bowling at a higher level. I remember being struck by their tattoos, and how often they said *fuck*. They were not many years older than we were, with other things to do in Vietnam.

"Not a Meeting of Minds"

While Nolting and Trueheart plunged into mission management, press management, and regime management, Nolting was also facing upward, dealing with increasing pressures from Washington to provide statistics about a military threat that was chaotic and unprecedented, to work with a government that was in paralysis and denial, and to generate positive news coverage about all of it. On top, Nolting was fighting, and losing, his first bureaucratic battle, which took the form of turf and authority and the chain of command, but the struggle spoke volumes about the inner contradictions of the early US approach to Vietnam.

An upshot of the Taylor-Rostow recommendations was a significant change in the military command structure in Vietnam. What had been the Military Assistance Advisory Group (MAAG) since 1955, led by a three-star American general, was being squeezed to the side by the creation of the Military Assistance Command Vietnam, or MACV. The new command came into being on February 8, 1962, and to head it President Kennedy appointed General Paul D. Harkins, who got his fourth star for this assignment.

This was a peculiar arrangement, another case of structures invented on the fly that went against norms. For one, as the United States was not technically at war, MACV really was not a command. Harkins answered to CINCPAC, the commander in chief of the Pacific, Admiral Harry D. Felt, a regular visitor to Saigon and an inveterate micromanager of the command, from his headquarters in Honolulu.

The new structure set off alarms for Nolting, and for Trueheart too, when they heard about it in January. Six years before, President Eisenhower had signed an executive order stipulating that all American agencies, including the military, were answerable to the president's personal civilian representative, the ambassador, in any country in the world. Early in his presidency Kennedy had reiterated this standing order as a message to the bureaucracy, and especially to the Pentagon, about civilian oversight of American missions.

The creation of a military command with a four-star general in Saigon struck Nolting and Trueheart alike as "a move by the military to get out from any control by the mission." They thought more broadly, Trueheart said, that MACV "tended to overemphasize the military aspects of the problem, which we thought was fundamentally a political problem."[17]

Here the special circumstances of Vietnam prevailed with a classic and clumsy bureaucratic finesse: "Wherever a military matter was concerned, Nolting was subordinate to Harkins; wherever political matters were concerned, it was vice versa," as Kennedy's new Vietnam man on the National Security Council, Michael Forrestal, later summed up the arrangement: "This never worked, because you can't distinguish in this kind of a war what is political and what is military. . . . In all honesty, if I were Ambassador Nolting, I would have read this [order] just the way he did read it. It made him a subordinate of the military establishment."[18]

During his January 1962 trip to Washington, Nolting made the rounds at the State Department, the CIA, the Pentagon. He met with newspaper editorial boards. He testified before the Senate Foreign Relations Committee. (On a side trip he visited his mother in Richmond and found time to pay a call on Trueheart's mother, who lived around the corner.)[19]

Not letting go, Nolting took up the chain of command issue with President Kennedy himself. At an Oval Office meeting arranged by Averell Harriman and joined by General Taylor, the president heard the ambassador out. Harriman stoutly supported Nolting's point of view, as it echoed his wariness of the military role.[20] Kennedy promptly told Taylor to change the instructions to reflect the point Nolting was pressing—the very point the president had reiterated to all ambassadors seven months before.

Even that presidential order hit the wall before Nolting got back to Saigon. Secretary of Defense McNamara gave the ambassador a lift as far as Honolulu. On the plane, during a private dinner, McNamara was blunt: his hands were tied. The Pentagon would never agree to a four-star general as a subordinate of an ambassador.[21] There had been a private understanding between Rusk and McNamara, and no piece of paper—or president!—would change it.

Yet Nolting persisted. On the next leg of the trip to Saigon, he wrote President Kennedy a plaintive, even patronizing letter of protest about the Rusk-McNamara handshake. He called it "an agreement on words, but, I am afraid, not a meeting of minds, which is more important." Nolting insisted that "one person must be clearly in charge of the conduct of our affairs in Vietnam and of our relations with the government of Vietnam." He concluded: "If the views expressed above do not accord with your own, or if there are scars which you think will impair my effectiveness, I hope that you will tell me so and accept my resignation which is, of course, readily available."[22]

Perhaps wisely, his superiors in Washington never showed Nolting's passive-aggressive letter to President Kennedy. The ambassador had pushed too many buttons. Secretary Rusk wrote him a soothing message that "there is no doubt you are Senior US Representative in Vietnam." But he concluded tartly that Nolting's "insistence" on putting his pre-eminent status on paper, "in absence of any actual misunderstanding, would almost certainly destroy the very relationships which are critical to success in Vietnam."[23]

That seemed to be that. But the genial Nolting was revealing himself to be touchy, irascible, wedded to principles. In the event, he and General Harkins got along famously. Not so Nolting and his own superiors.

The Diem Treatment

On February 15, 1962, Ambassador Nolting made a lunchtime speech to the Saigon Rotary Club, an audience of Vietnamese businesspeople, pro-fessionals, intellectuals, and government functionaries. Going somewhat beyond the State Department's expectations, Nolting declared: "What a marvelous transformation would take place in this country if all those who criticize their government would decide to work with it and for it." This caused ripples in Washington. Forrestal said Nolting's "instructions for the speech were to preach a bit of economic austerity at a time of war, but his speech was reported and read as a blanket endorsement of Diem—that was US policy, after all, even if more people were losing faith in Diem."[24]

A few days later, reacting to what he'd been told about the speech, Diem called Nolting in to the palace. He wanted help—or wanted to be seen to be wanting help—in drawing responsible anti-Communist dissident lead-ers to join the Vietnamese cabinet, another hoary American demand. "Let me see this list [of possible candidates]," Diem said. Nolting was startled but quickly produced one for the next meeting. When he showed it to Diem, the president said he'd be glad if any of them would serve—and would *Nolting* ask them to do so? Surely not a task foreseen by the dip-lomatic primer. "Having stuck my neck out, I agreed," Nolting said. "And not one of the people I spoke with was willing to join the government."

"You see, that is my problem," Diem told Nolting resignedly.[25]

Very often formal calls on Diem were to accompany visiting dignitaries from Washington. "They were unlike any courtesy calls I've ever seen any-where else," Trueheart said. "They lasted four hours and more and were always a monologue by Diem. . . . They were always the same thing: a long lecture on the history of Vietnam and the history of Ngo Dinh Diem. . . . You'd come out of these meetings with the chief of state and have absolutely nothing to report. We didn't even bother to report them, which says more than anything else" about their utility.[26]

A typical lecture might begin with Diem's days in 1922 as a district official; his readings of Communist literature published in Switzerland and insights gathered therefrom; the closeness between the Popular Front in France in the 1930s and Moscow central, which only encouraged Vietnamese Communists; the work of André Malraux; Diem's memories of living in America, which always included his delight at corn on the cob; and "the relationship of taxi dancers to espionage to Chinese Communist tactics in Guinea."[27]

There were always tales of the perfidy of Ho Chi Minh, who'd had the gall to offer Diem a post in his postwar government after arranging the execution of his eldest brother. Speaking as the pot facing the kettle, the president once carped to a US visitor that Ho Chi Minh "looks over your head when you're with him and does all the talking; if you try to say something he doesn't hear you."[28] Then Diem might turn to all the mistakes the United States had made since 1954, squabbles over rural development priorities and the experience of *agrovilles,* the impatience of Americans for quick results, Kennedy's sellout of Laos and the coddling of Prince Sihanouk in Cambodia, the scandalous personal attacks on the Ngo family by the American reporters, the poverty of leadership talent in Vietnam—no thanks to the French, and so on.

Nolting would take to the palace a list of ten or twelve items to cover but seldom got past the first one or two, because Diem would not stop talking. All the conversations were in French, with Diem interspersing his monologues with "*n'est-ce-pas?*," a tic so mesmerizing that some of the diplomats would keep count of the repetitions.[29]

"Someone Who Loves You Very Much"

The school bus picked me up at the corner, half a block away. It came very early, because school was out for the day by noon. This matched the business workday in Saigon, which came to a halt for three hours at midday for lunch and a siesta. My parents fell readily into this habit, which meant that we gathered often for lunch as a family, perhaps to compensate for the rarity of our dinners together.

While my parents napped afterward, especially in our first year in Saigon, I would while away the time in the front seat of the Ford Fairlane, with Sinh the chauffeur, both poised in the driveway to take my father back to the embassy. The DCM's official car had the Great Seal appliqués, and a place on the front sides to screw in flagpoles on the rare occasions when that might be needed. A DCM even had a flag—just the circle of stars sans the eagle within. All the US embassy cars in Saigon were outfitted with two distinctive local alterations. Their roofs were painted white, to deflect the sun, and their vinyl seats were covered in white broadcloth slipcovers, also to shield from the effects of the Saigon heat, which seldom dipped below 80 degrees.

In the driveway I'd find Sinh dozing behind the wheel, the doors open for the breeze. He would stir to life and turn to chat. Sinh was born in Hanoi. His family were among the hundreds of thousands of North Vietnamese refugees Dr. Tom Dooley and Colonel Lansdale had helped to shepherd to the South. Sinh was a Catholic, I knew from the small cross around his neck. I do not know whether he was a sleeper agent, as anyone might now wonder. He was well-read and well-schooled, with a place-marked French-language book on the car seat at all times. He had young children. Because of his kindness and my youthful obsession with cars, Sinh and I developed an improbable relationship, the only real one I had with anyone Vietnamese.

Across the street from our house, and down a bit toward a major intersection, was an open field. We lived in the city in a neighborhood of villas and small apartment buildings, but this triangular area was cleared and undeveloped. It was used intermittently for markets and sports events, a circus or *spectacle* now and then.

Mainly, it was a space where my American friends and I gathered for some rock-throwing and other preadolescent swagger. In so doing we drew the attention of Vietnamese boys our age. We began to taunt one another, group to group. We threw some stones at those boys, and they threw some back. No one was hurt. We scattered away.

As the land was visible from the house, Sinh may have seen the rock-throwing, or one of the white mice may have told him. Sinh reported the news to my father—surely not an easy thing for him to do—who admonished me. Gently, as I recall, but devastatingly. I can imagine now what it must have looked like to him, as he went to work every day to make things right between the Americans and the Vietnamese. When I asked who had ratted me out, he said, with his disconcerting frankness, "someone who loves you very much." And then, at my insistence, he told me who. Sinh and I never spoke of this. I threw no more rocks.

One of my prized possessions at the time was a transistor radio. These devices are a source of amusement to my children, as is my boyhood stamp-collecting, but they were the latest thing going—a battery-operated radio you could carry. I'd started with a little one in London, and on the trip to Saigon in the Tokyo airport I'd gotten an upgrade to one about the size of a small paperback book. I would bring the radio out to the car sometimes, and Sinh and I would listen to it together. He admired it. His own transistor was not as good, and it was held together with surgical tape.

One day Sinh asked me, just like that, if I would give him my radio. I was surprised and confused by this unimaginable request. Thinking fast, I said I had to ask permission. I begged (inside) for my father to tell me I could keep it. He told me it was my decision. He said that the radio would probably mean more to Sinh than it ever would to me. A hotly debatable point. Sinh never let me forget my generosity. He played the radio—tinny Vietnamese music—every day in the car waiting for my father to leave until the day we left for good.

Bombs over Independence Palace

Ngo Dinh Diem rose early, as was his custom, on Sunday morning, February 27, 1962, and went to his study to continue reading a biography of George Washington, whose struggles and victories he admired. At 7:15, he heard the roar of aircraft. The president ran to the balcony of Independence Palace, the wedding-cake former French colonial governor's mansion, to see the terrifying approach of two fighter-bombers with Vietnamese air force markings. For thirty-five minutes, while reinforcements were scrambled, the planes strafed the palace and dropped bombs on the wing where Diem lived with Counselor and Madame Nhu. Ships in the Saigon River a few blocks away eventually were able to shoot down one plane; the other pilot fled to Cambodia, where he was granted asylum by Diem's archenemy Prince Sihanouk.

As he had in the assassination attempt the summer before, Nolting showed remarkable sangfroid. After "the racket ceased," Nolting "pulled on some clothes, got into our car, and directed the driver to the palace." He flew the flags, which got them through a police cordon, but they were stopped by a phalanx of Vietnamese tanks surrounding the smoldering palace. "I impulsively jumped out and walked toward the gates. A sharp bayonet prick in my back stopped me. I explained who I was and was let through the gates."[30]

There was one fatality, an amah, who was found clutching the unharmed infant daughter of the Nhus. Madame Nhu herself was slightly injured when she fell through the cratered floor of her bedroom.[31] The ceiling of President Diem's bedroom also caved in, and with the cascading rubble tumbled a carpenter who'd been working on the floor above. (When told of the carpenter's unexpected encounter with Diem, Nolting quipped: "And how many hours did the president keep him?")[32]

Three Truehearts were not in Saigon that morning. With baby Josh left at home in the care of Thi Lan, his amah, the rest of us had left the day before on a trip to Bangkok. When the shooting and bombing stopped Sunday morning, Bittie Nolting rushed to the Truehearts' house on foot, three blocks away across that open field, collected Josh, and carried him back to the safety of the residence. Bittie laughed, telling the story fifty-five years later:[33] Thi Lan remonstrating and fussing behind her as she followed her tiny charge in the arms of the ambassador's wife through the streets of Saigon, hazy with the smoke of artillery fire and jammed with soldiers and armored cars. All nonchalance apparently, the other Truehearts went on to their next stop, Singapore.

In truth, the palace bombing was a rogue operation, and a fizzle. The pilots were delusional in believing, based on some critical coverage of the regime in *Newsweek,* that the United States would come to their aid in overthrowing the government if they got the action going. The attack represented no organized coup led by senior officers. But the US news coverage couldn't help construing the attack as more evidence that the Diem regime was not popular. Madame Nhu referred to the "ill-concealed regret" in the US press accounts that the Ngo family had not been eliminated. Diem and the Nhus moved out of the shattered palace for good afterward, to a smaller and more secure palace called Gia Long, a few blocks away, where they would live until the end.

Two days later Nolting went to see Diem in the company of yet another Washington visitor, William P. Bundy, an assistant secretary of defense and the national security adviser's older brother. The anecdotes Diem shared with them, as recorded by an American general taking notes, offer a rich glimpse into the odd chief of state and the cuckooland of his palace.

Ambassador Nolting asked President Diem several times if the attack had been the work of a disgruntled few or a sign of unrest in the South Vietnamese air force. Diem sounded magnanimous. The Vietnamese pilots were "not generally men of ill will," he told his visitors, but they were "young, excitable, and immature." Ngo Dinh Diem's idea for corrective action was characteristic of the professional mandarin: "there should have been a more careful selection made prior to training and . . . family, education, and background should be more meticulously examined." (The father of one of the pilots, he told them, had a long history of antigovernment activity, which Diem went into in detail, at the village and family level, for some time. Vietnam was a small country and Diem was encyclopedic in his knowledge of it.)

For two hours and forty-five minutes Diem disgorged seemingly everything he had been told or whispered or was determined to believe about the pilots, the army, the political opposition, the journalists. When Diem paused briefly to light another cigarette, Nolting seized the chance to offer specific advice. Nolting suggested Diem address the nation on radio "to express his confidence" despite the attack. Nolting said he had "noticed the pleasure of the people on hearing his voice. It could be seen on their faces." Diem demurred and said a planned demonstration would be "eloquent enough." The ambassador repeated his suggestion: an address by radio would reach the whole nation. Diem wasn't interested in any of this. He hadn't been interested even when his friend Ed Lansdale suggested it in 1955, as had every American ambassador since.

Ngo Dinh Diem was living in another world. The palace bombing was not a warning to him, as some journalists were saying, Diem declared. "It should be a warning to *them*"—the journalists—"an indication of the danger of *their* irresponsibility."[34]

Ophelia in the Rice Paddy

On March 21 Bill Trueheart was in charge again, as Nolting was in Honolulu again—the secretary of defense's Vietnam conference was an exhausting monthly dance—when unidentified aircraft were caught on radar supplying and reinforcing the Viet Cong near Pleiku, in the central highlands.

Trueheart immediately recommended to the State Department the dispatch of "aircraft with night-fighter capability . . . shooting down any unfriendly aircraft detected over SVN [South Vietnam]." He said it was the "minimum response expected by GVN." He said the US planes should remain "at least through present full moon period and that they be represented publicly as 'in transit.'"[35]

Two days later, President Kennedy approved the new rules of engagement, another significant step in the unacknowledged war. Tellingly, the first preoccupation was with appearances and alibis. In the State Department's telegrammed reckoning, "If US-marked plane actually destroys Communist plane, public handling will be simply that Communist plane crashed, thus attempting avoid problem of degree to which Americans engaged in active hostilities in VN. We feel confident Communists will in any event receive message loud and clear."[36] Roger Hilsman of the State Department's intelligence bureau, noted with asperity, and prescience, that American air strikes called in by the South Vietnamese army "on the basis of the flimsiest of intelligence" were leading to "a very large amount of what cannot help but be indiscriminate bombing. The whole business could blow up in any number of horrendous ways."[37] He pronounced such an approach "fruitless. It creates more Communists than it kills."[38]

Hilsman and Forrestal, who traveled to Vietnam together three times, were impressed with an American major general they met, Edward Rowny (a Yale classmate of Hilsman and many years later the US strategic arms negotiator). Rowny gave them a sober assessment of the war effort: there were too many American generals (by now twenty-two!), too many plans, too many programs, and no direct line to the Joint Chiefs of Staff because of the cumbersome fiction that General Harkins reported to CINCPAC in Honolulu.

And then there was the South Vietnamese army. Rowny described to the visitors a generic ARVN (Army of the Republic of Vietnam) sweep operation against suspected Viet Cong strongholds: a lot of noise and firepower at daybreak to announce an assault, which gives the enemy clear warning if they didn't have it before, and a chance to disappear into the maquis:

> After a while there is a flurry on the right and someone drags a peasant out of a rice paddy where he has been hiding. The peasant is bound and taken prisoner as a "suspected Viet Cong." . . . Some time later another flurry

appears on the left and a man runs toward the jungle. He is shot and killed and marked down as a Viet Cong since he ran. They then proceed to the village which is deserted except for an old man or perhaps an addlepated girl—an Ophelia, as Rowny describes her. Under interrogation the senile old man or addled girl points toward some spot in the jungle, or some cellar or something. The troops go there and drag out a man who is hiding who is then bound and captured as a "suspected VC." The operation has now reached noon. Everyone sits down, cooks their rice and meal. Patrols are sent around finding nothing. And then an hour or so later the helicopters come to pick the troops up and take them back to their regular billets.[39]

Rowny's conclusion, which never seemed to sink in with higher-ups: "They do not really want to tangle with the enemy."

"Not That Kind of General"

Fritz Nolting's high dudgeon early in the year about the chain of command in Saigon was always qualified by his clear willingness to give the military commander complete discretion in making military decisions. In the event, that approach seemed to work well with the commander President Kennedy had chosen to head MACV.

Paul Donal Harkins, fifty-seven, was a general of the old school, and more precisely a caricature of it. He was a cavalryman, a former aide-de-camp to General George S. Patton, a polo player who favored crisp uniforms and army rituals. Long after the debacle of his command, he told an oral historian, "I joined the Boston National Guard just to learn how to ride a horse because I figured only soldiers and millionaires could ride horses on the weekend. And I ended up 42 years later in Vietnam without a horse." Or a clue.[40]

Horst Faas, who worked as a photographer for the AP, was making arrangements to shoot the new commander for the wire services. He found Harkins attired for the appointment in dress whites. Faas suggested the newly minted four-star general might want to appear in fatigues. "Forget that kind of picture," Harkins said. "I'm not that kind of general."[41]

Vanity is hardly disqualifying in great generalship. But this general was by most subsequent estimates spectacularly unqualified for command of an unconventional, asymmetrical war. Neil Sheehan said the US commander "willed himself to believe what he wished to believe and to reject what he wished to reject."[42] Like Nolting, with whom he usually saw eye to eye on policy and protocol, General Harkins was amiable and upbeat. "I am an optimist, and I am not going to allow my staff to be pessimistic," he said at the outset, and he remained until the end the prisoner of his optimism. His relations with Fritz were "absolutely perfect" throughout, he recalled. "He's just my type of man. . . . We got along just hand-glove."[43]

More than anything, it seemed, Washington wanted from General Harkins numbers about Viet Cong strength and casualties. Such numbers as existed were notoriously unreliable, inconsistent, and usually unflatter-ing to the American cause. "It took but little observation of the ways of Vietnamese officialdom to realize that the answer provided was often not worth the cost of transmission," observed General Taylor.[44] Secretary McNamara, who wanted and trusted numbers more than anyone in Kennedy's circle, was making his first visit to Vietnam in May 1962. He had specified in Honolulu, en route, that he wanted to see maps reflecting government control versus Viet Cong control throughout Vietnam.

A. J. Langguth, in his excellent *Our Vietnam,* tells the story of the map as it was prepared for the high-level visit:

> Six feet high, three feet wide, it showed all of South Vietnam up to the Demilitarized Zone. Red acetate overlays with blue stripes represented the areas controlled by the Viet Cong; blue overlays indicated areas controlled by the GVN, the government of Vietnam. The other two categories were plain red for "VC in ascendancy" and yellow for "GVN in ascendancy." So much red dotted the map that the staff called it "the measle map," but it was not shown to Harkins himself until the night before McNamara was due to land. At a rehearsal of his briefing, Harkins was appalled. "Oh my god," he said. "We're not showing that to McNamara."[45]

General Harkins, not Ambassador Nolting, was on the cover of *Time* mag-azine in the spring of 1962. After Trueheart's mother inquired about the general she'd read about in *Time,* he wrote back, "He is a very nice man. We play golf together whenever we can—notwithstanding that *Time* says he doesn't have time for it."[46]

For reasons of style and substance, Harkins was no favorite of the American correspondents in Vietnam, but he made wacky copy and good satire. The reporters mocked Harkins for an order forbidding air-port goodbye kisses between American soldiers and their Vietnamese girlfriends—out of cultural sensitivity to the prim Ngos, reasoned Harkins.[47] Some American military advisers even composed this version of "Twinkle, Twinkle, Little Star":

> We are winning, this we know
> General Harkins tells us so
> In the delta, things are rough
> In the mountains, mighty tough
> But we're winning, this we know,
> General Harkins tells us so
> If you doubt that this is true
> McNamara says so too.[48]

A Diplomatic Education

In our earliest months in Saigon, I paid close attention to the obligations my mother was given and that she accepted enthusiastically. The first of these, as a newcomer, was to call on the wives of resident foreign ambassadors in Saigon at appointed hours for tea; reciprocally to receive lady callers from the diplomatic community; and at separate hours of every week, to receive the wives of US embassy personnel. One called on those of higher or equal station, and one was called on by those of lower. The American diplomats' wives worked for free, of course, and were evaluated as part their husbands' performance reviews. There were only a handful of women in the Foreign Service in those days.

Phoebe Trueheart had manuals, studied avidly, to learn such things as which corner to turn on a visiting card to indicate one had been present, or another corner to indicate a visit when the callee was not home. On our bookshelves at home was a well-thumbed Emily Post, now suddenly relevant in this distant outpost, as well as a State Department publication titled *Social Usage in the Foreign Service*. In these two catechisms could be found such exotic topics as how an invitation should be worded, and what the handwritten RSVP should look like. I learned terms of address (in person, on second mention, in correspondence, in listings, on place cards). I learned that an ambassador is an *excellency,* and that his full title is ambassador *extraordinary and plenipotentiary:* one of a kind, and full of power.

I learned that technically the *embassy* is where the ambassador lives, and the *chancery* where he and his staff work—but Americans didn't say that any longer. The embassy was the office, the residence the ambassador's house; chancery was what the British said. I learned where the guest of honor sits at a table, and the precedence that follows, and that when the number of guests is ten or fourteen or eighteen, the host and hostess couldn't be on both ends, and the hostess could sit to the right of the (invariably male) guest of honor, who was at the head of the table.

Later in our time in Saigon my mother found a Vietnamese leather worker who made her a rectangular board with a second oblong piece of trimmed and gold-embossed leather in the center. Into this dinner "table" could be tucked the little place cards with the names of the guests and shuffled around while deciding on the best arrangement, or dealing with a late-breaking no-show.

More than occasionally the parties Bill and Phoebe hosted were not for dinner but for a cocktail reception with anywhere from one hundred to two hundred guests, spilling out of our living room into the garden. Many Vietnamese attended these parties, as well as foreign diplomats of many nations, and lots of Americans. I was made to feel, and may actually have wanted to be, part of the team. I don't recall the slightest resistance to being outfitted for the kind of white sharkskin suit that all adult males wore to social functions in Saigon. In the flurry of activity before the arrival of guests, I would distribute cigarettes (my mother's L&Ms, but not my father's Gitanes) into silver boxes.

For these big receptions, often in honor of visiting senators or departing colleagues, the guests would arrive in a long procession of chauffeured cars, many of them flying flags. Just inside the gate, fifteen feet from the front steps of the house, they would be greeted by a little boy in a sharkskin suit with his hand outstretched.

I must have understood that most everyone found this charming, if at first disconcerting, or at least had reason to say so when they reached the entrance to the house and were met by my parents. But I relate this and much else here with due embarrassment. Dennis the Menace I was not, although I had those moments too. Normal I was not. But I was reveling in this strange life. I thought I was learning about the world, knowing how things worked and what adults knew. I had a vague idea that diplomacy was important, but I was preoccupied with what I could readily see and understand, which was the outward, formal, ritual expression, the vast system of codes and protocols to which I was becoming privy. My mother would later tease me that I had surely been the only child in Christendom who aspired to become the US chief of protocol. In that can be surmised how little I truly understood then about the work my father was doing.

The Hole in the Doughnut

The reporting of American correspondents in Vietnam in this period is a celebrated story, and it's told with verve by the late William Prochnau in his atmospheric book, *Once upon a Distant War.* David Halberstam of the *New York Times,* Neil Sheehan of UPI, and Malcolm Browne of the AP are the remembered triumvirate. Browne arrived shortly after the Truehearts did, Sheehan and Halberstam in mid-1962. Their fearless critical reporting of the American war effort and the embattled regime became one of the journalistic legacies of this period. In real time it influenced decision-making in Washington. They were journalistic heroes, but they were not the first.

When Nolting and Trueheart arrived in 1961, the resident *New York Times* correspondent was scarcely a lapdog. He was Homer Bigart, a crusty old newsman who had reported with distinction from both theaters of World War II and from Korea, where his work won a Pulitzer Prize, and from many another war zone during the 1940s and 1950s—including Vietnam, where he impressed the visiting Congressman Kennedy.

Bigart was a short-timer in Vietnam this time, six miserable months for him, but he was a hero to the younger reporters and "had established skepticism as the rule of thumb."[49] One visiting pundit called him "one of the great shit detectors" of the profession. It was Bigart who, despite his evanescent tour, coined one of the most memorable lines of the period. In a humorous ditty he composed to get a giggle from a *Times* colleague, his slogan to describe US policy in Vietnam was: "Sink or swim with Ngo Dinh Diem." (Diem, pronounced *ziem,* makes the rhyme smoother.)

John Mecklin, the new public affairs officer in Saigon, parsed the phrase to describe the syndrome: "Failure became unthinkable. . . . We were stuck hopelessly with what amounted to an all-or-nothing policy, which might not work. Yet it *had* to work, like a Catholic marriage or a parachute. The state of mind in both Washington and Saigon tended to close out reason. The policy of support for Diem became an article of faith, and dissent became reprehensible."[50]

I gathered early on that Bigart was not a favorite in the Nolting household, for I heard his name being taken in vain—by the two younger daughters, Frances and Jane, then in their early teens, and surely echoing their parents. At first I was confused, not having heard the name Homer Bigart before. But I knew what "bigot" meant, and that's what the word sounded like in Virginian. I thought they were calling him one. This animus may have been my first inkling that journalists could be pests or much worse, and also my first inkling that they were part of our world in Saigon, too, and not always in harmony with it. It may have been my first awareness of journalists as people.

Nolting, Trueheart, Mecklin, and the others found that they were expected to manage the unmanageable: the American correspondents reporting things as they heard and saw them. The presidents of the United States and South Vietnam, and their entourages, were being driven crazy by their reporting. They thought it was inaccurate. They thought it was tendentious. They thought it was simplistic. But at least some Americans knew it was accurate.

A bad-news story datelined Vietnam would prompt a "rocket" cabled from Washington demanding explanations, or a protest, or the disciplining of reporters. One embassy officer, exasperated by the instructions to correct the behavior of journalists, said it was like "trying to tell a New York cab driver how to shift gears." Equally impossible demands on the embassy might come from the presidential palace a half mile away. Diem could never shake the idea that the American journalists spoke for the US government; after all, most of the press in Vietnam spoke for the Vietnamese government.

While strenuously denying that, and reminding Diem about press freedoms and public opinion, US diplomats also had formal responsibilities to the American correspondents, who were being frustrated by the US military over access to battle zones or hassled by Vietnamese secret police for reasons unknown. The journalists in Saigon were accredited, like diplomats. Their presence in Vietnam was at the sufferance of the Vietnamese government, which was tested early and often.

In March 1962 Bigart's visa expired, and the government declined to renew it. His offense, it transpired, was a lighthearted paragraph in a miscellany that (like "sink or swim") the *Times* didn't even print. But Vietnamese government censors routinely reviewed the newsmen's dispatches, lifted from the telegraph office and translated for palace approval before being okayed for transmission. The paragraph was this: "Mme. Ngo Dinh Nhu will be going abroad soon. However, reports that she will be absent for several months have been discounted as wishful thinking by government sources."[51]

The other journalist being thrown out was thirty-three-year-old François Sully, the *Newsweek* stringer. Sully was French and had been in Vietnam for fifteen years. Just a short time before, he had reported on Operation Sunrise, one of the early stages of the much-vaunted strategic hamlet program. Touted by Vietnamese and American officials as a means of protecting the hamlets from the Viet Cong, the program was described by Sully as forced relocation. The magazine ran pictures he took of villagers' homes being torched by the army.

When he ran into Nolting thereafter, the ambassador asked him, "Monsieur Sully, why do you always see the hole in the doughnut?"

"Because, Monsieur l'Ambassadeur, there *is* a hole in the doughnut."[52]

Nolting, and Trueheart too, would have liked nothing better than to be rid of these nettlesome journalists. But the ambassador did his duty. On March 27 he went to Diem to protest, warning Diem these expulsions "could do nothing but harm to our mutual efforts." In Nolting's telling, after pouring out his grievances against Bigart and Sully and their "derogatory and insulting" coverage, the president ordered the visas renewed.[53]

Expecting gratitude from Bigart for this stay of execution, instead Nolting got invective. The notoriously irascible *Times* man told Nolting he'd been desperate to leave Vietnam for a long time, and "his expulsion would have made his exit sensational." Nolting responded, or perhaps just wished he had, "perhaps, he, too, would have to 'sink or swim with Diem' a while longer."[54] The war with the resident American press, of course, would only get worse.

Bigart left anyway of his own accord soon after, and not quietly. In his closing dispatch for the *Times,* he described Diem as "secretive, suspicious, dictatorial" and predicted that inevitably the United States would have to consider the option of "ditching Ngo Dinh Diem for a military junta." His last paragraph was just as pessimistic about the war effort: "No one who has seen the conditions of combat in South Vietnam would expect conventionally trained United States forces to fight any better against Communist guerrillas than did the French in their seven years of costly and futile warfare. . . . Americans may simply lack the endurance—and the motivation—to meet the unbelievably tough demands of jungle fighting." In his last days in Saigon, Bigart "got into his cups" with the columnist William Pfaff, who was passing through that summer on a reporting tour of the region. Bigart told Pfaff that Nolting was "the sorriest excuse for an ambassador he had seen in twenty years of overseas reporting." In passing this conversation along to a colleague, Pfaff said Bigart regarded embassy people as "Clerks, clerks, clerks."[55]

Bigart left Saigon, a place he hated and an assignment he found beneath his station, on June 30, 1962. If Nolting and Harkins thought the worst was behind them, that's because they hadn't yet met his successor, David Halberstam.

The Wives

Perhaps out of diplomatic duty—the chance to help their husbands and their country—and doubtless out of compassion, my mother and Bittie Nolting were involved in all manner of charitable work in Saigon. A group of embassy wives formally led by Bittie and overseen by Phoebe and others set about raising money to rebuild an orphanage for children with leprosy just a few blocks from our house. They wrote their friends and acquaintances in the United States for donations, my first exposure to fundraising. Among the solicitations was one to the vice president of the United States, who had made such a fuss over Vietnam on his visit the year before. I recall this only because my mother showed me Lyndon Johnson's eventual check—for fifty dollars. "They have *millions!*" she hissed.

I remember Bittie and Phoebe being inspired, and guided, by one of the more unusual celebrity visitors, Genevieve Caulfield. Then in her seventies, she had been helping blind children lead normal lives in Thailand for three decades. She had more recently brought her approach to Vietnam. The Friends of the Blind of Vietnam had opened a small school in Saigon that the American Women's Club sponsored. Caulfield, a Virginian, was almost completely blind, the victim of a careless doctor who had spilled corrosive medicine in her eyes when she was three months old. This horrifying story, and Caulfield herself, made a lasting impression. She carved a unique place in my autograph book by embossing her name in Braille, squeezed with a little pocket device onto a page, while also laboriously signing it below.

While visiting Saigon, as it happens, Caulfield learned that she had won the Presidential Medal of Freedom. "My goodness, whatever is that?" she exclaimed when she got the call from the embassy. Good question, as this was the first year of the Medal of Freedom, and Camelot was in full swing. Genevieve Caulfield's fellow recipients that year were redolent of a dwindling era. They were Thornton Wilder, George Meany, Ralph Bunche, E. B. White, Pablo Casals, Andrew Wyeth, Edmund Wilson, Edward Steichen, Marian Anderson, Felix Frankfurter, and Ludwig Mies van der Rohe.

The headline from the *Bakersfield Californian* read: "Reds Fire on Flight of U.S. Aides' Wives: Viet Nam Official's Son Slain." On June 26, 1962, Phoebe, Bittie, Betty Harkins, and two other ranking American wives took an official trip to inspect a couple of worthy military housing projects in Bien Hoa, just fifteen miles from Saigon, and then Can Tho, 120 miles to the southwest. Few American civilians (excepting reporters) drove anywhere outside the cities any longer, as most of it was Viet Cong–controlled. That morning the American women flew on two US-supplied ARVN helicopters. My mother recalled (in some jottings she saved) the noise and unrelenting vibration, and sitting all the way wordlessly, uneasily face-to-face with very young Vietnamese soldiers carrying automatic weapons.

There was heavy fog in Bien Hoa at eight that morning, the first stop on the schedule. While the helicopter carrying the wives hovered above the fog, the one carrying their host, a Vietnamese colonel, settled down through the thick cover to find a safe landing zone. Suddenly from the shrouded trees Viet Cong fire erupted. A single bullet pierced the fuselage as it pulled up and away. The bullet killed the colonel's seven-year-old son, who was along for the ride. The American wives, unharmed and unwitting in the other helicopter, proceeded to Can Tho for the second stage of the trip, hearing only that the first leg was canceled for security reasons.[56]

Photographs in an album prepared afterward by their Vietnamese hosts picture the ladies—cutting a ribbon for a maternity hospital; visiting dispensaries, a school, a tailoring shop; presiding at a big lunch—smiling steadfastly through a day they learned later was tragic. "Around 5 we learned of the boy's death," Phoebe said in these jottings.[57]

She and Bittie and the others might have been killed themselves. I have no real memory of this dramatic moment and doubt it was hidden from me, or could have been. Bill and Phoebe's preternatural calm in this violent place can sound like stone-cold indifference, or bad parenting, or black humor. "We were oblivious to what was going on so don't waste your tears,"[58] Phoebe wrote her mother-in-law, sort of missing the point. A note came from their old Paris friend Arch Calhoun—by then the US ambassador in Fort Lamy, Chad—expressing his relief that Bittie and Phoebe had "escaped without harm during one of their local knitting expeditions."[59]

My maternal grandmother, Thelma Everett, made sure her local paper knew. "Copter Carrying Mrs. Truehart [*sic*] Misses Red Fire," headlined the *Ledger-Independent* of Maysville. In her letter Phoebe sounded more concerned about the news coverage of the incident. The *Times*' Bigart (it was one of his last dispatches from Vietnam) had been "the only one who came close to accuracy," she wrote Bill's mother, asking her to send clippings. "I'd like to see how far off they were."[60] I have the clippings, and they have the key facts right—except that the little boy had *not* been sitting next to Bittie but on another copter entirely. ("Would you please look for a seersucker bathrobe for Charlie?" segued my mother.)

A very short editorial space-filler from an unknown American paper, perhaps in Richmond, is also among the clippings Phoebe saved. A writer with too much time on his hands, or to fill space, mustered two paragraphs of outrage from the incident. "It is incredible" that Ambassador Nolting and General Harkins, the husbands and ranking Americans in Vietnam, "should sanction such a trip on any excuse. We're glad they survived, but if we're going to teach defense against guerrilla warfare to the Vietnamese, rule no. 1 should be to keep American women out of front-flying choppers."

Rule no. 2 might have been: in Vietnam, there were no rules to follow.

5

★ ★ ★

Doubting Thomases

IN THE MIDDLE MONTHS of 1962, important reinforcements arrived in
Saigon. Even a child could sense the tide, especially the military one.
American soldiers and sailors and airmen, growing by more than a
thousand a month, highly visible in their uniforms and Jeeps, swelled the
commissary and movie theater.

New replacements at high levels of the embassy that summer included
a new political counselor and deputy political counselor, both from the
stable Nolting preferred. "You have managed to collect almost all of the
Paris [embassy] expatriates that have been floating around Washington,"
his friend and colleague Arch Calhoun wrote Nolting about the new senior
officers, Melvin Manfull and Robert Miller.[1] Also new on the scene, but
not Nolting recruits, were Rufus Phillips, ex-CIA, old Vietnam hand (and
Lansdale acolyte), to run pacification. Seasoned journalist John Mecklin
had arrived in the spring as the new public affairs officer, in time to deal
with two other mid-1962 arrivals, David Halberstam of the *New York
Times* and Neil Sheehan of AP.

In that summer changing of the guard, William Colby, the CIA station
chief since 1960 and close confidant of Nhu, returned to Washington; he
would remain at the crux of the Vietnam issue for the rest of his important career, which concluded with thirty months as director of the CIA. Bill
Colby was succeeded in Saigon by another seasoned agency hand, John
"Jocko" Richardson, who arrived that summer with his wife and two children, both too young to have been friends.

I was just eleven, but I knew about the Central Intelligence Agency.
A legendary founding father of the OSS (Office of Strategic Services),
Frank G. Wisner, recently had been CIA station chief in London and a
neighbor of ours in Belgravia; his son Graham and I were friends. Graham

filled me in about his father's trade, cross your heart and hope to die. In Saigon, my indiscreet mother let me know who William Colby and then Jocko Richardson really were, with their "special assistant to the ambassador" title. She would point out other "spooks" to me too, often adding "maybe." This was all pretty interesting.

I was at a friend's house one noontime after school got out. His father, I knew from that embassy manifest, was an assistant air attaché and wore the uniform of a US Air Force lieutenant colonel. One day the father came home to lunch with his boss, the air attaché. I noted they had ridden home from the embassy in one of the black Ford sedans with roofs painted white rather than in a military vehicle.

My obsession with cars had only been enhanced by the rich variety and significance of the official vehicles in my world and their vehicular place in the pecking order. US embassy CD (corps diplomatique) plates started with 200 for the ambassador, 201 for the DCM, and so forth in sequences representing the various embassy sections and agencies. Standing and waiting outside of cocktail parties, I could often distinguish among identical official cars by their license plates. The embassy car those two air attachés had taken home that day had a license plate whose numbers immediately followed those of Colby and his deputy. CIA cars.

A lightbulb went on. That evening I asked my father if my friend's dad was CIA. He gave me a sharp look. "Who told you *that?*" I told him how I had deduced it. He couldn't suppress a laugh. I don't know what else he said, such as "Keep it to yourself." In any case, I did not. I asked my friend point-blank if his dad were CIA. He turned red, using the same words as my father, with different emphasis. "Who *told* you that?" he said, swearing me to eternal secrecy. I protect his identity today.

The First Commandment

Bob Miller, the new number two in the political section, had no reservations about going to Vietnam or about the stated policy. He was a convinced hearts-and-minds-er.

"We were the Kennedy administration's shock troops, being sent to do unconventional battle in far-off Vietnam and other far-flung countries beset by externally-supported insurgencies," Miller dryly recalled years later.[2] "Crucial to victory was political and economic reform, not military might"—although neither was yet working. Miller recalled a *Peanuts* comic strip taped to a wall at the embassy: Charlie Brown marching up to a baseball mound saying, "How can we lose when we're so sincere?"[3]

Like Nolting, Miller, and most others in the US mission, Trueheart at first entertained few doubts. "I was sent out to help with organizing the embassy and the mission," Trueheart said later. "I accepted that I wasn't sent out there to make judgments about [the policy itself]."[4] (The casual and telling term *out* to locate this faraway—from Washington—place is one still in use today for American quagmires all over the world.)

Simply stated, the policy, newly dusted off by the Kennedy administration, and dubbed the "first commandment" by Nolting, was to get along with Diem. Tellingly, the four US ambassadors to South Vietnam to date had oscillated dependably between the carrots and sticks of the US approach to South Vietnam: between the tough and ultimately alienating love of General J. Lawton "Lightning Joe" Collins (1954–55) and Elbridge Durbrow (1957–61), on the stick side, and the patient and forbearing courtship of G. Frederick Reinhardt (1955–57) and now Fritz Nolting, on the carrot side.

"Sweetness and light was the rule during most of my tour in Saigon," said Mecklin. "We treated Diem and his family like a Latin lover seeking the favor of a crotchety, middle-aged heiress."[5] Yet the embassy was hardly oblivious to the unpopularity and ineffectiveness of their client. Trueheart recalled "no shortage of Vietnamese who were ready to tell you that the Diem administration was hopeless. In fact, it was hard to find anybody who wasn't a member of the regime, or employed by the government, who would have anything good to say about it."[6]

While Trueheart sounds cynical and world-weary, Nolting's response to all the Vietnamese bad-mouthing of Diem was indignant and righteous. He recalled two senior Vietnamese generals sitting on the sofa in the living room after dinner one night at the US ambassador's residence:

> They lit into President Diem and said he was unworthy to be president of the country . . . that this man is really no good. A bad character. It was shocking to me.
>
> I said, "Gentlemen, you are my guests and I am an accredited diplomat to the government which happens to be headed by your president, who was elected."
>
> I gave them the reply which not only I but my predecessors had always given to the dissident generals. "You have a chance to run for president next

time. Don't give us this stuff about revolt and supporting a revolt. Why don't you do your duty as military men? The United States is not going to get into this question of a coup d'etat."[7]

Nolting's guests that night became two of the three principal leaders of the November 1963 coup d'état.

Yet long before he arrived, those Trueheart called "doubting Thomases" were hardly scarce inside the embassy. Joe Mendenhall, the political counselor in Saigon whose tour ended that summer of 1962, was probably the one influential diplomat who had most soured on the Diem regime. When he composed his exit memorandum after returning to Washington in August, Mendenhall spoke a plain truth concisely: "To win against the Communists, the Government of Vietnam should be either *efficient* or *popular,* but the Diem government is neither. . . . *Conclusion:* That we cannot win the war with the Diem-Nhu methods, and we cannot change those methods no matter how much pressure we put on them. *Recommendation:* Get rid of Diem, Mr. and Mrs. Nhu, and the rest of the Ngo family."[8] Not shrinking from the implications, Mendenhall went on to describe—although "I have never carried out a coup, and am no expert in this field"—how a coup might be carried out. He thought it best to seize the whole family when Diem and Nhu were outside the palace and travelling in Vietnam, and even better at a time when Archbishop Ngo Dinh Thuc and Ambassador Ngo Dinh Luyen, two other brothers, were out of the country. Thinking of his own daughters, perhaps, and the rest of us, Mendenhall in the last paragraph of the memo highlighted the evacuation of American dependents "in advance execution of the coup plans. Otherwise we might find them hostages in the hands of the Diem Government which would not hesitate to use them."[9]

In his last days in Saigon, Mendenhall had called on the South Vietnamese vice president, Nguyen Ngoc Tho. The conversation turned to rumors already stirring of a coup that might catapult Tho into the presidency. Mendenhall passed along to Tho the scuttlebutt, probably picked up by the CIA station, that if Diem's hold on power were threatened, then "Ngo Dinh Nhu will see to it that the Vice President is eliminated through assassination during the attendant confusion. When the Vice President was asked why then he did not take measures to protect himself, he replied stoically that he preferred not to spend all his time under guard, but to live as normally as possible. The Vice President said he was prepared to die but would have preferred to be killed by the Viet Cong rather than by 'one of our own.'"[10]

Vietnam Cassandras were becoming more familiar at the White House. From New Delhi and on periodic visits to Washington, Ambassador John Kenneth Galbraith warned of a drawn-out and indecisive military involvement, effectively replacing the French "as the colonial force in the area and bleed[ing] as the French did." He decried a weak and ineffectual government in Saigon and "a leader who as a politician may be beyond the point of no return."

Galbraith's pitch to Kennedy was to seek a negotiated solution. He had always urged President Kennedy to "keep the door wide open for any kind of political settlement." The ambassador-don memorably told the president: "Politics is not the art of the possible. It consists in choosing between the disastrous and the unpalatable. . . . Any alternative to Diem is bound to be an improvement." Now he proposed that Averell Harriman, drawing on his ties from being the US ambassador in wartime Moscow, approach the Soviet leadership confidentially and arrange for a cease-fire and "general non-specific agreement to talk about reunification after some period of tranquility."[11]

Whether or not the Soviets had the ability, let alone the desire, to call off an indigenous insurgency, Kennedy was not going to talk about negotiations.[12] But he was provoked enough by what Galbraith said to ask Harriman and McNamara for their reactions. With acidity, McNamara said Galbraith's vision for a negotiated solution "contains the essential elements sought by the Communists for their takeover by providing a set of rules which the free world would be forced to obey, while the Communists secretly break the rules to gain their objective."[13]

Harriman's cautious reaction to the same letter, which Kennedy asked him to read in his presence, was "that while he thought that Diem was a losing horse in the long run, he did not think we should actively work against him, because there was nobody to replace him." This formulation was less catchy than, but fundamentally echoed, sink or swim. Until the very hours before the end of the Diem regime, this was the Americans' choice: the devil they knew or the devil they didn't.

Talk of negotiations was beginning to float in the air, some of it emanating from the United Nations, from European capitals, and even from right next door in Cambodia; the monarch, Norodom Sihanouk, another of Diem's bêtes noires, was calling for an international conference on Vietnam. Nolting wrote to the State Department that the idea should be "spiked"—that is, publicly repudiated. The Diem government could never hide its anxiety about American constancy, and talk of negotiations would feed that paranoia. The Vietnamese worries were hardly irrational.[14]

Weighing in again to Harriman from New Delhi on April 19, and licking his chops for Nolting, the lordly Galbraith declared:

> I take strong exception to the cliché which is so persistently damaging in our diplomacy that we must subordinate our policy to whatever will maintain the confidence of the regime to which we are accredited. This leads us to the absurdity that any action, however sensible, may undermine confidence if it doesn't fit the particular preferences of the government we are supporting. Nolting suggests that confidence of Vietnam people and war with Vietcong may begin to waver if we show disposition to diplomatic discussion. In fact there should never be any doubt about our preference for diplomatic settlement.[15]

He concluded: "I would also note typical tendency in telegram to identify the people with Diem and vice versa, an identification which no close observer of the South Vietnam scene can take seriously."

This is quite a rebuke to the resident ambassador, delivered to the ambassador's boss.

Nosy Parker

In Saigon, Bill Trueheart's almost sacred lifelines to the wider world were radio news broadcasts on the BBC and the Voice of America. In the cool early mornings before hot days of work and school my family enjoyed breakfast on the terrace overlooking the garden and listened to the plummy BBC newscasts on my father's enormous, barely "portable" shortwave Sony. The radio was a fifth presence at the table. I remember being shushed (or Phoebe being shushed) when something important was about to be uttered, and my father slamming his hand on the glass tabletop when he had missed it. He did this too when the vagaries of the shortwave connection led it to fade away or melt into squawks and honks. The patriarch's hand would slam again. My mother would look at me and, almost imperceptibly, roll her eyes.

Led by example, we were a news-aware family. The then-impregnable *Economist* came in the mail, along with *Time, Life,* the *Saturday Evening Post,* and the *New Yorker,* all quite delayed. Yet, mystifyingly, the adult reading material that absorbed me more fully, less abstractly, had to do with the US Foreign Service and the US embassy in Saigon.

I pored over the monthly *Bulletin of the Department of State,* a bland house organ of articles about the Foreign Service around the world and in Washington. One page of the magazine listed the American chiefs of mission in all the countries to which the United States was accredited. They were ambassadors, mostly, but in one or two instances "ministers" at "legations"—in smaller-fry countries—and also *chargés d'affaires* between ambassadors.

These American envoys appeared as points of reference on a mental map of the world that I was drawing. A few of these men were known to me already. Some had been my father's bosses, and now his contemporaries were becoming DCMs and ambassadors. Most were just names. I studied these exotic characters the way a regular American kid learns to name baseball players and follows them from team to team, in this case embassy to embassy. These champions, these diplomats of their day, bore fantastic names, so singular and striking they are easy for me to remember even now: Wimberley Coerr, Livingston Merchant, Archibald Calhoun, C. Burke Elbrick, Ridgway Knight, Leo G. Cyr, W. Walton Butterworth, G. McMurtrie Godley, and Outerbridge Horsey. ("Yes," my father replied to my incomprehension, "he likes to be called 'Outer.'")

It intrigued me, too, that quaintly (and vestigially even now) the US Foreign Service followed usages of diplomacy coined by the French: the *chargé d'affaires,* meaning the diplomat in charge in the absence of an ambassador, and the *attaché,* someone appointed (detached, we would say) from another agency. A *démarche* is a strongly worded official protest. Before a new ambassador can be appointed, an embassy seeks *agrément* (approval) from the host government. A *rapporteur* can sit in on meetings to record the proceedings. An important meeting may yield a *communiqué.* A briefing note can be called an *aide memoire,* while a social invitation may be sent *pour memoire.* Latin creeps in, weirdly yoked to the French, as in *chargé d'affaires ad interim,* for "in charge in the meantime." Or deployed for the ultimate banishment from a diplomatic posting: designation as *persona non grata.* My mother liked to use that or its abbreviation. If she was cross with someone, she'd say he or she (or I) was "PNG."

My Foreign Service curiosity was local and specific, too. For intelligence on the embassy in Saigon, I perused monthly registers of all civilian personnel. They were surely confidential documents, but they were left on the coffee table in the Blue Room or on my father's dresser. I pored through them. "Nosy Parker," my mother said, but she didn't stop me.

This meant that in addition to the titles and positions of every American in the mission, helpful in themselves, I could learn their civil service grades *and* their annual salaries—the salaries of every American adult male I knew, that is, many of them through their children. The ambassador was paid $25,000 per annum, the DCM $17,500, and all down the line, through the various sections, political, economic, consular, administrative.

My nosy parkering included close and frequent inspection of my father's dresser top. In one leather box he kept studs and collar stays and buttons, and a couple of old watches; in the other he kept old Zippo lighters, a couple of ex-pairs of glasses, and his military insignia, brass lieutenant's and captain's bars and multicolored decorations. Bill Trueheart was proud of his military service and often spoke of the doors and perceptions that military life had opened for him, to say nothing of professional opportunities. Through him I learned all the military ranks, puzzling (still) through the fact that while a major outranks a lieutenant, a lieutenant general outranks a major general.

I would describe Bill Trueheart as anything but a "military" kind of guy, the opposite of a Great Santini. Yet one of our conversations about his army days led us to agree on some role-playing, as we would call it today. He would play the master sergeant and I the buck private, and he would inspect my quarters every day. He taught me how to make hospital corners on my bed, waiving the rule that a quarter had to bounce on the tightly tucked-in blanket. According to a surviving page from a 1962 notebook, every week I was graded Excellent, Satisfactory, or Unsatisfactory on five counts: Room, Clothes, Cleanliness, Nails, and Behavior. (I was a nail biter.) The only U on this entry was for Behavior on February 21, 1962. On March 9, I was "promoted to corporal."[16]

No less interesting than the cuff links and chevrons on Bill's dresser was a wooden box nearby, concealed behind a floor-length curtain in my parents' bedroom. About the size of an attaché case, it locked with a padlock key "secreted" in one of the leather boxes. Inside was a big shortwave radio for emergencies, which my father had to test periodically to be sure it was working. "This is Mercury 4, this is Mercury 4, over," he would say, and back would come confirmation barks from an embassy security man. This was a primitive, easily penetrable arrangement. The network was named for the ambassador's car, not the early US space program.

More interesting yet, in an inside compartment of the box, was a Beretta pistol. I was not permitted to touch it, even in my father's presence. When I snuck friends in to see the radio, I didn't let them touch the gun either. I was not present the only times the radio and pistol were used and handled, respectively, by my mother.

"Explosion"

On September 7 at Gia Long, General Harkins proudly laid before President Diem his brainchild: an extraordinary US–South Vietnamese scheme to seize the military initiative. He dubbed it the "Explosion." The name made diplomats wince and snicker ("Shall we call it 'poof'?") at the same time.[17]

The idea Harkins pitched to Diem over the course of several hours, as William Prochnau caustically boiled it down, consisted in gathering "together every soldier, sailor, airman, civil guard, village self-defenseman, Montagnard scout, and paramilitary woman in Madame Nhu's troupe— some 450,000 fighters. . . . This force would be 'exploded' simultaneously on the unsuspecting and outnumbered Viet Cong. William Trueheart, the deputy ambassador who accompanied Harkins to the meeting, sighed many years later: 'I don't think he had had a new idea since the Second World War.'"[18] In 1991, Trueheart told historian David Kaiser that when Diem expressed fear in this meeting that the Viet Cong would descend from the central highlands and cut the country in half, General Harkins said, "Great! We'll pinch them off like the Battle of the Bulge!"

This did not make a favorable impression on President Diem is how Kaiser recorded Trueheart's words before sending a transcript to him for review. Trueheart replied to Kaiser that this sentence was the only error in the rendition: "That statement may be correct (about President Diem) but what I was trying to convey was that it did not make a favorable impression *on me!* I thought it conveyed a gross misconception of the nature of the military problem in Vietnam."[19]

General Harkins's own stenographic eight-thousand-word account of the same meeting, characteristically casting himself in the third person, suggests that it was Diem this time, and perhaps for the first time, who could not get in a word edgewise. That may be because Harkins spoke no French, which forced President Diem to exercise the serviceable English that he usually eschewed; the resort to English may have cramped his prolixity.[20]

It is hard to believe that my father, a most impatient man, at that long-awaited moment of escape from Diem *and* Harkins, would have asked the Vietnamese chief of state to sign my autograph book, but on that day he did. Trueheart being a diplomat, General Harkins's signature is in there too.

The Explosion plan eventually died quiet death.

Ink Blots

The strategic hamlet program was a kind of "solution" on which all seemed to agree at a time when they agreed about little else. It had the virtue of both pacification and security, if the solution worked. The hamlet plan operated on the theory of the inkblot, in which secure and self-sufficient hamlets would eventually proliferate and blot out the Viet Cong. There would be many thousands of them, eventually liberating the countryside from the thrall of the enemy. The bucolic-sounding hamlets were a natural expression of hearts-and-minds doctrine, but they had an intelligence quotient and a military objective. "We were using tactical defense in a strategic offensive," per William Colby.[21]

The concept dates to the Middle Ages, when vulnerable settlements fortified themselves against marauders. The French tried it in Morocco in the 1920s. With equally meager success, Diem had tried it already in Vietnam under another rubric, *agrovilles,* in the 1950s. Now they were rebranded. The strategic hamlet program in 1962 had many fathers, many enthusiasts, and many managers, each with his own motives and preoccupations and shortcomings.

The program's reinvention in 1962 was inspired and partially led by another of the many unexpected characters who wandered on to the Vietnam stage to give advice. Sir Robert Grainger Ker Thompson was a former British colonial official in Malaya. His work in counterinsurgency efforts, including a version of strategic hamlet, had succeeded against the local

Communists. He was a kind of British Lansdale. An expert with a legend and a record of success, he consulted frequently with President Kennedy (and then Johnson and Nixon) about the Vietnamese dilemma.

Bob Thompson moved to Saigon, about the time Trueheart did, to head the British Advisory Mission, the United Kingdom's gingerly participation in the Vietnam effort. Thompson and Trueheart, who ran the mission's Provincial Rehabilitation Committee, collaborated closely on the US embassy's oversight of the program—"oversight" being a vexed term for what was, like all things advisory, officially a Vietnamese program and ungovernable by definition.

The program was also Ngo Dinh Nhu's personal project—one of many. When Rufus Phillips arrived to take charge of rural pacification, he found Nhu claiming paternity. "Mr. Nhu said that although he had originated the strategic hamlet program, it was only an idea, a 'pipe-dream,' to him until the last four months," Phillips reported. (An interesting choice of words about a man suspected of being addicted to opium.)

Nhu viewed the strategic hamlet program much as its real progenitors had, and for the same basic two reasons: "a means to defeat communism while, at the same time, overcoming the problems of an underdeveloped country" and building loyalty to the regime, an essential ingredient in waging was against the Viet Cong. Nhu told Phillips that in addition to regrouping the villagers in safe zones, thus providing for their economic security, he wanted each village equipped with "commando" units "which would operate as guerrillas, in similar fashion to Viet Cong tactics." Another idea not likely to gain traction anywhere.[22]

Managing expectations, and developing the hamlets effectively, were preoccupations at the embassy, and for Trueheart in particular as the senior American cat-herder. Inside the embassy he began to express skepticism about its prospects for success. One visiting American official reported to the Joint Chiefs of Staff that Trueheart "was concerned that Brother Nhu, who is enthusiastic about the strategic village approach, might attempt to apply it simultaneously all over the country rather than systematically by phases. Ambassador Nolting, however, has talked with Brother Nhu about this specific question and has gotten some assurances that Nhu is aware of the danger of a blanket approach. Ambassador Nolting feels that it would be most unwise to raise with President Diem any question about Brother Nhu at this time."[23] So much there, and not just about the strategic hamlet program: the dubious DCM, the cautious ambassador, the bogus assurances from the palace, the eggshell-walking about the Ngo family. Nhu did indeed barrel ahead with a blanket approach, and the hamlets were never the success they might have been, even if that chance was slender.

Nonetheless, as 1962 drew to a close, the North Vietnamese leadership regarded the progress of the hamlets with deep concern, even ordering battlefield commanders to hold off on attacks that might be doomed. Ho Chi Minh went to Beijing to ask for more equipment and got it. Terrorist attacks diminished, and Viet Cong defections were rising. It was later revealed that Ho's leading confederate, Le Duan, had chalked up 1962 as a net win for the Diem regime.

The Ambassador and the Crocodile

It seems hard to reckon from the vantage of today, but in 1962 Laos still commanded as much attention, in the headlines and halls of power, as Vietnam. It was an open secret that Kennedy and his advisers were wary of making a stand in, or wasting much time on, this tiny landlocked country on China's border, whose military capabilities were anemic and whose civil service and infrastructure made South Vietnam's look like Austria's. President Kennedy had decided early in his administration to settle for a "neutralist" Lao state—a shotgun coalition of bitter enemies, royals, warlords, and Cold War puppets. He put Averell Harriman in charge of hammering out the terms of an unavoidably shaky and unsatisfactory deal.

Harriman was a formidable figure of enormous personal wealth and accomplishment—the scion of a railroad baron, Franklin Roosevelt's ambassador to the Soviet Union, secretary of commerce, governor of New York. He had badly wanted to be Kennedy's secretary of state, but it was never in the cards. He bravely settled for a nebulous title, "ambassador at large," and set out to make his mark with Laos.

In the fall of 1961, Governor Harriman, as he liked to be called, had swooped down on Saigon to persuade a skeptical Diem to see things Washington's way and endorse the Laos deal he was negotiating. Nolting found Harriman insufferable, as many did. The former wartime ambassador in Moscow told Nolting he had a "fingertips feeling" the Soviet Union would enforce the Laos accord. Nolting: "I said that my fingertips gave me precisely the opposite impression."[24]

Harriman drew two important conclusions from this early visit to

Vietnam. One was that Diem wasn't up to the job. The other was that Nolting wasn't up to his job either.

Laos was not an isolated theater. What happened there could not help but reverberate into Vietnam, with which it shared a 1,300-mile border. Quite literally, Laos provided the mountainous corridor for Communist arms and men to shuttle from North to South Vietnam. The skein of Viet Cong supply routes through the jungles would be dubbed the Ho Chi Minh Trail; those who thought the Laos deal a sellout to the Communists called it the "Averell Harriman Highway."

Just as importantly, the Laos settlement was an existential threat to Ngo Dinh Diem. He could only interpret its terms as an omen of his country's own fate at the hands of inconstant Americans. Explaining to Harriman and Nolting why he did not trust the Communist signatories to live up to their end of the bargain, Diem launched into one of his soliloquies. Harriman did what he always did when he was perturbed, or bored, or contemptuous, or all three—he removed his hearing aid and (per Nolting's recounting) "closed his eyes. He appeared to be asleep. Diem noticed this with some annoyance but continued his monologue. Sitting next to Harriman on the sofa, realizing he had had a long and tiring flight, I tried to nudge him into attention."

Harriman awoke and told Diem the same thing about his fingertips feeling: "The Russians will police this agreement and make the others live up to it. We cannot give you any guarantees, but one thing is clear: if you do not sign this treaty, you will lose American support. You have to choose."[25]

Nolting was appalled by Harriman's high-handed treatment of President Diem, whose confidence he had been nursing now for months, and now he had the task of persuading Diem to sign. Nolting saw the Laos deal for the calculated capitulation it was. "My conscience will not permit me to support" a coalition government in Laos that would be left "at the mercy of the Communists," Nolting told Harriman in the spring of 1962, at the regional US ambassadors' meeting in the Philippine mountain resort of Baguio. With all of Nolting's ambassadorial colleagues looking on, the merciless Harriman rejoined, "You are not working for God! You are working for the Kennedy administration!"

On a trip to Washington, Nolting had been asked to join a meeting at the White House. As the call was on short notice, he tried to hitch a ride from the State Department to the White House in the official car carrying

Secretary Rusk and Governor Harriman. It was a forlorn scene. Nolting waited in the State Department subterranean garage, chatting with the chauffeur, whom he happened to know from pre-Paris days. When Rusk and Harriman arrived,

> Harriman said, "What are *you* doing here?"
> "I'm going to the White House meeting," I said, "if you'll give me a ride."
> "Well, nobody's asked you."
> Yes, I informed them, the President had. So they indicated the front seat and promptly put up the glass partition between the front and back seats.[26]

To conclude the Laos negotiations in Geneva in 1962, Harriman needed Diem's signature (one of fourteen) on the deal. Rusk told Nolting that this request came from the "highest authority," meaning President Kennedy. Addressing Diem's deepest anxieties, Nolting was instructed to say to him, "I can assure you without reservation that this administration is not seeking a neutral solution for Vietnam." And failing to go along with this treaty would have "grave consequences for all the people of Southeast Asia."[27]

After a two-hour session at Gia Long, Nolting reported Diem to be "courteous but absolutely adamant against signing accords which he claimed would result in the communization of Laos by other means. He took the position, in essence, that it would be immoral to do so, and none of my arguments seemed to have any effect."[28] Of course, Diem knew that privately Nolting saw things just the way he did.

Even as he drafted that bad-news telegram to Harriman, Nolting got a phone call. President Diem had changed his mind and would not stand in the way of Vietnam's signature on the accord after all. *But* there was a condition, concerning one of the symbolic elements of the agreement: South Vietnam's diplomatic recognition of the Laos coalition government. In exchange for sending an accredited ambassador to Vientiane, the Lao capital, Diem wanted North Vietnam's representation in Laos to be downgraded to a trade and cultural mission. In sum, recognizing a government that recognized its enemy as an equal was intolerable to Diem.

This slippery recalcitrance irked Harriman to no end. "I must tell you frankly that it will be a diplomatic defeat if Diem severs relations with Laos," he wrote Nolting in terse and vaguely threatening language. "Diem cannot expect us just to accept his refusal, in affronting disregard of request from the President [Kennedy], to stay in the fight to preserve Laos, Laos being on his own doorstep."[29]

Nolting, either brave or foolish, wouldn't accept this order. He questioned whether Harriman's instructions were actually "Washington's position." He said the guidance he just got for his talks with Diem "advances no arguments not previously put to GVN and to Diem personally" and would "defeat our purposes here—on an issue which in itself cannot compare in importance to the United States with that of maintaining an independent, noncommunist Vietnam."[30]

Harriman had had enough. Nolting's reply, he cabled him, "indicates that you and I are not on the same wavelength."[31] Harriman was telling his most important ambassador that he was no longer in sync with the emerging policy. It's hard to say how seriously Nolting took this.

Washington, Rome, Beirut

In late September Trueheart accompanied Nguyen Dinh Thuan, President Diem's influential counselor, on a weeklong official visit to Washington and New York. Thuan and Trueheart were close, trusted each other, enjoyed one another's company. In Washington they met with officials at the International Monetary Fund, the CIA, and the Joint Chiefs of Staff; with Secretary McNamara, with Secretary Rusk and Averell Harriman, with Mike Forrestal and Carl Kaysen at the White House, and then on September 25 with the president. This was Trueheart's first and only close encounter with John F. Kennedy. He wrote his mother more than a month later, full of relief at the resolution of the Cuban Missile Crisis: "I hope you are as pleased and gratified as I have been at the way the President has handled it. . . . I was *most* impressed during the short time I was with him. I am now satisfied that he is going to be one of the really great presidents."[32]

Trueheart's assessments of the situation in Vietnam, shared with his colleagues in Washington during that visit, were remarkably positive given his growing doubts and his subsequent change of heart. "The military progress has been little short of sensational," and South Vietnamese intelligence capabilities were "greatly improved," he said. The strategic hamlet program had "transformed the countryside." The government was more willing to accept US advice. Interagency relations in the Saigon mission were excellent. Trueheart pronounced himself "tremendously encouraged" by all developments except press relations. This must mark the peak of his optimism, or the end of his willingness to muffle his real views.

He was also getting noticed in Washington. A ranking visitor from the State Department passed on a compliment from a "very senior US military officer," especially striking given the bad odor in which Trueheart would later find himself with the US military in Vietnam. "Trueheart comes closer to carrying out the day-to-day overall direction of the war as a whole than any other individual in Saigon," Alexis Johnson, a senior State Department official, wrote Averell Harriman.[33] I doubt Bill ever saw this description and in later years would have disavowed it strenuously.

After the business wound up in the United States and Thuan returned to Saigon, Bill Trueheart flew in the other direction to meet Phoebe in Rome, where they had lunch with the US ambassador there, Frederick Reinhardt, and his wife at the sumptuous fifteenth-century official residence, Villa Taverna. They were old friends; Reinhardt was Nolting's predecessor in Saigon once removed. Phoebe stayed on after Bill left for Saigon, then traveled alone to Greece and then Lebanon on her way home. One thing that may have kept her away were renovations at our house in Saigon—the creation of another bedroom by the enclosure of a square second-floor terrace. Once complete, Phoebe seemed to occupy it, at least when it was not needed for an official visitor.

Children typically have no way to know how their parents may differ from other couples. Mine were outwardly happy and fun, but they fought—not in front of me, but audibly, for as long as I remember. It was no more violent than raised voices, mainly Bill's, echoing muffled through the corridors to the bedroom where I slept. My mother was also a flirt, and a beautiful one. She liked to joke with me that my brother was in reality the son of a "white Russian." What impression she meant to leave by such fantastic remarks I cannot imagine.

Pied-noir, bête noire

In late August 1962, *Newsweek* ran a piece by François Sully, "Vietnam: The Unpleasant Truth," which termed the war against the Viet Cong "a losing proposition." With the story ran a photograph of members of Madame Nhu's paramilitaries. The photo caption, which Sully did not write, said, "Female militia in Saigon. The enemy has more drive and enthusiasm."

The palace erupted. Police tails were put on Sully. The *Times of Vietnam*, the English-language mouthpiece of the regime, accused Sully of spying, opium smuggling, and libertinism during several weeks of front-page diatribes, and called for his expulsion from South Vietnam. Although he represented an American newsweekly, and one with close ties to President Kennedy through his friendship with Benjamin Bradlee, its Washington bureau chief, Sully was French. Even at thirty-three he had a glorious history that he didn't shrink from burnishing. As a teenager he had been part of the French *resistance.* He had gone to Vietnam in 1947 as a paratrooper and stayed on as a reporter, even talking his way into the besieged garrison at Dien Bien Phu.

On August 28, after two weeks of calumny from the palace, Sully was served with an expulsion order. Trueheart went to see Thuan to protest the order the next day; Nolting did the same the day after. Sully's press colleagues, who had recently formed a Saigon press association, had a stormy meeting in Malcolm Browne's UPI bureau office to figure out what to do. Then they moved the meeting to the Caravelle Hotel bar and called in Sully. They asked him point-blank if he "was now or ever had been a Communist, and if he is now or had ever been a French intelligence agent"—common rumors about Sully that he liked to nurture. Now satisfied with his denials, the journalists voted to protest his expulsion to the White House and the presidential palace.[34]

Trueheart comes in for some unflattering treatment from Halberstam in this episode.[35] He supposedly cracked to the other reporters that Sully was a "*pied-noir*" and implicitly not worth the effort of rescue. *Pied-noir*— "black-foot"—was slang for a white French citizen of Algeria, but it might have been more like calling him a redneck. Trueheart insisted later to another interviewer that he had not understood *pied-noir* as a derogatory term.[36] As he had spent four years in Paris during the outbreak of the Algerian War in the 1950s, this explanation defies credulity.

Nolting had saved Sully from banishment six months earlier, but Diem, stiffened by Nhu, was not inclined to relent this time. The reporter was on a plane out of Saigon on September 9. Once in Hong Kong, Sully let loose in *Newsweek,* describing Diem as "reddish and bloated . . . a virtual prisoner in his own palace . . . the whole apparatus of the nation seems paralyzed." Nhu was "a vicious political infighter with an unquenchable thirst for power." His wife was "the most detested personality in South Vietnam."[37]

The night before Sully left, at a raucous farewell party at the Caravelle, everyone wanted to meet David Halberstam, fresh off the plane (from the Congo) for his new assignment in Vietnam. Sully told him when they met to keep reminding Nolting of the hole in the doughnut.[38]

Halberstam, still only twenty-eight, noticed something about the gathering that reminded him of his earlier days as a journalist in the American South: "We all seemed to be outsiders. There was no one there from the mainstream of the American embassy or the American military mission—just as in Mississippi comparable gatherings of reporters never included the leaders of the Chamber of Commerce, the mayor, or a local legislator."[39]

Frederick Nolting, Halberstam wrote, "came to remind me of some white community leaders I had known in Mississippi and Tennessee, men who—at a time when their communities were about to blow up in racial disorder—reassured me that all was well, that the Negroes were satisfied with the status quo, that the problem was entirely the work of outside agitators and that writing about it would make the situation worse."[40]

Halberstam had his first interview with Nolting in October 1962. It went poorly. The new correspondent kept asking the ambassador about problems in the Mekong Delta, where he had just spent some time. He kept bringing up bad news about the war effort and the Diem regime. Nolting asked him why he wasn't covering a press conference with a Viet Cong defector. Halberstam said he would let the wire services handle that. With that, Nolting turned red, jumped to his feet, told Halberstam he was wasting his time, and led the reporter—at six foot three, taller and wider even than Nolting—by the arm to the door of his office. This is all by Halberstam's account.

Later that day John Mecklin, the embassy press officer, stopped by to see Trueheart. He asked how the interview had gone. Sounding very much like himself, Trueheart said, "Oh, OK. Except the ambassador threw Halberstam out of his office."[41]

Halberstam became the bête noire of the embassy—and the White House. In Nolting's view, the greenhorn reporter just off the plane "quickly became leader of the 'get Diem' press group in Saigon." The ambassador believed that his superiors at the *New York Times* were egging him on to create "a crescendo of anti-Diem propaganda."[42] He had only slightly less flattering things to say about Neil Sheehan and Malcolm Browne. Nolting was flummoxed, rather naively it might seem to a journalist, by the lack of interest these correspondents might have shown in covering the opening of a new hospital or school. Indignantly Nolting recalled one reporter telling him "even if he wrote that story, it wouldn't be published, or if it did get published, it wouldn't be on page one, it would be on page 32."[43]

The diplomats in Saigon were so sensitive to the repercussions of news stories, observed Mecklin, that "a man from Mars admitted to official inner circles in both Vietnam and Washington could have been excused if he got the impression that the newsmen, as well as the Viet Cong, were the enemy."[44] Nolting deeply resented being held to an impossible standard by the reporters (and, he needn't have added, by his superiors in Washington): "to transform a new and divided country into a unified democracy, Western-style, and to do so promptly."[45] Elbridge Durbrow had told him as much.

Nolting's frustration—the embassy's frustration—is palpable in what he saw as too much attention to reporting from a mere handful of inexperienced journalists and not enough to the embassy's own professionals. "During this period our mission had more than a thousand pairs of eyes and ears of Americans, some of whom spoke Vietnamese, out in the provinces, in practically all the areas of Vietnam. . . . I myself visited most of the forty-one provinces and all the major cities." The reports from the field were "much nearer to the truth" than the news reporting, Nolting said.[46]

William Trueheart, in his oral history, remembered it quite differently. The American journalists "didn't know what we were doing [to pressure the government behind the scenes] and always assumed we were . . . not putting enough heat on Diem." But Trueheart concluded that "their information and reporting on what was going on in the countryside was on the whole more accurate than what we were reporting from the embassy."[47]

The reporters in Saigon had their serial problems with the embassy, but they directed special rage against the military because they controlled access to the battlefield. General Harkins had not helped his relations with the press corps by spreading the stupendously false assertion that Halberstam's colleagues were "eating out of his hand": Halberstam would hand out "mimeographs" of his dispatches to the others, Harkins claimed later, and they would dutifully write what he said, "change a few words here and there. But Halberstam was a Jew, and didn't like Diem."

Harkins's shocking free association suggests the crude anti-Semitism that infected his resentment of Halberstam's influence. The general said he put it to Halberstam directly: "I know you're Jewish, I know Diem is Catholic—are you letting that bother your reporting?" The correspondent turned to him and said, "How do you know I'm a Jew?" Harkins admitted he "wasn't sure of it at the time." But somehow he found peculiar comfort, in the next breath, in Halberstam's next assignment, in 1965, to Warsaw. "Poland kicked him out within thirty days. He should have been kicked out of Vietnam at the beginning."[48]

In fact, Halberstam was expelled from Poland—after a year—for writing critical articles about the Communist regime, which branded him a Zionist, and despite the personal cost: he had married Poland's most celebrated actress. Halberstam shared the 1964 Pulitzer Prize for his Vietnam reporting, with Malcolm Browne. Among his other badges of honor is that President Kennedy asked Arthur Ochs Sulzberger, the new publisher of the *New York Times,* to have Halberstam recalled from Saigon. Sulzberger ignored him.

In November 1962, the journalists had missed a major US-led military operation in "Zone D," just fifty miles from Saigon, because of the latest order banning them from helicopters. General Harkins had not had the professional courtesy to warn them about it. Neil Sheehan and Mert Perry of UPI pieced the story together anyway from shoe-leather reporting and sources they had cultivated in the middle ranks of the US Army. This made Harkins blow a fuse about "leaks." Yet there was no leak. Perry had observed the massive helicopter armada heading northwest from the roof of his apartment building.

At a briefing the next day, Sheehan asked the press spokesman for General Harkins's assessment of the Zone D Operation, to which the press guy said, "Uncle Paul doesn't want his name used."

"You tell *Uncle Paul,*" Sheehan shot back, "that he's in charge of the American military command here, that he's the man who released those helicopters, that those are American helicopters flown by American pilots, and that his name goes in my stories."[49]

A few hours later Halberstam stormed into Mecklin's office, shaking with anger, and slapped another letter on his desk to present to Ambassador Nolting. Halberstam said this Zone D incident had turned him from "a neutral observer into an angry man," although he was quite well known already for his squalls of anger. He told Nolting the press policy was "stupid, naïve, and indeed insulting to the patriotism and intelligence of every American newspaperman and every American newspaper represented here. Let me point out . . . that from the moment fifty helicopters landed at a given point in Zone D, certain aspects of the operation lost all classified status. You can bet the VC knew what was happening; you can bet Hanoi knew what was happening. Only American reporters and American readers were kept ignorant."[50] Mecklin naturally took their side. "I'm not sure we can live with this," he told Nolting. Individual cases were one thing, but "this time the GVN is deliberately harassing *all* foreign newsmen and, even more seriously, deliberately attempting to establish a blackout on news from Vietnam other than official communiques."

In case the problem was not clear enough to Nolting, Mecklin lectured on:

> This is not just another under-developed country or banana republic or what have you, rocking along in the usual intrigue and petty chauvinism. This is 1) the scene of a confrontation between East and West which could be decisive to the fate of Asia, and 2) an area of massive US involvement. . . . The GVN is infringing on a root American *right:* the right of the American people to be informed of the facts on which the policies of their government are based, and on the activities of US military personnel committed to combat.[51]

Nolting was in no mood for this idealism. He eventually became so enraged with Halberstam's reporting that he refused to see him at all, leaving briefings to Trueheart and others. Nolting vented to a visiting *Time* magazine editor from New York, Richard Clurman:

> "He's printing lies, so I won't talk to him."
> "Mr. Ambassador, you're aware that President Kennedy reads his stories before he even sees your dispatches."
> "It doesn't matter. I won't talk to him."[52]

At Work and at Play

The United States embassy building was a converted office block purchased by the US government in 1957. It was a ramshackle six-story affair with one curving facade pocked with window air conditioners. Mecklin called it "a disgrace to the United States . . . the building was flanked by a rundown apartment house so close that the American ambassador could look through a window . . . into a back terrace cluttered with refuse and the burned-out joss sticks of an unkempt Buddhist family shrine."[53] The offices on each floor were connected by open passageways—extended balconies, exposed to anyone who might like to take a shot (gun or camera) from an adjacent building. The embassy entrance was set right on the sidewalk at a busy intersection near the Saigon River. It was guarded only by the usual Vietnamese policemen (and plainclothes palace spies lounging about with the waiting taxis) and a contingent of US Marine guards, a protective fixture at all American embassies then and now.

Bill Trueheart typically worked seven days a week, a habit I latterly share with far less reason. In Saigon some Saturdays or Sundays I would "get out of the house" and go with him to do homework or read at Bill's absent secretary's outer desk, in a room that connected the DCM and ambassador. For hours Bill would drink coffee and smoke cigarettes and read and type and talk on the phone and meet behind closed frosted-glass doors with his colleagues. I had ears, but I honestly didn't know or think about anything he was doing. I was aware of just the outward appearance of urgency and responsibility.

At least once on one of these weekend jaunts I brought a friend, Greg Manfull; or perhaps his father, the number three at the embassy, had brought him along to work that day, too. On this day we decided to draw a Vietnam battle plan of sorts. Free-handing a map of the skinny S-shaped country ("that uvular peninsula" in *Time* magazine's hilarious phrase), we annotated the cities and spaces on the map with random arrows and numbers, and then played out some kind of war game, cowboys and Indians replaced by Yanks and Viet Cong. When my father eventually called it a day, Greg and I ripped up our maps and papers and threw them away.

The following Monday evening before dinner in the Blue Room my father sat down with his drink and told me he wanted to show me something. From his buckled leather briefcase he pulled a folder. Inside was Greg's and my map, painstakingly reassembled in a quilt of Scotch tape. Embassy security personnel had been alerted by the night cleaning staff to the presence of unsecured documents in open waste receptacles. My father had a good chuckle about this, although I felt the sting of knowing that someone had "stayed up all night" doing it.

On November 3, 1962, in response to a request from my grandmother, I provided her with my daily schedule as a sixth-grader in Saigon, or some idealized version of it.

5:30	Wake up
6:00	Breakfast
6:30	Get homework gathered
6:45	Catch school bus
7:00	School (very tough teacher)
11:45	School out (whew)
12:05	Get home—have Coke
12:15	Look for trouble (play, too)
1:30	Daddy comes home
1:45	Lunch
2:15	Go to my girlfriend's house
6:00	Get home from girlfriend's house
6:05	Homework
7:00	Look for more trouble (play, too)
7:30	Daddy gets home (if going out, I usually have a friend over for dinner)
8:00	Have drinks, or Daddy and Mother leave for dinner
8:30	Dinner over—sit in study
9:00	Do more homework or stay in study
10:00	Go to bed (listen to the news on AFRS)
10:30	Go to sleep

Coming across this today, I am astonished to read the claim of long afternoons with my girlfriend. I would have said they were spent with my male friends at the Cercle Sportif, or the bowling alley, or carousing around the city. Perhaps a girlfriend sounded more grown-up.

"Charlie is madly in love with a very cute, fun, girl, but don't tease him about it," Phoebe wrote Sallie. The girl, C. J. Bready, was a classmate and the daughter of the Pan American Airways chief in Saigon. C. J. had just come back from a holiday in the States, Phoebe wrote in one letter. "Charlie didn't meet her at the airport (midnight) but sent a note out to her by someone else. She was here the next day at 9 a.m."[54]

C. J. and I were eleven years old and had not passed the hand-holding stage. We made public evidence of our attachment in an exchange of totems redolent of the early 1960s: C. J. had my silver bracelet, bought cheap and engraved ("Charlie") at the teeming Saigon Central Market; from her, I received a work requiring considerable masticating: a chain of

Juicy Fruit chewing gum wrappers cleverly folded and linked, origami-style, into a strand longer than I was tall.[55]

Joshua Trueheart was christened at St. Christopher's Church in Saigon on Sunday, November 25, 1962. This time both Fritz *and* Bittie Nolting were chosen as his godparents, as sure a sign as any of a lasting family closeness. Josh's other godfather was Sir Robert Thompson, the strategic hamlet guru. In just a year in Saigon he had become close enough to Bill and Phoebe, apparently, to be accorded this honor. "We thought it would be good for Josh to have one British godparent, since he was born in England," Bill wrote his mother.[56] I have no evidence or recollection that Thompson ever was in touch with the family again after we left Vietnam.

"The First Nail in Diem's Coffin"

In December 1962, U. Alexis Johnson, one of the State Department's highest officials and the senior Foreign Service Officer in the corps, visited Saigon. Obviously carrying water for his colleagues, Johnson cabled to Washington a dramatic warning about congressional visits—eight separate delegations ("codels") over the space of a recent week: "Such a number of uncoordinated visits and the often-exacting nature of the visitors' demands not only impose extraordinary burdens on the staffs of the posts, but also on the good nature of local officials. For example, one delegation demanded that all members of the party, including wives and subordinate staff members, be present at the meeting with President Diem and established a strict time limit on the time they would make available for the meeting." Apparently they had not been briefed about Diem's logorrhea. Alexis Johnson deplored their "bad manners" and the impression left on leaders of the host country that "our Ambassadors abroad are expected to jump to the whim of any Congressional visitor. This is not good for the United States."[57] It still isn't, and it is far worse today.

Amiable and respectful as he was, Fritz Nolting had particular scorn for codels. "Some congressmen came to Saigon on nothing more than junkets. . . . As soon as they got off the plane, they would request the $500 in piastres they were entitled to draw from our aid program's counterpart fund and then would disappear into town, [returning] loaded down with china elephants and the like. . . . [T]hose people took out a lot of loot."[58]

Word reached President Kennedy about the problem—not only the codels but the Pentagon visitors and civilian brass and special envoys who took just as much time, if not as many china elephants. To Kennedy, their number and frequency appeared to suggest a greater US commitment to Vietnam. "That is exactly what I don't want to do," sighed the president. McGeorge Bundy passed down the word in a "National Security Action Memorandum" that the president directed that all visits to Saigon be "coordinated with Governor Harriman" and cleared with his office. This was bound to change absolutely nothing, as indeed it did not.[59]

Not all members of Congress were fools, and not all codels were junkets. Of all such visits to Saigon from Washington in this period, the most devastating to the Diem regime was one in the six-day cluster Alexis Johnson cited.

The trip was led by Senator Mike Mansfield, the Montana Democrat and former professor of Asian history who had succeeded Lyndon Johnson as Senate majority leader. The year before, he had written a confidential report about Vietnam to his friend Jack Kennedy that was, if anything, bleaker than anything Ken Galbraith had been saying—less hyperbole, but more gravity and knowledge of the subject, including a long-ago acquaintance with Ngo Dinh Diem and his family.

Mansfield's Saigon delegation in 1962 included his wife, Maureen, and three other senators: Claiborne Pell of Rhode Island, J. Caleb Boggs of Delaware, and Benjamin Smith of Massachusetts, who had been keeping Jack Kennedy's Senate seat warm for Edward Kennedy. They were in Saigon and in the provinces for four days. Their visit also put Trueheart in a brief spotlight which, among other things, revealed different ways in which he and Nolting saw things and said things.

The trip began badly before Senator Mansfield and company even reached Saigon. On their first leg, in Bangkok, a monsoon blew up in Vietnam. Ambassador Nolting thought to wire Mansfield about it, suggesting he might want to delay his visit. Mansfield believed he was being "waved off" by the ambassador and didn't like it. His party came ahead to Saigon; when the typhoon turned out to be a dud, Mansfield had reason to think his suspicions were correct. Then, the dinner President Diem was planning to give them on the first night was canceled due to what Nolting cryptically referred to as a "disagreement about a seating list."

The delegation was briefed by the Country Team at the embassy the next morning, Nolting wrote in his memoir, but "the briefing did not appear to interest them, and they asked few questions."[60] This account is belied by transcripts of the meeting, which show Mansfield leading the questioning and writing fifty-two pages of longhand notes about the answers over the course of four hours. It's not the way Trueheart remembered the briefing, either. In fact, something he said to the senators that day had an aftermath that Halberstam and other historians routinely note in their search for turning points within turning points.

It was Senator Pell who asked the question. Nolting and Trueheart knew Pell already: he had been a young Foreign Service Officer after the war before turning to politics in Rhode Island. In front of the Country Team, Pell asked Ambassador Nolting a hypothetical: if there were an election in South Vietnam today, how would Diem fare? For some reason, Nolting turned to Trueheart and said, "Why don't *you* answer that, Bill?"—to general laughter. Trueheart then said, "Senator, I'm not sure that's a meaningful question. I honestly think that if you went out into the boondocks of this country, not even half the people would even know who Diem *is*."[61]
This was not said in levity, but Senator Mansfield, Diem's old friend, heard it differently. He remonstrated with the DCM: "Diem has been head of this country for a long time." They moved on to other subjects. Trueheart is said to have "winced" from the rebuff, and Nolting to have been embarrassed at his deputy's impertinence.[62]
In the ensuing days Mansfield spent a lot of time with junior officers in the mission and in the field, and four hours with Halberstam, Sheehan, Browne, and Peter Arnett. "Halberstam did most of the talking: The ARVN was losing ground, not gaining; Diem was disrupting the war effort, not leading it; Nolting and Harkins were lost in their own hopeless optimism and misleading if not lying to Washington," as William Prochnau summarizes it. "Nolting stewed. He couldn't believe the majority leader of the United States Senate would dignify these troublemakers."[63]
Things didn't go well either when Mansfield saw Diem. Sitting in on the interview was Frank Meloy, who had been a young FSO in Saigon in the early days and was close to the Truehearts when they served together in Paris. Meloy reported to his superiors in Washington that Mansfield had been "miffed" because "Diem insisted upon recounting the whole history of his regime as though the Senator were a stranger to the Vietnam situation."[64]

At the end of the visit, the Country Team trooped to Tan Son Nhut airport to see off Mansfield's congressional party. "We were all standing around in a big circle there," Trueheart recalled, "and Mansfield walked all the way across the room, came up, shook my hand, and said, 'I think you were right.'"[65] Trueheart "winced again," possibly because Nolting was standing right there. Perhaps Mansfield was snubbing Nolting with the compliment.

In his parting remarks, Mansfield expressed personal esteem for President Diem but declined the guidance Nolting had offered that included praise for the regime's strides toward "justice and respect for human liberties." Halberstam's New York Times file that day said Mansfield was "the first high ranking official in a year who did not go out of his way to assert that considerable progress was being made against the guerrillas or Viet Cong." The historian Joseph Buttinger said by refusing the embassy guidance, Mansfield was "one of the few not sucked in by official self-delusion."[66]

In mid-December, Senator Mansfield gave President Kennedy an almost immediate assessment of the situation in Vietnam. It made a deep impression. Despite a year of seemingly good news, corners turned, momentum regained, successes chalked up, Mansfield wrote the president, "it was distressing on this visit to hear the situation described in much the same terms as on my last visit although it is seven years and billions of dollars later."

Outside the cities, Vietnam "is still an insecure place which is run at least at night largely by the Viet Cong." He questioned "the assumption that the great bulk of the people in the countryside sustain the Viet Minh merely out of fear or, at best, indifference." The government remains broadly unpopular, the senator told the president, and "it would be well to face the fact that we are once again at the beginning of the beginning."[67]

Success was possible, but Mansfield said it would require "an immense job of social engineering," dependent on huge outlays of US aid for years and "responsive, alert, and enlightened leadership in the government of Vietnam." And this was the problem. He tried to be kind to Diem, describing him as "dedicated, sincere, hard-working, incorruptible," but Mansfield also called him "depressed" and noted that he was showing signs of age (though Diem had just turned sixty) and yielding inexorably to the sinister powers of Ngo Dinh Nhu. Mansfield said the only alternative to a functioning Vietnamese government was a "truly massive commitment of American military personnel and other resources—in short going to war fully ourselves against the guerrillas—and the establishment of some kind of neocolonial rule in South Vietnam. That is an alternative which I most emphatically do not recommend." Of all the informal counsel President Kennedy sought during this period, none was taken more seriously than Mansfield's. Nolting himself gave it the ultimate mordant accolade: the senator's report to Kennedy was "the first nail in Diem's coffin."[68]

On December 29, Bill Trueheart closed a Christmas gift thank-you note to his mother with a line that must have sounded increasingly familiar to her: "Important visitors arriving New Year's Eve, of all things."[69]

6

★ ★ ★

Burning Arrow

THE NEW YEAR'S EVE arrivals were Roger Hilsman from the State Department and Michael Forrestal from the National Security Council. Kennedy trusted these two men, especially, to give him candid judgments about what they found in South Vietnam. At the outset of 1962, the president was still rattled by the bleak and unvarnished assessment Mansfield had given him privately upon returning to Washington before Christmas—an assessment the embassy in Saigon, and the public, would not hear about for several months. Now Kennedy wanted a political perspective, a counterweight to the reporting of Secretary McNamara and General Taylor, who had different stakes in the game.

Dating from this fact-finding exercise Hilsman and Forrestal would become the principal instigators, egged on and covered by the irascible assistant secretary of state, Averell Harriman, of the move to overthrow Ngo Dinh Diem.

Roger Hilsman was a pugnacious academic with the burnish of military heroism. Fresh out of West Point, he became a swashbuckling young guerrilla fighter against the Japanese in Burma with the famed Merrill's Marauders, a US jungle warfare unit in World War II's China-Burma-India theater. (Nolting dismissed him as "the Boy Wonder of Burma.")[1] Hilsman had earned medals and a robust sense of invincibility during the war and then joined the OSS after the peace.

Although Hilsman was a Jack Kennedy favorite and contemporary, his appeal was not just his intellectual and scholarly acumen, proven during the 1950s when he'd been teaching at Yale and working at the Rand Corporation. It was his ability to speak the military's language with authenticity. He also had one of the few résumés among senior Kennedy appointees suggesting familiarity with the region—he'd grown up in the Philippines, the son of an army officer—and with counterinsurgency, one of Jack Kennedy's favorite topics.

Hilsman's arrogance didn't wear well on some people. At a stag dinner in Washington in 1962, Roger Hilsman had lectured the chairman of the Joint Chiefs of Staff, General Lyman Lemnitzer, about how wrong he was about Vietnam. This so exasperated Vice President Johnson that he who broke in to say, "God damn it! Captain Hilsman, shut up and let the General talk!"[2]

Since the outset of the Kennedy administration, Hilsman had been running the State Department's Bureau of Intelligence and Research. Then, two months after his trip to Vietnam, Hilsman succeeded Averell Harriman as assistant secretary of state for Far Eastern (today East Asian and Pacific) affairs, becoming Nolting's direct supervisor. Hilsman reassured Nolting he'd be calling the shots in Washington on Vietnam policy now, and "not to worry about the 'Old Crocodile'"—Harriman. As Nolting recalled it, "I remember thinking that perhaps the new Assistant Secretary was protesting too much."[3]

Michael Forrestal, who always stayed at the Truehearts' in Saigon, was a young Kennedy confidant and frequent sailing companion. At thirty-five he'd been unable to say no to President Kennedy, who lured him from his law practice at Shearman and Sterling in New York. Forrestal's assignment was to work on the National Security Council under McGeorge Bundy, eventually becoming Kennedy's personal point man on Vietnam.

Forrestal's foreign policy expertise was slender, but his connections were compelling. After graduating from Phillips Exeter Academy in 1945, Forrestal got a navy commission—his father was secretary of the navy— and at seventeen was appointed assistant naval attaché in Moscow, at the special request of none other than Averell Harriman, then the US ambassador to the Soviet Union and a family friend. After Harriman left Moscow, Forrestal landed diplomatic jobs in Berlin and London, still without a college degree.

Meanwhile, his father, James Forrestal, had become secretary of defense in 1947 and then was fired by Harry Truman a year later for some political double-dealing—and recurring evidence of serious depression. A troubled man, James Forrestal was hospitalized at Bethesda Naval Hospital in March 1949 and two months later jumped to his death from its high tower. Averell and Marie Harriman immediately took his bereaved young sons under their wing and care.

So when Kennedy prevailed on Mike Forrestal to work at the White House in 1962, he made his real priority clear. He wanted Forrestal to serve, Forrestal recalled, as the president's "ambassador to the sovereign republic of Averell Harriman." Given the former governor's seniority, his dreams of becoming secretary of state, and his tendency to speak brusquely about whatever crossed his mind, Harriman needed managing by a sensitive and clever acolyte. But, as Nolting ruefully put it later, Forrestal's ostensible challenge was "like trying to tie up a stallion with a piece of string—instead of Forrestal keeping an eye on Harriman, he became Harriman's man."

In fact, Forrestal was Harriman's man from the start. Harriman couldn't have minded having such an obliging ward and ally in the White House with the president's ear. And as the Vietnam problem worsened in the spring and summer of 1963, Kennedy put more and more trust in Forrestal's judgment, knowing it reflected Harriman's.[4]

It reflected Trueheart's, too. In Saigon during Forrestal's trips in 1962 and 1963, the two men found they were of like minds and temperaments, and each useful to the other. They became very close and remained so for years after Forrestal rejoined his law practice. Trueheart in those days must have been conscious that Forrestal provided him one degree of separation from the president. He had reason to believe, months later, when his career was on the line, that their closeness provided hope of insulation.

As for Nolting, he was unimpressed with Forrestal, who "did not do much, did not say much" on this January 1963 visit. Forrestal kept insisting on pressing the Diem government to broaden its base and become more "popular." The ambassador was at pains to say that such an objective was "unrealistic and impossible to accomplish in a short time under existing conditions," he recalled. "I am sure Washington found me stubborn when I reported in this vein."[5]

During their ten-day trip to South Vietnam, Hilsman and Forrestal formed judgments that would carry weight in Washington in the months ahead. Hilsman, often drawing on Forrestal's own insights, dictated a series of memoranda for the record, often undated but sequential, which survive. The night of January 1, 1963, he recorded his first impressions, at that point dominated by their immediate conversations with Nolting and Trueheart: "I have the impression things are going much better than they were a year ago, but that they are not going nearly so well as the people here in Saigon, both military and civilian, say they are. . . . The trouble is, however, that the progress and the movement is highly uneven. One would wish that this is the fault of the Vietnamese, and it is to a considerable extent. But I am afraid that the great share of the responsibility belongs with the Americans."[6] This early judgment is a good summary of the report they delivered to President Kennedy three weeks and dozens of interviews and conversations later. That is, it temporized; it straddled the debate rather than steering it. Yet in Saigon they found the glass half-empty at best. As the days passed and their conversations multiplied—with military officers, diplomats, rural pacification experts, journalists—Hilsman and Forrestal wondered why the embassy was so optimistic.

The strategic hamlets they visited, supposedly signs of progress embraced by the Diem government and the embassy alike, appalled them. Hilsman acknowledged a few good signs—"cement pigstys, a good well, a new schoolhouse, and so on." Other outposts were "pitiful":

> Their defenses were a sham—a moat and a wall topped with barbed wire and bamboo spikes, meandering around fields and outlying houses for so many miles that a whole division would be needed to defend it. But the defenders were only a few old men, armed with swords, a flintlock, and a half dozen American carbines. One wondered where the young men were, and which of the many gaps in the wall they used when they came back at night to collect food and see their wives. . . . It seemed obvious that putting up defenses would do no good if the defenses enclosed Viet Cong agents.[7]

To Forrestal, the very idea of the hamlets was misconceived:

> They simply rounded up the peasants without any warning, . . . burned their farms behind them so as to deny their houses to the Viet Cong, and forcibly incarcerated them (that is the only word you can use) into half-built villages. They weren't even really villages. They were just areas surrounded by barbed wire. . . . In addition to being pretty frightful by Western standards, to do this sort of thing in Vietnam is foolish, because every Vietnamese peasant believes as a matter of religious faith that his ancestors live on the land which he has farmed.[8]

Although the hamlets had been a bright spot that even Trueheart celebrated on his trip to Washington a few months earlier, and Nolting remained a true believer, now Hilsman and Forrestal were reflecting the
growing gloom at the embassy about the efficacy of the program.

The two Washington visitors made the pilgrimage to Gia Long Palace for
the ritual audience with President Diem on January 3. The chief of state
had just celebrated his sixty-second birthday in a ceremony with monar-
chical trappings, wearing "long, silken Mandarin robes, a rare departure
from the white sharkskin suits of his daily presidency."[9] He heard syco-
phants call him "born to be a leader" and a president "whose genius is
outweighed only by his virtue."

When Hilsman got back to the Noltings' house that night, he told his
Dictaphone, "It is perfectly obvious that Diem regards these long conversations as a form of amusement. He schedules them when he has plenty
of free time and it is a substitute for bridge, movies, music, or social
evenings."[10]

Diem's obsession with detail, and his disgorgement of all he knew,
verged on derangement. When Hilsman told Diem he and Forrestal had
just visited a certain American Special Forces camp, recently overrun by
the Viet Cong, the stout president quickly took up pen and paper and
"drew us a remarkably detailed sketch of the defenses of the camp and
accompanied it with a devastatingly correct and completely fair critique of
the mistakes in siting weapons, in cutting fields of fire, and so on made by
the West Point commander of the camp. It made me squirm, particularly
when Diem recalled that I, too, was a West Pointer."[11] Saturday night they
all dined at the home of Secretary of State Thuan. Hilsman was seated
next to Ngo Dinh Nhu, the éminence grise, whose personality "hinted of
madness." At the table Nhu provided fresh evidence of his fearsome meg-
alomania. He told everyone that "he had conceived a grand strategy to
defeat world Communism once and for all—by having the United States
lure Communist China into a war with Laos, which was 'an ideal theater
and battleground.' It made me shudder."[12]

The report Hilsman and Forrestal gave President Kennedy was a few
weeks in coming. Their earliest impressions hadn't changed much. There
was some good news to report, but "the negative side of the ledger is still
awesome." The conclusions were bleak and would spread the miasma of
cynicism about America's Vietnamese client and America's military pre-
paredness and effectiveness.

"Is there a plan? The answer is no," Hilsman noted to himself privately in Saigon. "There are five or six plans, many of which are competing."[13]

A personal diary Phoebe started keeping in 1963, and regrettably abandoned a few weeks later, records with verve the social scene with Hilsman and Forrestal in town. The Truehearts and the Noltings took the visitors to a party at Bob Thompson's place, where the strategic hamlet guru was "well on the way to being drunk" when they arrived. On hand were "lots of horse-faced British secretaries looking for kisses." The British military attaché was "very naughty dancing in a little black room, also necking." A Colonel Steinberger was "a great twister. Bill and the two New Frontiersmen were the only ones who didn't dance. No *vigah*."

Around midnight "Bill got a message that a big battle was going on in the south. Four Americans killed so far. They ran into more than they had planned on. A big operation."[14]

"I Don't Take Orders from Americans"

Indeed. Hilsman and Forrestal were present in Vietnam for the most significant battle yet of the Second Indochina War: Ap Bac. In military terms it was a relatively tiny defeat for the South Vietnamese and American forces, but the immediate notoriety it gave the nascent war made it consequential out of all proportion. In that sense it foreshadowed the much bigger Viet Cong "Tet Offensive," just five years later, in laying bare all that was going wrong and changing hearts and minds in Washington.

The chaotic half-day confrontation happened only thirty-five miles from Saigon in the northern Delta in a hamlet named Bac ("Ap" means hamlet).

A coordinated US-ARVN military operation, dubbed Burning Arrow, was to attack a Viet Cong transmitter pinpointed in the village. What the American generals most wanted was what usually eluded them, the set-piece confrontation where the enemy stood and fought and could be beaten with superior numbers and firepower. This time, as Neil Sheehan described it, "one of those rare events in a conflict of seemingly endless engagements, no one of which appeared to have any intrinsic meaning, was about to occur—a decisive battle that would affect the course of the war. Today the Viet Cong were going to stand and fight."[15]

Because of fog, ARVN forces drove toward the stronghold without their expected air support. They were quickly pinned down by the surprisingly resilient Viet Cong, far more numerous than expected, who had prepared for the assault by digging a network of trenches. When US helicopters arrived at last, five were swiftly shot down. American efforts to extract the stranded crews and revive the assault were met with repeated refusals from the South Vietnamese commanders. A supposed showpiece of military counterinsurgency had turned into a humiliating, chaotic, infuriating disaster.

General Harkins had once described the Viet Cong as "those raggedy-ass little bastards." By the end of that terrible day at Ap Bac, Sheehan's devastating account reads:

> The "raggedy-ass little bastards" had obliged the Americans. The 350 guerrillas had stood their ground and humbled a modern army four times their number equipped with armor and artillery and supported by helicopters and fighter-bombers. Their heaviest weapon was the little 60mm mortar that had proved useless to them. They suffered eighteen killed and thirty-nine wounded, light casualties considering that the Americans and their Vietnamese proteges subjected them to thousands of rifle and machine-gun bullets, the blast and shrapnel of 600 artillery shells, and the napalm, bombs, and assorted other ordnance of thirteen warplanes and five Huey gunships.... With the weapons they held in their hands the guerrillas killed or wounded roughly four of their enemies for every man they lost. They inflicted about 80 killed and well over 100 wounded on the Saigon forces and also killed three Americans, wounded another eight, and accounted for five helicopters.[16]

That was only half of the catastrophic spectacle. The other half, no less damaging to the cause and perhaps more so, was the performance of the South Vietnamese military commanders, who in crucial moments in the battle declined the orders of their American "advisers" to attack enemy positions. Sheehan built his 1988 Vietnam masterpiece, *A Bright Shining Lie,* around the American colonel in charge of Ap Bac, John Paul Vann, who circled the battle in a little L-19 spotter plane all day hectoring his people on the ground to get their "counterparts"—the South Vietnamese officers, who often "outranked" them—to follow orders.

> "I've got a problem, Topper Six," the American Captain Jim Scanlon on the ground tells Vann on the radio. "My counterpart won't move."
> "God damn it, doesn't he understand this is an emergency?" Vann shouted.

"I described the situation to him exactly as you told me, Topper Six, but he says 'I don't take orders from Americans.'"[17]

Later, Vann was trying to coordinate the rescue of American and Vietnamese flyers in downed helicopters, lying sideways in muddy ditches and canals.

"I told you people to do something and you're not doing it. . . . Why can't you get the lead out of that son of a bitch's ass. He's got his order from the (ARVN) division commander. . . . That bastard has armored tracks and .50 cals and he's afraid of a bunch of VC with small arms. What's wrong with him?"

"We're doing the best we can, Topper Six."

"Your best isn't worth a shit, Walrus."[18]

This lively later account notwithstanding, Sheehan and Halberstam and the other correspondents in Saigon had missed the battle entirely, bogged down in expense accounts and battles with their bureaucratic overlords, and lacking any official heads-up. Sheehan and his fixer, along with Nick Turner of Reuters, sped to the scene that night in a Hillman Minx through territory only safe in daytime, badlands littered with mines and Viet Cong checkpoints by night. They got there at 10:00 p.m., rushed back to Saigon to file, then helicoptered back the next morning to the smoldering village. Sheehan and Turner wound up helping American soldiers carry the dead from the fallen helicopters after their Vietnamese colleagues declined to participate.

The reporters found their friend Colonel John Paul Vann thoroughly disgusted. Often more upbeat in his comments, Vann called the operation in Ap Bac "a miserable damn performance." (The reporters protectively kept Vann's quote unattributed, but no higher-up was in the dark about who was being quoted.) The phrase would be ringing in the ears of officialdom in Saigon and Washington for many weeks to come.

"These people won't listen. They make the same mistakes over and over again in the same way," Vann raged at the correspondents. He could have been expressing the thoughts of Nolting and Trueheart, facing the implacable Ngo family. Indeed, the obstinacy of the ARVN commanders could be traced directly to Ngo Dinh Diem, whose abhorrence of casualties and punishment of officers who incurred them had been translated, not surprisingly, into extreme caution on the battlefield, US "advisers" be damned. Madame Nhu, the reliable flame-fanner, indicated the hierarchical preoccupations of the palace by opining, of Ap Bac, that "everything would have gone splendidly had it not been for an American colonel who had flown around the battlefield all day in a little plane, countermanding the orders of her brother-in-law's senior officers."[19]

The defeat at Ap Bac, for the American correspondents and the influential people who read them, was a defining moment, presaging the collapse of credibility that would turn into an avalanche in years ahead. Sheehan's January 7 report in the *Washington Post,* with the money quote from Vann, was especially damning. For Sheehan, the Battle of Ap Bac marked "the end of the short era of innocence when the war was still an adventure."[20] For Halberstam, "Ap Bac epitomized all the deficiencies of the system: lack of aggressiveness, hesitancy about taking casualties, lack of battlefield leadership, a nonexistent chain of command."[21]

The incident also moved Vietnam to the higher ground of close scrutiny at home. "Prior to Ap Bac, the Kennedy administration had succeeded in preventing the American public from being more than vaguely conscious that the country was involved in a war in place called Vietnam," Sheehan recalled. Now, "Ap Bac was putting Vietnam on the front pages."[22]

The news stung. Kennedy and McNamara demanded explanations. Admiral Felt parachuted in from Honolulu. General Harkins was enraged by the coverage. Ambassador Nolting was undone by the blowback from home. "People keep writing me," he said a few days later, "asking, 'Fritz, what's going on out there all of a sudden? I thought we were doing so well.'"[23] Maybe he thought so too. That had certainly been the outward consensus at the embassy a few weeks before.

General Harkins turned up the day after the battle, "wearing street shoes, carrying a swagger stick, and using the long white cigarette holder he favored."[24] He insisted to the press scrum that Ap Bac had been a victory and that in fact the Viet Cong in the hamlet were trapped and about to be captured, even though they were long gone, and everyone knew it. At his airport arrival, Admiral Felt said he didn't believe what he was reading in the papers. "As I understand it, it was a Vietnamese victory—not a defeat," the admiral said, turning to Harkins, who said, "Yes, that's right, it was a Vietnamese victory. It certainly was."[25]

The great military historian Max Hastings, in his recent book on the

Vietnam War, is reminded of a maxim: "For all those who hold positions of authority, in war as in peace: Lie to others if you must, but never to yourselves. [Harkins] could make a case for talking nonsense to Halberstam and [Peter] Arnett, but he was peddling the same fairy tales in top-secret cables to Washington."[26] Sheehan found Harkins's performance "obscene." No less obscene was the general's repeated use of a lame witticism, echoing "Ap Bac," to suggest his I've-seen-it-all view of the problem: "My achin' back."

When Admiral Felt left Saigon a few days later, he stuck to the story. Malcolm Browne challenged him, and the admiral growled back words no reporter forgot: "Why don't you get on the team?" Joseph Alsop, the leading hawk in American punditry, said as much in a *Washington Post* column. In a letter to the editor published a few days later, David Halberstam's brother Michael compared this attitude to the "naïve theory" that if one "writes nice things about the high school team perhaps it will finally win some games."[27]

Ap Bac is a poignant moment of clarity—and conversion—in the journalists' accounts and memoirs. Before the battle, Sheehan wrote, "the American reporters shared the advisers' sense of commitment to this war. Our ideological prism and cultural biases were in no way different. We regarded the conflict as our war too. We believed in what our government said it was trying to accomplish in Vietnam and we wanted our country to win this war just as passionately as Vann and his captains did."[28] Their youth and inexperience, which made it hard for Nolting and Harkins—and even John F. Kennedy—to take them seriously, "made it possible for us to acquire what critical faculty we were displaying," Sheehan said later. "Vietnam was our first war. What we saw and what we were told by the men we most respected and most closely identified with—the advisers in the field like Vann—contradicted what we were told by higher authority."[29] Those colonels and captains and majors, their contemporaries, "discovered we were the only people who would listen to them."[30]

Sheehan put the journalists' perspective neatly: "Generals like Harkins and ambassadors like Nolting were not accustomed to reporters saying they were consistently wrong. Well, we weren't accustomed to generals and ambassadors who *were* consistently wrong, either."[31] But Trueheart was emerging in the reporters' eyes as one of those officials the reporters could trust, perhaps because he wasn't consistently wrong, perhaps because he listened to them.

Time's Up

There's retrospective irony that Fritz Nolting and his superiors seemed in perfect agreement at the beginning of 1963 that the ambassador's time in Saigon was drawing to a close.

In a private annex to President Kennedy appended to their January report on Vietnam, Hilsman and Forrestal said it was time to find a new ambassador in Saigon suited to the task of managing the exploding US mission. What was needed, they said, was "a single strong executive, a man perhaps with a military background but who understands that this war is essentially a struggle to build a nation out of the chaos of revolution." Better yet, he would be "a public figure whose character and reputation would permit him to dominate the representatives of all other departments and agencies," meaning especially just one, MACV.

"More vigor is needed," Forrestal subsequently told President Kennedy.

Although rumors of Nolting's premature withdrawal had circulated even in his earliest months in Saigon, the ambassador had always regarded his tour of duty to be for two years. (Three or four was and is more customary.) Nolting had made a two-year posting nearly conditional when he met with Secretary of State Dean Rusk to accept the assignment in 1961. Rusk had laughed off the question with the line about the mission not lasting even two years; Nolting heard this as assent.

During the Christmas holidays of 1962, nineteen months into his tenure, soon after the Mansfield delegation left Saigon, Nolting had written Rusk to remind him of their deal and to urge him to make arrangements for an orderly transition in May. His home leave—thirty months since the last, he mentioned in a cable to State—was on his mind, specifically a cruise through the Greek isles with his wife and four daughters. Hearing nothing in reply, he prodded through friendly channels.

In early February 1963 his friend Ben Wood, who ran the Vietnam Working Group at State, wrote a chipper message enclosing a news clipping from Reuters headlined "Nolting to Stay"—a story about rumors that he would be sacked because of pressure from the Pentagon. "The headline is right, the story wrong," said Wood, stroking Fritz with the promise that he would chat with Harriman about "relaxing Aegean cruises and refreshing home leaves for overworked ambassadors."[32]

Finally, on February 18, came word from Harriman: "It would be my hope," he blithely wrote, "that after home leave you would return to Saigon and stay on for some time." Nolting's proffer of "two-three months" in an earlier telegram was now "some time."

Nolting continued to be sensitive to what Diem and the palace thought about his future as ambassador, perhaps clothing his own anxieties in policy considerations: "I have said I have no orders. This has become embarrassing and, more importantly, has unfortunately been a factor in speculation here re continued US support for Government. Rumors re my recall . . . have begun to undermine my credibility and to affect mission's influence. . . . A prompt clarification is necessary here in light of political situation here." Nolting closed with, "Would also appreciate when possible indication of job possibilities in transfer to department."[33]

On February 28 the ambassador wrote again, pushing Harriman essentially to let him leave for good, implicitly in May, because of family pressures. Forrestal recalled that "he cited a personal problem. He had two daughters in school here, one of whom was in some sort of difficulty, and he felt that the problem was that he had been away from home so long that he really needed to get back."[34] The surviving Noltings say they recall no such problem, although proper schooling was always a worry.

"Because of distance and expense, we cannot bridge the family gap and provide the necessary maternal-paternal guidance," Nolting pleaded in a telegram, referring again to the Rusk conversation two years before.

As for managing things in his absence, he reassured Harriman, "We have a first-rate Country Team and an excellent DCM." This sounds like an ambassador with a unified mission and with confidence in his second. Nolting may well have misunderstood Trueheart's professionalism or reserve for intellectual agreement about Vietnam policy. Nolting would later regard this as a costly misjudgment.

"Everything Is Just Dandy in Saigon!"

Ten days after Ap Bac, outwardly unperturbed, President Kennedy told a press conference that "the spearhead of aggression has been blunted in Vietnam." The problem remained that the newspaper reporting suggested otherwise. As so often happens when the news media paint a picture that displeases those in power, someone will decide that the problem lies not in the policy but in the communications strategy. After Ap Bac, Harriman got on this bandwagon in a long and patronizing memorandum to Nolting about how he could improve the picture coming out of

Vietnam, citing specifically the embarrassment of Vann's remarks about a "miserable damn performance."

Nolting hardly needed to be reminded about the bad press raining down on his mission, but in his testy response he didn't hide his frustrations. The reporting of US news correspondents in Vietnam "is probably as good as average reporting of a stateside story like earthquake or Hollywood divorce." The ambassador in Saigon cabled that US newspaper editors and the stateside reading public "haven't been stirred by Vietnam, perhaps because remoteness, perhaps obscured by more pressing understandable crises like Cuba, perhaps, as they claim, by routine optimistic statements from American visitors here."

As for the Saigon press corps and its "inexperience"—by now the gospel dismissal—news organizations supposedly "have difficulty finding anyone at all who will agree to come, for essentially the same reasons that US agencies in Saigon have chronic recruiting problems."[35] Those who were persuaded to report from Vietnam, of course, turned out to be the most distinguished of their generation. And apart from the three most often named, the other reporters who covered the story were older or much older, and most of them, too, saw things the same way.

Nolting proposed to Harriman as one solution that he return to the United States for several weeks of consultation to do public relations work, meeting editorial boards and speechifying. He was politely refused.[36] "The administration has established a rule that no ambassador should be absent from his post for more than six weeks on account of the exigencies of the world situation," Harriman cabled back. "Your presence in Vietnam is too important."

His belligerence barely chained, Harriman also brought up with the stressed ambassador something else he heard from Hilsman and Forrestal. He suggested the embassy, and by obvious implication Nolting, had been negligent in its most basic duty to keep doors open to the non-Communist opposition, such as it was in a family-ruled state. That kind of political reporting is at the heart of what an embassy does and was of special and obvious interest to anyone in Washington ruminating actively about a successor regime. Or, as Forrestal put it to Harriman with insouciance, it would "eventually increase our alternatives in the event of an accident which results in a shift in the government."[37]

Nolting was capable of high dudgeon, even prone to it, and sensitive to slight. Even in the most courtly and courteous formulation, an insulted and exasperated man on the spot comes through in his reply to Harriman at the end of February.[38] It's Hilsman he didn't trust (and of course Harriman he couldn't bear), but Nolting starts in right away on Forrestal.

"I am sorry that Mike didn't voice these thoughts while he was here," he wrote, although it is nearly certain that he had, if not with Nolting himself then with Trueheart or the journalists. "In fact, I should have been glad to introduce him to dozens of non-Commie members of the Vietnamese opposition at our home . . . bankers, businessmen, labor leaders, landowners, lawyers, doctors, university professors—who would doubtless have had a field day criticizing the government . . . but what good would that have done—outside of demonstrating a point and possibly stimulating a coup—I don't know!" This was not the cool-headed telegramese of the professional diplomat. The ambassador went on: "I must confess to being somewhat astonished by the implication that we are living in cocoons here, dealing only with GVN officials and deliberately cutting ourselves off." Yet he reminded the State Department that conducting opposition research while trying to reassure a suspicious chief of state of American fidelity was a difficult challenge, stressing "the great difference between being accessible to oppositionists and giving them encouragement."[39]

Here Nolting came to his most serious point, a gauntlet laid down in an early act of the drama: "If the idea is to try to build up an alternative to the present government, I believe you already know that I am opposed." The ambassador saw no viable alternative, and any attempt at regime change would "ruin the carefully-built base of our advisory role here, which must rest on persuasion and on confidence in our integrity." Citing the "unequivocal public pronouncement" of Vice President Johnson and other senior officials in support of the regime, "which I myself thought right and proper, I would not find it possible to be the agent in a change of US policy away from forthright support of the legitimate government."[40]

What for Nolting was a point of honor was for those who read this outburst something else. Nolting couldn't have known it, but Forrestal sent a copy of his letter to a White House colleague, Carl Kaysen, with a cover note that read, "Everything is just dandy in Saigon!" More seriously, Forrestal told Harriman that the rap on poor performance with opposition outreach came from embassy people themselves, perhaps even

Trueheart among them. "I don't think it does any good to tell Fritz this, because I am sure he is sincere in what he says."

Arthur M. Schlesinger Jr., also in copy, was less sympathetic. "The letter from Nolting is one of the most dismal documents I have ever encountered. If Ed Gullion is leaving the Congo, how about sending him back to Saigon?"[41] Forrestal and Chester Bowles also sent their endorsements of Gullion, Kennedy's old friend.[42]

It was clear Nolting's days were numbered—and that he *wanted* them numbered. For Forrestal, in retrospect, the ambassador had gotten himself "into a deeply unfortunate position of being so thoroughly identified with the Diem regime that he had lost the capacity to influence President Diem." People from Washington had watched Nolting interact with Diem, Forrestal said, and "it was clear Nolting respected Diem but the reverse wasn't true. . . . Diem no longer really believed or took seriously what he said." Forrestal said Nolting was "a hell of a good ambassador, but just stuck on President Diem, and the more difficulties Diem raised, the more rigid Fritz Nolting became."[43]

Living on Paradoxes

The gloomy Mansfield report that Kennedy had seen privately in December was finally published in late February. That's when Ambassador Nolting saw it for the first time and recognized it as the nail in President Diem's coffin that it was.

The South Vietnamese president and the ambassador commiserated about it. Nolting told Diem it was a disservice to him and a gift to the Viet Cong. He also composed a plaintive note about it to Harriman: "It seems to me pertinent to recall the first commandment of our task force instructions issued two years ago"—to build confidence in the regime—"these basic instructions have not changed to my knowledge."[44] In his memoir, Nolting states disingenuously that "the Mansfield report was the first real indication we had in Saigon of negative thoughts in Washington about our policy in Vietnam."[45]

The new round of criticism in the press that followed the report's publication added more pressure on Diem, promoting a smart observation from John Mecklin in a telegram to Washington: "Paradoxically, we may have arrived at the point where negative criticism of the GVN is almost as useful in the present circumstances in Saigon as it is damaging to the

Administration's defense of its policy at home." But, Mecklin pointed out, "We can't live on paradoxes indefinitely."[46]

Bob Thompson, the British counterinsurgency expert, briefed a high-level group in Washington on April 4—Harriman, Robert Kennedy, CIA director John McCone, and Edward R. Murrow, head of USIA, among others. "The Governor kept his hearing aid in with the volume up" for seventy-five minutes, a friend reported to Nolting, referring to Harriman, who liked the title he had as governor of New York. "This is, I believe, a record for undivided gubernatorial attention."

About strategic hamlets, Thompson expressed the same worries that Nolting and Trueheart had been sharing for months—the danger of over-extension, "leaving pockets of Viet Cong control behind to subvert and harass the peasants" instead of "consolidating areas prior to pushing forward into insecure areas."[47] Even so, Thompson argued that withdrawal of some American forces by the end of the year was possible and desirable—"an indication we are winning." He said "a real white area"—free of Viet Cong—could be achieved by midsummer.

When he met with President Kennedy later that day, Kennedy probed Thompson's views on Diem's viability. "The question is not whether we could win with Diem but that without Diem we would probably lose within six months," Thompson told the president.

The US embassy spent much of its time and energy that spring in another standoff with the Diem regime, this one over control of US counterinsurgency funds—how shared and how disbursed. Diem was adamant that the latter be at South Vietnamese discretion. Without that authority Vietnam was a mere "protectorate," a designation that would "thus play into the hands of the Communists." Nolting insisted otherwise, pleading no "intention or act on our part to infringe on his government's sovereignty."[48]

The wrangle went on for hours each time Nolting saw Diem over many weeks. Diem cited case after case of US interference at the provincial and district level and the specter this raised of a "colonial mentality." Nolting wondered openly if Brother Nhu were the source of Diem's information and got no reply. He said to Diem he could "not accept the implication that our people were free-wheeling and out of control. . . . I told him bluntly this attitude would only arouse suspicions at home, as it did in my own mind, about the political motivations of the government. Was he really working for the benefit of the people or, as his critics charged, to perpetuate his own regime?"[49]

Despite "all the ammunition and personal persuasion I had," Diem was "courteous but immovable." The Vietnamese president "gave the impression of one who would rather be right, according to his lights, than president."

As usual, Madame Nhu didn't help. She had directed members of her Women's Solidarity Movement not to show gratitude for American aid because its purveyors undermined "our customs and habits and healthy laws" in order to "make lackeys of Vietnamese and to seduce Vietnamese women into decadent paths."[50] In response, Ambassador Nolting registered a complaint to Diem and broke a date he had with Madame Nhu to be her guest at Dalat.

Although Nolting was often portrayed as too complaisant with Diem, one historian observes that his real failing (really, Washington's) was to have ignored the symbolic importance of the funds issue to Diem—"some symbol of autonomous control of Vietnamese destiny"—which foundered over "absolute control of a min[u]scule pot of piasters."[51] In the quid pro quo Nolting had finally finessed with Diem on the counterinsurgency funding, the new terms of shared control were yoked to a public reaffirmation by the regime of the need for a US security presence in Vietnam for some time to come.[52]

"The Year of Victory"

In May, just back from another whirlwind visit to Vietnam, McNamara declared "the corner has definitely been turned toward victory . . . within three years." He too seemed to believe the fantasies General Harkins was nursing after Ap Bac and sharing with Diem: "The Viet Cong are still with us, but for the most part are not so bothersome. . . . [H]e is still a wily enemy and apparently is dedicated to his cause because he continues to put up a stiff fight under pressure. . . . [H]e is gradually getting to be like a rat caught in a trap with no place to go. . . . I am confident that 1963 shall be called the year of victory."[53]

Nolting was nearly as persuaded as Harkins that things were on the right track and that Diem was the key to its success. On regular trips into the countryside with the Vietnamese president, the ambassador noted "enthusiasm among peasants and officials . . . appreciation of American assistance. . . . Perhaps most striking was Diem's touch with the people. He spent two long hot dusty days talking with and seeking the reactions of farmers and their families. . . . I was nevertheless again impressed, as I believe my colleagues were, by the vast difference between what is actually happening in this country and the reflection of it in the outside world. . . . In my view, what is actually happening is a vindication of American and GVN policy."[54]

Disgusted with the course of the war, Richard Russell, the archconservative senator from Georgia, fumed: "We are trying to fight this problem as if it were a tournament of roses. I think it is time for the dirty tricks department to take over here." As for the Viet Cong, "we ought to catch them as if we were trying to run down Jesse James—$10,000, dead or alive. . . . We might promise them a couple of water buffalo, or a new wife, or some money, or three or four acres of rice land—almost anything would be cheaper than what we are doing."[55]

Not only was 1963 not to be the year of victory, but there was never to be such a year for the United States in Vietnam. While Nolting believed vindication was at hand, something else entirely was looming.

7

★ ★ ★

Out of Nowhere

I N A STORY WHOSE end has many beginnings and tide-turnings, the proximate event that sealed the demise of the Diem regime—and ultimately, paradoxically, the demise of American prudence and clear thinking—came out of nowhere. Or almost nowhere. There was nothing incremental or foreseen about it, in either Saigon (or Hanoi) or Washington. It had seemingly extraneous and spontaneous beginnings, an apparent distraction from the big questions of communism and democracy, neocolonialism and counterinsurgency—far from all the preoccupations of Americans and Vietnamese alike for the past two years, the past ten years. All concerned were ill-equipped to face it.

The Buddhist explosion was set off in Hue, the ancient capital of Annam, in central Vietnam. Hue (*hway*) was South Vietnam's second city, dominated by a citadel on the enchanting Perfume River just south of the 17th parallel, the "temporary" demarcation of northern and southern Vietnam by the Geneva Accords of 1954.

Hue was significant for other reasons. It was the seat of the Ngo family's ancestral homeland. It was a region of deep Buddhist traditions and a Buddhist majority, now ruled with especial authority by two Roman Catholics: the archbishop of Hue and ranking Catholic cleric in Vietnam, Msgr. Ngo Dinh Thuc, and the semi-autonomous political capo of the region, Ngo Dinh Can. Thuc and Can were brothers of Ngo Dinh Nhu and Ngo Dinh Diem.

During the first weekend in May, Archbishop Thuc celebrated the twenty-fifth anniversary of his ordination as a bishop—a measure of the Ngo family's influence long before Ngo Dinh Diem came to power. Word soon got back to President Diem that the white and gold flags and banners of the Holy See had been flown at the celebrations in Hue. Drawing on one of his constitutional mandates—dating to the colonial era, promulgated by the puppet emperor in 1950—the president upbraided the authorities and reminded them that religious displays were prohibited. The Vietnamese flag was the only one permitted.

May 8, three days later, was the 2,527th birthday of Buddha, another, bigger, regular occasion for religious celebration in Hue. Taking their cues from Diem's rebuke in a stern circular the night before, local police first attempted to enforce the ban on flags that had been ignored for the Catholics. Then under other pressures and stormy negotiations—Thuc wanted a tough line, Can was trying to find a solution, and Diem was caught in the middle—the police chief rescinded the order. The streets were already abloom with Buddhist flags and antigovernment banners. Several thousand people gathered at Tu Dam pagoda to hear from the emerging leader of the movement, the forty-year-old bonze (monk) Tri Quang, and others who denounced the suppression of freedom of religion and the government's favoritism of Catholics.

That evening the crowd moved, growing, to a radio station headquarters to hear the speech from Tri Quang to be rebroadcast on loudspeakers in the street. At the last minute frantic local officials blocked the transmission. A Vietnamese flag was torn off the roof and replaced with a Buddhist banner. At 10:00 p.m. police and Vietnamese army soldiers arrived in armored personnel carriers (APCs), surrounding the crowd and ordering it to disperse. Then the authorities waded into the demonstrators, firing weapons in the air and launching concussion grenades. One of the APCs rolled forward into the throng. In the general melee, eight young people were killed, including two adolescents crushed by the APC.[1]

The Diem regime did not hesitate to promote the idea that the killing was the work of the Viet Cong and that pagodas were infiltrated by Communists. "Terrorist Grenade Mars Buddha's Birthday in Hue," read the headline in the *Times of Vietnam*, the next day, over a brief article. The government persisted in this belief, or alibi, for months—to the end.

All the embassy, CIA, and independent reporting at the time, and exhaustive research ever since, has found no credible evidence of any Viet Cong involvement in the May 8 incident. Or of a US agent provocateur, as some Ngo brothers believed, or said they believed. But no one denied then, and the embassy reported as much, and much evidence has accumulated since, that the fragmented South Vietnamese political opposition to Diem coalesced quickly around the crisis and exploited it. "Under the press of the Buddhist protest, all the flaws, all the shortcomings, all the intolerance of the Diem regime came to the surface; so, too, did American impotence," as David Halberstam put it later.[2]

The Buddhists themselves were a mystery to the American diplomats and intelligence officers in Saigon, conspicuous nonplayers in their assiduous cultivation and analysis of oppositionists. There was plenty of evidence of a Buddhist revival of sorts in the months before, but the embassy and the press corps had more urgent matters to explore, they thought, than peaceful demonstrations of Buddhist monks. "We didn't even know who they were. We didn't have their names or the faintest idea of what their organization was all about," the National Security Council's Mike Forrestal realized with alarm.[3] Halberstam admitted he "knew no Buddhist priests, knew little about Vietnamese Buddhism, and had never been in a pagoda."[4]

What emerged was that many Buddhists in South Vietnam had long been resentful of their treatment, real and perceived, at the hands of a regime led by Roman Catholics. Senior military officers were known to have converted to Catholicism to improve their chances of promotion—and were called "1955 Catholics." Catholic numbers in the South (about 1.5 million) had mushroomed during the staggering 1955 exodus of a million Vietnamese from the north in the post–Geneva Accords population swap. What is more, the Ngos had been Catholics for generations, and there was no erasing the reality that their faith was a vestige of colonialism. The mandarinate itself, which President Diem embodied, was an import, too, the adapted heritage of centuries of Chinese domination.

Although official telegrams and news reports at the time (and even some histories long after) carelessly repeated the presumption, Buddhists were *not* in the majority in South Vietnam.[5] The country, occupied for a millennium, was a "syncretist" society of Buddhists, animists, Taoists, Confucianists, and followers of Cao Dai, a recent homegrown religion that was itself an amalgam of many world faiths, counting among its holy people not just Buddha, Muhammad, and Jesus, but Julius Caesar, Joan of Arc, and Victor Hugo.

Practicing Buddhists may have constituted no more than 30 percent of the Vietnamese population. But Buddhism in Vietnam as elsewhere was not "just" a religion. It was (and is today, under Communist rule) respected by the non-Catholic population at large as a historical and civic faith. "Somewhat like Hinduism in Gandhi's generation earlier, it was the reservoir of widely known cultural symbols in a fragmented society," according to one scholar;[6] it might also be compared to the way the secular French regard Catholicism today. Adherence to the tenets of the faith, in other words, was not a necessary precondition for a Vietnamese citizen fed up with Diem to feel solidarity with the Buddhists.

The May 8 killings had struck a nerve; in Tri Quang's words, the incident was "the drop that makes the bowl of water overflow."[7] Terse but vivid, the American consul, John Helble, cabled from Hue: "People seem to have taken seriously Bonze speech morning 8th 'now is time to fight.' . . . Student banner morning 9th 'please kill us.' Man on street expressing great desire the world to know of killings on 8th. While GVN line is VC responsible, no credibility this among population."[8]

Yet Nolting, then and since, persisted in this belief. "Some of these guys had just come into the pagodas, shaved their heads and put on saffron robes and had become monks, bonzes. And one could have very healthy and well-founded suspicions that they were no more bonzes than you or me. We had no hard, concrete evidence that it was a Viet Cong plot. I believed it was. I believe now without any question that it was," Nolting said in 1970.[9]

The APC that crushed the young Buddhists was a potent symbol. On its sides it bore the scrawled name (as fighter jets and fire engines are known to sport) of Ngo Dinh Khoi, the firstborn Ngo brother, who had been executed by Ho Chi Minh two decades before. It may not need to be added that the APC was supplied to the Vietnamese by the United States.

An Invitation to Leave

The following Sunday, May 12, Nolting and Trueheart accompanied Diem on a helicopter inspection trip to strategic hamlets in two Delta provinces, Long An and Binh Duong. They were unable to get a minute with the president on the Buddhist explosion. They flew back to Saigon to fresh alarums from Washington—about something else altogether. The *Washington Post* had just quoted Ngo Dinh Nhu as saying half of the thirteen thousand American military personnel now in Vietnam should leave.

The Kennedy administration was stunned—more so than it had been about the killings in Hue. "Nhu's action is incomprehensible. I wonder whether he will not repeat performance if not brought up sharply and immediately," Roger Hilsman cabled Nolting from the State Department.

Comments such as Nhu's, came the instructions, were "likely to generate new and reinforce already existing US domestic pressures for complete withdrawal from SVN." The administration was especially stung by Nhu's comment to Warren Unna, the *Post* reporter, that American casualties in Vietnam "are cases of soldiers who exposed themselves too readily." The State Department reminded the Saigon embassy, "It will not be taken well by US public or US forces in Vietnam to be told our casualties were needless."[10]

Nhu's threats were a new and especially galling iteration of the diplomatic dance the Ngo regime carried on: forever seeking reassurances of American constancy, and just as regularly protesting the American presence. The regime worried about being abandoned as Laos had been abandoned, in its eyes, but resisted any alliance or assistance that implied they were American vassals. They wanted the money and equipment to fight the Viet Cong, but they didn't want Americans calling the shots.

As before and after, the American commitment was deepening in tandem with official misgivings about it. When he was asked publicly about Nhu's comments to the *Post,* President Kennedy said the United States would withdraw troops any time the Vietnamese government requested it: "The day after it were suggested we would have some troops on their way home." Kennedy also said, as his political advisers had been prodding him to say, that "we are hopeful that the situation in South Vietnam would permit some withdrawal in any case by the end of the year."

The underlying point Kennedy could not have said out loud, as the scholar Ellen Hammer observes, was that "the Americans were not in Vietnam to oblige Diem; they were there to serve the interests of the United States and to demonstrate American credibility to the Soviets and the Chinese Communists in other parts of the world."[11]

The Care of a Prudent Man

There is no better illustration of the bet-hedging mentality in Washington than the last assignment Nolting was given before leaving on his family holiday. He may have done it with distaste. As requested, he submitted to the State Department a contingency plan in the event of a "change in government" in Saigon. It was reworked from older versions the embassy, the CIA, and the State Department had been churning out since at least 1960, if not 1954. (One of the drafters, Ben Wood, observed in a cover memo that such plans "should be made and reviewed with the same care that a prudent man devotes to his will," a pregnant turn of phrase.) Nolting made the paper sound less than urgent. "We will keep it for reference and will update it at least annually," he wrote.[12]

The document coolly laid out scenarios, including wildly unlikely ones: "Diem announces his intention of retiring"; "Diem killed by VC"; "Diem killed by non-VC opposition." Nothing on the list said, "Killed by South Vietnamese generals." Plausible contenders for replacing Diem were named: Vice President Nguyen Ngoc Tho, General Duong Van Minh. Another was named with a shudder—Ngo Dinh Nhu. The black humor of those days yielded a remark, which sounds like Trueheart, that among all the qualifications for a new leader of South Vietnam, "first of all, he should be an only child."[13]

As for the Buddhist crisis, Nolting had been cajoling Diem to take immediate steps to find common ground with the Buddhists, who had announced their five principal demands: rescinding the order against flying the flags; legal parity of Buddhists with Catholics; an end to arbitrary arrests of Buddhist activists; indemnification of the May 8 victims; and punishment of responsible officials. Each of these was seen as a tacit admission of government fault were the regime to consider them. With Nolting, once again, Diem was polite but unyielding. "He appears to feel that whole affair is far less serious matter than we do," Nolting cabled the Department.[14]

Privately, Fritz Nolting may have seen the Buddhist crisis the same way Diem did—as not serious enough to warrant changing his vacation plans. The Buddhists and the palace were talking. Grudging concessions seemed to be emerging. The street protests had subsided somewhat. He still trusted Trueheart. Washington had its mind on other things again, especially growing tension over desegregation and civil rights in Alabama and Mississippi.

The Noltings had already postponed their departure once, but the State Department seemed to offer no objections to his going ahead. He speculated later about "some kind of plot, but I didn't understand that then," to get him out of Saigon. "Bittie's antenna were better than mine, because she said 'Don't let's go.' And I said, well, we've got everything lined up." It was, he would say ever after, the worst mistake he ever made.

Bill and Phoebe Trueheart were among the usual delegations from the American community, the Vietnamese government, and the press corps who saw the Noltings off at Tan Son Nhut airport on May 23. Even vacations merited official sendoffs. The ambassador and his wife and their two younger daughters, Frances and Jane, were headed to New Delhi, the first stop on their vacation trip, where they stayed at the US ambassador's residence, although the Galbraiths were absent, before touring Agra and the Taj Mahal.

A few days later, Trueheart ran into Rufus Phillips, the young rural affairs czar, who was "thunderstruck" by the information that Nolting had left town—"incomprehensibly"—at a time like this: "Bill said Nolting was very tired, had long postponed his leave, and thought the crisis was on the way to resolution."[15]

There was to be no contact between the ambassador and the *chargé d'affaires* for the next six weeks. Trueheart was on his own. Nolting would not be back until July.

My father had been *chargé* in Saigon many times before, so there seemed nothing significant to me in his assumption of the role for this longest and most fateful interlude. He was just a great deal busier, and a great deal more absent. Although school was out for the summer in June, due to the press of diplomatic business and the deterioration of the Diem regime, we didn't go anywhere as a family except for a weekend in Nha Trang, the only time I ever left Saigon to go elsewhere in Vietnam. There the local CIA guy met us at the airport and took us to the embassy's colonial-era guest house on the beach, one of the most beautiful in the world. It was there that my mother and I first water-skied, and all of us but Josh got badly sunburned.

During these heated days of June 1963, assuming his mother's archiving was meticulous, the letters Bill wrote so dutifully to her for thirty years essentially stop. Phoebe, thankfully, picked up the narrative, finally giving a little emotional shape to what is absent from Bill's missives and can be only inferred from his telegrams. In apologizing to Sallie for Bill's silence, Phoebe also gives evidence of how much he was sharing with her about his work.

"You have to forgive him again," Phoebe wrote, still using up the family's teal-blue featherweight stationery from London. "You know, if he is not talking to Minister Thuan, or the President, or the newspapermen, he is writing cables to Washington—so he is 'all wrote out,' as you say." Phoebe lamented the phone "ringing all night long (and I refused to marry a doctor!). People at the door at 2 am. More people have seen me in a nightgown than I like to relate. But I am too old to care. I feel like a concierge. I let them in, get Bill out of bed (he never hears the doorbell), get their drinks, and wait outside the study with a book." Phoebe reports her husband working seven days a week: "He is running on nerves. . . . But don't worry. He really enjoys being in the thick of the fray."[16]

By the time the Buddhist dossier landed in the chargé's hands, Trueheart had concluded it was already too late for the concessions the Buddhists wanted from the regime, even if it would grant them. "Psychological moment to do so has long passed," he told Washington. "We are no longer dealing with a purely religious issue. . . . Those seeking to use Buddhist agitation can be counted on to keep the pot boiling if possible."[17]

The movement had taken hold across the urban pagodas of South Vietnam, where the active Buddhist protesters had sought refuge, now often surrounded by police and barbed wire. In increasing numbers, monks were observing hunger strikes. Boy scouts and girl scouts were praying in the streets under the baleful glare of armed security forces. Tear gas was sprayed into crowds in Hue, where on June 1 ten thousand people gathered to hear Tri Quang declare that the situation was "beyond compromise and, in direct confrontation with GVN, Buddhists should seek help from any source, including VC," as an embassy cable put it.[18]

Privately, Tri Quang told his US embassy contacts what was dawning on everyone: "The United States must make Diem reform or get rid of him. If not, the situation will degenerate, and you worthy gentlemen will suffer most." And he suggested they deserved to: "you are responsible for the present trouble because you back Diem and his government of ignoramuses."[19]

As the issue simmered, Trueheart was in all but constant contact with Washington and with Secretary of State Nguyen Dinh Thuan at the palace. The *chargé* delivered consistent and increasingly insistent counsel that President Diem had to make an immediate conciliatory announcement to calm the waters, and should do so in Hue, and in person, to dramatize it. Trueheart was instructed to emphasize "not only their own stake in amiable settlement with Buddhists but US stake as well." When he saw Thuan, "I felt bound to tell him that in my opinion US support for GVN could not be maintained in face of bloody repressive action at Hue."[20]

On June 4 Diem named an interministerial committee to deal with Buddhist grievances, headed by Vice President Tho, Secretary Thuan, and Interior Minister Bui Van Long, the most senior Buddhists in his government. They met with Buddhist emissaries, and within a few days an agreement seemed within reach. Trueheart's reports were upbeat and relieved.

But the moment was evanescent. On June 8 the *chargé d'affaires* telegrammed the latest incendiary declaration from Madame Nhu. A resolution passed the day before by the central committee of her Women's Solidarity Movement, and bearing all the trademarks of her invective, said Buddhist demonstrators were "exploited and controlled by communism and oriented to sowing of disorder and neutralism." The resolution labeled religious fasting as "blackmail" and called on the government to "immediately expel all foreign agitators whether they wear monks' robes or not."[21]

Trueheart wasted no time: "I am immediately seeking appointment with President Diem." Guidance flowed in from Washington while he left for the palace, but he knew it by heart. He found President Diem "entirely relaxed and friendly, and he permitted frequent interruptions in a way that is rare for him. Unfortunately, I have no reason to believe that anything I said to him moved him." He brought Diem a copy of Madame Nhu's resolution, and the president read it "line by line as if he had never seen it before." Diem finally told Trueheart that he could not disavow it, without saying why. "I fear that the general sentiments of the resolution are close to his own."[22]

This would be the pattern in the tumultuous weeks that followed: Diem would make assurances to satisfy his American or Buddhist interlocutors, who would then find the assurances contradicted and sabotaged in the government-sanctioned press controlled by Ngo Dinh Nhu and his wife. "The darker forecasts of the *Times of Vietnam* over a long period of time more accurately reflected the government policy than the official promises of Diem," as Halberstam put it. "Trueheart was beginning to learn the lessons of Durbrow."[23]

Nolting once compared any effort to separate the Ngo brothers to separating "Siamese twins."[24] For his part, Trueheart was once asked how he thought about Diem and Nhu and Madame Nhu. "While disclaiming any intention to be sacrilegious," Trueheart replied, "their relationship is analogous to the Holy Trinity. I see no real differences among them."[25] Interesting comparison, muddy theology.

Martyrdom

At midday on June 11, Saigon time—midnight in Washington, and at dawn on the Aegean Sea—the *chargé* in Saigon cabled the State Department that a Buddhist monk had set himself on fire in Saigon.

Malcolm Browne of AP was the only American correspondent on the scene, having turned up early that morning at a local pagoda on a tip about another demonstration. Browne stood around waiting for whatever was supposed to happen—his tipster had been cryptic: "Incense filled the room, numbing the senses, as did the ancient prayer droning over and over from a lean and ascetic monk . . . : *Na . . . Mo. . . . Ah . . . Di . . . Da. . . . Phat.*' For an hour the hypnotic prayer continued, the eyes of faithful and outsider alike glazing as its tempo slowly rose."[26] At 9:00 a.m., the crowd moved outside to a carefully organized procession of monks carrying banners condemning the Diem regime. Browne followed the procession as it made its way under police protection through the streets of Saigon. Though not a photographer, he carried a camera nonetheless.

Near the head of the procession moved a gray Austin sedan carrying several bonzes. At the intersection of Phan Dinh Phung and Le Van Duyet, in front of the Cambodian embassy, the procession stopped. One of the monks opened the hood of the car and withdrew a plastic five-gallon container of gasoline. The others led the oldest monk to the center of the intersection, where he was seated on a small brown cushion, hands folded in prayers, legs crossed in lotus position. The monk, seventy-three-year-old Quang Duc, then struck a match and went up in flames.

Twenty feet away, Browne trained his cheap Petri camera and began shooting pictures as "a wail of horror rose from the monks and nuns, many of whom prostrated themselves in the direction of the flames. From time to time, a light breeze pulled the flames away from Quang Duc's face. His eyes were closed, but his features were twisted in apparent pain. He remained upright, his hands folded in his lap, for nearly ten minutes as the flesh burned from his head and body. The reek of gasoline smoke and burning flesh hung over the intersection like a pall. Finally, Quang Duc fell backward, his blackened legs kicking convulsively for a minute or so. Then he was still, and the flames gradually subsided."[27] As the bonze burned, surrounding monks chanted, in Vietnamese and English, the message of the day, the message prepared for their banners: "A Buddhist priest burns himself to death. A Buddhist priest becomes a martyr."

As he kept Washington abreast of developments that day, Trueheart as acting ambassador closed the American Community School. The unexpected day off gave my friends and me a chance to bicycle to the intersection where the self-immolation had occurred and to ogle the brown stain on the street where the bonze had died. Trueheart also dismissed all the employees at USOM, as the US economic assistance mission was called then, because USOM headquarters happened to be next door to Xa Loi pagoda, in a quiet residential district only two blocks from the Noltings' house and three from the Truehearts'. It would prove a fortuitous listening post and escape route in the weeks ahead.

The *chargé,* after telling Washington that the "situation has drastically changed since self-cremation of bonze in central Saigon," went to see Thuan and told him the government's situation was "precarious." Again he urged "immediate, dramatic, and conciliatory move by President Diem personally." This was a stronger tune than he had been whistling, and Nolting before him, long before the immolation of Quang Duc. Trueheart told Thuan "as a personal opinion"—he didn't have his *démarching* orders yet, but Thuan had the president's ear—that if Diem didn't do something "this afternoon," he might be faced with US dissociation, "with quite possibly a strong overtone of disapproval of GVN handling of Buddhist problem since May 8."[28]

Diem addressed the nation on the radio that night, apparently heeding some element of US advice while oblivious to its spirit. With the overtones of *l'etat, c'est moi* so integral to his leadership, Diem declared that "Buddhism can count on the constitution, in other words, on me."[29] "Made bad impression here," the State Department flashed back.

As bad impressions go, it could not compete with the next day's utterance from Madame Nhu. She described the aged monk's self-immolation, in English, as a "barbecue," creating an international sensation and giving legs to the story. With her "unfailing instinct for the wrong word at the wrong time," wrote Marguerite Higgins, an American reporter who knew her well, Madame Nhu "never achieved an epithet more devastating than this one."[30] She later laid at the feet of Americans the blame for her use of "barbecue"—her English was poor—by saying she had heard it from her own daughter, who had overheard it at the American commissary. Madame Nhu also mocked the monks' use of "imported gasoline" and offered to provide matches for the next one. "Let them burn and we shall clap our hands!"[31]

The Buddhists seemed prepared to oblige her. Higgins, who happened to be in Saigon on a *New York Herald Tribune* reporting trip, got into Xa Loi with her White House press pass around her neck, which the monks mistook for a White House ID card, and she saw Tri Quang. He told her to tell President Kennedy to abandon Diem—or "he will see ten . . . forty . . . fifty bonzes burning."[32]

On June 12, the *Herald Tribune* carried Higgins's story and the Malcolm Browne photograph over three columns below the fold on page one, the first front-page news from Saigon in many days. In his memoir Nolting says he picked up a Greek newspaper with the news and photo when their yacht stopped on the island of Mikonos; this might have been the case if their cruise had diverged from the schedule he had sent the State Department in May, and was prolonged.[33] But if the itinerary was followed, the Noltings were already in Athens by June 11—and houseguests of the CIA station chief, who was an old friend, someone Nolting might have found useful as a source about the mood in Washington or the gravity of developments at his post. Even Greek television might have carried the news.

Nolting recollects inquiring at several ports in the Aegean, and again in Athens when they arrived, if there were any messages for him, and there were none. Instead, "I mistakenly relied on the assurances I had received" (from Trueheart, he says, among others) "that I would be notified if any unusual disturbances occurred in Vietnam. That proved to be a cardinal error on my part."[34]

Did he dismiss the Buddhist inflammation as unworthy of further investigation? Perhaps. As the family moved overland to Venice, off the waters, for four days, the ambassador might have been lulled into thinking the matter had passed—especially if he never sought information or clarification from Washington directly, a peculiar passivity.

From the outside, and looking back today, this was a week, as so many weeks were that summer, full of news from the American South and the standoff between President Kennedy and segregationist governors. Medgar Evers was murdered on June 12, the day after the bonze's suicide. President and Mrs. Kennedy were embarking on a photogenic European trip, including a historic visit to the family's ancestral homelands in Ireland. A papal conclave was meeting to select a successor to John XXIII. The *Herald Tribune*'s banner headline on June 17, while the Noltings headed to Venice, was, "Soviet Blonde Orbiting as First Woman in Space." Notwithstanding the shocking conflagration in Saigon, Vietnam was squeezed out of the news columns entirely for many days.

Yet the State Department had time for little else. That night Harriman and Hilsman approved Trueheart's recommendation to make an explicit threat of dissociation to Diem: "In our judgment the Buddhist situation is dangerously near the breaking point."[35] Trueheart thanked them for the timely instructions just as he was leaving for Gia Long, using words that revealed his own impatience and sense of the endgame: "They are of course very strong medicine and will be very hard for Diem to take. I would not care to predict outcome, but I believe we can be satisfied that we have done everything reasonably possible to get President Diem to save himself."[36]

The *chargé* saw the president at Gia Long that evening, with Thuan sitting in. This is one of those moments where I can't help reckoning with the singularity and stress of the occasion for Bill Trueheart, the bright, bespectacled boy from small-town Virginia, an envoy in a strange land, taking the otherworldly chief of state to the woodshed—in French.

Using diplomatic custom, Trueheart handed Diem "a paper, unsigned and headed 'Memorandum,'" outlining what he had been instructed to say. The president read the paper carefully without comment except to ask what the word "reluctantly" meant. The president's interactions with Americans always took place in French, but this was entirely a matter of pride. Diem had little trouble reading English, or speaking it, when he chose to.

After conferring with Thuan in Vietnamese, Diem told Trueheart that any statement of US disassociation would be disastrous for the Buddhist negotiations, set to begin the next day. Diem said he would take the whole memo under advisement and not make any decision until the negotiations had begun. But he was not happy with the pressure. After so many unpleasant visits, Diem had just about had it with Trueheart. He was not

Ngo Dinh Diem, who became president of the Republic of Vietnam in 1956. His image on postage stamps was part of a broader cult of personality engineered by his family to establish Diem as the father of his country. (Trueheart family archives)

President John F. Kennedy confers in 1961 with his two most senior advisers on Vietnam, General Maxwell D. Taylor (*left*), soon to become chairman of the Joint Chiefs of Staff, and Secretary of Defense Robert McNamara. (Abbie Rowe, White House Photographs/John F. Kennedy Presidential Library and Museum, Boston)

Ambassador Frederick E. Nolting and Deputy Chief of Mission William C. Trueheart in the ambassador's office at the US Embassy in Saigon, July 1962. The two diplomats had just received promotions in grade in the US Foreign Service. (Trueheart family archives)

Fritz Nolting as a student visiting the Great Wall of China in the summer of 1929. (Courtesy of Lindsay Nolting)

Bill Trueheart in a studio shot, probably at the University of Virginia, from the late 1930s. (Trueheart family archives)

The author, aged ten, on a family trip to Angkor Wat in Cambodia, 1962. (Trueheart family archives)

Bill and Phoebe Trueheart at a US Embassy reception in Saigon, 1962. (Trueheart family archives)

Joshua Trueheart with the embassy driver Nguyen Van Sinh, 1961. The DCM's official Ford Fairlane, where Sinh and the author spent many hours in conversation, is parked in the background. (Trueheart family archives)

The Nolting and Trueheart families in the garden of the US ambassador's residence in Saigon, Christmas 1961. Bittie Nolting is at front left. To her left are Lindsay Nolting, Phoebe Trueheart, and Jane Nolting. To Fritz's left are Frances and Molly Nolting. Missing from the empty chairs in the photograph are the author and his father, coaching Charlie on the use of the camera. (Courtesy of Lindsay Nolting)

Trueheart, US chargé d'affaires, and Ngo Dinh Nhu, President Diem's brother and counselor, greeting US Attorney General Robert F. Kennedy in Saigon, February 1962. In an allusion to the younger brothers' special importance to the two presidents, Americans in Saigon were known to call Nhu "Bobby Nhu." (Trueheart family archives)

Tran Le Xuan, the wife of presidential counselor Ngo Dinh Nhu and first lady to her brother-in-law, the bachelor president Ngo Dinh Diem. Madame Nhu was a force to be reckoned with during the Diem years and a source of constant irritation to the US government. (CPA Media Pte. Ltd./Alamy Stock Photo)

The young American reporters covering the Vietnam War and the dissolution of the Diem regime in 1963: David Halberstam of the *New York Times* (*left*), Malcolm Browne of the Associated Press (*center*), and Neil Sheehan of United Press International (*right*). (AP Photo)

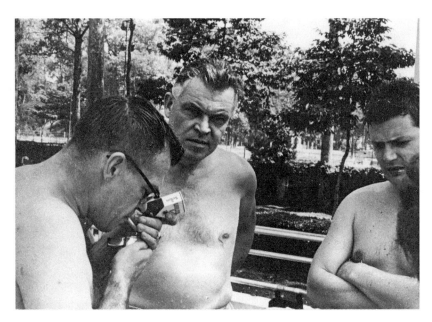

Fritz Nolting poolside at the Cercle Sportif Saigonnais in 1962 with the future champions of the US-sanctioned coup, Assistant Secretary of State Roger Hilsman (*left*) and White House assistant Michael Forrestal. (Trueheart family archives)

Trueheart, in Nolting's absence, delivering one of many bracing US messages to Ngo Dinh Diem at Gia Long Palace, June 1963. (Trueheart family archives)

The self-immolation of Thich Quang Duc, 11 June 1963. The photo, which drew the attention of the world to the Buddhist crisis in South Vietnam, outraged President Kennedy and won the photographer, Malcolm Browne, a Pulitzer Prize. (AP Photo/Malcolm Browne)

U.S. Ambassador Frederick E. Nolting, Jr. is met at the airport by Charge d'Affairs William Trueheart who acted as Mission Chief during the Ambassador's absence.

Ambassador Nolting walks with Trueheart at Tan Son Nhut airport, July 1963, upon his return to Saigon to make a last-ditch appeal to President Diem to meet Buddhist demands. Such official departures and arrivals were regularly covered by the local English-language daily, the pro-regime *Times of Vietnam*. (Trueheart family archives)

Nolting and Trueheart with other guests at President Diem's farewell dinner for the Noltings at Gia Long Palace, August 1963. (Trueheart family archives)

Henry Cabot Lodge, the new US ambassador, presents his credentials to President Diem on 26 August 1963. (Trueheart family archives)

Bill and Phoebe Trueheart with Lodge at his new ambassadorial residence, November 1963. (Trueheart family archives)

Outside Gia Long Palace after the November 1963 coup d'état. (AP Photo)

Looters in Saigon at the end of the fighting that overthrew the Diem regime. (AP Photo)

Trueheart, as chargé d'affaires in Lodge's absence, receives spontaneous delegations of Vietnamese citizens expressing condolences on 23 November 1963, the day after the assassination of John F. Kennedy. (Trueheart family archives)

the genial and trusting Fritz Nolting, and he was not the US ambassador, even if he was under instructions.

Or was he? Or, put differently: whose instructions? The coming months would be marked by President Kennedy's agonized ambivalence about tightening the pressure on Diem, both impulses fed by deep divisions among reasonable men he trusted about the risks and consequences of doing so—or not doing so. Kennedy was furious, for example, when he heard about Trueheart's démarche to Diem from the CIA's intelligence briefing two days later. He ordered that "no further threats are made and no formal statement [of disassociation from the regime] is made without his personal approval."[37]

But the damage was done. The *New York Times*' Max Frankel, in Washington, published a front-page story on June 14, clearly conveying Trueheart's threat of dissociation to Diem. The leak almost certainly came from the pugnacious and undisciplined Harriman, although any number of people who wanted to tighten the pressure on Diem could have done it. Implicitly it reflected on the approach Nolting had been taking: Washington was "losing faith in the effectiveness of quiet, backstage pressure." The story, to the embassy press officer, John Mecklin, read as if Frankel "had been shown the file of classified cables from Saigon." The palace was outraged.

Following the embarrassing story, and Kennedy's eruption, Trueheart was instructed to tell Diem that there had been no change in the US policy of support—the kind of hand-holding and there-there-ing that he and Nolting had been doing since 1961. Yet on the very same day that Harriman was ordering the *chargé* to deliver these hollow assurances, he brought up "contingency planning" again. He ordered Trueheart to get word discreetly to Vice President Tho—a message the United States would deny if it were exposed—that "in event situation arises due to internal political circumstances (in which US would play no part)," the United States would want to back Tho as the constitutional successor to Diem and would "assume he would need military support."[38]

This coup talk, as such it was, had gone beyond brainstorming. Trueheart saw Tho on June 18 and delivered the message. Viewing the unassuming Vietnamese vice president in this new light was a stretch for the *chargé*. Tho had the special virtues of being a Buddhist and not being a Ngo, but he was widely regarded as soft and ineffectual—precisely the qualities Diem desired in his adjutant. Disillusioned as he was with the Ngos, Trueheart pronounced himself "not impressed" with Tho (or anyone else) as an alternative to Diem, "nor do I think are any of my colleagues American or foreign."[39] This would be a theme of discussions at the highest levels in Washington for many months, long after Tho had been dismissed as the engine of any coup: if not Diem, who? The great fear in these days was that it would be Nhu.

Seemingly unaware of the disaster in Vietnam, or relying on someone else to tell him about it, the next day Nolting and his family boarded the 1,000-passenger ocean liner SS *Constitution* in Genoa, bound for a nine-day passage to New York.

The Conversion

It was in these heady days and weeks that Bill Trueheart had his conversion experience about Vietnam—or at least about the government of Ngo Dinh Diem. His "bitter opposition" to the escalation of American combat forces in Vietnam would come later, although not much later.

David Halberstam's take, in *The Best and the Brightest,* was that after Nolting left, Trueheart as *chargé* and Melvin Manfull, the political counselor and acting DCM, "opened up the embassy reporting" to dissidents and Buddhists, suggesting truth-tellers unchained. Their diplomatic reporting to Washington had turned abruptly from being "blindly pro-Diem" to "being skeptical, cool and iconoclastic in its appraisal. . . . The Embassy began to doubt that Diem could handle the Buddhist crisis . . . and also cast doubt upon Nhu's sanity, doubts which were accurate."[40]

"The change in Trueheart was crucial," Halberstam wrote, always a bit breathlessly. "It let loose a floodgate of doubts. For the first time, American diplomatic reporting in Saigon resembled the American diplomatic reporting from China" after World War II. A few months earlier, "only American journalists had been pessimistic about the war." Now they were joined by "the State Department people in Saigon." And the CIA too, he added, a little prematurely. "Only the military held devotedly to the line of optimism"—all the way up to Secretary of Defense Robert McNamara, to whom Rusk had ceded primacy in the conduct of the war. That much is very true.

What Halberstam doesn't quite say is that the upper ranks of the embassy were beginning to come around more openly to the journalists' point of view. Theirs was a symbiotic relationship between information-gatherers. Trueheart's calendar throughout suggests almost weekly appointments with Halberstam, Browne, and Sheehan, and frequent dinners which included Phoebe and others. Phone calls were dicey.

Reflecting on what made Neil Sheehan say, at his memorial service, that our father was a brave man, my brother Josh suggested, "maybe he meant the way Bill was treating reporters. It was dangerous territory. I assume he was listening to them and talking to them, engaging them and not giving them bullshit."[41] Marguerite Higgins noted that "the press had as allies many members of the US embassy, most of whom were junior-grade, with one astonishing exception, William Trueheart, deputy to Ambassador Nolting."[42]

Embassies don't report to Washington in a vacuum. They report about what the State Department wants to know, which in these days was beginning to be driven by what was appearing in the US news media. In that sense diplomats can't help reflecting the approbation and encouragement they are getting from headquarters.

My own reading of the cables from Nolting, and then Trueheart, in May and June (and in the many months before) reflects that byplay between headquarters and field command—another symbiotic relationship. My reading doesn't bear out a 180-degree turn in the reporting but rather a gradually sobering assessment—in Washington and Saigon—of the Diem regime's inability to handle, or even understand, a political crisis, and all that that said about its ability to win the war.

William Sullivan, watching his colleagues from Washington that summer, saw that "a certain head of emotional pressure built up in the Ebassy which finally erupted into the open after Fritz went on home leave and while Trueheart was in charge."[43] For Bob Miller in the embassy in Saigon, it was simpler than that: "I think Bill Trueheart was convinced, and most of us in the political section were convinced, that Diem was so isolated from reality that he was not really aware of how bad things were getting. . . . Fritz felt that somehow in our reporting the glass should have been half-full rather than half-empty. My own feeling was that the embassy was reporting things as they saw it—that Diem had lost control."[44]

The Buddhists had exposed the fragility of the government. They had struck a nerve. And in June 1963, any careful newspaper reader would have understood what then-secret contemporaneous cables made clear.

The Kennedy administration was deeply worried, and it was preparing warily to throw its ally overboard if things didn't improve dramatically.

Mecklin said, "It will remain one of the unanswerable 'ifs' of history that Nolting's low-key way, at the moment of ultimate challenge, might have been more effective."[45] Nolting believed he might have saved the day if he had been notified and brought back to Saigon immediately. Trueheart doubted this, of course. The fact is the policy had changed: the message had become tougher. Trueheart had become the new messenger of the new policy. He happened to approve of it, and he could reasonably believe that he had had a hand in galvanizing it.

Mecklin's dramatic recitation of these confrontations is that Trueheart applied "direct, relentless, table-hammering pressure on Diem such as the United States had seldom before attempted with a sovereign, friendly government."

The table-hammering is so powerful an image that it is quoted or echoed by many other historians and journalists who read Mecklin's lively and nearly contemporaneous *Mission in Torment*.[46] Nolting may have been among them. Nearly two decades later, still angry, and still echoing the Diem party line about Communist infiltration of the Buddhist movement, Nolting said:

> What happened was the United States all of a sudden began to hammer the table on hotheaded instructions from Washington, burned into action by the American press, to . . . tell this guy to apologize and eat crow and do things that he couldn't possibly afford to do as president of the country, which also would not have done any good. Because by that time the Buddhist movement had come into the hands of those who had only one objective, and that was the overthrow of the government. Well, that objective was the exact objective of the Viet Cong.[47]

I don't see my father doing any such thing as table-hammering—with a chief of state, anyway. What he did tend to do, to emphasize a serious point or ensure he was being heard, was jab his index finger, making little thuds, on a tabletop. I suspect (as my father liked to say) that this is a distinction without a difference. Hammer or jab, the offense to the brittle Diem was the same.

Mecklin wrote afterward that Diem might have survived if he "had immediately heeded Trueheart's advice," but "the regime bitterly resented

Trueheart, both because of what he said and because its pride was hurt by the fact that he was only a *chargé*." Trueheart's final warning to Diem was "an insufferable humiliation" for the government, "and such influence as Trueheart may still have possessed was dramatically weakened." Mecklin quoted "one officer at the time" (political or military, he doesn't say) who declared, "No government in the world can take this kind of treatment. Diem could well declare Trueheart *persona non grata,* and I hope he does."[48]

Rufus Phillips told me he admired both Nolting and Trueheart but agreed with Nolting that the aggressive approach was "very counterproductive." The gist of the instructions Trueheart got was "insulting: 'Go tell Diem this!' This was reverting back to General Collins, to the French. . . . There was nothing that would cause Diem or any other Vietnamese to dig in their heels more than some American or other paleface telling them what to do."[49]

For Francis X. Winters, the Georgetown University professor whose book *The Year of the Hare* closely examines the events of 1963 from a moral perspective, Trueheart was the "scourge" of the affair. While "riding high in Saigon" as the ambitious henchman of Harriman and Hilsman, Trueheart delivered "fulminations" in "two months of hectoring" while "issuing imperial edicts on the conduct of South Vietnamese internal politics."[50]

Winters attributes Trueheart's appetite for attacking Diem to "the carrot of rapid promotion in the department that Harriman held out to him."[51] This is close to Ambassador Nolting's view of his old friend. In a vaguely passive-aggressive formulation, Nolting added in longhand to an oral history interview transcript he was vetting: "I myself had requested [Trueheart's] assignment as my deputy two years earlier. I knew well his hard work and his efficiency. I also knew how ambitious he was. So in the final analysis I have only myself to blame for my misplaced confidence."[52]

Nolting also vigorously disputed the notion that, before his departure, any daylight existed between his analysis of the regime and Trueheart's, or that the scales were falling from Trueheart's eyes. Yet the DCM's dissident noises during the Mansfield visit the autumn before might have given him an outward clue, and surely it was not the only one.

I have to ask, here and throughout this tragic fracture: did these two close friends of twenty-five years *never* sit down together in the winter and spring of 1963 and speak frankly to one another? Air their doubts, test their analyses, explore their differences? Working ten paces from one another on the top floor of the embassy, going to the same appointments and diplomatic parties, on the same inspection trips, they had nothing but opportunities. And they were old friends!

Making the case for Trueheart's ambitious overnight conversion, Nolting declared: "We had completely agreed on policy up to the time I left on home leave." Nolting said, "Trueheart had read and approved the speeches I was to make in the States" immediately upon disembarking from his holidays in New York at the beginning of July. "Then I found that Trueheart had shifted with the winds blowing from Washington—he had joined the Harriman-Hilsman cabal. He had adjusted his views." Nolting went on to assert, "The Mission's views were divided when I got back in July. Before, we had been united."

When an interviewer pressed Nolting for more details about the conflict between the two men, Nolting pulled back: "I'm not sure . . . to what extent I want in this interview to go into all of this. . . . It involves friends— or former friends."[53] He preferred to put it this way, no less condemnatory: "The embassy in Saigon when I was away had broken the bridge of confidence by which we had worked with the Diem government."[54]

What happened to the supposed "Ambassador-DCM combination made in heaven"?[55] For one of Trueheart's younger colleagues at the embassy, Robert Barbour, the answer was that "Trueheart developed the kinds of impressions that everyone else was living with: 'It isn't working, boss, and we have to recognize certain basic weaknesses in our policy and what we are doing.' Nolting, I guess, just didn't want to hear it from his best friend. . . . Trueheart was very loyal when he arrived; he is very perceptive and I think after a while it all got to his intellect, he reached some very profound personal conclusions."[56]

More than twenty years later, in one of his own oral history interviews, Trueheart also turned uncomfortable when his rupture with Nolting was brought up, urging the interviewer to move on, but not willing to say nothing: "He was very upset. . . . It's a very painful thing to me because we were friends for so many years."

But Trueheart justified his actions crisply, getting right to the question—the philosophical quandary, if you will—of loyalty: "I think Fritz felt that my responsibility during his absence was to *him,* whereas I felt my responsibility was to Washington when I was in charge during his absence. I did not feel I should be guided, in his absence, by doing what I supposed *he* would do."

On his own, Trueheart also had realized in the course of the confrontations with Diem that the United States had no chance of winning with this person in charge: "I concluded this long before Nolting came back. . . . I said at the time and I would still say: I don't have a guarantee that anybody else will do better. But we can be sure that this man will lose. And if it's not going to work, you don't start putting more money on the table."

Trueheart told his interviewer he didn't remember how his thinking developed, but by June 1963, he understood the fundamental problem and the dilemma it posed. He stated it eloquently:

> Every head of government in Vietnam, starting with Bao Dai and going through Diem and right up to Nguyen Van Thieu, never really regarded himself as the governor of Vietnam. He regarded himself as administering the country for somebody else. Not one of these people looked for his support, his ultimate support in office, to the people of the country. They looked to France or to us as the source of their power. That being the case, the more we did, the more we made this even more true. The more involved the United States became, the more it became impossible for whoever was the nominal ruler of the county to be a real ruler, both in fact and in the eyes of the country.[57]

Trueheart's friend and Saigon colleague Bob Miller applied the same analysis to the subsequent prosecution of the war: "One of the biggest mistakes we ever made was to take the war away from the South Vietnamese. They became a subordinate command in their own war. We took away their stake in their own survival."[58]

Diem struck a deal of sorts with the Buddhists on June 16, but as Trueheart had warned, it was too little, too late. He had hoped to persuade Diem to get ahead of the accord and make more dramatic moves—to use the crisis as a "blessing in disguise" to carry out big reforms—but found instead that the Nhus were actively working to sabotage it. They were ignoring both the spirit and the optics of the agreement—for example, by going ahead with a three-day Catholic jubilee in Hue, a reprise of the celebrations of Archbishop Thuc's anniversary that had set the Buddhist issue on fire in the first place.

Trueheart laid out the evidence before Diem on June 22: "Diem let me do most of the talking. If he was irritated by my bluntness, he did not show it." In "businesslike" fashion President Diem rebutted Trueheart's specific points about the Nhus stirring up trouble, repeated his view that the Buddhist agitators were Communists, balked at releasing prisoners, and brushed off any suggestion that the *Times of Vietnam* was publishing tendentious material.

Referring to his instructions from Washington, Trueheart also tried to make it sound personal: "I said I hoped he would believe I was speaking as a friend but . . . I had to tell him that he was in a very grave position, in my opinion, and had to take drastic measures, going beyond religious questions, if confidence in his government was to be restored." He reminded Diem of the military progress of recent months and that the Buddhist affair "could overturn everything that had been accomplished."[59]

These were not easy days for Diem, embattled by the Buddhists, the United States, the Viet Cong, and, most conspicuously and painfully, his own brother and sister-in-law. According to an inside account given to Halberstam, when Madame Nhu read the news of the agreement the government had struck with the Buddhists, she exploded at her "jellyfish" brother-in-law over a palace lunch of chicken soup: "You defeated the Binh Xuyen, you defeated the Hoa Hao, you defeated the paratroopers, and now you have lost to a few miserable unarmed bonzes. You are a coward," she supposedly said. When Diem demurred, reminding her that the crisis demanded a settlement, she flung the tureen of soup across the table.[60]

"Terminal Phase"

At dawn on June 12, President Kennedy was brought the morning papers and saw Malcolm Browne's photos of the burning bonze in Saigon. "Jesus Christ! Who are these people!?" he roared at his brother the attorney general, who'd called him while he was still in bed to talk about the big news of the day, the administration's confrontation with the governor of Alabama over desegregating schools.

The president was still seething when his old friend and rival Henry Cabot Lodge Jr. walked into the Oval Office for a scheduled meeting later that morning. He was the grandson and namesake of the senator and secretary of state who famously called the Spanish-American War "a splendid little war" and drove a stake through the League of Nations. Henry Cabot Lodge Jr. had been Richard Nixon's running mate on the Republican ticket in 1960, President Eisenhower's ambassador to the United Nations before that, and a two-term US senator from Massachusetts before that—until Representative John F. Kennedy unseated him in 1952. These two men had a past.

The subject on the official agenda that day was anodyne—Lodge's retirement project, a talking shop called the Atlantic Council—but Kennedy had something else on his mind. He wanted to send Lodge to Saigon to replace Frederick Nolting. Gesturing to that morning's newspapers, the president told Lodge, a former newspaper reporter, that he wanted him to take charge of the press effort in Saigon, among other challenges. He did not hide from Lodge that he thought the Diem government was in its "terminal phase."

Lodge said he would talk over the idea with his wife, but there was little doubt he would take the job, which he had been hinting he wanted for some time. Lodge was sixty-one, and, with his career in limbo since the Republican defeat in 1960, he had been angling to get back into action, preparing himself for engagement as a major general in the US Army Reserve studying counterinsurgency.

In addition to Emily Lodge, who was game for Saigon, he sought the counsel of Dwight D. Eisenhower. The ex-president was lukewarm about the idea. Eisenhower understood, he thought, what Kennedy was up to. By naming prominent Republicans to important and potentially messy jobs—McNamara at Defense, Douglas Dillon at Treasury, John McCone at CIA, now Lodge in Saigon—Eisenhower groused, his Democratic successor was insulating himself politically. Kennedy's aide Kenneth O'Donnell recalled hearing the president say as much, in mirth. "The idea of getting Lodge mixed up in such a hopeless mess as Vietnam was irresistible," said O'Donnell, as was the idea of deflating Lodge's famous pomposity.

Everyone including Lodge appreciated the political subtext of the move. It may have also been a round of family rivalry, ruminated one scholar. Grandfather Lodge long ago had insulted his fellow Bostonian Joseph P. Kennedy, the president's father.[61] Then young Edward M. Kennedy thrashed Henry Cabot Lodge Jr.'s son George in the 1962 Massachusetts US Senate election; according to the family theorists, that apparently was insufficient payback.

While Lodge considered the private offer from Kennedy, the president asked Mike Forrestal what he thought of Lodge as ambassador to South Vietnam.

"It would be a disaster, Mr. President. You cannot do it."

"Why do you think that?"

"First of all, he's a Republican, and he's an insensitive man. His experience in the UN was not good. He can't work with his staff. He can't work with the Department of State. And he's just too complicated a person to have over there at this particular time."[62]

As Forrestal recalled, "The President said absolutely nothing. He just looked at me. He had a way of looking at you with his eyes suddenly opened very wide, and he just stared directly at you and said nothing."

The idea of installing Lodge had not been Kennedy's, but Dean Rusk's. He wanted to head off a bureaucratic push for the president's old friend Ambassador Edmund Gullion, who'd been serving ably in the Congo. "Of course, the paradox of this story is that Lodge turned out to be an extraordinarily able envoy, and most of us who worried about it turned out to be wrong," Forrestal said. In truth, the Lodge record in Saigon was quite mixed.

When an ambassador is about to be nominated, the US embassy in the accredited country confidentially seeks the government's consent to the appointment—in diplomatic parlance, reliably French, the host nation's *agrément*. This was one of Trueheart's other errands with Diem on June 22. Under instructions, he reassured Diem that Nolting's departure was a normal rotation and the choice of such a distinguished character as Lodge a sign of the importance the United States attached to its alliance with Vietnam.[63]

The Vietnamese president had no choice but to agree, but like everything else he was hearing, the news could only have been ominous. After the encounter, President Diem vented at Thuan (who repeated it verbatim back to Trueheart): "They can send ten Lodges, but I will not permit myself or my country to be humiliated, not even if they train their artillery on this palace."[64]

Lodge's appointment was announced by the White House on June 27. The news returned Vietnam to page one. By this time the SS *Constitution* ferrying the Nolting family was halfway across the North Atlantic. That day or the next there came a knock on the door of the Nolting stateroom. It was a ship's steward holding a scrap of newswire about Lodge's appointment. Lindsay Nolting, then twenty, remembers the steward "looking supercilious. He knew he had a devastating piece of news and he was enjoying it." Lindsay says the family was "dumbfounded" and "aghast" at the news. "It was just awful."[65]

This was a needlessly insulting way for Nolting to have learned he was out. It was just the kind of shabby treatment he'd gotten before and resented deeply. But, I asked Lindsay recently, how could it have come as such a surprise, given her father's much-bruited desires and plans to conclude his assignment after two years—in large part for his daughters' sake? In his communications to Washington all spring, he seemed almost desperate to go home.

Lindsay said she remembers nothing of this: "I don't think my parents would have deliberately deceived their children. I had no sense of two years as being a cutoff point." Foreign Service families are protective of their children, so accustomed to being uprooted, and may choose not to share all the contingencies and possibilities until they are certain. But the wound to Nolting's pride must have been hard to hide, and it would never heal.

Assuming Sallie would have read the news of Fritz's replacement in the Richmond papers, Phoebe wrote, "Everyone is very sad about the Noltings." According to her, the news was not surprising, as the end of his two-year tour was "on the books." Phoebe added, "we are all agog that Mr. Lodge has consented to come here."

Channeling Bill's own understanding of how Fritz must be feeling, or the way he rationalized his own silence as things fell apart, Phoebe wrote: "He did get a letter off to Fritz Sunday, his first since F. left. But the situation was changing so fast he thought it was hardly possible to give him any *idea* of what was going on." Those words sound guilty.

She told her mother-in-law: "I just can't tell you how difficult it is (I mean Bill's task; *we* are in *no danger*). Someday when you have four hours with nothing to do but listen, Bill will tell you. I wish he had kept a diary of the last month for his grandchildren."[66] Phoebe, I second the motion.

The pressure on Trueheart in Saigon to make progress with Diem continued even as the *chargé*'s efficacy was waning as his sense of frustration grew. They had another two and a half hours together at Gia Long on June 27, during which Diem "parried all efforts" to speak frankly and directly about the Buddhist crisis, preferring instead a monologue that encompassed Laos, military operations, the Chieu Hoi movement, the Republican Youth, the strategic hamlets, all with an undercurrent of support for Ngo Dinh Nhu, whose removal from power was becoming the focus of the State Department as the last obstacle to Diem's own.[67]

Although there is no record of it in the State Department volumes devoted to this period, in the last days of June, Diem sought to send a message to Nolting seeking his immediate return to Saigon. And then a second message. Nolting never got either one.

"Upon timely notification, I could have returned within twenty-four hours and I believe I could have helped to prevent the tragedies that followed," said Nolting of this white-knight scenario.[68] He said he found it "incomprehensible" that Trueheart didn't let him know what was happening.

Nolting was especially bitter when he was told that Trueheart had "refused" to send the telegram from Diem requesting his immediate return. "Or, according to Thuan, he said he'd do it and never did. It sounded like instructions to me," said Nolting. When his interviewer offered that Trueheart was "on a very short leash," Nolting became direct: "That still doesn't explain why Trueheart didn't let me know. He was under an obligation to do so. He had all the information. I suspect he was ordered not to." He told author William Rust, "It seems obvious to me that those who wanted to let Diem hang himself didn't want me back in Saigon."[69]

This is the crux of the betrayal. One has to wonder when professional boundaries would trump a quarter century of friendship, and I don't doubt that Bill agonized over it. But these were men who had lived compartmentalized and hierarchical lives since World War II. Nolting may be right that Trueheart was under specific instructions to keep him in the dark, or he may have just acted on instinct.

My brother Josh is impatient with Nolting's plaintive attitude. He heard Bill tell the whole story of "the business with Fritz," unvarnished, to cousins at dinner in the late 1970s. Here Josh may be echoing what our father said, adding his own gusto: "Give me a break. It's in the newspapers Nolting sees two days later. It's not like he's on a fucking desert island. If Bill can get in touch with him, so can the embassy in Athens. So can the State Department. It's up to *one guy* [Bill] to find him on a sailboat? Nobody *wanted* to tell Nolting what was going on."[70]

On Saturday, June 29, the SS *Constitution* steamed into New York harbor. The six Noltings had rooms reserved at the only hotel they knew, the Henry Hudson, from a jaunt to New York as a young couple twenty years before. By 1963, it had become a dump, Bittie and Lindsay recall, with strange people peeking out their doors in the corridors; the place added insult to their sense of injury, their fall from grace made tangible.[71]

At the hotel they found a packet of letters awaiting them, including Thuan's earlier plea for help from Diem and the personal letter Phoebe described to my grandmother—and I would think handwritten—from Bill to Fritz.

One phrase Nolting remembered from Trueheart's letter was "mea culpa," for his old friend's long silence. The other was, "I'm afraid you have another Joe Mendenhall on your hands," Trueheart's black humor about his conversion experience. Mendenhall was their former colleague in Saigon whose unhidden disgust with the Ngos had begun years before Nolting or Trueheart ever got there. Between the two friends, Bill was telling Fritz he had gone over to the dark side.

Nolting was not mollified: "I was so mad. I tore it up and threw it away. I wish I hadn't." He said he should have fired Trueheart "forthwith, but I didn't." Instead, he waited to respond until he saw Trueheart back in Saigon: "I had a very straight talk with him. But I won't go further than that."[72] Then, after he left Vietnam for good, he finally lowered the boom.

Nolting's Reprieve

For now, for better or worse, Fritz had been granted a reprieve of sorts—as he saw it, a last chance to turn things around. He would go back to Saigon for a month with Bittie, pack their things and say goodbye, and give a last breath to the conciliatory approach the administration was abandoning.

Although Nolting later said to an interviewer he returned to Saigon "three days" after getting Diem's plea,[73] and the State Department said they wanted him back in Saigon by July 5 "at the latest," and although he routinely described his last period in Saigon as six weeks long when it was four, Nolting did not return to Saigon until July 11. "He has severe family problems which make it almost inhuman to require that he leave [for Saigon] earlier," Forrestal explained to President Kennedy, although, again, these problems remain a mystery to the surviving Noltings.

His schedule does not suggest a man in a hurry to get back to his post. Ambassador Nolting went ahead with his New York speeches to the Far East–American Council on July 1 and the Council on Foreign Relations on July 2, pronouncements redolent with what seemed like simpler days in the middle of May. Nolting had drinks with Tillman Durdin and John B. Oakes of the *New York Times,* warhorses of the newsroom. The Noltings proceeded as planned to Washington on July 3, then to Danville for Independence Day, and then Fritz went back to Washington for a round of briefings. He had lunch with Henry Cabot Lodge. The Hilsmans gave the Noltings a dinner party, and so did the Chuongs, the Vietnamese diplomats who were Madame Nhu's parents and, of late, archenemies.

The Senate Foreign Relations Committee gathered in executive session to hear Nolting's take on things, after six weeks out of action. His folksiness betrayed a certain skittishness about what he was saying. He spoke of the regime's "bonehead plays" and making "more booboos than one can imagine." The ambassador said, "One of our constant problems is to get them to put their best foot forward and, by golly, they put the wrong one forward nine times out of ten."[74] Nolting assured the senators the South Vietnamese government "has a winning program" requiring only patience and perseverance. "Events in Vietnam unfortunately are often judged in terms of simple, dramatic and sometimes unpleasant episodes, when the only true measure is the long-term trend, which is favorable," Nolting declared, as Maggie Higgins summarized it in the *Herald Tribune.*[75]

Nolting called on all the relevant leadership in Washington: McNamara at Defense, McCone at CIA, Rusk, Ball, and Hilsman at State, and on July 8, President Kennedy at the White House. Kennedy liked Nolting and would keep his counsel flowing into the decision-making for a while longer. The president said he found it "almost miraculous the way he had succeeded in turning the war around from the disastrously low point in relations" between the United States and South Vietnam when he arrived. Kennedy told Hilsman he hoped an appropriate position could be found for Nolting in Washington "so that he could give his children a suitable home in the years immediately ahead."[76]

The first person Nolting had called on at the State Department was Averell Harriman, who lost no time telling him that if he had his way, Nolting would have been out in May—just as Nolting had asked in the first place! As Nolting recounts: "I said that, however that may be, I could not understand the State Department's failure to let me know about the troubles that had broken out in Vietnam while I was on vacation." Harriman said he doubted Nolting's presence would have made any difference. "The implication was clear—he wanted to see a revolution there," Nolting said, underlining his suspicions about Harriman's pivotal role in the whole affair, down to the timing of Nolting's leave.[77]

Passing through Washington, and now back in the official loop, Nolting was among those in the chain of clearances for a cable to Saigon instructing Trueheart to warn Diem that more demonstrations, bloodshed, and suicides, which the Nhus were provoking by "openly daring Buddhists to carry out further burnings," would compel the United States to publicly dissociate itself from the regime. A broken record of a threat already made: "We are acting to help him preserve his government. We do not believe GVN can survive prolongation of Buddhist crisis at same time it is engaged in life and death struggle with Viet Cong."[78]

Trueheart was at Gia Long to see Diem by 5:45 p.m. on July 3 and delivered the message: "Meeting lasted less than half an hour, which may be a new record." Diem was cryptic about what he was going to do. "Had the time not arrived, however, for him to take matters into his own hands?" Trueheart said he asked the Vietnamese president. After he had studied the letter Trueheart had composed from instructions and listened to another US protest about insults in the *Times of Vietnam,* President Diem "brought [the] interview to a close, ushering me out with great, but perhaps forced, politeness."[79] Thuan told Trueheart the next day that he had no idea what Diem was going to do but was wary of the politeness the *chargé* reported: "I would rather have him red in the face and pound the table; after he cools down he may accept. The least encouraging posture is polite immovability."[80] Diem may not have pounded tables either.

This was the kind of threat President Kennedy had forbidden just a few weeks earlier. When Forrestal told the president about the latest démarche, he noted that "Ambassador Nolting does not agree with this approach and argues it will succeed only in destroying the last vestiges of Diem's confidence in us." Forrestal also spelled out the division, clarifying in Washington: Harriman, Hilsman, and Forrestal "feel otherwise." He also told Kennedy that Nolting would not be returning to Saigon as early as they had hoped. He praised the "outstanding" performance of the *chargé d'affaires* but noted—the barn doors having swung shut—"the inappropriateness of having our Ambassador away from his post during a crisis period."[81]

That day Trueheart also got a personal note from Forrestal at the White House: "Everyone here thinks you are doing a grand job. Keep up the good work." But he was under strain. He told his colleagues in Washington that he had confided to Thuan "that I was beginning to feel helpless in this affair." His friend Ben Wood on the Vietnam desk jotted in the margin of the telegram: "From Bill, this is serious."

8

★ ★ ★

Malice in Wonderland

EARLY ON THE MORNING of July 4, 1963, Secretary of State Thuan called the US *chargé d'affaires* to make another plea for Ambassador Nolting's immediate return to Saigon. President Diem was "sentimental" about Nolting, Thuan told Trueheart. He thought Nolting could be helpful now because his lame-duck status made him more "detached." Trueheart pointed out that "would normally be considered a disadvantage, but Thuan insisted it would be an asset."[1]

Trueheart returned to the embassy to be told of another attack on US correspondents by Madame Nhu, this one in a signed jeremiad in the *Times of Vietnam.* To his superiors in Washington, Trueheart weighed the merits of the standard protest to Brother Nhu himself. Just the day before, with President Diem, Trueheart had delivered his latest blistering démarche about Brother Nhu's incitements against the Buddhists. What more could be accomplished? Nhu would just say his wife was a private citizen. In a cabled response, the State Department told him to use his own judgment: "To Nhu or not to Nhu is up to you."[2] Trueheart would see Nhu in a few hours anyway.

In the Noltings' absence, it was the Truehearts who hosted the American Independence Day reception that evening at the ambassador's residence. As was the custom in the merry-go-round of national days at all the embassies, flags were unfurled on the official cars that climbed the gentle slope to the porte cochere in front of the residence, dropping off the diplomats and generals and their wives. All the ambassadors in Saigon—fifteen were accredited and resident[3]—and most of the Vietnamese cabinet were on hand.

I may have tired of my curbside greeting routine by this point, but Bill and Phoebe stood at the entrance and shook every hand as a photographer recorded the hundreds of encounters. It was the biggest party Phoebe had ever organized—five hundred Champagne glasses had to be rented—although she had Vietnamese staff to do the serving, Foreign Service personnel to handle the invitations and responses, and a team of embassy wives to help her greet and mingle. That way she could think of important things. She boasted to her mother-in-law that she would be wearing "one of those dresses you can't wear often, as it knocks people's eyes out."

The cadaverous Brother Nhu was the most powerful Vietnamese official present, but the traditional toasts were exchanged between the *chargé d'affaires* and the foreign minister, Vu Van Mau. As Trueheart raised his glass with Mau to salute President Diem, David Halberstam was heard to mutter in the back of the crowd, "I'll never drink to that son of a bitch."[4]

The *Times* correspondent, more of a bad boy every day, also refused to shake General Harkins's hand at the party. In a Saigon restaurant a few weeks later, a just-arrived American Foreign Service Officer was treated to the spectacle of Halberstam shouting about "what a swine General Harkins was for faking reports and throwing away American and Vietnamese lives." As the young diplomat looked nervously around to see who might be hearing this outburst, he heard Halberstam say, "Paul D. Harkins should be court-martialed and shot!" This new arrival, in the first post of a long career in American diplomacy, was Richard Holbrooke.[5]

Another larger-than-life American guest at the Independence Day reception was doing a piece of historically momentous business. He was about to become the linchpin of the coup d'état.

Lucien Conein was, in the phrase, an international man of mystery. Born in 1919, out of wedlock, in Paris, he'd been sent to Kansas City to be raised by a French aunt who'd married an American doughboy. Conein joined the French army in 1940, and after the fall of France enlisted in the US Army. His language skills drew him right into the OSS, and, with special training in sabotage from the British Special Operations Executive, he parachuted into France in August 1944. A year later he was in Hanoi, fighting the Japanese forces occupying French Indochina. He'd returned in 1955 with Colonel Lansdale after Vietnam was divided, doing dirty tricks in Hanoi and getting to know Ho Chi Minh and Vo Nguyen Giap.

Conein returned again to Saigon in 1961 (with his fifth wife, a Vietnam-born Frenchwoman) about the time the Truehearts arrived; Elyette and

Luigi, as he was usually called, became neighbors and close friends of my family. In this Vietnam assignment Conein was operating under military cover, as a US Army lieutenant colonel, working a day job on the main priority of the embassy: pacification. His contacts with the local French and Vietnamese communities were gold to the CIA and the embassy, and he took special care to renew his ties to the Vietnamese officers he knew from as long ago as Hanoi in 1945.

At the July Fourth party, one of those old acquaintances sought Conein out. General Tran Van Don, now acting chief of staff of the Vietnamese armed forces, said they needed to talk immediately, and elsewhere. They chose the subterranean nightclub of the Caravelle Hotel, about as indiscreet a place as can be imagined. At the club Conein found Don and three other generals, all of whom he knew well: Don's number 2, and brother-in-law, Le Van Kim; the army chief of staff, Tran Thien Khiem; and the most senior officer in the Vietnamese army, Duong Van Minh—known as "Big" Minh because of his size, unusual for a Vietnamese, and to distinguish him from another, slighter General Minh. These middle-aged French-trained officers were the eventual core of the plot to overthrow the government.

Some historians have speculated that the generals were moved to contact Conein by reading a dispatch by Halberstam in the *New York Times* that had appeared the day before. "Some American officials are reported to favor a new Vietnamese government," he reported, suggesting that US criticism of the regime's Buddhist policies would be a catalyst for a military coup. Which American officials? In Saigon, Trueheart, perhaps, and the embassy political section. But not Nolting, not Harkins, and not John Richardson at that point. Yet the Vietnamese generals treated the *Times* as a semi-official organ, as well they might have. Were coup contingency not becoming a priority in Washington, and even Saigon, there wouldn't have been any such leaks to Halberstam.

At the Caravelle the generals railed against the regime and told Conein they were ready to launch a coup. They said the whole family must go, not just Madame and Brother Nhu. They sounded serious now. They wanted to know the US view. Conein said he would find out on the double. That huddle at the Caravelle launched four months of sub rosa contacts, virtually entirely in Conein's hands, between the US embassy and the dissident generals. He much later described them as "corporals with stars on their shoulders" who were incapable of organizing "a two-car funeral."[6] And yet.

Double-Seven Day

Every July 7 in Vietnam was known as "Double-Seven Day" (7/7), rich in good fortune. The Ngos had contrived to mark that date as the anniversary of President Diem's accession to power. In a public proclamation on that ninth anniversary, Diem declared that the Buddhist problem had been settled. Not leaving well enough alone, he went on to excoriate the "underground intervention of international red agents and Communist fellow travelers who in collusion with fascist ideologues disguised as democrats were surreptitiously seeking to revive and rekindle disunity at home while arousing public opinion against us abroad."[7] Madame Nhu couldn't have said it better.

That same day Trueheart received a letter from the leading Buddhist group requesting US military protection of Xa Loi pagoda, predicting that "nothing will withhold our government when it wants to achieve its aim, and a St. Barthelemy Night is not to be excluded from our assumption." The *chargé* needed no guidance to turn down the request in private—and in public if the letter were published.[8]

That very morning Trueheart had reported to Washington an altercation between plainclothes police and American news correspondents covering a pagoda ceremony in Saigon. Peter Arnett, the young Kiwi reporter, had his camera snatched away and was thrown to the ground and kicked in the kidneys. Uniformed police made no attempt to stop the assailants— doubtless members of Colonel Le Quang Tung's special forces—"and in fact tacitly abetted the plainclothesmen," Trueheart cabled Washington. "There is also no doubt that reporters, once the fracas started, acted in belligerent manner towards police." Trueheart was being euphemistic. As he knew, the brawny Halberstam had charged the Vietnamese goons and pulled them off Arnett, brandishing his fists. "Get back, get back, you sons of bitches or I'll beat the hell out of you!"[9] The plainclothes police didn't just take Arnett's camera, they smashed it to the ground. Browne and Arnett were charged with assault.

In a rambunctious session in Trueheart's office later that morning, the American newsmen demanded an official protest to the Vietnamese government. Trueheart declined, saying he didn't yet have enough information. Feeling betrayed, the reporters decided to go over the *chargé*'s head— way over. By lunchtime they had fired off a message to the president of the United States: "The inescapable conclusion is that the government of

South Vietnam, a country to which the United States is heavily committed, has begun a campaign of open physical intimidation to prevent the
covering of news which we feel Americans have a right to know."[10]

By way of context, and perhaps coverage for his refusal to protest,
Trueheart cabled three days later, "resident correspondents have become
so embittered towards GVN that they are saying quite openly to anyone
who will listen that they would like to see the regime overthrown. GVN no
doubt has this well-documented."[11]

Fence-Sitting

Oblivious to the optics, but in their minds showing coup plotters it meant
business, the next day the Diem regime opened the long-delayed trial of
nineteen former South Vietnamese military officers involved in the failed
coup of 1960. In the current climate, this was an awkward juxtaposition.
With some heat, Trueheart was instructed to deny US complicity in that
earlier plot and to remind the reporter who asked that then US ambassador "Durbrow's actions may well have saved Diem's life." When the
presidential palace was surrounded by artillery, "Ambassador Durbrow
had used every means at his disposal to urge both sides to avoid a bloodbath."[12] For the Ngos, this was just the problem—the equivalence implied
in the "both sides" line.

Trueheart briefed the American correspondents about this development: "I told them for attribution that I could deny 'flatly, officially, and
unequivocally' that Americans in any way involved in attempt to overthrow GVN." A CIA agent named George Carver, who had been whisked
out of Saigon right after the failed 1960 coup, had been named in the trial.
Trueheart was not telling the truth, or should have had reason to be
skeptical of the denial he was uttering. *Time* magazine's account, summarized immediately to Trueheart from the State Department, said the
chargé's flat denial "was made out of ignorance of reality situation [*sic*]
as it existed." Of course, Trueheart also knew well that coup plans were
brewing in the present moment.

The next day in Washington Mike Forrestal gave President Kennedy
some blunt advice, passed along from Harriman and Hilsman: "The
United States must avoid allowing its own interests to be confused with
those of the Diem regime." Because of his "political ineptitude," Forrestal
told Kennedy, Diem "cannot be expected to hold out much longer."

While waiting to see "if our estimate of Diem's survivability turns markedly adverse," the administration's "policy must be one of fence sitting." Kennedy's young aide held out the possibility, were Nolting's last efforts with Diem to fail, of recalling the ambassador immediately and leaving Trueheart in charge until Lodge arrived: "Trueheart has handled the situation with great skill and with somewhat less personal involvement than Nolting . . . which would give Lodge a reasonably clean slate to start with."[13]

One of only two photographs I have found of the two men together in Saigon, with no one else, appeared in the *Times of Vietnam* the day after Nolting returned from his ill-scheduled leave. It shows Fritz and Bill walking together, in conversation, across the tarmac to the VIP terminal at Tan Son Nhut. Nolting is reaching into his jacket, probably for a cigarette. They are smiling and seemingly unperturbed (see illustration gallery).

Presumably the "straight talk" between them came later that day at the office, where, in Halberstam's raw account, Nolting "turned his fury on his old friend Trueheart and accused him of having destroyed the trust which Nolting had so carefully built up. Trueheart's protestations that he had worked loyally for the policy, but that the months since May had seen the disintegration of that fragile hope, fell on deaf ears. The more Nolting realized that Trueheart's reporting was accurate, the more he blamed Trueheart for not holding it together. If Nolting was impotent, then it was Trueheart's fault, not the fault of history or of the policy."[14] For his part, Trueheart professed to recall no such fury, no such confrontation. In a 1982 interview, he said, "I know that he was upset with me, although he never directly said this to me." The more we get to know these two gentlemen, the more this unlikely statement seems plausible.

Nolting seethed enough about Trueheart's apostasy to repudiate his own *chargé d'affaires* to the Vietnamese chief of state, a serious breach of protocol. Over the next two days, after an emotional reunion at Gia Long, Nolting spent seven hours with President Diem, during which inter alia he "strongly deplored Trueheart's resort to threats as a substitute for diplomacy."[15] To the State Department, Nolting turned in a mostly sunny report on Diem's prospects, and the war's, echoing the regime's view that the Buddhist affair had been blown out of proportion.

On his return to Saigon Nolting had found, among much other correspondence, a personal letter waiting from the syndicated columnist

Joseph Alsop. He was a fan of Nolting and of Diem, too, if more gingerly so of late. Alsop had written Fritz only hours after the news of Lodge's appointment had broken. After effusive congratulations on a job well done, Alsop got to what was most on his mind: "I am ashamed to add a request" for Nolting to purchase four plaster elephants—a common fixture as end tables in expatriate living rooms in Saigon—specifying which kind, two blue and two white, that "you might almost mistake for Chinese pottery of the Ming period." When Alsop wrote again to ask why they were late in arriving, Nolting snapped at his personal assistant, Dixon Boggs, "Tell Joe, God damn it, I'll bring the white elephants" in his personal effects (on the government dollar, of course).[16]

Bittie Nolting had stayed on a few days in Virginia to be with her family in Danville. In a handwritten spousal letter rare in the collection of his mostly official papers in Charlottesville, the beleaguered ambassador wrote his wife to share his sadness about what he knew was happening. "My darling," he wrote Bittie, "I feel as if two years' work and building is teetering on the brink and I am doing all I can to help shore it up. I am more hopeful of success than most others, but that may be either an asset or the reverse."[17] This was self-knowing. Fritz could be counted on to bring optimism to even the bleakest situations, and it could be taken as naivete. After a session with Thuan on July 24, he told the State Department he was reassured and encouraged that "the heat is slowly going out of this crisis," as it surely was not.

A week later, Bittie arrived back in Saigon. Peculiarly it was Bill who met her plane at Tan Son Nhut, standing in for Fritz, who had been meeting with Thuan and couldn't get away. As she recalled that day fifty-five years later, "I knew Bill blamed Fritz for going on the trip and Fritz blamed Bill for not keeping him closely informed. I said, 'Hi, Bill. What's going on?' and Bill said, 'Mea culpa.'"[18] I asked Bittie whether those were not the same words Bill had used with Fritz in the letter he tore up in New York, which she might have been thinking of. Bittie said she didn't remember any such letter. That's just what Bill said to her. It must have been a long ride into Saigon from the airport.

"Alice in Wonderland Miasma"

After the Saigon press altercations that wound up with the fiery missive to President Kennedy, the State Department sent its chief public affairs officer, a seasoned journalist named Robert Manning, to Saigon to assess the situation. Manning arrived two days after Nolting, saw Nhu and Diem, then spent hours with the Country Team and the journalists.

Manning's report was part of Kennedy's reading the last weekend of July. It can't have been a surprise to read of "the serious deterioration in the credibility attached by American correspondents to the information and assessments given to them by the United States military and political authorities in Vietnam, and to a certain extent in Washington."[19] Looking on the bright side, Manning noted the "mature and unexcitable" public reaction to all the bad news preoccupying policymakers. He recommended easing some of the reporting strictures imposed by the embassy and the military command since Ap Bac. Easing up would help to "reduce the somewhat sullen Alice in Wonderland miasma" in Saigon.

In Saigon Manning spent hours hearing out the American correspondents, listening to their fears about their personal safety in carrying out their duties. He heard their open disdain for General Harkins and his optimistic pronouncements. He heard them say they had been lied to by the embassy. Underneath all that, Manning saw the journalists were unanimous in feeling "the Vietnam program cannot succeed unless the Diem regime (cum family) is replaced; this conviction, though it does not always appear in their copy, underlies all the reports and analyses of the correspondents."

But he stressed, in italics, what was probably still true of their collective view: "the US involvement in Vietnam is a necessary free world policy." The journalists were "all decent, patriotic Americans who are striving to do credit to themselves and their profession." Diplomatically he agreed with most of the embassy people he talked to that "the personal manners of some [journalists] vis-à-vis the Vietnam officials leave something to be desired, and they suffer the common newspaper tendency to let the immediate dominate the long view."[20]

Their "bitterness and contempt" for the Ngo regime "is fervently reciprocated," Manning went on. What Nhu told him at Gia Long matched what he inferred from the "incorrigible" journalists: "These young reporters want nothing less than to make a new government. This is an exalting ambition, a stimulating pastime for three or four of them to get together to overthrow a government." Nonetheless, through Manning's efforts, the charges against Arnett and Browne were dropped and various pledges of openness were extracted from the palace and the embassy. The arrival of Henry Cabot Lodge seemed to offer hope of a new press policy that would get results.

That weekend Ambassador Nolting made the wrong kind of news. He gave an interview to Neil Sheehan of UPI on July 28 in which he expressed weariness that the Buddhist crisis was causing everyone to take "his eye off the ball," meaning the war effort. "I myself, I say this very frankly, after almost two and one half years here, have never seen any evidence of religious persecution."

He may not have. Of Diem's catalogue of sins—official corruption, messianic obstinacy, executive incompetence, gulags of political prisoners—this one had never been high on the list. But Nolting's formulation was ill-timed and tin-eared at a minimum. It would color the remainder of his dwindling days in Vietnam.

The Buddhists exploded with a telegram of protest to Kennedy and harsh denunciations of Nolting. "The ambassador would probably want to be presented with nearly 6,000,000 corpses of Jews before being convinced of religious discrimination," the letter said. On August 1, Harriman phoned Hilsman and roared that Nolting "ought to be recalled at once." Hilsman talked him down but fired off a withering telegram to Saigon: "Your statement is, as you can imagine, unfortunate," even granting that it might have been taken out of context. Hilsman told Nolting specifically to clear any further farewell remarks with Washington.[21]

In an odd coda to this incident, Nolting apparently was jangled enough by the blowback from his earlier remarks that when a CBS television crew was setting up cameras in his office for its turn at an exit interview, the ambassador was heard to tell an aide to replace the portrait on his office wall of Thomas Jefferson, the ur-Virginian, with one of George Washington—because he was "less controversial."[22]

"Just back from Quang Tin with Diem," Nolting hastily messaged Washington on August 2. Appearing to him "receptive . . . determined . . . confident," President Diem elicited "much apparently spontaneous enthusiasm" from the ten to fifteen thousand people rounded up for the occasion. Echoing the Vietnamese president's own view of things, Nolting said, "Buddhist problem has been misrepresented and misunderstood at home, . . . will be surmounted by GVN, and . . . it should not repeat not throw us off the course here."

Then Nolting turned to the date of his departure. He told the State Department he wished to extend it a few days for "my wife and me to make an orderly and polite departure" involving a shower of farewell dinner invitations. With remarkable serenity, Nolting proposed to cross the Lodges in Honolulu and cited the need for extra time to collect his thoughts for that handoff: "I do not want to attach too much significance to my staying an extra five days here, but I have a definite feeling that it would be useful psychologically and politically i.e. continued influence re Buddhist affair, politesse, (which counts for so much here) and not appearing to be 'yanked' in face American (and now Buddhist association) press criticism."[23] How much of this was really about his own shaken pride, his unwillingness to let go, and how much about fine points of etiquette and unruffled feathers?

Hilsman was brisk if not brusque in his immediate reply—"I reluctantly agree to your departure August 15"—and extravagantly disingenuous: "No important policy changes under consideration here." The latter was the answer to a question Diem had put to Nolting about whether his replacement by Lodge augured a different policy toward Vietnam. When Nolting relayed Hilsman's response, Diem told him, "I believe you, but I don't believe the message you have received."[24]

"I Will Not Shut Up"

After a hiatus of nearly two months marked by constant rumors of Buddhist self-immolations, they began again. Five more monks burned themselves to death after Nolting's return—on August 4; on August 13; on August 15, the day Nolting left Vietnam; and one each the following two days. Their deaths were greeted with pantomimed delight by Madame Nhu: "If they burn thirty women we shall go ahead and clap. We cannot be responsible for their madness. They incite people to hari kari. It reflects such a low intelligence level. Either they are communist-minded and very cynical . . . or they are very stupid people who have never coped with the world."

These words were spoken on August 7 to David Halberstam, in an interview long sought, and plenty long, where Madame Nhu unloaded on everyone. Halberstam's archived readout of her monologue—five single-spaced typed pages, no caps, barely trackable between the reporter's haste and Madame Nhu's poor English—for some reason starts right out with

Trueheart, who'd been back as DCM and out of Diem's face for a month. Trueheart had "threatened and blackmailed" Diem, she said, to get him to get her to "shut up." "Since they cannot oblige the Buddhists to shut up, then I will not shut up."[25]

So she didn't. She defended herself personally: "It is absolutely not true that I am devious. I am not a woman of intrigue." She called the nepotism charges against the ruling family "very unjust" and protested the depictions of the Ngos as dictatorial. Every day, she said, she witnessed inside Gia Long Palace a "democratic" family—that is, everyone had a say, including her. Madame Nhu said her husband was "the sweetest man, a real holy man." She said he was "tougher than Diem," who was "much too scrupulous. He worries too easily. My husband has a soothing effect. I do not have a soothing effect. On the contrary. I never sugarcoat." Her relationship to Diem? "He is very shy around women, which is a great disadvantage to me." On the contrary.

Then back to the American reporters and the American embassy. Trueheart had "waved" his June instructions at President Diem ("maybe in case we don't believe him"), but the instructions were bad: "The reporters hypnotize Mr. Trueheart, and Mr. Trueheart hypnotizes the State Department." Fritz Nolting, on the other hand, had had excellent results upon his return, "so good they even doubt them, but it is a miracle. Nolting is a good American. He is very idealistic. He isn't at all like a politician, just an idealist."

The praise was no favor to Nolting. He was sent in to protest something else she said that proved quickly prophetic, possibly something she heard at the breakfast table, that the government would "crush" the Xa Loi pagoda if the Buddhist leaders kept up their behavior. Brushing off his wife's latest salvo—"she does not speak for the government"—Brother Nhu gave Nolting "categoric assurances" of his support for conciliation with the Buddhists. Invading the pagodas would be counterproductive, he told Nolting, and said he favored more concessions instead. He painted himself as the peacemaker in contrast to the Vietnamese military, which wanted to use an iron hand with the Buddhists.

"I told him, as I have once before," Nolting reported to State, "that if he was telling me the truth, he is a most misunderstood man."[26] What a courtly way to call someone a liar.

By the next day the Kennedy administration had seen the Halberstam profile and the cover story about Madame Nhu in *Time,* and the guidance

for Nolting got very specific: "Tell Diem frankly that at this crucial juncture most convincing action vis-à-vis both Vietnamese and US opinion
would be to remove Madame Nhu from the scene," suggesting "a Hong
Kong convent," for example.[27] Nolting could only agree: "Madame Nhu is
out of control of everybody—her father, mother, husband, and brother-
in-law." The alibi that Madame Nhu spoke only for herself, Nolting told
Diem directly, "would not wash in the outside world and I did not think
it would wash in Vietnam." He asked Diem "to remove the appearance of
schizophrenia from his government."[28] One of Diem's responses was to
ask *Nolting's* advice about what to do with her.

The next time he saw him, on August 12, Nolting begged the impassive
mandarin to take charge of the fracturing situation. With hours ticking
until he quit the scene, this was the moment of truth for Nolting: "I drew
heavily, perhaps exhaustively, on store of goodwill and confidence, spoke
absolutely frankly from point of view partner in joint enterprise, could
detect no resentment but rather a great sense of struggle between family
loyalties and public duty."[29]

Halberstam, in *The Best and the Brightest,* put it more starkly. "Nolting,
who had acquiesced to Diem on so many things in order to have money in
the bank for just such an occasion as this, now found he had little influence after all."[30] In *The Making of a Quagmire,* his earlier, slighter Vietnam
book, Halberstam sounded more sympathetic: "The policy had failed, not
because of the ambassador's lack of dedication or skill as a diplomat, but
simply because his faith [in Diem] was never reciprocated; it was accepted,
but never returned."[31]

Ngo News

Across town, or even down the hall, President Diem was giving an interview to Marguerite Higgins of the *Herald Tribune.*

Marguerite Higgins was not one of the boys; the Ngos knew her to be
more sympathetic than the male journalists. Higgins was a hard-bitten
and unglamorous veteran of war reporting—she'd won a Pulitzer for her
Korea coverage—who didn't toe the same line as the other reporters,
young and old. She was infamous among her colleagues for claiming (to
Charley Mohr of *Time,* over dinner at l'Amiral one night) that "reporters
here would like to see us lose the war to prove they're right."[32] Higgins was
a dogged reporter, and her well-sourced files were noticed by Halberstam's

editors at the *New York Times.* They would gingerly ask their correspondent for a follow-up on one point or another Higgins had made. After
one of those sallies, Halberstam cabled New York: "If you mention that
woman's name to me one more time I will resign repeat resign and I mean
it repeat mean it."[33]

When they sat down to talk, President Diem startled Higgins by
"recalling the dressing-down he had received from Trueheart, who had
twice threatened to abandon Diem if he did not measure up to American
standards of pluralism," in the dyspeptic phrase of scholar Francis X.
Winters.[34] Diem wondered aloud to Higgins, "Am I merely a puppet on
Washington's string?"[35]

A few days later Higgins saw Madame Nhu, who said of the self-
immolations, "if you start to give status to suicide, you only encourage
impressionable, credulous people to seek false glory." She sneered again
that the Buddhists "had done nothing but barbecue a monk" and were re-
duced to using "imported gasoline" for the task.[36] "The lash, even the rack,
if need be, is the proper answer to Buddhist opposition."[37] She claimed
not to have spoken to her brother-in-law the president "in three months."

Lies, Lies, Lies

The *Times of Vietnam,* the only newspaper I read closely in those days, was
a bizarre window into the soul of the Ngos, and the subject of regular
hilarity and occasional alarm in the Trueheart household. Thanks to the
Times of Vietnam, ever since I have had a template of a state-controlled
press.

The country's only English-language newspaper was owned and run
by an American couple, Gene and Ann Gregory, who'd been in Saigon for
longer than Diem had been in power. Ann Gregory was especially close
to Madame Nhu. She had become in essence her English-language editor and speechwriter. Gene Gregory, who went on hunting trips at Nhu's
mountain lodge, ran the business side and was mixed up in Ngo-protected
local business schemes that he marketed in the news pages of the *Times.*
As open collaborators with the regime, the Gregorys were not part of the
expat scene in Saigon.

The real American journalists were contemptuous of the paper, while
reading it closely. When his editors in New York suggested he file a feature about the *Times of Vietnam,* David Halberstam cabled back: TO DO

ANYTHING AT ALL ACCURATE ABOUT THOSE PEOPLE WOULD BE LIBELOUS AND TO DO ANYTHING NON-LIBELOUS WOULD BE TOO CHARITABLE. As the UPI man in Saigon, Neil Sheehan had to do farcical double duty servicing the Gregorys as local clients of the wire service. He had to cajole them to sign up for *Bugs Bunny* comic strips and collect on their unpaid bills, while enduring such classic headlines as "UPI LIES, LIES, LIES."[38]

While attacking the US government regularly, the paper, oddly, sought to be useful to the American community in Saigon. It ran church and movie listings, flight and radio schedules, American baseball scores, comings and goings of ambassadors, generals, and other US officials, *Peanuts* and *Dennis the Menace* and *Beetle Bailey*. The residents of Gia Long Palace received the paper's most lavish coverage, as did the activities of the Catholic Church: entire papal encyclicals were reprinted on successive pages in very small type. The paper's primitive Sunday magazine regularly extolled Madame Nhu's Women's Solidarity Movement and her pet projects. One cover story in 1963 depicted a girl in humble dress holding a rifle in a rice paddy: "typical and atypical, modest and self-confident, fun-loving and serious—the daughter of counsellor and madame Ngo Dinh Nhu." This was seventeen-year-old Le Thuy (Beautiful Spring), a pal of the younger Nolting daughters ever since their arrival two years before.

Looking back now on my daily reading matter, on microfilm at the Library of Congress, I am mystified anew by this crude product, and by the reader the Gregorys conjured. Two-inch wire copy items were flung into the paper with abandon: "Prince Philip Is 42." "Hotel for Fish Opens." "Surgeons Give Boy New Ears." "Malta Faces Uncertain Future." "Increasing Baldness among American Women." "German Cuckoo Clock Popular in Afro-Asian Countries." "Sex Life of Eel Unusual."

Perhaps too long gone from the United States, the Gregorys had an affinity for curiously inane locutions; when an American astronaut completed a perfect ocean return from space in May 1963, the banner headline on page one of the *Times of Vietnam* was: "Cooper Down Right on the Bazoo." Kevin Wells, a student at the American Community School we attended, never forgot a local society-page item about the marriage of two diplomats, unnamed. The wedding, the *Times of Vietnam* reported, "was consummated on the embassy lawn, much to the delight of the assembled guests."

"Mighty Big Shoes to Fill"

The gods remained unkind to Fritz Nolting until the very end. The sham-bolic denouement of his ambassadorship crystallized, or brought uncom-fortably to mind, so much of what had gone wrong and would continue to go wrong in this benighted mission—not just Nolting's, but Kennedy's, America's.

To honor the outgoing envoy in a highly symbolic way, the persistently blinkered regime told Nolting about the farewell gesture they wished to bestow on him: dedicating a strategic hamlet in his name. A national essay-writing contest about Nolting's contributions to Vietnam would determine the "winning" village.

Nothing good, Nolting knew, could come of this. He tried to beg off, citing the press of business in his final days. The palace said, in effect, name your day, and Nolting was cornered into accepting. The American reporters said as much in their dispatches about the upcoming dedication ceremony; this somehow enraged Nolting, even though it put him in a more sympathetic light, relatively speaking, for wanting to avoid it.

The news of the day itself, August 9, was tragic, and a good deal more enraging. According to the lede of the AP story that flashed in Washington, "A US Jeep convoying US Ambassador Frederick E. Nolting on an official inspection tour ran over and killed a 3-year-old boy here Thursday."

Nolting cabled the State Department a torrent of corrections: "Jeep in question was not convoying me, but was part of ARVN convoy. Incident occurred before my arrival. Victim was 7-year-old girl not 3-year-old boy. The victim was injured not killed. Incident occurred Friday not Thursday." Also, *that* story had been conflated with another incident the day before, in a nearby hamlet, which was worse: A US Army helicopter accidentally fired a burst of machine gun bullets into the village, killing a little boy and wounding five others. An American soldier had tangled his microphone cord around the machine-gun trigger.

Nolting was nevertheless congenitally determined to put a brighter face on the dedication ceremonies in the strategic hamlet: "People in ham-let and surrounding territory were touchingly cordial despite accident. No hint of resentment. No evidence whatsoever of religious tension. These 200 people were enthusiastically focused on subduing VC and improv-ing their village."[39] Halberstam, covering the story, said the villagers' "enthusiasm was as ersatz as the occasion itself; they looked pathetically confused and frightened, and with good reason—naming the hamlet after an American ambassador would make it a prime target for the Vietcong."[40] Indeed, after Nolting left Vietnam, the hamlet was overrun.

Yet for all that, in the photographs of the farewell dinner for twelve in the Noltings' honor at Gia Long Palace, it looks like everyone is having a good time. Fritz and Bittie sat on either side of President Diem, the Truehearts and Harkinses down the line, along with Foreign Minister Mau and his wife. Phoebe noted in a letter home how sweet President Diem had been when they chatted before dinner.

Out of his sincere affection for the departing ambassador, when the dinner broke up Ngo Dinh Diem personally escorted the Noltings to their car outside. As they walked, Bittie told President Diem she and Fritz hoped he might visit them in the United States in October, when the turning leaves are so beautiful. Diem said to her, wearily, that in October he would more likely be taking a much longer voyage.

When Bittie told me this story fifty-five years later, I asked, *Do you think he meant he would die?* "I do," she said.[41]

Ambassador Nolting paid his farewell call on Diem early in the morning of August 14. The "rather strenuous goodbye" he recounted to the State Department can only have been excruciating. Here the ambassador beheld a man for whom he had fought so vigorously and at such personal cost now slipping back into his weathered tropes of victimization. In another grim and wordy recitation, Diem painted himself as a misunderstood man, beset by relentless attacks from the Buddhists, the American press, the American embassy, the Viet Cong. Nolting had a familiar démarche to deliver.

Sounding very much like Trueheart umpteen times before and, like Trueheart, under explicit guidance from State, Nolting "stuck to the position it would be impossible for the US Government to continue our present relationship . . . if he did not promptly make a declaration which would show clearly who was running the country, would undo some of the damage done by Madame Nhu's statements, and would restore faith in GVN's intention to carry out its announced policy of conciliation."[42]

Diem promised to make such a statement before Nolting got on the plane the next day. The meeting ended on a grace note. Ngo Dinh Diem told Nolting that his ambassadorship had been one of the great *souvenirs* of his life. As usual, the *Times of Vietnam* spoke more forcefully and colorfully about Nolting's departure in the edition he read on the way to the airport the next morning, August 15. Although he later professed embarrassment at the editorial's unflattering references to his predecessors in Saigon, Nolting printed it in its entirety at the conclusion of his Vietnam memoir, *From Trust to Tragedy.*

"The first American Ambassador to Vietnam really worthy of being addressed by his title is being recalled from Vietnam," the editorial began. "Ambassador Nolting somehow seemed intuitively to know how to represent in its Sunday best the greatest power of the free world in this newly independent nation." In the future, when the Viet Cong threat had shrunk to a "policing problem," the Vietnamese people would look back on the "Nolting era" as "the beginning of all the programs that spelled success." Henry Cabot Lodge, the editorial concluded, "has mighty big shoes to fill."

Before he left Saigon Nolting got word that Diem had lived up, at least technically, to his goodbye pledge for a public statement of conciliation to the Buddhists. He did this with classic obliqueness, in an interview with Marguerite Higgins, who always gave the palace a good shake. Diem's cryptic formulation was that "the policy of utmost reconciliation is irreversible."

This was a way of saying he had done nothing wrong in the first place, and that the policy had not really changed. But even if it meant something, as President Kennedy's intelligence briefing put it, making the statement in a US newspaper meant "it could be disavowed if need be, and few Vietnamese are likely to be aware of it anyway."[43]

The evening before he left, Fritz Nolting came by our house alone to say goodbye to his godsons. I recall this special if awkward occasion distinctly—even if it was my godfather Fritz, it was still the ambassador himself coming to call on me (Josh at two not really tracking). Bill was absent, not uncharacteristically. We sat down in the Blue Room, my mother and I, as Fritz told us warmly that he would miss us and looked forward to seeing us back in the States. There were hugs. I knew none of what had happened between Fritz and Bill.

I don't recall going to the airport to see the Noltings off. To Halberstam that day in the VIP lounge at Tan Son Nhut, Nolting seemed a lonely figure as he delivered his final remarks. "My wife and I are sad, naturally, to leave a job not yet finished, a victory not yet won," said the ambassador before he boarded a Pan American plane to Honolulu.

Sometime that morning as they said a dry-eyed farewell, Bill may have asked his old friend for the traditional signed photograph—he kept other such framed photographs from his career near his desk in his embassy office. Or perhaps Nolting took it upon himself to add Bill to the photographs he was signing. If you were looking for tension or ill will—as of course I was—you would not find it in the words Fritz scrawled beneath the picture "to Bill—with vivid recollections of strenuous and exciting work together. My friendship, thanks, and all good luck. Fritz. Saigon Aug. 15 1963."

That day Nolting and Trueheart had to co-sign a routine document for the files, clockwork custom as embassies change hands around the world, but perhaps not an easy box to check for this departing ambassador.

CERTIFICATE OF TRANSFER

The undersigned jointly certify that on August 15, 1963, at 11 a.m., Frederick E. Nolting, Jr., Ambassador, relinquished charge of the Embassy of the United States at Saigon and that William C. Trueheart, Minister-Counselor, assumed charge.

"Getting the Right Fella"

Henry Cabot Lodge paid his farewell call on John F. Kennedy that same day, August 15. Their twenty-two-minute meeting in the Oval Office was captured by the White House recording system, installed the summer before. Kennedy activated it himself when he wished conversations preserved. This was a courtesy call—Kennedy saw off many of his ambassadors personally, even to flyspeck countries—with momentous consequences. It's worth listening in.[44]

Lodge is ever so slightly obsequious to the man who unseated him in the Senate a decade earlier and was now in the White House, a place still a latent gleam in Lodge's eye. He is grateful for the new lease on his public life, eager to show he has boned up on his new dossier. President Kennedy has just read Halberstam's latest bleak battlefield report in the *New York Times,* "Vietnamese Reds Gain in Key Area," the Delta, puncturing again the optimistic assertions that, for all the mess of the Buddhist crisis, the war was being won.

Lodge tells Kennedy he has just had dinner with Madame Nhu's mother in Washington. Despite their official diplomatic roles, Madame Nhu's parents, Tran Van Chuong and Than Thi Nam Tran, known as Madame Chuong, have been issuing thunderous private denunciations of their daughter, their son-in-law, and President Diem to any American who would listen. Madame Chuong assured Lodge the family "cannot be saved."

After hearing some of Lodge's plans for Saigon, Kennedy shifts the conversation, using generalities, to what's most on his mind: "The time may come . . . to do something about Diem." Kennedy asks if Lodge is "prepared" for what's going to happen: "It's just a matter of getting the right fella and getting it done." The president means a successor to Diem. Perhaps uncomfortable with names he can't pronounce, Kennedy uses the same generic to describe Diem: "I just want to be sure there is some-body who would be better than this fella." Kennedy wanders to Chiang Kai Chek, and Korea, and Thailand, and muses that every dictator the United States patronizes "turns out to be a son of a bitch."

They talk for a while about Halberstam and the other Saigon correspondents, then Kennedy steers back to Diem: "So, I don't know, I assume that probably this fella's in an impossible situation to save, but I want to be sure we are not getting our policy made for us by a couple of smart young reporters." Kennedy tells Lodge he's going to leave the matter "completely in your hands and in your judgment," a pretty bald-faced assertion, which turned out to be eerily predictive.

The president reminds Lodge of Nolting's view that Diem was better than any alternative: "They said Nolting was soft . . . but maybe it was the right policy." The policy is already in the past tense. "So, I don't want us to get carried away [with replacing Diem] until you've had a good chance to look at it."

Lodge thanks Kennedy for giving him "the most interesting assign-ment in the government." From here on, Lodge sounds like he's running out the clock. He's trying to think of things to say—about improving "cul-tural contacts"; about getting color-coded maps, like he used to have at the UN, showing shrinking Viet Cong areas; about putting government "suggestion boxes" in the villages like they do in the Philippines—while

Kennedy clucks metronomically through Lodge's soliloquy: *ya . . . ya . . . ya . . . uh . . . uh . . . huh . . . ya.*

Kennedy doesn't sound like he's listening but then snaps back to the Buddhist crisis: "How much is political, how much is religious, how much is subversive. How do you judge it?" Lodge says he thinks it's "only *pahtly* religious," and then explains something to Kennedy about the broad appeal of Buddhism: "Buddhism isn't a religion that makes great demands. It isn't a religion that has a lot of discipline. Ahh, a little bit like Episcopalians."

They both have a good laugh. They talk about the weirdness of a French-educated Catholic minority in charge and the sense of injustice it breeds, but they seem sympathetic to the Ngo family's predicament. Kennedy agrees when Lodge declares, "I don't think they've persecuted the Buddhists. I think it's just a natural thing to give the posts to the best-educated people, who were the people educated in France—who naturally happen to be Christians." They talk about what Lodge calls the "comedy of errors" with the flags and the killings in Hue in May: "The heart of the matter is they've established a police state and they are interfering with the liberties of the people and you have resentments born of that."

They touch somewhat breezily on the possibility that Ngo family members might be assassinated if things went wrong.

It's time for photographs. While the photographers fuss, the two Massachusetts pols start dissecting the prospective Republican candidates for president in 1964.[45]

And with that, John F. Kennedy took a step that, whether he knew it or not, would outsource extraordinary power over Vietnam to a personality unlikely to be harnessed by even presidential directive. With the dispatch of Lodge to Saigon, the countdown to Ngo Dinh Diem's final days had started.

9

★ ★ ★

The Guns of August

D URING THE BRIEF INTERREGNUM between American ambassadors, and not coincidentally, Buddhist demonstrations swelled across the country. There were open calls in the streets for the overthrow of the regime, including personal denunciations of Madame Nhu. Xa Loi pagoda, Saigon's largest and most important, had drawn thousands of new bonzes and thousands more sympathizers, including many students. The pagoda had become a permanent, bristling nexus of protest. American correspondents were struck by the telephones and mimeograph machines in the Buddhist war rooms. Among the forests of street placards in Vietnamese a few stood out with slogans in English. A spontaneous protest had professionalized itself rapidly.

The embassy reported to Washington that a phalanx of younger, more radicalized bonzes was coming to the fore. Most alarming to the US government, the Buddhist revolt had seeped into prosecution of the war. In cables from the Saigon embassy and CIA station, there came "a veritable flood of extra intelligence and reporting on the near collapse of the administration of government in Saigon," Mike Forrestal recalled not long afterward.

Vouchers were not being signed to get food and materials out to the front. Munitions were being held up. Civil servants were going on vacation, or at least refusing to turn up at the office. We began for the first time to get reports from the field . . . that the war was grinding to a halt. That troops were not moving. What was actually happening was the troops were being redeployed to support a coup. This gave a sensation in Washington that this whole thing could collapse rather quickly, so there was considerable amount of tension for practical reasons, plus a certain amount of emotion. Could the United States long remain associated with this kind of suppressive activity?[1]

Feeling the heat, on August 18 and again on August 20 Diem gathered his senior military leadership at Gia Long to take stock of the crisis. The embassy's own sources had suggested that the senior Vietnamese officers were deeply unsettled at the effect of the crisis on Vietnamese troop morale. To meet the challenge of growing anarchy, Diem sought the generals' concurrence in a decree he planned to announce imposing a state of martial law in Saigon—a necessary first measure to restore order. The decree set curfews, shut newspapers, and suspended habeas corpus, such as it was in South Vietnam under the Ngo regime.

The generals' quick consent to the move was not mere subservience, and not surprising. Some of them had urged the idea on the president. And the Gia Long consultation was indispensable, paradoxically, in focusing the generals' inchoate planning for a coup d'état. On this day they were showing respect to the chief of state, sharing their concern about national unity and confronting the enemy. At the very least, too, the key plotters did not want to be out of the room—out of sight of each other—when anything important was said or decided.

Diem's martial law decree was to take effect at the stroke of midnight on August 20.

By that time, Bill Trueheart had been *chargé d'affaires* again for less than a week. At the embassy, as at the presidential palace in Saigon, all was anticipation about the arrival of Henry Cabot Lodge, the symbol of a new leaf turning in Washington's approach to Vietnam—and for Bill Trueheart, a new boss with an outsized reputation.

Not all of the advance word on Lodge was reassuring. Thelma Everett, Phoebe's mother, wrote to repeat gossip she claimed to have heard from Maysville's *other* Foreign Service in-law, James Moose, who had just retired after a distinguished career in the Middle East. "All that Jimmy Moose told you, we have heard," replied Phoebe. "But we hope for the best. He is called 'the imperious Mr. Lodge' etc. I am almost sure what they say is true or otherwise he wouldn't have such a reputation. He is bringing in some young hotshots as 'special assistants' but they in no way take Bill's place. Lodge will find he is dealing with some strange characters here and no amount of bullying or cajoling will move them. It's all been tried before."[2]

Following Foreign Service practice, Phoebe Trueheart had been corresponding with Emily Lodge—what to wear in Saigon, the state of the residence, the talents of the household staff, the immediate social calendar. No doubt with Bill's concurrence, she composed and proposed to Emily a series of dinner parties in the first days after the Lodges' arrival. Emily gently declined these, no doubt with Cabot's concurrence. He was going to do things his way.

Meanwhile, Phoebe and Bill went ahead with their own small dinner on Tuesday, August 20, with "only people we wanted, just some gay young Americans . . . attractive ones." They had declined a dreary reception at the Indian ambassador's. The dinner party ended in time for everyone to get home before the witching hour of midnight.

Within minutes of their goodbyes came the Diem regime's dreaded swift strike. Convoys of trucks packed with helmeted police converged on Xa Loi pagoda. As they smashed down the temple's iron gate, Stanley Karnow reported in the *Saturday Evening Post,* the bonzes within "shouted and banged pots, pans, drums, and gongs. . . . Some 400 monks and nuns cowered before the onslaught. There were screams, shots, and explosions as the police attacked. Some monks were thrown off balconies onto the concrete courtyard, which was hung with banners reading: THOU SHALT NOT KILL." Tipped off by their fixers' police sources, American correspondents were able to witness the whole thing. Neil Sheehan said the operation was "flawlessly executed." It put him in mind of a Gestapo raid on a French resistance hideout.[3]

The crackdown was happening simultaneously in two dozen other Vietnamese cities. In Hue, ancestral seat of the Ngos and locus of the May Buddhist uprising, saffron-robed bonzes barricaded themselves inside Dieu De pagoda and fought off paratroopers for eight hours. "They ripped down barbed-wire barricades with their bare hands while soldiers beat them down with rifle butts," Karnow wrote. The young US consul in Hue, John Helble, told the State Department that the ransacking of the pagodas had prompted "ugly incidents between highly excited crowds and security forces. . . . Anti-US feeling at an all-time high."[4]

The number of arrests of bonzes and students at Xa Loi in Saigon approached 1,400. The number of dead, or missing and never heard from again, was in the dozens.[5]

Here Phoebe Trueheart, three blocks from the action at Xa Loi, in the middle of the night on the most dramatic day yet of the year, wrote it all down in installments for Thelma—and herself: "Someday this may be of historical interest to my grandchildren. As you see it is 2 in the morning."[6]

After their dinner party guests had left, "we'd been in bed ten minutes when the phone went off. After three such calls, Bill proceeded to dress as he felt he might not get to the embassy at all if he delayed. While he was dressing, Reggie Burrows, the British DCM, called with the same information. Also Mal Browne (AP or UPI I forget) called with even worse news. I called Mel Manfull and got him cranked up, also got Johnny Jones (colonel military attaché) out of his bed." Note Phoebe's close involvement in the drama, speaking on behalf of her husband to people she knew well.

Sinh, the DCM's driver, had gone home hours earlier after dropping Bill off for dinner. So Bill drove himself to the chancery in the family car, the old Mercedes 220S shipped from London, through barricaded streets swarming with police and redolent of tear gas. "He took with him his faithful little 'friend'—he'll probably shoot his toe off with it. And it's loaded!" This was the pistol Bill had shown me in its wooden box. Phoebe told her mother that she had heard explosions and small-arms fire in the streets around the house "through all the air conditioner noise. I must have inherited my ears from you." (Apparently my little brother and I did not, as we snoozed through the night.) She called Suzie Manfull, the political counselor's wife and an old friend from Paris, "because I knew she was awake. She was brewing up some coffee for herself and Lisa (age 17). I told her I wished I could have coffee with somebody but only had Charlie to wake up. . . . There is no question of going to bed even if I could go to sleep. The phone keeps ringing."

Phone lines across Saigon had in fact been cut, but the residences of senior American officials were equipped with second phone lines, extensions on the embassy switchboard allegedly impervious to Vietnamese tampering. The calls from the diplomats and reporters, whom she knew well, put Phoebe clearly in the picture about what was happening. It's easy to infer, as well, the confidence into which her husband and his colleagues took her: "Mal Browne reported when he called that he tried to file a story through the PTT (post office) and met with bayonets. It sounds like a coup

working up. We have heard these rumors for so many weeks we are practically immune. When they take over communications, that is *it,* brother."

At 3:30 a.m., Phoebe resumed writing: "I couldn't bear it any longer so
I called the embassy extension. Mel Manfull answered and said the situa-
tion was 'in hand' but 'it' was 'not good.' That's all I know. I am going nuts.
But those poor devils down there hacking away at cables to Washington.
Don't ever say we don't earn our pay!"

Even as all hell is breaking loose, Phoebe clung to, or is comforted by, a
mirage of eventual relief: "All we need is two weeks out of here, but I cannot bear to leave the children in this hell-hole. I may send Josh to Suzie
and take Charlie, if we can get off after Lodge comes—and go to Kashmir.
It's our only salvation. Bill is so tired and irritable with all of us. But I try
to be understanding because he is really doing a grand job." I cannot help
observing that, writing to the sound of explosions and small-arms fire
outside the windows, my mother was daydreaming about leaving her two-
year-old behind to go on holiday to Kashmir.

Bill Trueheart's telegram on the pagoda raids, written that night on deadline with feeds from US officials all over Vietnam, signaled important first
facts to Washington.

"Expertness, speed, and coordination with which operations carried
out against Buddhists in widely separated cities," the *chargé* wrote, suggested contingency planning well ahead of the events—too well ahead
to have been triggered only after Diem met the generals, for example.
Trueheart noted that the immediate display of army banners in the streets
of Saigon also indicated careful preparation as did, he added dryly, the
"remarkably expeditious appearance of ARVN psywar pictures purporting
to show evidence of VC penetration of Buddhist movement."[7]

When Rufus Phillips saw Trueheart that day, he was "shaking his head
and saying, 'Now the fat's really in the fire.'"[8]

In his telegrams that day—there were twenty of them out of Saigon
in those twenty-four hours—Trueheart did not yet make distinctions
about who carried out the raids. He mentioned Colonel Le Quang Tung's
Special Forces, Ngo Dinh Nhu's fearful CIA-funded squads, only in passing. But he had no trouble reading Diem's mind: the president believed he
had been pursuing a policy of conciliation and that it had only made the
situation worse: "Diem probably concluded that this policy had become
one-way street to catastrophe for him, his family, and his government.

Early action against Buddhists would also have advantage of presenting Ambassador Lodge with a fait accompli."[9]

The serious prospect ahead, Trueheart told Washington, was that this "very amorphous and anomalous situation" would be the opportunity for the military to strike with a coup. The CIA the same day gave the Kennedy administration a rundown of their information on the coup plotting, letting drop that Madame Nhu had told an Australian correspondent she expected a coup any day. And, the CIA added, "the possibility of a takeover by Nhu cannot be discounted."[10]

Trueheart and Harkins collaborated on a local message broadcast on the Armed Forces radio network "advising all American dependents remain in quarters until situation clarified." On his own General Harkins delivered his take on all the turmoil, providing Washington some inadvertent comic relief. "It's a bit premature to crystal ball the hidden machanisms [sic] and internal machinations of this mixed-up country," he wrote Maxwell Taylor Thursday morning, sounding like someone who'd been drinking the Ngo family Kool-Aid: "A few bones were bruised as the police and the military took over the main pagodas. . . . Not that I'm for the military taking over—no indeed—but . . . things were getting out of control, and some measure of authority had to be established. That it was done without firing a shot and thru the nominal chain of command precluded a lot of bloodshed which would have spilled if rival factions tried to take over."[11]

Shots had been fired, and blood, of course, had been spilled. Harkins mentioned to Taylor, almost by the way, that "we have accomplished our part of everything we set out to do after your visit in the fall of '61—all except ending the war, and that is not far off if things continue at present pace."

With the regime going for broke, the American journalists heard from palace sources they might be its next targets. Purported assassination lists were proliferating. Halberstam and Sheehan showed up at the embassy, deeply shaken, at 4:00 a.m. as they struggled to file their stories on the raids in a city with severed telecommunications. They asked for physical protection; John Mecklin, with Trueheart's permission, offered them sanctuary in his own residence. Both Mecklin and Trueheart knew the optics were not good for Mecklin or for the United States: the regime's and the

administration's fiercest critics being sheltered on US government property. But Halberstam and Sheehan bunked in the Mecklin compound for
several weeks, much to the consternation of higher-ups in Washington.

In the melee of the raids, two bonzes at Xa Loi jumped over the wall
into the adjacent compound, serendipitously the headquarters of USOM,
the American aid mission in Vietnam. The US military protective detail
refused to let Vietnamese police enter the building, so the police cor-
doned off the compound. Foreign Minister Vu Van Mau called Trueheart
in at noon the next day to demand the monks be handed over. The *charge*'s
forthright guidance from Washington, repeated to Mau, was: Whatever
you do, don't hand them over.[12]

Trueheart was surprised to learn, only two hours after this démarche,
that Foreign Minister Mau had resigned in protest at his own government's descent into bloody repression. He refused to continue as "the
devil's advocate." Mau shaved his head in solidarity with the Buddhists.
He made haste to leave the country on a plane for India for a Buddhist
retreat. Trueheart and other Western diplomats went to the airport to
see him off late that afternoon; some rituals were not dampened even by
martial law and geopolitical crisis, or perhaps they were showing crisp
solidarity. But Mau never showed up after leaving his house at 5:00 p.m.
He had been arrested. One of the diplomats told Sheehan, "Saigon seems
to have a lot in common these days with the Chicago of the 1920s."[13]

Two other significant resignations happened the same day: those of
Mr. and Mrs. Tran Van Chuong, the South Vietnamese ambassador to the
United States and that country's observer at the United Nations. This was a
shock only to those who had not heard their diatribes against their daughter, her husband, and President Diem. Henry Cabot Lodge had heard them
in person on the eve of his last meeting with President Kennedy.

As in the aftermath of the Hue killings that ignited the crisis, and all
the crises that followed, the regime's first resort was to a lie, the carefully prepared one Trueheart had alluded to. The government told the
Americans and the Vietnamese people that the raids on the pagodas had
been carried out by the armed forces. Yet Sheehan and the other reporters
could see for themselves that these "squads of ARVN Special Forces troops
in trim camouflage fatigues and berets with submachine guns held high"
were no ordinary soldiers. They were Brother Nhu and Colonel Tung's palace guard. "For this work they were using their household troops," wrote

Sheehan. "The family had hoodwinked the CIA into forming a Praetorian guard for them."[14]

After another exhausting day and night at the embassy, and preparing to be relieved of his command by Lodge within hours, Trueheart went home through the deserted city, the avenues lined by military vehicles and police checkpoints. Later the next day, Phoebe picked up the narrative in the same letter to her mother:

> Bill came in at 5:30 and at 6:00 am the phone rang—a telecon at MacV with CincPac at 7. So Bill showered and dressed and we had breakfast. The lines are cut. I can't call out except to the embassy on the extension. I was incommunicado all morning. . . . Nobody knows anything. Bill can't see Thuan until 5. . . . Washington hasn't said 'boo.' . . . Curfew at 9 to 5. . . . They cleaned out the pagodas, killed and wounded bonzes (all hearsay) and packed the rest in trucks. Some say they've been shipped to an island prison.
>
> Bill went off to embassy again after an early supper (so the servants would get home before 9). . . . Bill flew the flags, which he seldom does. . . . So on the way to Mel's they were *arreté* by two goons with machine guns. But were let thru. Then after Mel got out Bill was stopped again by two more. I guess they don't recognize the American flag. . . . They are really trigger happy.

Some routines nonetheless continued:

> This morning I played tennis at 8 around the corner. Three goons were standing at the corner of *rue Mayer* and *rue d'Arfeuilles*. Boy, they are really rough and tough looking. I've not seen such faces since I've been here. Bayonets at the ready. We quit playing in the middle of the third set as we kept hearing rumbling of crowds and a loudspeaker. Don't know what that is. Sounded like a pep rally. . . . Bill called at 11:30 and said Lodge is coming at 6:45 tonight. I am preparing dinner in case they will come here, only have a piece of tough beef. *Tant pis.*

Once again, and not even for the last time, Bill Trueheart was the American *chargé* at a critical moment in the downfall of the regime. It would be so interesting to know in his own words what he was feeling, but we must rely in part on the excellent narrator he married and with whom he shared all he knew.

The New Ambassador

The news about the nighttime raids in Saigon came over the wire in Honolulu the same morning. Roger Hilsman was there with Fritz Nolting as they looked at the copy chattering out of the wire service teletype. Hilsman heard Nolting say *shit* under his breath as he read the news, news he took personally. "This is the first time you have ever gone back on your word to me," Nolting would write Diem, generously for a man so wholly betrayed, the next day.

Nolting was at Hickam Air Force Base in part to confer with his successor, who was about to leave for Tokyo on his multistop procession to Saigon. One of Lodge's aides recalled that he had declined any briefing at all from Nolting—"he had nothing to learn from him"[15]—which seems even ruder than one might expect. Bittie Nolting remembers that Lodge's immediate reaction to the frightful news from Saigon was, "good—this makes it easier for us," meaning, the situation was more clear-cut because more dire, and firing Diem for cause more logical.[16]

The Lodges flew on to Tokyo. There, the ambassador-to-be got a call in the middle of the night from Washington ordering him to proceed immediately to his post. A military plane was being rushed to take him to Saigon directly. While he awaited its arrival, Lodge proceeded to receive a delegation of Japanese Buddhists expressing their solidarity with the oppressed brethren in Vietnam. He also arranged for four American reporters to join him on the plane for the nine hours to Saigon, landing himself not just gratitude for access but a chance to get their briefing to him about Vietnam.

Henry Cabot Lodge's plane touched down in Saigon at 9:30 the next night, August 22. The Truehearts were at the bottom of the steps when Lodge appeared at the top of them, lifting his straw hat in recognition at snapping flashbulbs. It was a small party of greeters, given the state of martial law; apart from a few US officials and the Vietnamese chief of protocol, the greeting party consisted of reporters. A television cameraman captured Bill and Phoebe at Lodge's side on the tarmac as they were the first to welcome him to Vietnam.

After these hellos Lodge's first question was, "Now, where are the gentlemen of the press?" He proceeded to greet them in a warm huddle and spoke of their value to democracy. Then he climbed into the new official car ordered for the new ambassador, a roomy Checker sedan (painted black with a white top) to accommodate both his and Emily's height. On the way into the city through the deserted streets, Lodge recalled "the hot tropical blackness from the airport to the embassy, the only human beings we saw were soldiers edging the street, but facing the houses, with guns ready to use."[17]

The Truehearts went directly to the ambassador's residence on Hien Vuong with the Lodges. My mother wrote: "Bill and Lodge went into the study. Mrs. L and I had a drink and I showed her the house. She *loves* it. Thrilled with it all."[18]

The new ambassador was a master of symbolic moves. The next morning, August 23, he made his first official outing to visit the USOM compound next to Xa Loi where the two monks had taken refuge. He inquired after their health and ordered them supplied with fresh vegetables for their no-meat diets (Lodge, amazingly, had a Buddhist cousin). By the weekend three more bonzes forced their way into asylum by rushing past US Marine guards at the doors of the chancery building. One of them was the unofficial leader of the Buddhist revolt, Tri Quang. He would live with his confreres in an embassy conference room for the remainder of the Diem era and play a nettlesome role in Vietnamese politics for years to come.

Lodge came to trust some of his new colleagues, including Trueheart. But he brought with him to Saigon a pair of special assistants, whom Phoebe and her pals dubbed "Cohn and Schine" (after Joseph McCarthy's unsavory thugs Roy Cohn and G. David Schine). Freddy Flott was a French-speaking Foreign Service Officer (FSO), a friend of his son George Lodge and of Robert Kennedy. Mike Dunn was a swashbuckling military guy with a Harvard degree. They became a kind of palace guard; for weeks they even lived in the residence, and took turns sleeping on rugs outside the Lodges' bedroom door, armed, in case of an attack.[19]

As soon as he saw his (spacious but grim) corner office in the downtown chancery, the Yankee in Henry Cabot Lodge ordered the brass plaque on the door—AMBASSADOR—removed and replaced with one that read MR. LODGE. His first appointments there, beyond the obvious (Trueheart, Manfull, Harkins, Richardson, Mecklin), were Rufus Phillips, who had special access to and perspicacity about Ngo Dinh Diem and a clear-eyed view of the situation, and Lucien Conein, whom Lodge deputized at once as the coup go-between with the plotting generals.

Lodge's first lunches were with reporters—the triumvirate Halberstam, Sheehan, Browne, one by one—at the residence with Emily, whose judgment of people he trusted. After Sheehan had shared with Lodge his scathing analysis and gloomy prognosis about the government and the war, over coffee in the living room after lunch, he asked, "What's *your* impression, Mr. Ambassador?" Sheehan recalled Lodge "sitting on the couch beside his wife, his legs crossed lazily and his arm extended behind her. He smiled. 'About the same as yours.'"[20]

A Lodge biographer, Anne Blair, comments astringently that Sheehan, "at first skeptical of the influence that a reporter might have on ambassadorial thinking, came to believe that Lodge had based much of his subsequent analysis of the ills of the Diem regime on what he, Sheehan, and his group had told him."[21] Be that as it may, as a former newspaperman himself, Lodge came to his conclusions with breathtaking speed and the kind of judgments that reporters, too, don't have the luxury to ponder indefinitely.

Lodge immediately sought out other exotic creatures in the Saigon zoo of 1963. One was P. J. Honey, a British scholar of Vietnamese culture on a three-month sabbatical in Saigon, and probably a British intelligence asset as well. Another was Giovanni d'Orlandi, the Italian ambassador, whose European urbanity appealed to Lodge. Monsignore Salvatore Asta, the apostolic delegate (the pope's nuncio, or ambassador) in Saigon, happened to be an old friend.

Lodge understood instinctively that the Roman Catholic issue, for President Kennedy, was a keen and sensitive one. Deep-sixing Ngo Dinh Diem, a fellow Catholic and recent hero of the American Catholic establishment, could come back to bite Kennedy in the upcoming election. Lodge's early political career in Massachusetts had been helped by his assiduous courtship of the Catholic vote and the Catholic heirarchy.[22] Lodge made the astonishing statement in his own memoir that in Saigon he felt he had to make sure that "every action Kennedy took in relation to the Diem regime had the approval of Asta, and therefore the Vatican."[23]

Years later, Trueheart spoke of being "full of admiration" for the way Lodge took over in Saigon: "I have never in all my career seen anybody move into such a complicated, messy situation and take charge so quickly and so effectively. . . . He simply hit the ground running. He made decisions and moved ahead. He had certainly been well briefed and knew what he wanted to do. He had full confidence that he was in charge of everything and was not going to tolerate any sort of suggestion that he was not."[24]

Phoebe was equally impressed. "He is the most handsome man I have seen in a long time," she wrote her mother-in-law. Emily Lodge is "a peach . . . she wants my advice on everything, from eating the lettuce and brushing your teeth in the (tap) water to her calling duties." Feeding her mother-in-law's pride, she said Henry Cabot Lodge, "when they were alone, told Bill he had no idea how many admirers he had in Washington—right on up to JFK."[25]

Flattery was getting Lodge everywhere. And as it turned out, when it came to what to do about the Diem regime, Cabot and Bill were peas in a pod.

The August 24 Telegram

"The most famous cable of the Vietnam war"[26] is a much-studied document in American diplomatic history, sometimes compared to the Zimmermann Telegram, an intercepted message that reputedly goaded the United States into entering World War I.

The August 24 Telegram to Henry Cabot Lodge followed in a straight line the tightening pressure and sharpening threats that Trueheart had been delivering for months, and Nolting too, in his gentler way, and all the way back to Durbrow before them. The new instructions, however, did contain one important new wrinkle of menace: an explicit willingness on the part of the United States to engage with the military plotters against the sovereign government, and an open acknowledgment that the Diem regime itself was dispensable.

In the famous cable, Lodge was told: "US government cannot tolerate situation in which power lies in Nhu's hands. Diem must be given chance to rid himself of Nhu and his coterie and replace him with best military and political personalities available. If, in spite of your efforts, Diem remains obdurate and refuses, then we must face the possibility that Diem himself cannot be preserved."[27] Lodge was further given extraordinary operational discretion—and preemptive cover. He was instructed to "urgently examine all possible alternative leadership and make detailed plans as to how we might bring about Diem's replacement if this should become necessary. . . . You will understand that we cannot from Washington give you detailed instructions as to how this operation should proceed, but you will also know we will back you to the hilt on actions you take to achieve our objectives."

The telegram's composition and dispatch are a sobering window, case study material, on the vagaries of decision-making at the highest levels of government. For on this late summer weekend, the principal deciders were absent from Washington. It was their seconds and deputies, the aides and bureaucratic players, who wrote, cleared, and delivered the instructions to Henry Cabot Lodge on his second day of work. To those who truly didn't like its consequences, the August 24 Telegram is regarded as a violation of process on a matter of state—a high-level runaround that set important policy in a single stroke. The procoup cabal, if you read it this way, outmaneuvered the principals to clear the way for the overthrow of Diem.

Mike Forrestal, thirty-five, was in the bureaucratic cockpit, nearly alone in the West Wing of the White House all weekend, shepherding the telegram forward. He remembered a consensus building on Thursday, August 22, the day after the pagoda raids, to deliver a forceful response.[28] It would also be marching orders for the new ambassador—at that moment in the air between Tokyo to Saigon—and a test of Lodge's ability to carry out instructions.

Averell Harriman, Forrestal's mentor, was in accord with the new instructions. Hilsman, just back in Washington after the Lodge-Nolting handoff in Honolulu, "for some time had felt this way strongly." Forrestal himself was convinced. Maxwell Taylor—like everyone else, really—was worried about Washington's lack of intelligence on who had the forces and wits to carry out a coup, let alone lead the country. Secretary of State Dean Rusk was in New York part of the day at a Yankees game. "McNamara hadn't addressed himself to the situation" and was hiking the Tetons. John A. McCone, the director of the CIA, was on a yacht in Puget Sound. President Kennedy, the great sphinx at the heart of this matter, "had never expressed an opinion one way or the other." The next day, Friday, August 23, he was leaving Washington for a weekend in Hyannisport. "So you didn't have much of a Government" left in Washington, Forrestal recalled.[29]

That Friday morning, Roger Hilsman caught a ride to work with his neighbor Tom Hughes, who had succeeded him as head of the State Department's intelligence and research bureau. Hughes had been reporting gloomily on Diem's prospects, and Vietnam's, for months. He remembers that, on the way to Foggy Bottom, Hilsman told him about the telegram he was about to write: "This is going to be one of the days that separates the men from the boys."[30]

At the end of that long day Forrestal sent Hilsman's draft cable to President Kennedy on Cape Cod. He brought the president up to date about who had carried out the raids, notwithstanding earlier suppositions: "It is now quite certain that Brother Nhu is the mastermind behind the whole operation against the Buddhists and is calling the shots." He noted that among Kennedy's senior advisers "there is disagreement on whether Diem has any political viability left, and on whether he could ever be brought to acquiesce in the removal of his brother."[31]

Forrestal told Kennedy that the cable had been endorsed by Harriman, Hilsman, and George Ball, the acting secretary of state in Dean Rusk's absence. He stressed the urgency of sending the message, given rife coup rumors and Lodge's own request for immediate guidance. Richard Helms at the CIA, acting for the absent McCone, had signed off. ("It's about time we bit this bullet," Helms remarked.)[32]

Forrestal told Tom Hughes that day, when he broke for lunch with him, that the military leadership was being recalcitrant about approving the cable. Evidently in a fighting spirit himself, Forrestal said to Hughes: "'What is it about that great gray citadel,' meaning West Point, 'that turns those guys into such cowards? It's like pulling teeth to get the Pentagon to agree that action has to be taken."[33]

But not all the military. In a surprise note of skepticism, Admiral Felt in Honolulu had confidentially told Hilsman the military situation in Vietnam was dire enough to remove Diem. Forrestal called Roswell Gilpatric, the number 2 at the Pentagon, at his farm in Maryland and read the draft message to him twice. Gilpatric said the Pentagon couldn't take a position on a matter of this kind but sought Forrestal's assurances that senior State Department people were in concurrence. And then he asked, "Has the President seen it?" Forrestal told him they were waiting for his response.

While they waited on Kennedy Saturday afternoon, Harriman and Hilsman decided they needed to find George Ball. In a touch a screenwriter would savor, they learned the acting secretary of state was on the golf course—a public course, Falls Road, outside Washington—playing eighteen holes with his deputy, U. Alexis Johnson. Hilsman and Harriman drove out to intersect with them as they approached the ninth tee. They prevailed on Ball to leave the game and took him back to his house.

Now unwilling to clear the telegram without the president's explicit concurrence, Ball got Kennedy on the phone in Hyannisport. The president conditioned his agreement on Rusk's and Gilpatric's, who, believing Kennedy was for it, then gave their cautious approval. Finally, in this dizzying round of clearances, Forrestal got word from Victor Krulak, a top Vietnam aide to Maxwell Taylor, that the chairman of the Joint Chiefs had signed off. "Yes, he has seen it, and it's all right with him if everybody else is in agreement."

It was, in short, a hall of mirrors.

When Forrestal called Kennedy to say the clearance was complete, the president asked if the matter shouldn't wait until the following week. Forrestal said Harriman and Hilsman insisted on a prompt response. "Send it out," the president wearily replied. The cable was dispatched at 9:36 p.m. that Saturday in Washington, mid–Sunday morning in Saigon.[34]

It did not take long for the shaky "consensus" on the telegram to Lodge to come apart. Some of the principals whose seconds had acted over the weekend professed shock about the telegram and set about trying to undo it, or at least to cover for themselves. After the fact, Forrestal was rueful: "I had not had enough experience in organizing—orchestrating—this kind of matter to realize that you had to get these men together. And that a weekend was no time to do it, especially when many were off on vacation." What's more, the instructions themselves were opaque. "I don't believe that the full thrust of the Saturday cable was ever communicated in full effect to anybody."[35]

Forrestal was distraught. He told Harriman, his unofficial godfather, that he thought he should resign. The Crocodile, never warm and fuzzy even to those he loved, told Forrestal to "quit being a god-damned fool" and "get back to work."[36] Forrestal went ahead and offered his resignation to the president. "You're not worth firing," Kennedy snapped. "You owe me something, so stick around."[37]

Kennedy was also reckoning with a divided government, his own. The military wanted nothing to do with a coup. Vice President Johnson was insisting it was better to stick with the devil we knew. "My god! My government's coming apart!" Kennedy told his chum, the columnist Charles Bartlett.[38] "It was the only time, really, in three years, the government was broken in a very disturbing way," Robert Kennedy recalled.

When he gathered his leadership on Monday, President Kennedy went around the room asking everyone if the Saturday instructions should be changed. "John, do you want to cancel it? Bob, do you want to cancel it, Dean, do you want to cancel it?" None did. One can picture sheepish faces. Taylor, who had been indignant about the telegram, said, "I wasn't for calling it back. You can't change American policy in 24 hours and expect anyone to ever believe you again."

George Ball, in his memoir *The Past Has Another Pattern,* has wise words about this famous telegram—which he, as acting secretary of state, had signed: "Because our deep involvement in Vietnam was such a ghastly error, a thousand myths have been spun to explain our failure. . . . Then there is the large club of the reconstructed who—seeking an excuse for preordained failure—seize on the August 24 telegram as an exculpation. Had that telegram not been sent, they contend, Diem would have remained in charge; we would have won the war; and everyone would have lived happily ever after. Myths are made to solace those who find reality distasteful."[39] The reality, for Ball, was that the ruling family in Vietnam were "poisonous connivers" whom "America could not, with any showdown of honor, have continued to support."

After conferring with the Country Team, Ambassador Lodge requested from Washington a significant modification to his new instructions. He sought permission to go directly to the plotting generals, bypassing a last-ditch ultimatum to Diem altogether. Lodge feared an ultimatum might tip the ruling family off to the scheming and the US hand in it (although they were well aware of it). Believing the chances of removing Nhu were "close to nil," he said he would tell the generals that, so long as the Nhus were gone, they could make their own decision about whether to keep Ngo Dinh Diem as their figurehead. The new guidance Lodge proposed was accepted quickly in Washington, though misgivings about his approach lingered a long while.

Then, at midweek, Lodge heard that Maxwell Taylor had told General Harkins that "authorities are now having second thoughts" about the August 24 instructions and soliciting the commander's views. Lodge was livid. With less than a week in Saigon, he wrote to Washington some of the plainest and most fateful words of the period: "We are launched on a course from which there is no respectable turning back: the overthrow of the Diem government. . . . US prestige is already publicly committed to this end in large measure and will become more so as the facts leak out.

In a more fundamental sense, there is no turning back because there is no possibility, in my view, that the war can be won under a Diem administration."[40] The August 24 Telegram had taken on a life of its own.

The personal authority Henry Cabot Lodge had accreted in just three days on the ground is impressive, given that he was a man on the sidelines of power just a few weeks before. Yet without demurring about the approach his new ambassador favored, Kennedy wrote Lodge an eyes-only message reminding him that as president he reserved a "contingent right to change course and reverse previous instructions." In an unmistakable allusion to the Bay of Pigs, President Kennedy said, "I know from experience that failure is more destructive than the appearance of indecision. . . . When we go, we must go to win, but it will be better to change our minds than fail. And if our national interest should require a change of mind, we must not be afraid of it."[41]

Robert Kennedy said that at this moment his brother had deep misgivings about the course on which they were launched. "A change in government wasn't really what he wanted to have. He wanted to bring pressure on Diem to change his ways. That was his intention," said the attorney general, perhaps protectively, of his late brother.[42]

In Robert Kennedy's retelling, a year after the fact, the president was beginning "to have serious doubts about the *whole* effort. . . . Was the United States capable of achieving even the limited objectives that we then had in Vietnam? Did the United States have the resources, the men and the thinking to have anything useful to do in a country that was as politically unstable as Vietnam? Was it not possible that we had overestimated our own resources and underestimated the problem in South Vietnam?"

Arthur Schlesinger Jr. wrote of this moment: "The question hovered for a moment, then died away, a hopelessly alien thought in a field of unexamined assumptions and entrenched convictions."[43]

There was no learning curve for Lodge. He had arrived in the afterwash of the pagoda raids, received the dramatic August 24 cable, successfully altered the tactics in his instructions, and by Monday morning had another crisis to deal with: the Voice of America had inadvertently blurted out the truth. A broadcast that morning said that the Vietnamese military had not been responsible for the pagoda raids, that in fact Nhu's shock troops had been, and that a US aid suspension was under serious contemplation. Lodge was angry about the lapse, as it tipped the US hand and jeopardized the generals he was trying to coax into action. Profuse apologies to him from Washington ensued.

Later that morning, the new ambassador was scheduled to present his credentials to President Diem at Gia Long Palace. This is musty diplomatic custom, but it is unusual for such a ceremony to take place when everyone present, including the chief of state, is expecting a military coup d'état at any moment. Before Lodge and his entourage set out to depart for the palace, Trueheart advised the ambassador that Harkins and Richardson should stay back. The putative fear was that the Americans in the official party might be held hostage. Given that those two members of the Country Team were known for their closeness to Diem and Nhu respectively, Trueheart's recommendation may have had other subtleties. In any case, Lodge agreed. Later that day at Gia Long, the new ambassador suffered through his first Diem monologue, two hours, and decided that if he could do anything about it, this one would be his last.

The coup plotters, meanwhile, were stymied. They wanted assurances, through Conein, that Lodge was behind them and that if a coup failed, they would have safe passage to exile. Rumors were rife that Nhu planned to arrest all the conspiring generals. At the White House all week the same cast of characters met once or twice a day to assess and anticipate a coup they believed—because the embassy and the CIA station were telling them so—was coming any day. Some at the table feared a bloodbath or civil unrest. CINCPAC moved ships closer to the Vietnamese coast to exfiltrate thousands of American noncombatants. "If necessary," Hilsman told Kennedy, "we should bring in US combat forces to assist the coup group to achieve victory."

On Wednesday night, August 28, while the Truehearts (on their fifteenth wedding anniversary) hosted a black-tie dinner at home in honor of Cabot and Emily Lodge, Richardson cabled the CIA: "Situation here has reached point of no return. Saigon is armed camp. Current indications are that the Ngo family have dug in for a last-ditch battle. It is our considered estimate that General officers cannot retreat now."[44]

Whatever the considered estimate of Wednesday, it didn't hold. By Friday the generals had stood down, cold-footed. "This particular coup is finished," Richardson reported. Lodge fumed in his cable home. "There is neither the will nor the organization among the generals to accomplish anything," he explained to Washington. He compared goading the Vietnamese generals into action to "pushing a piece of spaghetti," a line he might have picked up from Trueheart, who liked the phrase. General Harkins, typically: "You can't hurry the East."[45]

"Get Out!"

When Fritz Nolting reached Washington on Tuesday morning, August 27, he found in the mail piling up for him at the State Department the customary letter from the president of the United States accepting his resignation as ambassador to South Vietnam. The brief letter was warm and congratulatory about his service. He had only just read it, Nolting recalled, when he got an urgent telephone call from the White House: "A public relations staff member asked me to give the letter no publicity. I said that I had no intention of doing so. 'That's fine,' he said. 'The President would find it awkward and embarrassing because of his references to the close relations you established between the Government of South Vietnam and the United States.'"

Nolting could smell what was up. A few minutes later he stood in Hilsman's office and for the first time read the famous telegram to Saigon that had gone out over the weekend. As Nolting saw it, "a plot had been launched to overthrow the constitutional government of President Diem, and President Kennedy was aware of it, if not entirely sympathetic. Naturally, he did not want to be caught in the contradiction between his former policy and the emerging one."[46]

This was, of course, the contradiction in which Nolting himself had been caught.

Although he doesn't mention it in his memoir, he had another jarring encounter that first day back at the State Department. When Nolting appeared at his open office door, Averell Harriman looked up sharply from his desk.

"What are you doing in here?"

"Well, I came to say hello."

"*Get out!*"[47]

About to mark his fifty-third birthday, Fritz Nolting was in the end times of his diplomatic career. But on that first day back, seemingly in ignominious defeat, Nolting was the man President Kennedy wanted to see.

When Kennedy gathered his advisers on Monday to thrash out the consequences of the August 24 Telegram,[48] the can-kicking decision was to go back and ask Lodge and Harkins what they thought, again. Then Kennedy suddenly asked, *Where's Nolting?* "At his farm in Virginia," someone said. "Let's get Nolting back here tomorrow," Kennedy decided. Then Averell Harriman drawled to life to say scornfully that Nolting thought that "if Diem goes, we're finished. He's very emotional about this." Kennedy snapped, "Maybe logically so. I'd like to hear what he thinks." Hilsman persisted, "He's a man deeply shocked. Diem double-crossed him."

At the White House the next day—he'd come from Danville, actually, because he no longer had a farm in Chantilly—Nolting was surrounded by the most powerful men in the United States government. Spurred by the August 24 Telegram, they were holding the very deliberations that should have preceded it. These were first discussions yet of such thoroughness, constituting so many powerful officials, under the pressure of an imminent coup and a chain of events they couldn't control. Were the stakes comparable, these meetings could be compared to those during the thirteen days of the Cuban Missile Crisis the year before. The White House tapes were rolling.

The former ambassador seemed to have seen the handwriting on the wall about the Diem regime's fate, as anyone could, but he put on a brave performance, day after day, all week.

On Tuesday, after listening to Bill Colby's rundown of the Vietnamese generals involved in the coup planning, President Kennedy asked, "Do you know these generals, Mr. Ambassador?"

"Yes," Nolting replied, and none of them had "the guts or the sangfroid or the drive of either Diem or Nhu."

On these scratchy recordings, Nolting sounds more than subdued. His words come slowly, but he doesn't shrink from his stubborn fondness for Diem. "I'd give him an E for effort on everything, on most things. I never considered him a liar, but a man of integrity." Reaching back to his last full day in Saigon, August 14, one week before the disastrous pagoda raids, Nolting described the "categoric assurances" both Diem and Nhu gave him of their commitment to reconciliation with the Buddhists, which was "irreversible" again.

Then, as two dozen important pairs of eyes look on, Nolting picked up from his papers a long account of these Diem-Nhu conversations that he himself set down after he left Saigon. Startlingly, he said, "If you have the time I'll read it to you," and proceeded to do so without interruption while four agonizing minutes tick by.

Kennedy remained skeptical. He asked if the Ngos "changed their minds" between August 14 and the raids, or "were they just covering up what they were already planning?"

Nolting: "This is the $64[,000] question." Although it had been answered in telegrams from Saigon.

Kennedy pressed him on Madame Nhu—why have there been no efforts to curb her?

Nolting is audibly weary, worn out from making excuses for her. "There've been efforts, Mr. President, over and over. She's a strong-willed woman."

Kennedy: "Is she under Nhu's domination?"

Nolting: "I don't think she's under anybody's domination."

Kennedy also wanted to know more about Nhu: "Is he anti-American?"

Nolting: "No, I think he's pro-Vietnamese."

Kennedy inquired about rumors that Nhu wants to take over the government. Nolting's extraordinary answer: "I asked them, and they both said no. . . . They both looked me straight in the eye and categorically denied it."

On this day Nolting had the floor for about thirty-five minutes, offering his judgments on the separability of the Ngo brothers and the Nhu couple. He was wary of ultimatums. Nolting even brought a laugh from President Kennedy and everyone else when he reminded them that the last time an American ambassador tried to order Diem to exile Brother Nhu, it was the ambassador—Elbridge Durbrow—who got quickly exiled. Someone joked about that kind of a quick round-trip for Lodge.

Overall, Nolting stuck to his main point: Lodge should have it out with Diem, "all cards on the table," and give persuasion another try.

Averell Harriman had been silent throughout, acting the crocodile who seems to slumber until he snaps. Finally, after George Ball made a forceful case for removing Diem, Harriman came to life. Interrupting, he declared himself "utterly convinced we can't win with the combination of Diem and Nhu." He spoke an uncomfortable truth: "We created them, after all . . . and they have betrayed us and double-crossed us."

The next day, as the deliberations resumed and Nolting continued to advise prudence, the recordings from the National Archives and Records Administration indicate (as they often do) an excision "on grounds of national security." Usually, by inference, these are references to CIA assets, or information gleaned from "sources and methods" that remain privileged decades after the fact. But not every excision.

It's no secret that during one of them, abruptly, Averell Harriman broke into something Nolting was saying and lit into him—*"Shut up! Nobody cares what you think!"*—with a brutality no one at the table forgot.[49] Roswell Gilpatric, the deputy defense secretary, said it was "the only time I remember in the presence of a president where anybody took the tongue-lashing that Nolting did from Harriman. . . . [I]n effect [he] was charging Nolting with having been taken in by Diem and not really adequately representing the interests of the United States. . . . I don't think from anybody else it would have been tolerated by the president."[50] Indeed, President Kennedy pushed back at Harriman, saying he, for one, cared what Nolting thought, and let him go on.

The momentum in these sequential meetings is toward abandoning Diem, but Nolting was persistent to the point of redundancy. This may be because Kennedy encouraged him, repeatedly turning back to hear his views. After one meeting, when the president gathered just four of the principals for a private huddle without the others, Rusk told Kennedy grimly that "Fritz is in a state of minor shock. He keeps coming full circle, answering his own arguments, and comes out with zero." Kennedy disagreed and said Nolting's record in Saigon had been pretty good until the Buddhist crisis.

The president was there through Thursday, until he left for a long Labor Day weekend in Hyannisport, but the meetings of the Diem-era Wise Men went on without him (and without recordings). At the last one, on Saturday, an FSO named Paul Kattenburg was asked to speak about the situation in Saigon, whence he had returned the night before. As he listened to "men at the top of our government like Rusk, McNamara, Taylor, and Robert Kennedy, who simply did not know Vietnam, its recent history, or the personalities and forces in contention . . . I finally, and imprudently for such meetings, blurted out that I thought we should now consider 'withdrawal with honor.' Dean Rusk and Lyndon Johnson's responses, cavalier dismissals of this thought, were indicative of precisely what I felt: that these men were leading themselves down a garden path to tragedy." Kattenburg saw this moment as "the last best chance the United States had to examine in a concerted and systematic way whether or not it ought to continue in Vietnam," and punted.[51]

10

★ ★ ★

Silent Treatment

T HAT PARTICULAR COUP MAY have been finished, but it did not remain a secret. The Nhus blew the whistle on the CIA in the *Times of Vietnam* on September 2. "CIA Financing Planned Coup d'État," read the banner headline. "Planned for Aug. 28; Falls Flat, Still Born."

Channeling Madame Nhu's prolix ravings, the *Times of Vietnam* said the CIA's "detailed plan . . . had the blessing of high officials in the State Department." Since January "American secret agency experts who successfully engineered the *coups d'état* in Turkey, Guatemala, Korea, and failed in Iran and Cuba, began arriving in Vietnam" to organize another one, whipped up during Ambassador Nolting's absence by persons unnamed. "Now faced with an embarrassing dilemma created by gross errors of assessment of the situation here," the United States "has a choice of doing an about-face or losing plenty of face, and maybe both." The palace organ called on the United States Congress—"watchdog of the American dream"—to take action.

In fact, Senator Frank Church and his colleagues were doing just that— only in protest of the Diem government. A sense of the Senate resolution with twenty-two signatories and growing called for cutting off military and economic assistance unless the regime undertook significant reforms. The White House and State Department, far from fighting the resolution, worked closely with Church and other senators to bend it to its coincident objectives, and Ambassador Lodge found it a helpful turn of the screw on the Diem regime.[1]

On the same day as the CIA blast from the *Times of Vietnam,* September 2, Labor Day in America, President Kennedy sat on the lawn of his house in Hyannisport for an interview with Walter Cronkite of CBS News.

It happened to be the inaugural broadcast of the first half-hour-long network evening news program, previously contained in fifteen minutes. Along the way, Kennedy was asked if he thought the South Vietnamese government had a chance to regain the support of its people. "I do," he replied. "With changes of policy and perhaps of personnel, I think it can win. If it doesn't make these changes, I would think that the chances of winning it would not be very good." General and indirect as the words read, this statement was heard, and was meant to be heard, as a bracing ultimatum.

On September 9 Ambassador Lodge called on Diem—for the first and last time until the eve of the next, and this time successful coup—to add new bite to the official warnings. On the mind of both allies was the looming cudgel of a United Nations resolution condemning the regime's treatment of Buddhists. As a former US ambassador to the UN, Lodge could speak with personal authority. Diem could not have missed the gravity of what Lodge was saying: that "it was obvious that public opinion could not condone the idea that American loss of lives and American aid were being expended for the repression of human rights."[2]

In response, President Diem treated Lodge to some of the wildest speculation yet about the Buddhists. Diem said he would be prepared to go to New York himself to show the United Nations General Assembly that "the pagodas had been turned into bordellos, that they had found a great deal of female underwear, love letters, and obscene photographs. . . . They knew of one priest who had despoiled 13 virgins."

Lodge gave Diem a now-familiar piece of advice: lose Nhu. Get him out of the country while the US Congress weighed further military and economic assistance to South Vietnam and until the United Nations investigation had run its course. Yet Diem still was adamant that his brother had been "unjustly accused" of masterminding the pagoda raids and that the strategic hamlet program that Americans so loved would run off the rails without Nhu. Diem said, "If American opinion is in the state you describe then it is up to you, Ambassador Lodge, to disintoxicate American opinion." Lodge replied, "I would be only too glad to do so if you would give me something with which to work."

Reading this account, Assistant Secretary of State for Far Eastern Affairs Roger Hilsman told Lodge to "continue frequent conversations with

Diem, although all recognize how frustrating these are."[3] The instructions were clear enough, but Lodge had no appetite for the "extremely time-consuming procedure" of a call on President Diem: "It seems to me there are many better ways in which I can use my waking hours."[4]

Lodge on his own recognizance thus adopted the approach that confounded not just President Diem but President Kennedy and his men: Lodge would kill Diem with silence. Even when Washington begged him to engage, Lodge declined: "I would rather let him sweat for a while and not go to see him unless I have something really new to bring up."[5]

John Mecklin, for his part, said, "Lodge's strategy suggested a shrewd understanding of human nature. He knew that any approach to him from the palace, especially in face-conscious Asia, could only be tantamount to surrender. The technique not only preserved but exploited American dignity, in effect turning an Asian characteristic against Asians, yet it never closed the door to reconciliation—on American terms."[6] Ambassador Lodge would work with symbols, with actions and not words.

The storming of the pagodas and a state of martial law had not brought peace to the streets. In September, "a form of madness seemed to take over in Saigon," recalled David Halberstam. "Having crushed the Buddhists, the government had moved against college students, and having crushed them, moved against high school students, and after they were crushed, and finding rebellion in [Vietnamese] elementary schools, it cracked down on them, closing those schools too. In hundreds of homes, brothers and sisters had been arrested."[7] Many were the offspring of South Vietnamese civil servants and military personnel, not a good move or sign for the regime.

Buddhist self-immolations went on, too, with more of them constantly rumored. Mordant humor reigned among the American diplomats, with brittle talk of "Buddhist cookouts" and "hot cross bonzes." Mecklin said he heard that a boy at the American Community School, an embassy officer's son, had "poured gasoline on his clothes and struck a match" and was seriously burned. "I wanted to see what it was like," the boy was quoted as saying.[8] I feel very sure I would have heard about this if it really happened, but I didn't. But I was playing with fire, too. My pal Greg Manfull and I figured out how to make Molotov cocktails using empty Coke bottles and gasoline stealthily siphoned out of the Mercedes. We tested the incendiary devices against the wall of an empty lot next to my house, with what I recall were disappointing results.

A Separate Peace

As summer turned to autumn another singular character was maneuvering in the Saigon shadows. Mieczysław Maneli, a Polish lawyer and diplomat newly posted to Vietnam, would personally engage another significant what-if of the history of the Vietnam morass: the possibility in late 1963 of a negotiated settlement, or a "neutralist" coalition, between South and North Vietnam—and an off-ramp for the United States from the road to a wider war.

The idea of negotiating with the North was not exactly new. Averell Harriman had had an elaborately secret meeting with the North Vietnamese foreign minister at the Hotel Suisse in Geneva the year before while the Laos negotiations went on. It came to nothing. Ngo Dinh Nhu had been preaching the idea for months, rattling American diplomats, as was his intention. Whether Diem believed in the idea is a mystery, but Washington continued to doubt it, given his deep-rooted anticommunism; their older brother, after all, had been executed nearly twenty years before on orders of Ho Chi Minh.

But as Diem's position weakened in the summer of 1963, Brother Nhu's stature and menace could only grow. Evidence that Nhu was preparing his own takeover proliferated. Supposedly official photographs of Diem in government facilities around Vietnam were being removed and replaced by ones of Nhu wearing military regalia. Some in the embassy, and thus in Washington, feared a fratricidal coup that might deliver South Vietnam into a neutralist arrangement with North Vietnam.

Whether any of this was a serious prospect or not, the hypothesis went as follows, per Georgetown University's Francis X. Winters in his book *The Year of the Hare:* Ho and Diem had each concluded that "the cost being exacted by China from Ho and by the United States from Diem was too high a price to pay." Stating the matter with intentional melodrama, Winters went on: "Now was the dangerous hour of emancipation . . . from the colonial controls of Washington and Peking. Now Diem had decided that it would be 'sink or swim with Ho Chi Minh.' Independence would be an all-Vietnamese dream."[9]

Making matters more vexing yet for the United States was the president of France, the redoubtable Charles de Gaulle. On the fourth day of Kennedy's daily crisis meetings about Vietnam, August 29, the French president had made a subtle but, to Washington, deafening public call for a negotiated settlement to the Vietnam War. De Gaulle's diabolical scheme, as it was seen in Washington eyes, was to wrest his country's former colonial domain from the hands of the Americans and reintroduce it to dependence on the great civilizing and economic power that was France.

However much the United States wanted to end or extract itself from the conflict, doing so on anything that resembled de Gaulle's terms, let alone Hanoi's or Moscow's, was a great deal to swallow.

Mieczysław Maneli was not a conventional diplomat. A Jew who had survived Auschwitz, a law professor and author who had been in Saigon in the mid-1950s, and a stalwart member of the Polish Communist Party, Maneli was posted in early 1963 to a tripartite international entity in Vietnam called the International Control Commission (ICC).

The ICC was a three-headed diplomatic beast created under the Geneva Accords to monitor the observance of their terms by North and South Vietnam, notably proscriptions against the introduction of foreign troops or forming military alliances. Composed of three flavors—pro-Washington (Canada), "neutral" (India), and pro-Moscow (Poland)—the ICC representatives might be compared to high-school hall monitors, who really don't have any power except ratting out the truants, if they could agree on the truancies, or count them.

The monitoring was largely a farce. Both Hanoi and Saigon had walked away long since from their Geneva commitments, with their patron-paymasters looking the other way. Yet the ICC triad remained useful. They had letters of transit, as it were, a plane at their disposal, and entrées in Hanoi to match those in Saigon, which made them valuable sources of information, back-channeling, and occasional mischief.

With the encouragement of his superiors in Warsaw, who would not have been acting without the tacit approval of theirs in Moscow, Maneli that spring of 1963 and again in July had gone to see Ho Chi Minh and Pham Van Dong, the North Vietnamese prime minister and, along with Le Duan, the power behind the throne in Hanoi.

Maneli noted the aging Ho's apparent warmth for his longtime adversary Ngo Dinh Diem, whom he called "a patriot in his own way." What conditions, asked Maneli, would the North set on negotiating with the South? "One thing is sure," Pham Van Dong replied: "The Americans have to leave. On this political basis, we can negotiate anything"—including a coalition government, and the personal safety of Diem and Nhu. "We are realists," said Dong.[10]

To take the key next step, Maneli was introduced into the orbit of Ngo Dinh Nhu by a colorful Saigon trio of would-be peacemakers consisting of the French ambassador, the Italian ambassador, and the papal nuncio. The moment of contact finally came in late August at a huge diplomatic reception in Saigon hosted by the brand-new foreign minister of South Vietnam, his predecessor having quit in protest three days before.

When Maneli was drawn "accidentally" (his quotes) into a circle around Brother Nhu, the latter made it clear he knew exactly what Maneli was up to. A private meeting was fixed for six days hence. But the evening before that rendezvous, Maneli was summoned urgently to the residence of the French ambassador, Roger Lalouette, who'd been in Saigon since 1958. The Frenchman told his guest he doubted the Nhu meeting would take place because the rumored coup d'état was to take place "*tonight*"! Maneli wrote: "I tried to remain calm and remarked only, 'We have expected this for a long time. Since Lodge's arrival, the regime's days have been numbered.'"[11]

What emerged that night from Lalouette's triste soliloquy, as his hopes and Charles de Gaulle's seemed to be crumbling, was this: a coup to remove Diem would wreck the chances for rapprochement between North and South, and "the last—small, it is true—chance for peace would be lost."

The French ambassador offered Maneli further evidence that the interest of the North Vietnamese in a settlement was real: a dog that didn't bark. Hanoi had not taken military advantage of the summer turmoil in the south—holding back, Lalouette thought, to be sure they had a sovereign partner to deal with in the putative peace talks. A strange twist, but no stranger than many other that summer. The enemy wanted to overthrow the Diem regime but seemingly not just yet, not when they could do it at a negotiating table one-to-one, "without the participation of the Great Powers."[12]

Maneli is a winning memoirist: "If Lalouette wished me to inform 'the socialist camp' of all these happenings, I did not disappoint him." Within half an hour his report had reached Hanoi, Warsaw, and Moscow.

The imminent coup having been only the latest mirage, Maneli saw Brother Nhu the next day as scheduled. In the course of a long monologue

Nhu painted himself to the Polish Communist as a highly flexible patriot, a postcapitalist who accepted "certain Marxist theses."

Comrade Nhu explained: "Capitalism is a spiritual and economic format foreign to our nation. The Saigon plutocrats . . . are strangers to me. I have no intentions of defending their interests. Their fortunes should serve all the people, and I will be the first to carry this out, even before the Communists and more consistently than the Communists."[13] As for Marxism, the personalist guru declaimed, "I agree with Marx's final conclusion: the state must wither away—this is a condition for the final triumph of democracy. The sense of my life is to work so that I can become unnecessary."

Those in the CIA and embassy who believed Nhu was losing his mind would have had more fodder for that dossier with this conversation, which they may well have overheard. Maneli reported the exchange to the Soviet ambassador in Hanoi and his military back channel with the North Vietnamese government. They responded enthusiastically and called the contact "momentous," as indeed it was, seen in historical and counterfactual light. They told Maneli to come at once to Hanoi for consultations on next steps.

The shifty Nhu told quite a different version of the meeting when he saw the CIA's John Richardson on September 6. Reporting on his parley with Maneli, Brother Nhu said he had responded coolly, with words to the effect of, "SVN is allied with US and it would be 'immoral act' to explore such a problem unilaterally behind backs of Americans." Richardson cabled that Nhu insisted he was "adamantly opposed to neutralism, although [I] had not brought up this subject" and ruled out negotiations with Hanoi "either openly or secretly, except after having won guerrilla war and . . . seeking to incorporate North Vietnam within free world order."[14]

In Maneli's telling a more senior Polish diplomatic official soon scotched the incipient plan for negotiations, and events in South Vietnam quickly took their course. Maneli believes he knows why a settlement was anathema to Moscow, and Peking too, for that matter: because it posed the threat of another intractable nationalist—"Titoist," in the term of the day—state. In Maneli's judgment, "Neither of them wanted peace and a sovereign, independent Vietnam. Rather, both wanted the Americans to remain embroiled in Southeast Asia indefinitely so that they could make political capital at their expense."[15]

Thomas Hughes, the State Department intelligence chief, said everyone was fully aware of the supposed parleying between North and South in this period. "Some of us thought it was a very good idea because it'd get us out of the place."[16] Looking back twenty-seven years later, Robert Miller was scathing about the American official mind-set on a settlement: "We were convinced this was not in the US interest. 'How *dare* they negotiate a compromise of some kind with Hanoi!' Today that seems almost unbelievable."[17]

What thought our two Virginians of this? Asked many years later by oral historians, they sound much like themselves.

Nolting said he had a tolerant view of Nhu's dalliances with the North. He knew that his view was at odds with the alarm he sensed from Washington. He understood that emissaries from Hanoi could visit Nhu in his office under "a gentleman's agreement that they wouldn't be nabbed while they were there." Nolting thought it a useful channel to keep open. He said he had tried in vain to tell the State Department, "Wait a minute, maybe this isn't so treasonable. Maybe this is the way to compose this thing. Give them a chance. They're not all that stupid, and they're not going to betray us."[18]

Of Brother Nhu's separate-peace boomlet, Trueheart said, "I think it was a lot of horseshit." Ultimately, "I don't think the VC would have given Nhu the time of day. It's just something he would put out, you know—disinformation. . . . To confuse people, he was quite ready do anything, say anything."[19]

The Go-Between

Now that he had a confident ambassador in Saigon, with clearance and swagger enough to act, the CIA's Lucien Conein pursued his coup facilitation with new vim. Wholly bucking procedure, and cutting out John Richardson, the station chief, Ambassador Lodge dealt with the CIA agent directly and privately. In congressional testimony a dozen years later, Conein recalled that Lodge "would fold a piece of paper [to show] what pertained to you for instructions. He would let you read that, and that alone, so that you didn't know who was sending it or where it came from. He said, 'These are the instructions, do you understand them?' 'Yes, sir.' 'All right, go carry them out.'" The deniable communications ran in both directions. Conein was a notoriously incompetent typist—and with reason, as he had lost two fingers on his right hand. So he would read to Lodge from his indecipherable scribbled notes.[20]

Dealing with the slippery cast of plotting Vietnamese generals was a memorably unsettling experience for Conein: "If you had three Vietnamese generals sitting and talking to you, one general would go out of the room to go to the john, and the other two would tell you, 'Don't trust that one.' And finally the one would outwait the other two so he was the only one left, and he would say, 'Don't trust those two.'"[21] Conein had to live by his wits. He was the only conduit the Vietnamese generals trusted.

On September 4, Lucien Conein had a four-hour meeting with the newly named military governor of Saigon, Brigadier General Ton That Dinh. Dinh's loyalties were known to be fluid, but in mid-August, the Ngos had felt confident enough to put him in charge of 2,500 paratroopers, 1,500 marines, and 700 military police in the South Vietnamese capital. Colonel Tung's special forces, presidential guards, and combat police were the other defensive bulwark for the regime, and a marginally more loyal one.

Conein had known Dinh a long time, but on this day he found the general unhinged, paranoid, megalomaniacal. His report on the meeting, describing himself in the third person, is a mesmerizing glimpse of the unreality of that time and place:

"Flanked by soldiers [who] continued to point their submachine guns at Col. Conein throughout [the] meeting and during lunch," General Dinh was "exultant, ranting, raving," calling himself "the man of the hour" and the "Napoleon of Vietnam." He "rushed around the room gesticulating wildly at maps on the wall insisting that entire city was surrounded by Communists." He called the American reporters all Communists. Also John Mecklin. Also the American "trash" protecting the Buddhist asylees in the embassy. "Dinh demanded to know if Trueheart and Richardson were on Dinh's side" and "was assured (at gunpoint) that they were." He "screamed" that he had a "figurative *bombe atomique* to drop on the Americans, quite possibly in the next two or three days."[22]

Before Conein could leave, Dinh insisted on taking an incriminating photograph of the two of them toasting one another. He said he would give the photo to Conein after Dinh triumphed as Vietnam's "man of destiny" because it would have marked "a moment of great historical significance." In her husband's presence the manic general got Elyette Conein on the telephone and "congratulated her on her opportunity to converse with the military governor of Saigon." He dropped the phone to order that flowers be sent to her. Then he insisted Conein drink "liquid vitamins mixed with whiskey. This, according to Dinh, was to make Conein strong like the general."

Such reports from inside the plot, featuring characters the United States was risking its credibility to thrust into governance, could have done nothing to inspire confidence in anyone in the embassy or in Washington. The other senior Vietnamese generals, however, had Dinh's number.

A Death in the Family

As intense maneuvering continued in the shadows, on September 10, 1963, William Cheatham Trueheart died in Chester, Virginia, at the age of eighty-seven, after a hip fracture and a long period of frailty. My mother told me the news. When my father came home from work, I ran up to him in the Blue Room and put my arms around his waist and blurted out, "I'm sorry about your father." Bill hugged me back and said, almost correctively, "He was your grandfather too."

Bill did not go back to Chester for the funeral. He asked the State Department that his half sister Rose be telephoned in Leesburg with his excuses: "Overseas telephone service Saigon suspended during martial law. Not possible for me to leave post and family at this time. Deeply sorry not to be able to help." I always assumed it was because Lodge couldn't spare him during a highly charged moment. Fritz Nolting likewise had not been able to return for his mother's funeral the year before, when things were far less tense. That seemed the price far-flung diplomats paid. But in a letter that week to Sallie, the deceased's long-ago ex-wife, my mother suggested another reason Bill stayed in Saigon and let others bury his father: he was concerned about his nuclear family's safety.

Thanking Sallie for the obituary clippings from Virginia newspapers, Phoebe wrote: "Bill felt so sad not to get there, but as you know it was impossible. He didn't want to leave us (situation here VERY delicate). He hopes to get home this fall to settle the estate, but it looks pretty dire as of today. (Read Alsop's columns from Vietnam.)"

In this letter, Phoebe recorded a recurring scene in the Blue Room that gives electric evidence of the strain my father was under, not to mention the sanctity of the cocktail hour and the indispensability of the amah. Josh Trueheart, not yet three, "drives Bill out of his mind—and often has to be removed from the study at cocktail time because he makes papa so nervous. He is *very* loud and boisterous, knocks over drinks (although he is *not* clumsy). He brings his trucks in and Bill is too weary to be amused. He flies like the wind, whizzes around the coffee table, and Bill is 'too old' to cope. Charlie thinks I let Josh get away with murder, which I guess I do."

This could not have been entirely reassuring to Bill's mother, nor Phoebe's reference to the latest news Sallie had doubtlessly read about in Richmond. In mid-September, a Viet Cong terrorist burst through the swinging rear doors of the Capital Kinh Do movie theater, an American community magnet, and set off a bomb that killed a US Marine. I was on my bike five minutes away, five minutes late to arrive for the show and for the bombing. "I can't tell you why I am so calm," Phoebe wrote. Her husband, *chargé* again while Lodge was in Honolulu, made the call to keep the theater open. Per Phoebe: "We *can't* demoralize 20,000 Americans by closing."[23]

Phoebe may seem to get short shrift in this narrative, but she was very present in my life at the time, perforce more present than my father. He was more of a distant example, she more of an active tutor. Upliftingly, sometimes shockingly, Phoebe pushed the boundaries of my age in naming things that were generally unacknowledged. By example and encouragement, she taught me skills (or hobgoblins) of discernment, good taste and bad, the power of the written word and the joy of its exercise.

She was unself-consciously fun. Waiting in the Blue Room for Bill to come home, she would put a Chubby Checker record on the Victrola so we could learn the Twist together. In contrast to her husband she was a physical person, proud to have been a tomboy, and a versatile athlete disappointed that I took no interest in such. A young lifetime of unlearned "lessons"—golf, tennis, riding, judo—went to apparent waste.

In the same letter of late September Phoebe shared with Sallie the news that the Trueharts would be returning to Washington in the spring: "We'll be sorry to leave here in spite of the hell-hole it has become. Charlie has suffered the most. He hates it." I would have said just the opposite; she may have been projecting, or I may be forgetting. Meanwhile, she was taking me to Hong Kong in a few days. "I had promised him the trip for his birthday instead of a party. Bill will be busy with McN. and Taylor, and we are keeping Mike Forrestal, so they don't need me."

I looked forward to a few days away with my mother (and out of school), staying in a fancy hotel in Hong Kong and shopping for an English bicycle and a watch. On the plane to Hong Kong, the bar service having made its rounds, she told me for the first time about the business with Fritz, the story of the last few months, the rupture, the awkwardness (had I noticed?) of the Noltings' departure, the sadness in our families. I was engrossed, bewildered, and began a lifetime of stewing about the whole thing.

The Efficiency Report

One day in September, Bill brought home from the embassy mailroom a letter to me from Jane Nolting, writing from Danville around the time of the pagoda raids. Apparently this was the first any of us had heard from any of them since they left Saigon.

Considering what you might expect from the foregoing, and what other Noltings say now about what the family had been through, it's surprising now to read Jane breezily telling me: "I guess you heard about our terrific trip back from mama and daddy. If you come back by Greece take a sail. It was wonderful. (If you have a tough stomach: poor mama and Lindsay and Molly were seasick most of the time.) Saigon sounds terribly agitated (by the press). How do you like the sounds of H. C. Lodge? Yesterday we saw him on TV but he obviously had his mind on his nose, which he kept scratching, and not on the questions of his interviewers."

Jane reported they'd also seen their father on television: "He was very good and made a good impression. I have been indoctrinating the people of Danville on VN. They know very little about anything and almost everybody here is pro-Goldwater for '64, which is proof of their ignorance. . . . I am by far the best talker at the golf club poolside." Having just turned fifteen, Jane had gotten her learner's permit to drive—"up and down grandmama's driveway and her flowers have suffered many casualties." She was preparing to enroll at Chatham Hall, a proper girls' school in southern Virginia, and she wasn't looking forward to it. She longed for news of Saigon—"something to cheer me and enlighten my heavy heart." She closed: "When are yall getting a transfer? . . . You'll hate America. I do. People treat you like a nut. I'm developing a superiority complex. With cause. Love, Jane."[24]

I was not the only member of the family who heard from a Nolting. A few days after his father died, Bill received a personal letter from Fritz on State Department letterhead. It was probably the first communication between them in a month. The cover note made a stab at concealing or softening the shiv the envelope contained: his final report on his deputy's performance as *chargé:*

"I have thought about you all constantly during the last month. Since getting back to the Department some three weeks ago, I have been doing what I could to help on Vietnamese problems here. I have also put a self-restraining order on myself against public speeches, etc."

In the second paragraph, before signing off with "our love to Phoebe and the boys," Fritz turned formal: "I am sending you herewith a copy of a report which I have made today to the Personnel Division. I regret having to do this, but feel it is my duty to do so. I, of course, want you to have the opportunity and to feel free to comment on my report."

Curiously the report he enclosed was dated August 17, just two days after Nolting left Saigon, when he was crossing the Pacific.[25] But seemingly it had been delivered only recently, uncooled by the passage of time. (Bill could hardly complain about being kept out of the loop.) In the formal, impersonal language of a performance assessment—"efficiency report" was then the State Department term of art—Nolting wished to record "the following reservation" to his earlier consistently superlative evaluations of his deputy, "the highest efficiency ratings I have ever given."

Nolting stated that his travel schedule during his absence from Saigon from late May to early July "was known in detail to Mr. Trueheart," whom he had asked to "advise me, en route, of any changes in the situation in Vietnam in order that I might be up-to-date upon my arrival in the United States." Nolting went on to say that Trueheart, "through no fault of his own," faced a crisis after his departure that "was of such magnitude as to threaten to destroy the base on which United States policy in Vietnam was founded."

Trueheart had furthermore "failed to let me know of these developments. This was contrary to our understanding and, in my view, not in keeping with the responsibilities and loyalties of a Deputy Chief of Mission to a Chief of Mission, irrespective of previous understandings."

Nolting wrote he and Trueheart had "discussed the matter thoroughly"—gentleman talk for their angry confrontation after Nolting returned to Saigon—and he granted that there were "certain extenuating circumstances." But, he concluded, "neither the fast-moving and unpredictable situation in Vietnam, nor his heavy workload, was sufficient in my view to justify or excuse his failure to let me know, inasmuch as these matters clearly affected my responsibilities and my duty as ambassador."[26]

This was probably the last thing Nolting ever communicated to his old friend. I believe it is the formal questioning of his "loyalties" that Trueheart found most outrageous, knowing it would blot his permanent record. What to some eyes might seem a mild rebuke, and Nolting himself cast as a mere "reservation," appears to have been the bone of contention, the mortal insult, that Bill took to his grave.

Is it possible that Bill never imagined his old friend would make his anger so official and so personal? Or that Bill had misjudged the depth of Fritz's ire? And when they had hashed it out together in Saigon in July, did Bill never tell Fritz that the decision not to keep him posted was not his own? Perhaps because it had been? Or that the situation with Diem was hopeless and that Washington had concluded as much as well?

Not long ago I showed this 1963 efficiency report to a distinguished American foreign policy veteran. Anthony Lake had been in his first Foreign Service posting in Saigon that long-ago summer and worked, way down the line in the consular section, for Fritz and Bill. Reading the report with me over dinner in early 2020, Lake at eighty gamely volunteered exegesis to Nolting's text: "It's a classic anal-retentive American diplomat who was really pissed, and really feeling betrayed if he was willing to go to this length." Lake mocked Nolting's disingenuousness: "'neither of us anticipated any changes in the situation . . .' On August 17, 1963? Are you effing kidding me? . . . 'threaten to destroy the base on which United States policy in Vietnam was founded' . . . a base which was fatally flawed ever since Diem came to power! And we knew it!"

In a situation like the one Trueheart was in, Lake told me, "You're not caught between a rock and a hard place. You're sitting on the rock, which is the hard place at the same time." As for the official condemnation of his deputy, Lake said, "If you're a professional, you don't go outside and trash the people you're working with. It's tribal. You may disagree with them, but you're a tribe."

But what about Trueheart's failure to keep Nolting informed? That was something else. Lake seemed to find Bill's lapse as confounding as I did. "Chargé is French for something, after all. You should keep the ambassador informed—especially if he's your best friend. Unless, of course, he was being told not to."[27]

Perhaps the weight of Nolting's decorous damnation of his old friend may be judged better by the immediate reaction of Trueheart's defenders. They were alarmed by Nolting's report, knowing it was the kind of thing that could sink a Foreign Service career. They knew, too, that if Trueheart was tarnished, the tarnish had originated with *them*, with the coup-plotting cabal that gave Trueheart his orders.

Referring to Trueheart's seven weeks of crisis management as *chargé d'affaires* in Saigon, Averell Harriman wished "to state for the record my admiration of his performance. Not only did he carry out his instructions skillfully and forcefully, but he displayed unusual resourcefulness and imagination in analyzing the developing situation and making recommendations. . . . Mr. Trueheart's performance under pressure leads me to the judgment that he is fully qualified to become head of a diplomatic mission at an appropriate time."[28] Harriman later said the report had been "very unfair of Nolting. He put in the record that Trueheart had been disloyal to him. . . . It's a very bad thing for a man to do that."[29]

For his part, Roger Hilsman wrote the director of personnel a specific rebuttal to Nolting's displeasure "that he was not called to return to Saigon during the Buddhist crisis." Hilsman said the subject had come up repeatedly "whether he should not be recalled from leave and sent back to take charge." Hilsman said that in each case, in consultation with the secretary of state, he decided "that it was not necessary."

To Trueheart directly Hilsman wrote, "Everyone here in Washington thinks you've done an outstanding job in very difficult circumstances." Making concrete that esteem, Hilsman got to the point: Knowing that Trueheart's Saigon tour was up the following spring, he said he thought he "should now serve a couple of years in Washington to get the feel of this end of things at a high level." He offered him, "if you are interested," the job of running Southeast Asia at the State Department, as one of Hilsman's principal deputies. "If all goes well, I think you can look toward following that to an ambassadorship."[30]

Trueheart received this letter on September 16, possibly even before he had seen the Nolting report itself.

I do not know whether my father replied to Nolting. I would guess not. It was over between them.

A Sinking Ship of State

Also on September 16, Mike Forrestal wrote McGeorge Bundy a long memorandum baring his frustration with the "stall in our attempts to develop a Washington consensus" about Vietnam. His description of the forces and personalities in tension "within the President's official family" perfectly mirrors the ones that developed inside the Country Team in Saigon during the spring and summer of 1963: "On the one hand, Averell sees a world in which the only successful way to resist the Communist menace is to provide the people concerned with an alternative worth fighting for. On the other hand, to Bob McNamara the issue is . . . if enough of the enemy can be identified and killed by methods his department has been so successful in developing there will be time to concentrate on the political and social welfare of the people. Each fundamentally views the other's position as an impractical one."[31] More fact-finding and more information, Forrestal said, won't change anything. What's needed was "presidential guidance," he told Bundy, a nice way of saying Kennedy was wavering and uncertain about the best path forward. Kennedy needed to "grasp the nettle." As time went by, making a choice "will become more painful."

Wise counsel, but President Kennedy was not ready. He wanted more fact-finding missions to Vietnam. The first of them was a lightning visit by a lower-profile tandem: Major General Victor "Brute" Krulak of the US Marines and FSO Joseph Mendenhall, the ex–political counselor in Saigon. Dean Rusk had insisted on adding Mendenhall just as Krulak, Taylor's eyes and ears, was about to head to Saigon alone. Both Krulak and Mendenhall were respected, experienced hands, and they couldn't stand each other.

They left Washington on September 6 and were back to the White House to report what they had found by September 10. They barely spoke during the ten thousand miles out, went their separate ways in Vietnam, and barely spoke on the flight back. Their back-to-back assessments were so laughably at odds that President Kennedy famously remarked, when he had heard them out, "The two of you did visit the same country, didn't you?" Yes, they had. Krulak had embedded with the senior US military in the provinces, where the view continued to be optimistic, whereas Mendenhall had embedded with his former colleagues in the US embassy—and stayed with the Trueharts—in Saigon, where most everyone thought the regime was doomed.

Back at the White House, citing Bill Trueheart as someone who shared his view, Mendenhall told the president and his circle that a "reign of terror" existed in Saigon and that the war against the Viet Cong could not be won with the Ngos in power. Fritz Nolting, present for the penultimate time at a White House meeting on Vietnam, challenged his former political counselor. He reminded him that he had been bearish on the regime from the outset—how could Mendenhall "rationalize how, in the ensuing years, so much progress had been made by a government which he forecast could not survive?"[32] President Kennedy interrupted, and Mendenhall didn't have a chance to answer.

John Mecklin, the embassy press officer, and Rufus Phillips, the pacification czar, had joined Krulak and Mendenhall on the plane back to Washington. Both Mecklin and Phillips were given lengthy hearings at this White House meeting. Phillips said neither Krulak nor Mendenhall had painted an accurate picture of what was going on. When President Kennedy asked for his view on the military situation, Phillips said, "I am sorry to have to tell you, Mr. President, but we are not winning the war, particularly in the Delta."[33]

Krulak mocked Phillips for "putting his views over those of General Harkins." Nolting was furious at Phillips, telling him privately afterward that he had "ruined everything." When word got back to Harkins in Saigon about Phillips's gloomy assessment at the White House, he, too, was enraged. He declared at a dinner party hosted by the Truehearts that he was going to "get that god-damned Rufus Phillips." Phoebe's "sweet" reply in her "soft southern accent" forever won Phillips's heart: "But General, he doesn't work for you."[34]

By now Nolting's star had faded, and it was easy to see why. When he was asked by a Kennedy aide at his next, and last, White House meeting to jot down three things the administration could do to get things "back on the track with Diem," Nolting was bold to propose, as item three, "a concrete demonstration of our President's purpose—specifically, replacing Lodge and Harriman."[35]

Kennedy glanced at the piece of paper and, as he left the meeting, muttered sideways to Nolting, "You don't expect me to do *that*, do you?"

Weighing in from Saigon, Lodge was as gloomy as Mendenhall. "The ship of state here is slowly sinking," he wrote in a long and eloquent analysis of the situation. He explained the deterioration of Diem's support among South Vietnam's elites, civilian and military, with this powerful illustration: "Consider the lieutenant in the Vietnamese army whose father has been imprisoned; whose mother has seen her religion insulted, if not persecuted, whose older brother has had an arbitrary fine imposed on him—and who all hate the government with good reason. Can the lieutenant be indifferent to that? Now come the high school demonstrations and the fact that the lieutenant's younger brother has been dragged off in a truck (bearing the US insignia)."[36] In a personal message back to Lodge, Kennedy said "your courageous and searching analysis has already been of great help, and . . . the strength and dignity of your position on the scene are clear."[37]

General Harkins, however, wasn't buying any of this doom and gloom. In a message to General Krulak after the visit, the commander of US forces in South Vietnam reliably served up a glass more than half full of silliness:

> The battle here is not lost by any manner of means. In fact it's being won. . . . We are fighting a ruthless, crude, brutal enemy who is using every known trick in the Communist bag. In 1960 he saw he was losing the initial round so he openly flexed his biceps. . . . We're stronger physically, mentally, and morally than the enemy. We must be stronger in our will, determination, and sacrifice. No, we haven't lost this one by a long shot and we must not take counsel in our fears. Perhaps some of the tools are tired and worn . . . so it's another must for us to sharpen the cutting edges of the old or come up with something new, and get on with the offensive. "Amen."[38]

McNamara and Taylor were unpersuaded by Mendenhall and Lodge's doomsaying, too—so Kennedy sent *them* to Saigon two weeks later.

"Lousy, General"

Lodge rapidly reached the same conclusion as his forebears about the utility of high-level visits from Washington. Ahead of the big McNamara-Taylor tour, Lodge sent the secretary of state a dyspeptic dismissal that echoed the Saigon embassy's message traffic of a year before: "It is inconceivable to me that direct questions asked on a whirlwind tour of the countryside can possibly elicit any new and deep insights into the situation which you do not already possess." Trueheart felt just the same way: "They were mostly wheel-spinning. When you couldn't make up your mind what to do, you'd always send another team out to Vietnam to talk to the same people, ask the same questions, and go back."[39]

Lodge wrote President Kennedy personally on September 18 to object to the McNamara-Taylor mission. Such a visit would necessitate a visit to President Diem with Lodge in tow and "will be taken as a sign that we have decided to forgive and forget." And "it would certainly put a wet blanket on those working for a change of government."[40] The ambassador wrote with pride that his "policy of silence" was working to put the Ngos "into the mood to make a few concessions"—an advantage lost if the McNamara and Taylor mission went ahead.

As it did, after Kennedy wrote endearingly and flatteringly to Lodge to reassure him the visitors wouldn't undercut what he was trying to do. "Having grown up in an Ambassador's house," Kennedy wrote—his father, Joseph P. Kennedy, had been President Franklin Roosevelt's ambassador in London—"I am well trained in the importance of protecting the effectiveness of the man on-the-spot."[41]

The McNamara visit lasted seven days, a much bigger and longer affair than the Krulak-Mendenhall drop-by of just two weeks before. Also on board were Mike Forrestal from the White House and the three Bills: Bundy from the Pentagon, Colby from the CIA, and Sullivan from the State Department. (Colby would be immediately shut out on arrival; Lodge, assuming his prerogatives as the American viceroy, forbade him to meet any of his former Vietnamese contacts, and that made Colby sore.)[42]

McNamara and Taylor met all the Saigon players, including the coup plotters (not billed as such, of course), and ranged around the country. According to hospitality protocol, General Taylor stayed with General Harkins, and McNamara stayed with Lodge. In one of their daily debriefings at the residence, the ambassador (and reserve major general) gave a warning to the secretary of defense: "I do doubt the value of answers which are given by young officers to direct questions by Generals—or, for that matter, Ambassadors. The urge to give an optimistic and favorable answer is quite insurmountable—and understandable."[43]

Yet some younger officers got through. While visiting a remote Vietnamese military camp where captured Viet Cong arms were on display for the visiting dignitaries, McNamara pointed to a weapon and asked, "Is this Chinese?" The South Vietnamese officer leading the tour had to tell the American secretary of defense that it was "a regular 57-mm. recoilless rifle which they captured earlier from us." In another encounter with

American officers in Can Tho, General Taylor asked a young major how things were going. "Lousy, General," came the answer. When he explained his negative assessment, the other officers jumped in to add theirs. "All hell broke loose," said Forrestal.[44]

Meeting with Diem for two hours, McNamara pressed him on Madame Nhu's outrageous and unhelpful comments, which Diem dodged in the usual manner: "One cannot deny a lady the right to defend herself when she has been unjustly attacked."[45] President Diem came away from the meeting believing he had cleared everything up, making it obvious even to those who wanted to believe in him that he had heard nothing. "You could just see it bouncing off him," Taylor said.[46]

Calling on Vice President Nguyen Ngoc Tho, the evergreen "constitutional successor" to Diem the Americans always talked about, General Taylor was taken aback when he heard (through interpreters) Tho's frank assessment that "there are not more than 20 or 30 properly defended strategic hamlets in the whole country," this at a time when Nhu was claiming more than a thousand existed.

Vice President Tho's next comment, as Lodge repeated it back to Washington, was just as sobering: "Why do you gentlemen think that the Viet Cong is still so popular? Two years ago there were between 20–30,000 in the Viet Cong army; for these last years we have been killing a thousand a month; and yet the Viet Cong is even larger today. Why is this true? . . . The answer is they stay in the Viet Cong army because they want to, and the reason they want to is their extreme discontent with the Government of Vietnam."[47] Yes, this was Diem's handpicked sitting vice president.

The strangest moment on the trip was a tennis game. Duong Van Minh, the senior general leading the coup plotting, had expressed interest in direct contact with the visitors from Washington. Taylor and McNamara met him at Saigon Officers' Club, and they played tennis for two hours. Maddeningly, surreally, Minh refused to be drawn into any discussion of any coup. "As far as he was concerned, the occasion was simply a game of tennis," Taylor told McNamara.[48] A subsequent private meeting between Taylor and Minh also yielded nothing of interest. Minh and the other generals were more comfortable dealing with the CIA's Lucien Conein.

The report the visitors cobbled together on the plane back to Washington was, for Forrestal, one of its authors, a "mishmash of everything," from rosy scenarios to thinly veiled despair. It did give President Kennedy one thing he wanted—a horizon on the war. Its first iteration was the withdrawal of one thousand American military personnel by the end of 1963, as a prelude to total withdrawal—contingent on a stable government and a thriving war effort—by the end of 1965.

After the visit, the astute Bill Sullivan put his views starkly to Harriman. "The ultimate objectives of the United States in Vietnam do not coincide with the Diem-Nhu objectives"—that was his premise:

> The question is not, therefore, whether we can win with this regime but rather whether we want this regime to have the benefits of such a victory for purposes which are contrary not only to our objectives but also to our interests. The fact is that Nhu is exploiting two principal elements of power to produce his totalitarian state. The first is the Vietnamese establishment—that educated, propertied leadership class which makes up the military officer class, the bureaucracy and the Vietnamese portion of the business community. The second is the military power of the United States.

Sullivan said Nhu would dispatch the establishment through "liquidation" and the Americans "by a deal with North Vietnam." He said, "I therefore conclude that it is in our interest to make common cause with [the establishment] to overthrow the current regime."[49]

Sanctuary

It is seldom that one glimpses (or that I remember) Phoebe interacting on a serious level with Vietnamese people. But in a characteristically discursive typed letter to three couples, the Truehearts' best friends in Washington, she talked about their life in Saigon in late September 1963 in respects that were entirely lost on me at the time.

Writing with more gravity than in her flightier accounts to her mother, Phoebe captured the siege of apprehension gripping Saigon in the end days of the Diem era:

> Bill is definitely "*mal vu au palais.*" [in bad odor at the palace] Mme Nhu has called Bill a "*dur*"—tough customer. She told one reporter she blames the whole thing on Bill. The majority give us a wide berth as they are so scared of being "seen" with us—little eyes and ears are everywhere. Our phone is definitely bugged. We play loud music when anyone comes to call, Americans or Vietnamese. Anybody Vietnamese has to be brave to see us at

all. . . . They are petrified. They have to be pretty desperate to come here. It must be their last chance.

I've received two visits from Vietnamese ladies, which in itself is amazing for these times. These two ladies, one week apart, sought sanctuary.

One is a leading businesswoman, a widow, who is known to be anti-Diem. She wanted me to get her on a plane, military or CIA I guess, over the frontier and into Cambodia. I talked to her for two hours, in French, explaining that I had my little children to think of, did not want police beating down my doors, and more important we are not *supposed* to keep people who are wanted by the GVN. She pointed out we were keeping three bonzes in the Embassy. She had me there—but it isn't the same. I turned soft after two hours, then went off to a reception where I tried to enlist another friend of hers, a Canadian brigadier, to help—*he* had a plane. Don't you love me in the role of Mata Hari? With no fun attached, I might add.

In the meantime Bill came home, heard the same story, and showed her nicely and firmly to the door. She was ready to *stay*. She said it would be on his conscience when she was tortured. Anyway, she is still alive—but says that's only because she came to see us, and "they" know!

The second visit was more serious. Wife of a very powerful man in the government (or was)—pregnant—five children. *She* wanted to seek sanctuary. That's all I need. But I would do it for her as she is a *good* friend. She lives across the street, so if she flees in her nightgown with those five adorable children I'll naturally do the Christian thing. Her husband has been sent out of the country, ostensibly to go to Cairo but he is stuck in Bangkok.

I was well aware of the Tuyen family across rue d'Arfeuilles in their contemporary villa, like ours walled, fortified, and protected. Play dates arranged for me with their age-appropriate offspring after we arrived had led nowhere. But the husband in question was no ordinary official. He had long been, until August, one of the shadowy figures in Ngo World. Tran Kim Tuyen was the physically tiny head of SEPES. With its charmingly bookish name—Service d'Etudes Politiques et Sociales—SEPES was the palace's intelligence and security service. SEPES reported to Brother Nhu about suspected opponents inside the Vietnamese civil service. His sinister powers won him the label of "Diem's Goebbels."

During the summer Tuyen, disaffected with the regime, had begun hatching his own coup, which came to nothing except his expulsion to a sinecure as Vietnamese ambassador in Cairo, which he never reached. He was given sanctuary in Hong Kong and after the coup, returned to Saigon to be with his pregnant wife, only to be arrested and jailed for five years for being a suspected Nhu puppet. The family came to no harm.

In her letter Phoebe then turned to Nguyen Dinh Thuan, Bill's now-close friend—they'd gone to see President Kennedy together in Washington—and Diem's right hand. Thuan had been telling Trueheart and others at the embassy how pessimistic he was for the regime's survival and how frantic he was about the safety of his own family as his own feelings became unconcealable.

"Thuan," Phoebe wrote their Washington friends,

> is on the outs. Bill purposely has avoided him because he thought he (Bill) would be harmful to him. He saw him at the Malaysian reception and said as much, and his friend said thanks—and laughed bitterly, but understood and *was* thankful. Which is pretty sad. They are still great friends, but no telephone calls or visits or calls in the usual way. This makes Bill I think most ineffective here. He is a pariah vis a vis the government. Bill has explained this to Lodge and offered to leave sooner than April, but L won't have it.
>
> To look at me, I am the picture of calm and tranquility. Inside I am churned up. When I do sleep I have horrible dreams of blood, soldiers, and little children torn apart—and falling out and down. The only time I sleep is when I've had lots to drink or taken Seconal. I don't mean to excite your pity. Actually, I wouldn't have missed it for the world. And Bill would say double in spades. Not many chargés have had the chances he has had to get their names in front of JFK. But I do worry about the children, especially Charlie, who is everywhere and hard to keep at home.[50]

That last observation rings true. I was a seventh-grader determined to enjoy my freedom at a juncture when new temptations were arising and my parents were deeply preoccupied with the crisis at hand.

11

★ ★ ★

Waiting for the Generals

RT BUCHWALD, A NEWSPAPER humorist who was great in his day, wrote a silly column in late September 1963 about the Vietnam standoff, including bits such as this one:

"We've asked Diem to fire his brother."
"What did he say?"
"He said he'd fire his brother only if President Kennedy fired his."

The Truehearts had known the Buchwalds in Paris in the 1950s. Art Buchwald, unable to resist riffing, wrote Bill Trueheart in Saigon on October 1 to thank him "for the love letter about my piece on Vietnam. You probably have the most interesting job in the world right now. Probably anybody who has anything to do with Vietnam will never be able to get a post again. . . . Don't get discouraged. General de Gaulle is going to save the day for all of us." Buchwald also told Trueheart that everyone in the United States was eagerly awaiting the arrival of Madame Nhu. "She is going to be on 'Meet the Press,' 'Face the Nation,' 'Youth Wants to Know,' and 'I've Got a Secret.'"[1]

Madame Nhu's departure from Saigon was most welcome at the US embassy, which would have preferred that her husband accompany her and neither of them return. But as with everything Madame Nhu did or said, her trip to the United States made an impossible situation much worse.

Accompanied by her seventeen-year-old daughter, Le Thuy, Madame Nhu stopped first in Belgrade to represent Vietnam at the congress of the Interparliamentary Union. During subsequent leisurely stays in Rome and Paris, recounted *Life* magazine, "she has seen the sights, shopped, and sounded off with the frequency and delicacy of a piledriver on her favorite subjects." The statement that rocketed around the world, from a newspaper interview in Italy, was that junior officers in the US military mission in Vietnam were "acting like little soldiers of fortune." This resulted in a withering protest from Ambassador Lodge, making him break his autumn vow of silence regarding the ruling family.

Madame Nhu arrived in New York on October 7 for a twelve-city trip across the United States. It would last twenty-two days. Crowds of students heard her speak at Columbia and Fordham, at Harvard Law School and Radcliffe College, at Princeton and Sarah Lawrence. In Washington, she spoke at the National Press Club. She appeared on *Meet the Press.* She met no one in the US government, which did its best to ignore her formally, though it had decided against denying her a visa lest it look cowardly and close-minded.

Critics of the Kennedy administration, however, found her useful. In Dallas, she participated in a far-right confab that included John Birchers and Minutemen and, in the audience, a man about to become infamous, Lee Harvey Oswald. She sojourned at the ranch of a right-wing mogul named Dudley Dougherty near Beeville, Texas, where one of Dougherty's nephews, Bruce B. Baxter III by name, was smitten with Le Thuy and courted her as far as Los Angeles, the Nhus' last stop.

Madame Nhu, thirty-eight, was a sensation. The press fell in love with her, or with the idea of her. She was petite and feminine but also sinister. She was compared to Lucrezia Borgia, to Marie Antoinette, to Scarlett O'Hara, to a James Bond villainess. "As for the pistol-packing lady of the script," mused a *Herald Tribune* editorial, "she doubtless has her country's good at heart. But it's of stone."

Protesters swarmed her appearances, pelted her limousine with eggs. "Phu on Nhu," read the placards, as well as the cleverer "How many killed per diem?" Over a photograph of deadly mayhem in the streets of Saigon a caption read, "The Nhu Frontier," a play on Kennedy's New Frontier. Senator Stephen Young of Ohio said Madame Nhu had gotten "too big for her britches." Congressman Wayne Hays, also of Ohio, said, "It is bad enough that every two-bit dictator around the world reviles and insults the US at will, but it is too much to let this comic-strip Dragon Lady do it under our very noses." The *Los Angeles Times* was magnanimous: "We have little to lose by acting toward Mme. Nhu with dignity."

American coverage of Madame Nhu would constitute a trove for a gender studies dissertation. The *Dallas Morning News*: "Whether her actions are sinister, as her foes claim, or misunderstood, as she claims, there is no doubt that they are 100 percent wifelike." When she appeared before the Overseas Press Club in New York, *Time* magazine quoted a "matron" remarking, "You don't have nails like that and do much work around the house." A cartoon in the *Denver Post* showed a sultry Madame Nhu coming on to a frightened Uncle Sam, who pleads, "Please, madame, I'm a happily married man."[2]

Although she said plenty of provocative things in America and grated deeply on officials in Washington, Madame Nhu tried to follow the advice of her friend Marguerite Higgins to curb her tongue. She seldom had anything good to say about the American press, yet on this trip she cultivated them daily. To reporters at the Barclay Hotel in New York, she complained bitterly about Bill Trueheart's impertinence during the summer, and said Fritz Nolting "was the only one who believed the Vietnamese government's version of the Buddhist affair." She seemed to sense the worst that was to come when she said, amid her ramblings, "I refuse to play the role of an accomplice in an awful murder."[3]

Most bizarre of all, she led about twenty American reporters to an unusual outing in northwest Washington, DC, to the Western Avenue colonial residence that her parents had occupied when they had resigned in disgust two months earlier as Ngo Dinh Diem's envoys. Ngo Dinh Nhu had said in an interview with an Italian magazine that if his father-in-law, Tran Van Chuong, were to return to Saigon, "I will have his head cut off. I will hang him in the center of a square and let him dangle there. My wife will make the knot on the rope because she is proud of being a Vietnamese and she is a good patriot."[4] Madame Nhu's own mother, Tran Thi Nam Tran, had called her a monster and supposedly urged members of the Vietnamese community in New York and Washington to run her "over with a car."[5]

As reporters looked on, Madame Nhu knocked at the front door of the darkened house. She led the cameramen around to the backyard and tried the back door, peering through the kitchen windows. The Chuongs had been alerted, apparently, and were either crouching in the dark or long gone.[6]

Blown Cover

Lodge had frozen Diem out, much to the consternation of the State Department and the White House—and, of course, the presidential palace. As he waited for his gamble to pay off, Lodge made another symbolic move. Even though he had struck out in his first effort to move the CIA station chief, Jocko Richardson, aside, in the first days of October Lodge delivered dramatic evidence that he meant business.

The maneuver was triggered, fittingly for the maestro of the press, by extraordinary leaks to a journalist. This one, Richard Starnes of the *Washington Daily News,* was not otherwise known for his work on Vietnam. On a reporting trip to Saigon, he followed the scent of the *Times of Vietnam*'s scathing revelations about CIA coup plotting. Nosing about the American crowd, Starnes uncovered and published information about the August pagoda raids that suggested the station chief was running a rogue operation in Saigon, tacitly in league with Ngo Dinh Nhu and his special forces.

The story ("'Arrogant' CIA Disobeys Orders in Viet Nam") said Richardson had refused twice to carry out Lodge's instructions. And it named him as the station chief. The source of the leak was clear to Rufus Phillips: "Only Lodge was ruthless enough for such a hatchet job."[7] Lodge had made his attitude crystal clear as soon as he landed in Saigon: "the leak is the prerogative of the ambassador," he said as he gave John Mecklin his new marching orders. Yet this CIA leak struck others as the handiwork of Averell Harriman.

The station chief was damned either way: Richardson either had been unaware of the special forces' role in the raids (though he golfed regularly with Colonel Tung) or had been all too aware and complaisant about Nhu's scheming. Since the CIA funded the special forces—supposedly as commando units for anti–Viet Cong operations, but now as the personal police of the repressive regime—Starnes steamed, "It may not be a direct subsidy for a religious war against the country's Buddhist majority [*sic*], but it comes close."[8]

In those days, the identities of CIA personnel were closely guarded, as they still are, usually in tacit league with journalists. Now Richardson had been exposed, his cover blown, even if his real job in Saigon was well known to anyone, Vietnamese or American, who needed to know (and some who didn't, like me). The damage done, and as if to confirm the story, Richardson was sent home immediately, without even an explanation to his family, who followed later.

Why did Lodge fire Richardson? He may have seen the CIA station as a rival power center in the mission. He may have believed that Richardson was too close to Nhu, too trusting, to be objective about him—an echo of the rap on Nolting and Diem. Richardson thought mobilizing the generals for a coup, which he was being ordered to do (via Lucien Conein) when Lodge showed him the August 24 Telegram, was "hasty and unwise, even an act of betrayal," as he told his son much later. "For all his flaws, Diem was our ally in a time of war."

This sentiment, redolent of Nolting's view, would not have sat well with Lodge had Richardson uttered the words before him. Instead, the professional intelligence officer says—and here he was following explicit instructions from the CIA director in Washington—he "placed my station at the complete disposition of Ambassador Lodge and invited him to assign a senior foreign service officer of his own staff to participate in all station actions and decisions relating to the immediate matter at hand."[9] That is, orchestrating the generals' coup.

According to his son John's memoir, by this time Richardson had come around to the prevailing view that the Ngos were no longer viable. But like Colby before him, the station chief's most significant contact was Ngo Dinh Nhu, his alter ego in the shadows of power. The spook-to-spook connection is the bread and butter of a station chief's work. As the CIA funded and trained Nhu's special forces—the ones that had sacked the pagodas, the ones now defunded—theirs was a contractual relationship in the most basic sense. But "that close relationship, which was sanctioned and had a long history, was bound to lead people on the Vietnamese side to wonder if we had two policies," said Trueheart in a later interview.

Perhaps in subliminal empathy, Trueheart was stout in his defense of his CIA colleague: "I'm confident that Richardson was an absolutely 200 percent loyal follower of policy and was not double-crossing anybody. I don't believe Lodge thought he was either." The reason Richardson was removed, Trueheart believed, was to make it clear "to Diem and Nhu and even more importantly the [Vietnamese] military that Lodge was speaking for the [US] government. . . . It was the only kind of really believable signal Lodge could give."[10]

Richardson's excommunication rippled into the Truehearts' domestic life. Since their arrival, despite what Emily Lodge first told Phoebe about being "thrilled" with the ambassador's residence, the Lodges found they couldn't stand the clamor of traffic on Hien Vuong. The Saigon villa's dowdy colonial formality was furthermore not to their taste: embassy wives had been undone on hearing that Emily Lodge, not long after occupying the residence, had the formal mahogany dining room table and chairs *painted white.*

The chief of station's Saigon residence not far away happened to be in a quieter and more secure setting, next door to a cemetery, and was by some measures a more gracious place on expansive grounds with pool and tennis court.[11] So Henry Cabot Lodge took Richardson's house for himself, again making manifest his authority. At the embassy there was joking that this was the *real* reason Lodge wanted Jocko gone. The new ambassador had even railed in envy, in his private diary, that the "CIA has more money, bigger houses than diplomats; bigger salaries; more weapons; more modern equipment."[12]

The consequence of that decision was a three-way residential pivot. The Lodges would occupy the CIA villa on Phung Khac Koan; the Truehearts would move three blocks away into the now-former ambassador's residence on Hien Vuong; and Richardson's eventual successor would take the DCM's house on Nguyen Dinh Chieu. Those housing assignments persisted through the rest of the Vietnam War.

I was thrilled at the move into finer quarters. But I recognized, even in the moment, how it might have looked to the Noltings: here was the Judas family usurping the space from which they had been banished.

The house was grand, but we were not there long.

Not Stimulate, Not Thwart

By October, the regime was feeling the squeeze triggered by the decisions of late August, reinforced by Lodge's preference for imposing painful sanctions rather than engaging in fruitless palaver. The commodity import program that funded the Vietnamese government's cash needs was cut off. The CIA's aid to Ngo Dinh Nhu's special forces was sharply curtailed, giving further meaning to Richardson's departure.

Every week the embassy in Saigon received instructions from Washington that could only have left them shaking their heads at the policies in tension, and the indecision behind the tension. "No initiative should now be taken to give any active covert encouragement to a coup," said one cable, while yet demanding "urgent covert effort . . . to identify and build contacts with possible alternative leadership as and when it appears."[13]

Or, as the yin-yang was repeated and recast, in a CIA message to Lodge on October 9: "While we do not wish to stimulate a coup, we also do not wish to leave impression that US would thwart a change of government or deny economic and military assistance to a new regime if it."[14] Not stimulate, not thwart.

Duong Van Minh, the coy tennis player who had mystified Secretary McNamara and General Taylor during their September visit, had emerged as the Vietnamese general in charge of the coup plot. His top confederates were Tran Van Don and Le Van Kim, the brothers-in-law. The troika was all-Buddhist. Don, the French-born acting army chief of staff, was really the brains behind the operation and the key outside interlocutor, but General Minh literally had the stature. Other than his height, and like his American cutout Conein, Big Minh had another striking physical characteristic. When as a French army officer in 1945 he was captured by the Japanese occupiers, the dreaded Kempeitai military police broke off his upper front teeth. He refused to have them replaced, wearing his smile as a military decoration.

Minh's heroic reputation stemmed too from having helped Diem bust the criminal sects and gangs in Saigon eight years before, even though he had since been sidelined repeatedly from any command responsibilities. Many thought him a shallow dilettante, preferring his orchids and tennis games to decision-making. As for his aptitude for governance, "I knew Duong Van Minh, and thought he was a total blowhard, without a useful idea in his head," said William Colby long after.[15]

On October 5, Big Minh pressed Conein again on the two things that made the generals the most nervous: Further bona fides that he was acting on direct US instruction and that the plotters would not be betrayed to the Ngos. Minh and Conein talked about the fate of Ngo Dinh Diem after a coup—figurehead president? Exile? Dead man? Then they turned to the generals.

Big Minh assured Conein that none of them wanted power for themselves—except, he added with a laugh, Ton That Dinh. This was the deluded martinet who had put on such a crazy performance for Conein in September. But since his installation as Saigon's military governor, he was an essential player in any successful coup. Big Minh said he thought Dinh was being "played the fool" by the Ngos.[16]

Something else came up. Alarmed by the prospect of harm coming to Diem and Nhu in any military coup, CIA director McCone had instructed Conein to make it clear to the generals that the United States wanted no part of any assassination. When Conein passed the message back to General Don, he replied, "All right, you don't like it. We won't talk about it any more."[17]

On the same day in Saigon, another Buddhist bonze arrived at the Central Market in a taxi, got out with a jerry can in his hand, drenched himself in gasoline, and set himself ablaze to die. There was no entourage and no crowd, at first, but David Halberstam and two other journalists, John Sharkey and Grant Wolfkill of NBC, had been alerted. When they began to shoot pictures of the self-immolation, they were set upon by police and slightly injured. Ambassador Lodge protested.

American journalists were under great pressure in these days, and a backlash about their reporting was discernible. It was in this period that President Kennedy asked leadingly if the publisher of the *New York Times* might want to bring Halberstam home. When *Time* magazine received a file from Charles Mohr that began, "The war in Vietnam is being lost," the managing editor, Otto Fuerbringer, turned it around into an attack on the journalists themselves in the press section.[18] Echoing a line Nolting and Harkins had espoused for two years, the establishment-oriented weekly said, "The press corps on the scene is helping to compound the very confusion that it should be untangling for its readers at home. . . . They pool their convictions, information, and grievances. . . . They have covered a complex situation from only one angle, as if their own conclusions offered all the necessary illumination."[19] Mohr resigned over this professional calumny in his own magazine.

The censorious syndicated columnist Joseph Alsop, too, blamed the Saigon correspondents for Diem's evident demise: "The reportorial crusade against the government has (also) helped mightily to transform Diem from a courageous, quite viable national leader into a man afflicted with a galloping persecution complex, seeing plots around every corner, and therefore misjudging everything."[20] It's fascinating to read how the ghastly portrait of Diem's frailty is the fault of the journalists covering him.

On the same weekend, President Kennedy took home with him a memo addressing one of his preoccupations: the divisions in the US mission in Saigon, which had only deepened since Lodge's arrival. In the memo, William Sullivan delivered a keen psychoanalysis of the clashing mind-sets and an insight into the ways policy was being made on the fly, finessing its internal contradictions. It is not hard to imagine these issues later riving US missions in places such as Iraq and Afghanistan.

For the military, "Any suggestion that success is not being attained is considered a personal affront, a reflection impugning the achievements of the US armed forces," Sullivan wrote. For the diplomats, "any effort by the military to reach essentially political or intelligence conclusions is considered an incursion into, or even the pre-emption of, a field of activity which should be properly civilian."

It was about "the pecking order." When he had visited Saigon the year before, Sullivan saw General Harkins as the "top banana." He ran a bigger, more impressive establishment than Nolting did, and "he was the executor of the main US drive of the day in which there was invested a great measure of US prestige." Nolting, by contrast, Sullivan went on, was "a fairly junior US Foreign Service Officer of no particular international reputation or prestige . . . undertaking his first assignment as an ambassador in a part of the world in which he had no depth of experience . . . with limited resources at his disposal and a relatively small staff."

Sullivan gave Nolting due credit for his handling of the situation: "With good common sense and discretion, Fritz 'got on the team' and made no contest to assume prerogative of control. This does not suggest he was a doormat; it merely means that he chose what he quite sensibly considered to be the most effective way to exercise his talents and to utilize his resources."[21]

The leaks about the CIA station that so irked President Kennedy had metastasized into general coverage of a mission in dissension and disarray. UPI ran a story calling the Country Team in Saigon a "five-headed monstrosity"! The Truehearts took special notice of a wacky syndicated newspaper column by Robert S. Allen and Paul Scott. As part of the torrent of codels, Representative Clement Zablocki, Democrat of Wisconsin, had junketed to Vietnam in mid-October with seven colleagues from the House Foreign Affairs Committee, which he chaired. The congressmen had "discovered," said the Allen-Scott column, that while Ambassador Lodge "is supposed to be running the show . . . minister-counsel [*sic*] William C. Trueheart appears to be calling the shots" in Saigon.

The largely fact-free column said Trueheart and Mecklin tried to channel congressmen toward "US civilian officials strongly biased against President Diem." They described Trueheart as a "former intelligence official" who had a "major role" in the Richardson recall. Trueheart and Mecklin were "ringleaders" in the August noncoup. The columnists said Trueheart had been "caught . . . frantically signaling Lodge not to discuss sensitive questions raised by the committeemen. . . . While sitting strategically behind the legislators Trueheart was sighted several times waving his hands furiously or shaking his head 'no' when Lodge began discussing differences between his staff, the military, and the Central Intelligence Agency."

I recall mirth in the Blue Room a few evenings later when Bill and Phoebe showed me a clipping of the column. The mirth surprised me, as this did not strike me as a flattering portrait of my father. I was reassured it was not to be taken seriously—any more than I should have been by critical comments about him in the *Times of Vietnam,* which had also unsettled me. From the clippings that my mother saved, I see that the *Maysville (KY) Ledger-Independent* covered the Allen-Scott column as news. Its account, entirely missing the columnists' point, carried this classic local-angle headline: "In Saigon, Trueheart Given Credit for Running the Show."[22]

"If I Am Assassinated . . ."

In their letters to their mothers, Bill and Phoebe carefully neglected to mention the assassination target list that had circulated in August and September. Allegedly drawn up by Ngo Dinh Nhu—and passed around by his wife's semi-deranged brother—the hit list included Lodge, Trueheart, Harkins, Richardson, Mecklin, Conein, and more, to name only the Americans. I was not aware of such a list at the time, but frankly would have been disappointed if my father had not been on it. I see now that Phoebe retailed this rumor to her Washington friends.

That was only one of many rumors swirling around Saigon in the tense autumn hiatus between the pagoda raids and the coup d'état—rumors of a military plot to assassinate the Nhus as they motored into Saigon from the airport, of killing Diem and Nhu in a suicide bombing at a Gia Long meeting, of capturing Nhu on one of his tiger hunts and exfiltrating him from Vietnam.

Another concerned Lodge's own prospective assassination. According to Radio Catinat, the local term of affection for the Saigon rumor mill, a Nhu-inspired mob would storm the US embassy and capture the ambassador. Evidence for this plot was said to be the sudden clandestine purchase of "a large quantity of orange cloth" to allow Colonel Tung's thugs to pose as parading monks in the putative embassy assault.

Lodge advised Washington at length about this story, echoing his predecessors by underscoring the fact of a pitifully undefended chancery. "If the crowd tries to enter the building by throwing ladders or other catwalks from the Chinese house next door over to our outside balconies, we will try to throw the ladders off and use tear gas there," wrote Lodge. "I plan no shooting."[23]

The assassination threat "comes as no surprise, as I realized the possibility of this when I accepted the post," Lodge wrote pridefully. "For Diem and Nhu even to be thinking of my assassination is so unbelievably idiotic that a reasonable person would reject it out of hand." Then why hadn't he? Henry Cabot Lodge even saw a plausible bright side to his untimely death. It "might give us a chance to move effectively for a change of government using methods which would now be rejected by US and world opinion, but which would then become acceptable."

The ambassador said he had instructed the acting CIA station chief to tell Ngo Dinh Nhu that were this to happen, "American retaliation will be prompt and awful beyond description." Referring to the "record of US Marines in the Pacific during WWII," Nhu was to be asked candidly "whether GVN wishes to have such a horrible and crushing blow descend on them."

McCone in Washington told Harriman he thought the Lodge cable was "rather hysterical."

"You Get What You Pay For"

Two months after the pagoda raids and the coup that didn't happen, and one week before the one that did, President Kennedy and his men were still wringing their hands about their options, which they realized were narrowing and largely beyond their control. The White House was desperate for more information about the coup leaders, suspicious about Brother Nhu's maneuverings, tempted to micromanage the coup but wanting no fingerprints, and resigned to the appearance, whether it succeeded or failed, of American complicity and whatever it ushered in.

Feeling increasingly helpless to dictate events, the president and his senior advisers instead focused on elements that they *could* control. At a minimum, and most ineffectually, this meant refining the US ambassador's instructions. Lodge was scheduled to be in Washington for consultations the first weekend of November, so at the White House on October 25 they brainstormed inconclusively about what to tell him to do. As they were out of ideas, Kennedy's advisers focused instead on personalities, starting with the shadowy Lucien Conein, now the indispensable link between the president of the United States and the plotting generals: "How did we wind up with this guy? And who is he? Can we do better—for example, send in Bill Colby to take charge of the coup?" That is, the coup the US has nothing to do with.

Robert McNamara sounded anguished and angry about the way the operation had been handled—"like a bunch of amateurs." McNamara said the particular "amateurish hands" running the coup that he had in mind were Lodge and Conein. "We're dealing through a press-minded ambassador and an unstable Frenchman—five times divorced. That's the damnedest arrangement I've ever seen." (In fact, just four times divorced.)

McCone, a fellow Republican who knew him well, echoed this dim view of Lodge's reporting from Vietnam—hampered by "this correctness of Cabot" in giving the Ngos the cold shoulder: "The total intelligence we've gotten from him as to what Diem and Nhu are thinking of are second-hand reports of their discussions with some newspaper people . . . or the ambassador of a third country. Furthermore, he has stood down contacts by the station. . . . So there has been a breakdown of substantive intelligence on just what these people are thinking about," McCone said in a transcribed recording of the meeting.

McCone had also soured on Lodge because of the Richardson affair. As Kennedy's men piled on, black humor surfaced.

McCone picked up a copy of a recent telegram: "You see, Lodge reports here, he says [the CIA station] has been punctilious regarding [my instructions]. I have personally approved each meeting of General Don and Conein, who has carried out my orders in each instance explicitly."

McGeorge Bundy was amused: "Lodge is his own press relations officer. He is his own case officer. He's really quite an economical investment in that sense."

McCone rejoined: "You get what you pay for." The transcript cites "[Group laughter.]"

As was his custom, President Kennedy had been listening to all of this, and tried to bring the conversation to order. Henry Cabot Lodge, he understood, did not suffer instructions any more than fools. Acknowledging "more or less unanimity" of misgivings around the table about Lodge's conduct, Kennedy said, "But he's there, we're not going to fire him, so we're going to have to give him some direction." The president pointedly added, "we've got to get him to end up with where we want him to go, and not end up where he wants us to go."

The president also had other questions about personnel in Saigon. "Do we want Mecklin out of there? Do we want Trueheart out of there? Do we want Conein out of there?"[24]

"An Even Bet"

General Harkins ran into General Don at a British embassy reception on October 22. Having been deliberately kept out of the loop by Ambassador Lodge, when Don felt him out about the coup, Harkins felt no compunction in saying it was a bad idea. Don, who was about to roll the dice with what he thought was tacit US encouragement, was incredulous to hear from Harkins that "it was the wrong time to stage a coup because the war against the Vietcong was progressing well."[25]

Conein had to scramble to reassure the skittish generals that Harkins didn't know what he was talking about. Lodge believed the Harkins stumble even "may have served the useful purpose of allaying the generals' fears as to our interest." When Conein pressed General Don for information about their planning and timing—"the US Government could make no commitment to the coup leaders until it had studied their plans in detail"[26]—the general promised two days' notice. He said the coup would happen no later than November 2.

By this point Lodge was thoroughly committed to the coup and found himself trying to give the ExCom in Washington some spine. "It seems an even bet that the next government would not bungle and stumble as much as the present one has." The ambassador deemed it "extremely unwise in the long range for us to pour cold water on attempts at a coup. . . . This is the only way in which the people of Vietnam can possibly get a change of government."

In reply, McGeorge Bundy candidly acknowledged that what really concerned President Kennedy was the "hazard that an unsuccessful coup, however carefully we avoid direct engagement, will be laid at our door by public opinion almost everywhere."[27]

Robert Kennedy, for his part, told his brother at that meeting, "I don't think that this makes any sense on the face of it, Mr. President. . . . We're putting the whole future of the country, and really Southgeast Asia, in the hands of somebody that we don't know very well . . . we're just going down the road to disaster."[28] The attorney general, a reliable Cassandra, was asking pointed and gloomy questions. The right ones.

A Day in Dalat

President Diem finally took Lodge's bait, too late, by inviting the American ambassador to the family retreat in Dalat, thinking perhaps of the halcyon days when he received the Noltings there.[29] Lodge's report to Washington about "my day with Diem"—Sunday, October 27—covered all the issues that had been simmering since August. As they dined alone at the mountain retreat, Ambassador Lodge navigated Diem's stream of consciousness, steering his way against a powerful current.

President Diem mentioned to Lodge that UNESCO wanted to build a university in Vietnam, which "gave me the opportunity to discuss the UN commission," which had just arrived in Saigon to investigate the regime. Lodge said he wanted permission of the government of Vietnam to let the UN observers see Tri Quang at his US embassy asylum (afforded to him in the first place without the government's permission). Lodge said it would be in Diem's interest to show the world he had not prevented them from talking to anyone.

By his account, Lodge pushed hard on the bargain implicit in his instructions. "Would he open the schools, would he liberate the Buddhists and others who were in prison, would he eliminate the discriminatory features" of the law that treated Buddhists differently from Catholics? Diem waffled. Even though it was too late, certainly too late in the ambassador's own opinion, Lodge pressed Diem to do something, anything, to satisfy American public opinion.

Diem said, "I will not give in." He praised Brother Nhu as "so good and so quiet, so conciliatory and so compromising." Lodge told Diem the

Nhus should undertake "a period of silence," as Mme Nhu wended her way unsilently across the United States. Diem retorted that American press coverage of her visit was "a concert of lies orchestrated by the State Department." Lodge explained freedom of the press again: "When there is something sensational to report, an American newspaper is going to report it or else it will cease to be a newspaper. The way to stop the publicity is for Madame Nhu to stop talking."

At the end of their exhausting parley, Lodge said, "Mr. President, every single suggestion which I have made, you have rejected. Isn't there some one thing you may think of that is within your capabilities to do and that would favorably impress US opinion? He gave me a blank look and changed the subject."

Changing Horses

When they met on October 29, Lucien Conein told General Don that Ambassador Lodge was leaving for Washington consultations two days later and wanted a "complete grasp" of the coup planning before he left. (A "complete grasp"—but "no fingerprints.") General Don was evasive. He reminded Conein it was a Vietnamese affair. It could be any day now. He backed off his commitment to give Conein a signal forty-eight hours before the coup, shrinking the notice to just four hours. Don wanted to know exactly when Lodge's plane was leaving and told Conein to stand by and "remain at home from Wednesday evening onward," meaning October 30. He reassured the CIA cutout that the conspiracy was determined to "win the war against the VC and re-establish the prestige of Vietnam and the Army . . . before the Americans leave in 1965."[30] A coup was the prerequisite for that.

Conein's rendition of the encounter in a top-secret telegram went to everyone who counted in Washington, "eyes only," so any suggestion that the timing of the coup took the United States by surprise is, of course, nonsense. Conein was also told something else that would turn out to matter: "The Generals are aware that there are two underground tunnels of escape from Gia Long Palace."

On that day in Washington and the next one, too, the president's men debated that old symbolic standby, now in the context of a coup d'état: Who was in charge of US interests in Saigon when Lodge left for Washington? The State Department wanted the ambassador to stick with his travel plans and be out of the country when the coup came down, with Trueheart "as chargé the senior US representative in Vietnam." Some favored a troika of Trueheart, Harkins, and the acting CIA station chief, David Smith.[31] McCone, protectively, didn't like the idea of a threesome; better for CIA to "take direction rather than participate in a decision-making group." Then Secretary McNamara argued that "Trueheart should head the Vietnam Country Team until the coup was initiated. At that time, General Harkins would take over with Trueheart becoming his political adviser" ("POLAD" in the parlance).[32]

A smaller group met at 6:00 p.m. to review the new instructions to Lodge, who would be waking up in Saigon in a few hours. The president said Lodge should come ahead to Washington at his discretion on a plane that could leave Saigon as late as Saturday afternoon. McGeorge Bundy also telegrammed Lodge to bring Harkins into the picture and get his assessment and the CIA's of the "balance of forces" for the impending coup. "Highest authority desires" that General Harkins participate in all coup contacts as he would "become head of the country team and direct representative of the President" when the action began.[33]

That same day Harkins griped to Taylor about Lodge's treatment of him: "I will say Cabot's methods of operations are entirely different from Amb Nolting's. . . . [Y]ou are correct in believing that the ambassador is forwarding military reports and evaluations without consulting me." As for the coup itself, Harkins reverted to form—Nolting's form—prolonging an argument long since closed. The general thought it was "incongruous" to get rid of Diem after eight years:

> The US has been his mother superior and father confessor since he's been in office. . . . I'm not opposed to a change in government, no indeed, but I'm inclined to feel that at this time . . . I have seen no one with the strength of character of Diem . . . certainly there are no generals qualified to take over, in my opinion. . . . I am not a Diem man per se. . . . I am here to back 14 million SVN people in their fight against communism and it just happens that Diem is their leader at this time. . . . I would suggest we not try to change horses too quickly. That we continue to take persuasive actions that will make the horses change their course.[34]

Meanwhile Lodge, sensing cold feet in Washington, said there was no power available to him to discourage or delay a coup. He expressed his admiration for the Vietnamese generals' determination: "These men are obviously prepared to risk their lives and they want nothing for themselves."

With mendacious delicacy Lodge responded to the guidance about Harkins this way: "Time has not yet permitted substantive examination of this matter with General Harkins." But Lodge insisted on the chain of command issue: "It does not seem sensible to have the military in charge of a matter which is so profoundly political as a change of government." Lodge insisted he was speaking "impersonally . . . since General Harkins is a splendid general and an old friend of mine to whom I would gladly entrust anything I have."[35]

At the end of the telegram, Lodge noted coolly that "General Harkins has read this and does not concur."

Lodge's final instructions from Washington that day twice contradicted him: 1. "We do not accept as a basis for US policy that we have no power to delay or discourage a coup." And 2. In the ambassador's expected absence, when a coup got under way, General Harkins would be in charge, not Trueheart.[36] In any case, Lodge remained in Saigon for the coup.

With Nolting long gone, and Lodge hardly a sympathetic substitute, Ngo Dinh Diem felt utter isolation from his American patrons. After all these years of separation, Edward Lansdale still felt like a missing limb. The one American in Saigon Diem felt he could trust was Lansdale's protégé Rufus Phillips, another steady, seasoned hand who'd been there for him in 1955. On Wednesday, October 30, President Diem summoned Phillips to Gia Long Palace. The president offered his condolences to his visitor for the recent death of his father. He inquired wistfully about General Lansdale. Phillips was struck by his grim serenity:

> There was none of the agitation I had seen in him during the height of the Buddhist crisis. He seemed philosophical about what fate might bring. We sat in silence for a moment while he looked down and puffed on his ever-present cigarette. There was no more to say, I thought.
>
> Then he looked up directly at me and asked softly, "Do you think there will be a coup?"
>
> I looked him in the eye. I couldn't lie to him.
>
> "I am afraid so, Mr. President."
>
> I felt like crying.[37]

12

★ ★ ★

All Saints' Day

HENRY CABOT LODGE ROSE early on Friday, November 1, to accompany the latest American dignitary to come calling on Ngo Dinh Diem. Admiral Harry D. Felt turned out to be the last one.

For the Vietnamese generals gathering at the offices of the Joint General Staff, near Tan Son Nhut airport, this could only have been a moment of high anxiety. The coup could not start until Admiral Felt and Ambassador Lodge—and General Don—had left Gia Long. Diem was known to keep visitors.

The embassy knew that a coup would come at any moment. Lodge's own planned departure from Saigon looked imminent: President Kennedy had sent a berth-equipped military plane to bring him to Washington on a moment's notice. White House meetings with the ambassador were on Sunday's schedule.

In a scene soon to be evidently surreal, with only a day to live, President Diem performed his usual monologue for more than an hour. It was so nearly identical to what he had told McNamara and Taylor five weeks earlier that, in his obligatory telegram about the discussion, Lodge merely referenced the September 29 cable number. He sent it to Washington with such a routine classification that it was not delivered for days.

At the end of the meeting, after the admiral hastened to the airport with General Harkins and General Don, President Diem pulled Lodge aside. On Diem's mind that morning were the same topics he had raised in Dalat. The questions the UN commission in Saigon was asking, for example. Diem asked Lodge for the names of people he should bring into the government to broaden its base, a well-worn feint. He pleaded the case for his misunderstood younger brother, "a flexible spirit . . . always so full of good advice." Would Lodge, once in Washington, please tell President Kennedy that he had in Diem "a good and frank ally, that I would rather be frank and settle questions now than talk about them after we have lost everything"?[1] As they parted, Lodge said he expressed his admiration for Diem's courage and for his kindness to Emily and him, and then went home for lunch.

At 12:30 p.m., the long, low wail of the airport siren announced the beginning of Saigon's daily three-hour break for lunch and the ritual siesta. November 1, All Saints' Day on the Roman Catholic calendar, was a half-day holiday in South Vietnam, so most people in Saigon were not going back to work. As usual, Bill Trueheart was dropped off at home for lunch about 1:00 p.m. He was just putting his lips to his midday martini when his chauffeur returned unexpectedly, out of breath. Sinh had just passed the central post office and seen it aswarm with soldiers. Trueheart, remembering the moment years later: "It was clear to me what this meant."

With Sinh back at the wheel, Trueheart raced to the ambassador's residence nearby, where he found the Lodges having their lunch. Because "we had very good communications between the residence and the chancery," they agreed that Lodge would stay put. Trueheart would go downtown to the embassy, where he could keep Washington up to the minute through flash messages on the CIA communications channel. Lodge asked Trueheart to send a reinforced US Marine detachment for the protection of the residence. Lodge's departure for Washington was put on hold.

Tony Lake, the young foreign service officer new to Saigon and to the trade, said the "opening shots of the coup were fired from my driveway, [at] 7 Mac Dinh Chi, half a block from the presidential guard barracks." Like everyone else, he'd been having lunch when the shooting started. He and his wife, Antonia, pushed a mattress up against the window, "as if a mattress was going to stop bullets." Out another window the Lakes saw a street vendor selling pho from a cart, business as usual: "When the machine gun would open up, they would lie down. Then they'd stand up and start selling pho again. I thought, this is a tough neighborhood, this Vietnam."[2]

All afternoon at the fully exposed US chancery, Trueheart, Manfull, Miller, Mecklin, and their colleagues watched carefully from the rooftop as the artillery barrages against the palace rattled the windows. The resistance was stiff but short-lived. The post office, the police station, the radio station, the airport were all soon in rebel hands. But the palace was not yielding. Loudspeakers planted around the besieged grounds of Gia Long periodically ceased their martial music to declare, in Ngo Dinh Diem's own voice, "We shall not give in."

Beverly Deepe, the only American woman reporting from Saigon that day, filed to *Newsweek:* "At 3:30 p.m., Diem's tanks raked the central avenues with gunfire. Pedestrians scattered indoors; women cried hysterically; I noticed one bicycle rider dive into the gutter as the branches of trees fell all around him, then get up and pedal away. Soon the city was rocking to the staccato rhythms of ack-ack: two rocket-firing T-28 fighter-bombers swooped down on the palace, and were met by 20-mm. shells from rooftops and naval guns in the river. Mortar fire reverberated throughout the city."[3] Murray Gart told readers of *Time* about "grimly humorous sights: outside the Hotel Caravelle, a Diem policeman seated in a tiny European car struggling desperately to get out of his uniform before the rebels spotted him; a pedestrian dashing madly around a corner, bullets kicking up sparks at his heels; a man scooting into a sidewalk pissoir an instant before it was riddled with machine-gun fire."[4]

Huddling in the top-floor offices at the embassy, Trueheart and the other diplomats tried to keep up with the news. Helpless to do much else—and with their vulnerable families on their minds—they argued intermittently about the protection of American dependents in Saigon. On the Armed Forces radio station General Harkins broadcast a warning to Americans to stay off the streets. The Pentagon had contingency plans for the airlift of two thousand American dependents if the need arose. But the diplomats decided against trying to assemble so many Americans for extraction. "We didn't do anything because we didn't think we could improve on their safety, but I daresay if anybody had been hurt we would have been blamed for it," remarked Trueheart later.[5]

After school let out at noontime that Friday, I rode the school bus to my friend Alain Perry's house for lunch and a Friday afternoon of play. Alain lived a few blocks from us, across the street from the five-house US political section compound on Tu Xuong Street. While we were having lunch, my father phoned Alain's mother, told her the coup was under way, and asked that she keep me there for the duration. It was a lucky break to spend this thrilling moment with a pal rather than with, say, my mother and baby brother, who spent the night of the coup alone on rue d'Arfeuilles.

Through the night the periodic outbursts of artillery fire continued. I had heard the likes of it in the safe distance for two years but never so loud or so close. Shooting in arcs through the hot night air were what I first took to be rockets but then learned were tracers to mark the path of artillery fire. Alain remembers his mother shooing us under their dining room table during the worst of it. I remember being on the upper terrace of the Perrys' house, crouching and watching, alarmed, agog. I had no communication with my parents for twenty-four hours.

The Ngo brothers had a plan. Their scheme was to stage a bogus coup to thwart the real one. Their confederate among the generals—Ton That Dinh, self-styled "Napoleon of Vietnam"—would command a phony revolt and declare victory, whereupon the regime's loyalists would stage a successful countercoup, exposing and executing the generals who rallied to the first one. This plan was dubbed Bravo One. It was outlandish, but anything was possible in the paranoid hothouse of Gia Long.

It might not have mattered, but the brothers had not counted on the vanity and vengefulness of the megalomaniacal General Dinh, who had been installed as Saigon's military governor after the August pagoda raids. No slouches at scheming themselves, General Don and the other real plotters, in the days before the coup, had played to Ton That Dinh's ego. They urged him to present himself to Diem as his savior and to ask, as a reward for his loyalty as the instrument of Bravo One, to be appointed minister of the interior. He did so. President Diem brusquely dismissed the idea. Angered, his pride wounded, General Dinh told the plotters all about the fake coup. The other generals promised him the same important job if he joined them. He did—and they were good to their word after the coup. Sold out by the generals, General Dinh was then rescued by them.

Meanwhile Bravo Two, as the plotters had dubbed the real coup, proceeded. Bravo One gave them a cushion, in fact. As the revolt got under way, Diem assumed all the troop movements and gunfire constituted their own mock coup, being carried out by General Dinh. Too late, the Ngo brothers realized they had been betrayed.

Lucien Conein got the summons at home, at lunch, from General Don's trusted dentist, whose office had been one locus of their secret rendezvous during the summer and fall. Fearing he might be detained in civilian clothes, Conein switched into his US Air Force grays. He called Rufus Phillips to come to his house to look after his wife and children. Packing a .38 and a satchel with sixty-eight thousand dollars worth of Vietnamese piasters (more than a half million dollars today), Conein rushed to the Joint General Staff (JGS) headquarters near the airport, the nerve center of the coup.

Conein would be embedded with the revolting cabal throughout the operation, an extraordinary piece of access (and incrimination) that made him the most important CIA agent in the world for the next twenty-four hours. With communications equipment he brought in his jeep, Conein was able to relay to Washington in real time the disposition of the forces arrayed against the vulnerable points in the regime's defense, all the generals and senior officers involved, and their progress through the day and night. One of Conein's first reports to Washington that afternoon was that Colonel Tung had been lured to JGS and forced to broadcast to his own Special Forces troops, the Ngo palace guard, and tell them he had switched his allegiance to the plotters. Having done so at gunpoint, Tung was taken outside and executed.

"Conein gave us reports every 20 minutes as soon as the shooting started. It was the most extraordinary communication," Mike Forrestal of the White House staff recalled. "He telephoned the Embassy, and the Embassy put it right on the wires. We got it in the White House Situation Room 10 or 11 minutes later. This was rare. Not like the Cuban missile crisis where there was a seven-hour delay in the transmission of messages."[6]

By late afternoon, Big Minh finally got through to President Diem and gave him an ultimatum—resign and surrender in exchange for safe passage to exile, or face an attack on the palace. Diem dithered. Proposed conditions. As he had before, he thought he could palaver his way out of this bind. Impatient, Minh ordered another assault on the palace.

At 4:30 p.m., President Diem phoned the US embassy to speak to Ambassador Lodge. He got Trueheart first, who connected him to the residence extension, probably staying on the line. When the call was over, Lodge called Trueheart back and dictated the contents of the conversation he had just had. It is the only record of what was said between the president of South Vietnam and his last American interlocutor.

Diem came right to the point: "Some units have made a rebellion and I want to know what is the attitude of the US?"

Lodge prevaricated, saying he'd heard shooting but didn't have any information. He served up this lamest of formulations: "It is 4:30 am in Washington and US Government cannot possibly have a view."

"But you must have some general ideas. After all, I am a chief of state. I have tried to do my duty. I want to know what duty and good sense require. I believe in duty above all."

Lodge poured on compliments, which sound vaguely elegiac: "No one can take away from you the credit for all you have done." He said he was concerned for Diem's "physical safety" and then let on that he actually had information—the generals' offer of safe conduct. "Had you heard this?"

"No," said Diem, and then after a pause, "You have my telephone number."

Diem's next phone conversation was with the generals, gathered around a conference table at JGS. Each in turn took the phone, expressed his solidarity with the revolt, and guaranteed to the Vietnamese president that he would have safe conduct if he resigned.

As night fell, the troops defending Gia Long Palace still refused to surrender. At 9:30 p.m., from home, Lodge called Trueheart at the chancery, where he was surrounded by his colleagues. As a colleague overheard it, it sounded like this:

> "Yes, Mr. Ambassador."
> "No, I can't think of anything. No change."
> "No, I see no reason why not."
> "Yes, of course we'll call if necessary."
> "Good night, sir."[7]

Henry Cabot Lodge was going to bed.

After an eerie silence in the barricaded palace grounds, the final rebel barrage began at 9:45 p.m. and lasted through much of the night, with counterfire from Diem's loyalist troops fighting to the last. At the embassy, someone found a case of C rations, which the diplomats broke into, along with a bottle of bourbon, which they drank in conical paper cups from the water cooler. Then another phone call came. It was Nguyen Dinh Thuan, of late in desperate, fearful straits—Diem's loyal right hand, Trueheart's closest Vietnamese friend.

Thuan told Trueheart he'd heard about the offer of clemency to the Ngos if they surrendered by 11:00 p.m. He'd also heard the offer applied to officials like himself. Those who did not surrender to the generals would be considered enemies of the new regime. Thuan had a wife and children. He wanted Trueheart's advice about trusting the generals. He was asking for help.

In *Mission in Torment,* John Mecklin recorded Trueheart's end of the excruciating conversation that night. Speaking on an open line, the DCM could not imply that the United States knew anything about the coup or the plotters, even to a trusted friend.

"Mr. Minister, we know only what we have heard on the radio." Thuan evidently pressed, with emotion, for more guidance than that. Gripping the telephone with fingers that were sticky from cold C ration pork and beans, Trueheart repeated: "We know only what we have heard on the radio." Thuan persisted. Trueheart repeated the same sentence several times more, increasingly embarrassed. After perhaps five or six minutes of this, he said, "Good night, Mr. Minister." Then he put down the phone, looked around the room noncommittally, and reached for a soggy cup of bourbon. Nobody spoke.[8]

For better and for worse, as we have seen, Trueheart was a man who could separate his personal loyalties from his job.

All Souls' Day

President Kennedy's Vietnam council—Rusk, McNamara, McCone, Robert Kennedy, Harriman, Taylor, Hilsman, Bundy, Manning, Colby, Forrestal—had been up most of that Friday night following the unfolding coup in Saigon, twelve hours ahead on the clock. While they briefed the president around the Cabinet Room table that Saturday morning, Kennedy excused himself for half an hour to attend a mass at a nearby Catholic church. On the Christian calendar, November 2 is All Souls' Day, the day of the dead.

By now, based on a stream of reports from the embassy, it appeared the generals' coup was succeeding. The White House pummeled Embassy Saigon with instructions and questions—information about the composition of the new government, the conditions to be placed on US recognition, statements the United States would like to hear made by the generals, and so forth.

General Harkins checked in with Maxwell Taylor around 5:00 p.m. Saigon time. He speculated that the Viet Cong would take advantage of the turmoil to carry out acts of terrorism in Saigon. This didn't happen. At the end of the cable, General Harkins signed off this way: "All I can say is, there is never a dull moment here in Saigon. Warm regards. PS . . . Sounds like tank fire has just started. Oh me!!"[9]

Before dawn Saturday morning in Saigon, having spent the night desperately trying to find a loyal general with troops, or a friendly country that would grant the brothers asylum, Diem phoned General Don to say they now were prepared to surrender and wanted only safe escort to the airport and exile.

By this time, up all night themselves and sure of success, the generals were in no mood for conditions or for the formalities that came so naturally to Diem. The generals' forces had just expended considerable unnecessary firepower and manpower to surround and take Gia Long Palace, only to find it empty of the ruling family. Diem, a forward planner, had used a phone line from his secret lair through the Gia Long switchboard during the night to give the pretense of still being in place. But Diem and Nhu were long gone.

The brothers may have escaped the palace through one of the two tunnels, possibly the one that led to the old cemetery across the street from the CIA station chief's house, soon to be Lodge's residence. General Don, in his absorbing memoir, *Our Endless War,* disputed this. Per Don, Diem and Nhu merely walked out the back entrance of Gia Long into a waiting Citroën and drove off. By some accounts, Nhu and Diem discussed the tactical advantages of splitting up, but brotherly solidarity, live or die, prevailed.

By prearrangement and reactivation, Diem and Nhu were discreetly welcomed at a house owned by a wealthy businessman, Ma Tuyen, in Cholon, the Chinese-majority twin city of Saigon. On the phone from there, after a sleepless, chain-smoking night, the brothers told the generals that they would be at the St. Francis Xavier Catholic Church at 8:00 a.m. for their ride to the resignation ceremony and their flight to exile. At the appointed hour Ma Tuyen drove them to the church, said a dry-eyed farewell, and watched them enter the sanctuary. After the All Souls' mass, Diem and Nhu, dressed in gray suits, went outside to meet their escort.

Accosted by officers of lesser rank, their hands then bound in rope behind them, the chief of state and his counselor were directed not into the sedan they expected but into an M-113 US-supplied armored personnel carrier (APC), one of five in the convoy. Nhu is said to have objected to the insulting treatment and continued to argue with their captors in the APC. They set off. At a railroad crossing the APC stopped to wait. In the din of the passing train the Ngo brothers, lying bound and gagged, were sprayed with machine gun bullets. They were stabbed for good measure.

When the head of the escort detail got back to Joint General Staff headquarters, he strutted into Big Minh's office and—in his excitement not noticing General Don's presence in the room—told his boss: "Mission accomplished."[10] The bodies were brought back to JGS headquarters, where Conein was offered the chance to view them and confirm their identities. He declined.

At 9:00 p.m. Washington time, as Lodge was waking up in Saigon, Secretary Rusk sent "warm thanks for a day of brilliantly quick reporting." He wanted immediate guidance for press backgrounding in Washington, trotting out the line the United States would take: "not a coup in the sense that it is merely the product of a few scheming officers. . . . Diem has yielded to virtually unanimous determination of military and civilian leadership of his country . . . underlining absurdity of notion that this national decision could have been merely a foreigner's trick."[11]

In reply, just before lunch Saturday in Saigon—and either still ignorant of the death of the Ngo brothers or ignoring the early rumors—Lodge urged that emphasis be given to the popularity of the coup: "Every Vietnamese has a grin on his face today. Am told that the jubilation in the streets exceeds that which comes every new year. . . . When I drove to the office with a very small US flag flying, there were bursts of applause from the sidewalk, people shaking hands and waving. The tanks which were standing at the street corners were being covered with garlands of flowers."[12]

Newsweek's Beverly Deepe was an eyewitness to the exhilaration in the streets of Saigon that morning. Buddhists flocked to the pagodas to greet leaders who had been released from jail by the military: "As the monks, many of them thin and weak, were helped from army vehicles, they were embraced and lifted bodily into their temples." Deepe made her way into the darkened palace, where Vietnamese soldiers were milling, searching the rooms by candlelight: "Mme Nhu's three-room suite was cluttered with letters, family photo albums, and files of her old speeches. In her wardrobe I saw eighteen silk-embroidered ao dais hung next to one of her husband's battle jackets. French perfume bottles and spray net were strewn around her bathroom, replete with pink tub and black marble washbasin."[13]

As the sun rose, other intruders flocked to Gia Long, its stucco blackened and pocked by artillery fire. They encountered shattered mirrors, drapes torn to the floor, soldiers pawing at Madame Nhu's silk negligees.[14] Americans were among the rubberneckers. Freddy Flott from Lodge's office entered the palace alone and came across "the body of the first man I ever saw who was shot in the head with an M-16 rifle. . . . [I]t looked just like a tomato that somebody had stepped on."[15] Flott put some ashtrays in his pocket. As he was exiting the palace, he crossed paths with David Halberstam carrying a ten-foot-long elephant tusk. Halberstam's version is that he had lifted one of Nhu's Lao swords.[16] When Rufus Phillips went to Gia Long for a look, just a few days after his sad farewell to Diem, "the two seats that we had been sitting in were riddled with bullet holes."[17]

Among the other immediate looting targets were Saigon's Catholic bookstore, established by Archbishop Thuc, and the Ngo family mouthpiece, the *Times of Vietnam*. It did not take long after the shooting was over for crowds to invade and ransack the newspaper offices. The violence drove one-half of the lickspittle publishing couple, Ann Gregory, to seek asylum in, of all places, the embassy of the United States of America. Lodge quickly arranged a visa for her safe extraction. Gene Gregory was on business in Tokyo when the coup came. Their subsequent trajectory is a mystery.

Apparently given an all-clear, my pal Alain Perry and I, joined by other preadolescent friends, joined the party, although not inside the palace gates. We went out that Saturday afternoon to take pictures and collect souvenirs in the streets—spent shells, discarded military insignia, helmets, shrapnel. We made our way to the riverfront. The spectacle there surrounded the tall modern statue of the two Trung sisters, national heroines at the founding of Vietnam, commissioned by the Ngo family and bearing the likeness, on *both* of the sisters' faces, of Tran Le Xuan, Madame Nhu. Working with acetylene torches and wire cables, the crowds had brought the statues crashing down into the traffic circle—much as, forty years later, crowds in Baghdad felled the statue of Saddam Hussein.

That afternoon also brought news to Washington that Diem and Nhu were dead. The first bit of nonintelligence, sourced to the generals, was that they had taken their own lives. No one believed this story of devout

Roman Catholics. (After learning the grisly details, McGeorge Bundy noted drily, "this is not the preferred way to commit suicide.")[18]

Mike Forrestal rushed into a White House meeting Saturday morning bearing the bad news from Saigon. President Kennedy was said to have blanched, leapt to his feet, and left the room to compose himself. "He had been led to believe or had persuaded himself that a change in government could be carried out without bloodshed," Maxwell Taylor wrote. Two days later, alone in the Oval Office, President Kennedy took the extraordinary step of recording his troubled thoughts on the coup. "I feel we must bear a good deal of the responsibility for it, beginning with our cable" of August 24, the president said, revisiting the weekend merry-go-round of clearances and no meetings, and nudging responsibility a bit toward his ambassador. "While we did redress that balance in later wires, that first wire encouraged Lodge along a course to which he was in any case inclined."

That All Souls' Day in Washington, Bill and Barbara Colby, serious Roman Catholics, went to mass at Church of the Little Flower near their house in Bethesda. Bill Colby joined his wife late and whispered to her in the pew that Diem and Nhu were dead. "We prayed fervently for the souls of President Diem and his brother," she recalled.[19] That evening, they went ahead with a scheduled dinner, a sad Saigon reunion of sorts, with John and Eleanore Richardson and Fritz and Bittie Nolting.

Bill Colby described it as "probably the only American wake over the deaths of Diem and Nhu."[20] John Richardson said the couples had wondered together "how our government could have been so blind to have contributed directly to his overthrow and death."[21] "It was good to be with trustworthy friends on that tragic day," Nolting recalled.[22]

Blood on Their Hands

As all this shocking news—and the first photographs of Diem and Nhu's bloodied bodies in the APC—came tumbling down, Madame Nhu was in her suite at the Beverly Wilshire in Los Angeles, recovering from an operation to remove a cyst from her eye. After attending services at a nearby Catholic church, wearing recuperative dark glasses, she met the news media. "Judas sold the Christ for thirty pieces of silver. The Ngo brothers have been sold for a few dollars. . . . President Ngo Dinh Diem's face was serene in death, and my husband had a slight smile though his face was all streaked with blood. . . . I cannot be less serene than they," she declared.[23]

She and her daughter Le Thuy had been awakened during the night with a call from the Vietnamese embassy in Washington. She could not reach her three other children, Trac, fifteen, Quynh, eleven, and Le Quyen, four. They had been sent to Dalat, protectively; when news of the coup came, they hid in the woods, not sure whether to trust the military guards. Madame Nhu frantically phoned her friend Marguerite Higgins: "Are they going to kill my children too?"[24] Higgins promptly called Roger Hilsman, still in the middle of the night: "Congratulations, Roger. How does it feel to have blood on your hands?" Said Hilsman, "Oh, come on now, Maggie. Revolutions are rough. People get hurt."[25]

At Lodge's instructions, Trueheart organized a C-54 to get the three younger Nhu children out of South Vietnam.[26] Lodge's man Flott accompanied them to Bangkok, then on Pan American to Rome. "Because they had no passports," Lodge swaggered, "I took it upon myself to issue them an impressive-looking 'travel document' . . . to which the clear-headed Italian ambassador, Giovanni d'Orlandi, affixed an Italian visa . . . on thick, expensive-looking paper on which scrolls, eagles, and stars had been engraved."[27]

On the flight to Rome, teenaged Trac, the eldest, read newspaper accounts of the murder of his father and uncle. Flott remembered the young man as stoic. When he read that the heads of Diem and Nhu had been "squashed" by rifle butts, Trac asked Flott what *squashed* meant. "*Ecrabouillé*," Flott told him in French and told him not to believe it. "He took it very calmly. . . . He wasn't crying, it was sort of an Asian outward passivity." In Rome Archbishop Thuc, the children's uncle, met the plane. Flott said, "He wouldn't speak to me, wouldn't shake hands, nothing."[28]

With those significant exceptions, the overthrow of the Diem regime was miraculously nonlethal. The civil insurrection Rusk and Nolting and others had feared, the evacuation of American dependents, didn't happen. Perhaps one hundred Vietnamese soldiers from both sides of the revolt, and a handful of bystanders, lost their lives in the battle.

Archbishop Thuc had been sent out of Vietnam to attend the Vatican II councils in Rome, conveniently.[29] His brother Ngo Dinh Can, the capo of the Hue region, surrendered to the army, having been promised safe passage out of the country and asylum in the US consulate in the meantime if

he needed it. Evidently skittish about getting in the way of the new leadership in South Vietnam, the Americans handed Can over to the provisional
military government. Can was "tried" and executed several weeks later.

Lodge on Sunday evening credulously told Washington that there was
no question the now-ruling generals deeply deplored the assassination of
the Ngo brothers, which was "contrary to their wishes and was, unfortunately, the kind of thing which will happen in a coup d'etat."[30] This may be
an accurate dictation of what Don and Kim said, but Henry Cabot Lodge
seemed to take it at bald-faced value: "I am sure assassination was not at
their direction."

Around this time he spoke more cynically and honestly to David
Halberstam, who described Lodge as "not unhappy" that Diem and Nhu
had declined the offer of safe conduct to exile. (Which they hadn't, in fact.)
"What would we have done with them if they had lived? Every Colonel
Blimp in the world would have made use of them."[31]

There's some dispute about the sincerity of US efforts to prepare the
Ngo brothers' safe passage out of Vietnam. With all the American attention and preparation for the generals' coup, "the impression remains that
American officialdom was content to leave Diem and his brother to the
post-coup mercies of the plotters," Tom Hughes of State's intelligence
bureau said later.[32]

As the coup unfolded, but oddly not before then, Conein was asked
by the generals about an American aircraft for this critical purpose. After
checking with the acting station chief, David Smith, he was told that the
closest one was a KC-135 tanker in Guam. It would take twenty-four hours
to arrive, too late to be useful. Yet Lodge had a berth-equipped plane
standing by at Tan Son Nhut to take him to Washington. General Harkins
had his own plane, too. Wouldn't either have sufficed?

It appears that the State Department may have been more cold-
blooded about the brothers' fate than Lodge and others later let on. The
US government wanted Diem and Nhu not just on any plane but on one
that had the potential to fly very far from Vietnam to an unspecified asylum country without refueling. Conein believed American leaders, like the
generals themselves, feared Diem and Nhu would disembark somewhere
in Southeast Asia and establish a nearby government in exile.

On Sunday afternoon, the American ambassador had his first meeting
with the new leaders of the country whose rump government the United

States was preparing to recognize quickly. Fittingly for the tipping point that had just occurred, the meeting took place in Ambassador Lodge's office. FSO James Rosenthal said he would "never forget the sight" of the generals' arrival: "This car pulled up to the Embassy, and the cameras were grinding away. Conein hops out of the front seat, opens the back door, and salutes, and these guys come out. As if he were delivering them to the Embassy, which he was. I went up with them in the elevator, and Lodge greeted them. . . . Here were the guys who had just carried out a coup, killed the chief of state, and then they walk up to the Embassy as if to say, 'Hey, boss, we did a good job, didn't we?' "[33]

The junta—another word I learned in these historic days, along with *ouster*—wanted economic assistance to start flowing. They told the American viceroy of their plans for a figurehead prime minister (the inevitable Nguyen Ngoc Tho) to serve under the real president, General Minh, who was not present at the meeting. They made strong noises about their collective unity and Minh's primacy. They discussed Tri Quang, holed up in the US embassy now since August with two other bonzes, and Lodge took the generals down to the second-floor quarters that had been outfitted for them. It was a joyous reunion.

Lodge was ebullient about the performance of the Vietnamese generals, saying the coup "could be profitably studied" for its operational finesse. The concentration of the coup forces on switchboards, radio stations, and communications facilities "showed a realism not possessed, for example, by those who attempted the coup against Hitler."[34] The revolt had been pulled off "without a single piece of paper having been kept. All papers were burned; everything was memorized."[35] Lodge reported the comment of an "observer" who, "watching the performance of the ARVN, said if these men can perform like this when their hearts are in it, why isn't it reasonable to believe that they can do equally well against the Viet Cong?"[36] *When their hearts are in it* is the key phrase here.

The laundering of the US role in the coup was already under way. State Department spokesman Richard Phillips said, "I can categorically state that the US government was not involved in any way." Another State Department official, unnamed in *Time*, averred, "It's their country, their war, and this is their uprising."[37] That's the way President Kennedy wanted the world to interpret the news.

Dallas

Another Honolulu conference on Vietnam was called for November 19–20, the first one under dramatically changed circumstances. Even though there was a new government in Saigon, and a new day dawning, to Forrestal the Honolulu conclave was "shaping up into a replica of its predecessors, i.e., an eight-hour briefing conducted in the usual military manner . . . 100 people in the CINCPAC Conference Room, who are treated to a dazzling display of maps and charts, punctuated with some impressive intellectual fireworks from Bob McNamara," he wrote in a cranky memo to McGeorge Bundy on November 13.[38]

Trueheart accompanied Lodge and Harkins to Honolulu. All ears were on prospects for the generals' success in pacifying the country and waging the war. Lodge explained why things were improving but urged the decision-makers to lower their expectations: "If we can get through the next six months without a serious falling out among the generals, we will be lucky."

General Harkins began his peroration by assuring everyone that he and Ambassador Lodge saw eye-to-eye, even as Lodge was privately pressing Kennedy for the commanding general's removal, as he had been doing and would continue to do. Called upon to assess the strategic hamlet program in the post-Ngo era, Trueheart gave a cautiously positive prognosis, with the usual caveats: overextension under the Ngos, alienation of the populace. Echoing Harkins, he denied that any hamlets were under permanent VC control.

The Honolulu meetings broke up on Thursday, November 21, and everyone went their separate ways: McNamara and Rusk to Tokyo for meetings with Japanese leaders; Lodge and McGeorge Bundy to Washington to report to President Kennedy; Harkins and Trueheart home to Saigon, accompanied by Forrestal, who was going to Vietnam again, and then Cambodia, at President Kennedy's request. "I want to start a complete and very profound review of how we got into [Vietnam], what we thought we were doing, and what we now think we can do," President Kennedy told Forrestal on Thursday, "I even want to think about whether or not we should be there."[39]

In Washington early the next morning, before he boarded Air Force One for a political trip to Texas, President Kennedy was briefed by Bundy on the Honolulu meetings. Bundy raised a key point about viability: not the competence of the Vietnamese generals but the competence of the US ambassador.

After just three months, the bloom was off the rose. Henry Cabot Lodge's imperious behavior seemed directed at his Washington masters, all the way up to the president. The ambassador was refusing to take orders, declining to answer messages, going his own way. "It was an impossible situation," Robert Kennedy said. The president "discussed with me in detail how he could be fired, because he wouldn't communicate in any way with us." Bobby reminded his brother that he had warned him that Cabot Lodge would cause him difficulty in Saigon. The president snorted that "it was terrific about me [Bobby] because I could always remember when I was right."[40]

Now, on the last morning of his life, John F. Kennedy was told the problem was getting worse. Lodge's treatment of Harkins, his obvious disrespect under a veneer of patrician cordiality, was a sign of much bigger trouble—the kind of jurisdictional trouble Nolting had warned about when MACV was created but that he had skillfully avoided until the end. Now things were different, McGeorge Bundy told him:

> Lodge is clearly the dominant personality, but it is not at all evident that he can handle the job he is now faced with. He is a strong-willed close operator who keeps only his personal staff involved. This was just the type needed during his first months in Saigon when he was supposed to create a posture [of neutrality about Diem]. . . . Now, however, what is needed is a good manager who can develop a team to do a very complex job. Lodge apparently has neither the inclination for nor the interest in this type of management task.[41]

When President Kennedy was shot to death in Dallas a few hours later, it was the middle of the night in Saigon. My father had just gotten home from Honolulu. Mike Forrestal was ensconced in the new guest room. At daybreak on Saturday, November 23, my mother came into my bedroom to wake me, which was unusual. I made room for her as she sat on the bed. She was in her bathrobe. She looked exhausted. She spoke gravely.

"Charlie, something terrible has happened."

I imagined immediately that something terrible had happened to *my father*. I steadied myself. So upon hearing the news of the assassination in Dallas I felt, first, shamefully, an evanescent pang of relief. Then came the shock. Phoebe's tears and hugs conveyed a great deal. My mother told me she had watched Mike Forrestal cry, too, after she and Bill woke him in the middle of the night. The president and his aide had been very close.

Phoebe said I should go on to my regular Saturday piano lesson a few blocks away. I was taught by the kindly wife of an American general, but when I got there on my bike she said she was too upset to teach me piano and sent me home. When I got back, I wandered out to talk to the servants behind the house. They gathered around me in spontaneous sympathy, jarringly all smiles in their evident grief. I later asked Phoebe why. She explained that the smiles were not about what they felt; they were meant to make *me* feel better.

Downtown at the embassy later that morning, hundreds of Vietnamese mourners convened in the street to pay their respects to President Kennedy. In a wire-service photograph among the jostle of post-traumatic images of Dallas, the American *chargé d'affaires* in Saigon stood at the door of the old chancery accepting flowers and tributes presented by three students. "Near tears himself," his colleague Bob Miller noted, Trueheart invited everyone to sign a condolence book. Using a microphone proffered by the students, he said, in French, "I'd like all of you to know how touched I am, and I know Mrs. Kennedy and the president's family and the American government and all the American people will be touched by your coming here."[42]

Recriminations

In the days after he became president, Lyndon Johnson's views about what had just happened in Vietnam and Texas were emotional, fantastic, seldom far from his neurotic obsessions with the Kennedys. Although he had not spoken much in the Vietnam huddles he had attended at the White House, Lyndon Johnson had not hidden his opposition to a coup. Now, as president, he would have to live—miserably—with a fait accompli.

According to Robert Caro, Johnson's ongoing biographer, the new president told Pierre Salinger, the late president's press secretary, something that he meant Salinger to repeat to Robert Kennedy: that he believed his brother's assassination was "divine retribution" for the murder of Diem. Salinger did pass this on, and Robert Kennedy was indeed appalled. He, too, had opposed the coup. When Senator Hubert Humphrey came to see Lyndon Johnson at the Elms, his home in Spring Valley, in north-west Washington, the new president gestured at a picture of himself with President Diem on that long-ago May 1961 visit. "We had a hand in killing him. Now it's happening here," muttered President Johnson.[43]

Johnson's own press secretary, George Reedy, said Johnson was ob-sessed with Diem's murder: "He felt he had made a personal commitment to Diem and this is the way it was answered." Johnson told Reedy, "One of the greatest mistakes this country ever made was when we encouraged the South Vietnamese to assassinate this president."[44]

Of all people, Henry Cabot Lodge insisted meretriciously then and there-after that the United States did not have any fingerprints on the generals' coup. Two days after he took office, President Johnson gathered Rusk, McNamara, McCone, and others to hear Lodge say that "we were not in-volved in the coup," though he acknowledged that economic pressures and the thousand-man withdrawal plan might have had an impact on events. Lodge said that Diem and Nhu would be "alive today" if they had followed his advice and accepted safe passage out of the country.[45]

Writing in the wake of the 1971 publication of the *Pentagon Papers,* which took a forensic approach to the disaster then coming to a boil in Vietnam, Lodge claimed that the August telegram setting such a coup in motion had been "cancelled"—in truth, it had and it hadn't—which "in effect removed the basis for the charge of US complicity in the Pentagon Papers account." In his 1973 memoir, *The Storm Has Many Eyes,* Lodge blithely scrubbed the record of culpability: "Because of our lack of involve-ment in the intricacies of Vietnamese political life, we could not have started a coup if we wanted to. Nor could we have stopped one once it started. Our policy, under instructions from President Kennedy, was 'not to thwart' a coup. . . . Being tolerably well informed is not the same as 'authorizing, sanctioning, and encouraging' the coup."[46]

Exit the DCM

It's said that a coping mechanism for tragedy is to get on with business. The grieving New Frontiersmen, now working for an alien president, wasted surprisingly little time doing so. On the morning of November 23, Secretary McNamara—he and Rusk had turned their Tokyo-bound plane around after the news from Dallas—wrote an urgent note to President Johnson, who was about to have his first meeting with Lodge. The secretary of defense was concerned, as were many, about "back-biting and sniping" about Harkins in Saigon—mostly generated now by Lodge—and a lack of cohesion in the Country Team in general.[47] "A key element" in the solution, McNamara said, was the selection of a new deputy chief of mission—"a good chief-of-staff type"—to succeed William Trueheart.

Trueheart knew his tour would soon be up. He had already gone to Lodge to tell him of Roger Hilsman's proffer of the key job at the State Department. Lodge told him, "If you want to, if it's a step up, why yes, I'll agree to it." And they quickly fell to talking about "who might replace me," Trueheart recalled.[48]

The State Department soon proposed two DCM candidates to Lodge: William Sullivan, Harriman's adjunct and a future American diplomat of great distinction, and Norbert Anschutz, the seasoned political counselor in Paris. Lodge didn't care for the suggestions, or the fact of them. He whined to Roger Hilsman that he "cannot understand why any other department or agency of the government should have a voice in the appointment of his DCM." Instead, Lodge chose another Foreign Service Officer, David Nes, whom he had run across in Cairo and at the United Nations, and who had made a good impression. Nes had already been a DCM in Tripoli and Rabat, and like Lodge, was both a former newspaperman and to the manner born. David Nes arrived in Saigon very quickly, enough to overlap with Trueheart, who relinquished his duties in mid-January 1964. As a Foreign Service family, we were accustomed to changes of plans, but this departure seemed hasty. The talk had always been about April or May, and we had barely moved into the new house.

Was my father pushed out the door? Some historians of the period speculate so, and so did Trueheart: "By the time I left there were plenty of people who were keen for me to go sooner rather than later. . . . The military were clearly anxious to see me out of there." He also thought it "very clear that Johnson was very much involved in the decision to replace me in Saigon. I think he may have been encouraged by the military, but it was his decision."[49]

General Harkins and unnamed others in the Pentagon associated Trueheart, not alone but correctly, with the Country Team skeptics who found military statistics and claims of progress against the Viet Cong increasingly difficult to credit. For the reputation he gained alienating Diem during the Nolting hiatus, Bill Trueheart was associated more than implicitly with the downfall of the regime. Harkins had abhorred it, and events were proving the coup no panacea. That reputation would soon have more serious consequences than a quick departure.

Made Boy

Looking back, it's easy enough to deduce that the war and the violence that surrounded me in those years had an impact on my young psyche. The rock-throwing against Vietnamese kids, the Molotov cocktails. How much was preadolescent hormones and sheer hijinx is impossible to say. But Saigon was a petri dish for more, especially in the fall of 1963, when I turned twelve.

The clandestine purchase of choice for my friends and me that autumn was a switchblade knife. We found they could be purchased, expensively for our allowances, at the Central Market. You had to ask the vendor, and he would bring out the selection surreptitiously, as the switchblades were "illegal." By now we each had one, which we would flick open menacingly in boisterous play with one another.

It was at this time, and also with help from the Saigon Central Market, that another group of seventh-graders formed a "gang"—*West Side Story* had just come out as a movie—called the Unsociables. Their members each wore faux-silk black motorcycle jackets emblazoned with dragons and other standard Vietnamese imagery, and, across the backs, their names embroidered. The Unsociables became instantly very cool in our school.

Feeling competitive, my circle followed suit. We organized our own gang, which we christened the Mafia. Instead of more expensive silk jackets we ordered custom-made cloth badges, which were small and black with gold lettering. We pinned them to our shirts as one would a name tag. The badges read: MAFIA, and below, in smaller letters, *Charlie,* or *Robert,* or *Greg,* or whoever. Our two gangs never did anything, of course, except hang out warily together and vaguely discuss the "rumble" we were going to have. With our badges.

My gang life came to an abrupt (and switchblade-free) conclusion. It was late in the autumn, probably December, because by now we had moved to the ex-residence on Hien Vuong. The coup was several weeks behind us.

My friend Robert Reardon and I, and perhaps one or two others, were wandering around my new precinct when we came to an alley. All the villas in the area were enclosed by high walls, plastered and whitewashed, topped with broken glass or barbed wire or both. One stretch of wall in a deserted part of the alley had begun to peel in great sheets of plaster. My pals and I began to help the process along, pulling off thin shards of plaster with satisfaction.

On a return visit to the scene of the crime a couple of days later, now just the two of us, Robert and I realized we could also remove some of the masonry itself, loosening the bricks behind the fallen plaster. As we started in on this, the owner of the house burst out of a gate in the wall: an elderly Frenchman, screaming bloody murder. We ran, zigzagging through the Saigon streets. He chased us down—in a taxi—and caught up with us a few blocks away. A few Vietnamese, perhaps from his own household staff, straggled up to watch the confrontation, conducted in French. I'm not certain whether Robert or I had this brilliant idea and which one followed suit, but when the angry Frenchman took down our names we provided him with those of the two leading guys in the Unsociables.

Several days later all of us Mafia boys were called into the principal's office at the American Community School. There we were told that the Unsociables we had named had solid alibis—one was even in Bangkok at the time. These boys had suggested that perhaps this "mistaken identity" was the work of the Mafia. The principal said that anyone who was not present at this incident in the alley could leave the room. The others left the room without a backward glance. Robert and I remained. A confession ensued.

That night, I was already in bed and in the dark when my father got home. He came into my room and sat on the bed. I felt his weight but couldn't see his face. He was not angry but appalled, wounded, worried. I believe all I could say was that I was very, very sorry. I was ashamed of myself and as shocked and puzzled by my behavior as he was. He either extracted a promise, or I made a silent promise, that it would not happen again—not that specifically, but anything like it. I believe it was the moment I decided I would keep my nose clean and eschew the path of the juvenile delinquent.

As I try to recall his deep hurt and my mortification, I understand now that this absurd vandalism happened at a juncture when Bill Trueheart might have felt his life was falling apart: working around the clock, under enormous pressure in a critical historical moment, being hurried out of his job, having cut the cord with his best friend, and having lost his own father. Now his firstborn had been fingered as a petty criminal and liar. This was not a good moment.

★ ★ ★

Endings

FTER A LONG ROUND of farewell parties and a flurry of packing, the Truehearts left Saigon on January 16, 1964. It was an emotional parting from the household staff, a family to us now. They lined up in the driveway to say goodbye just as they had greeted us twenty-seven months before. Josh's amah, Thi Lan, wept as she handed her charge off to Phoebe. In the car on the way to the airport, with me in the front passenger seat for the last time, my mother told Sinh how much we would miss him. At this Sinh lapsed into tears, his mouth twisted in grief as his affection tumbled out. That image of my friend reverberates in memory, as it did frequently as I watched Vietnam engulfed in war in the years that followed.

The journey home was leisurely, five weeks, taking in many of the sights that my mother had wanted to see, taking advantage of what might be the last time we would be in this part of the world. We started in New Delhi, with side trips to Agra and then Jaipur, where a family movie shows my brother crying because forced to ride atop an elephant. After a refueling stop in Tehran, where Josh saw snow for the first time, we landed in Beirut for a few days. We then flew to Egypt, our main destinations Luxor and Aswan.

News from Saigon reached us while we traveled. I felt a pang about being gone from the action, the Vietnam story continuing without me. On the last day of January, while we were in Abu Simbel, in Egypt, the November military junta was overthrown, bloodlessly. Ten days later terrorists set off a bomb at Pershing Field, where American soldiers and dependents played softball, where I had been a batboy, killing two US servicemen and wounding dozens. On February 16, another bomb went off at the Capital Kinh Do theater, my Bijou of the last two years; three Americans died. It would be a full year yet before President Johnson ordered all American dependents out of Vietnam.

We flew on from Cairo to London and stayed two weeks, seeing old friends, before boarding the SS *America* for what was to be my last ocean voyage. After ten years abroad, I remember the homecoming in New York harbor vividly, the charcoal immensity of the place we slowly approached in the harbor. Miraculously by father was able to rent from Hertz a black Plymouth convertible with red leather upholstery. We drove to Washington—why, I don't know, as it was a very long day's drive in those days. Possibly it was to remind us of America after a decade overseas.

Bill remarked in a quick note to Henry Cabot Lodge that "the trip was worthwhile, but I was reminded from time to time of Robert Benchley's remark that travelling with children is equivalent to travelling third class in Bulgaria."[1]

Since our departure from Saigon, Lodge had leapt into national consciousness as the surprise winner, as a write-in candidate thousands of miles away, of the New Hampshire Republican presidential primary. This was certainly fascinating news in the Trueheart household. My father's ex-boss and close colleague was on the cover of *Time* and *Newsweek*. Sucking up in his own way, Bill Trueheart wrote Lodge the day after the primary: "I hope it is not a violation of the Hatch Act for me to say that there was considerable rejoicing in the Trueheart household as the results came in last night."[2]

From Hawk to Dove

When Trueheart reported to work at the State Department six weeks after he had left Saigon, three significant things had happened:

1. The military junta in Saigon that carried out the November coup had itself been overthrown at the end of January, with US acquiescence. Lodge and McNamara embraced the new military leader, General Nguyen Khanh. The coup Khanh led was the second of a half-dozen nonviolent coups by fractious Vietnamese generals that would roil Vietnam's governance and Washington's public relations for the next three years. John Kenneth Galbraith's advice to President Kennedy as he had weighed the first coup—that "nothing succeeds like successors"—was proving to be funnier than it was true.[3]

2. Those who had believed in the necessity of the first coup thus were not in the best odor in the new Johnson regime. The most prominent of them, the godfather of the coup, Averell Harriman, saw his dreams of becoming secretary of state go up in smoke after the August 24 Telegram. The next to go was the coup's Washington mastermind, Roger Hilsman, Trueheart's patron, protector, and prospective boss. By the time the Truehearts reached American soil, Hilsman was out. The pugnacious intellectual might have appealed to Jack Kennedy but not to Lyndon Johnson.

3. Most concretely, the Bureau of Southeast Asian Affairs had been reorganized—shrunk. Vietnam was peeled off into its own high-level directorship. It left Trueheart, as he liked to remark, with "just the dominoes": Cambodia, Laos, Thailand, Burma. The deputy assistant secretary title that Hilsman had dangled did not go with this position.[4]

Reflecting on this years later, Trueheart said a case could be made that splitting the bureau made sense, given the primacy of the Vietnam dossier—but in that case it would have been logical to give *him* the Vietnam piece rather than the four countries he knew much less about: "I think it was very clear what they were trying to do. I was never under any misapprehension about that."[5] As Trueheart put it elsewhere, his "name was mud" with the military; a relationship of trust between the State Department and the Pentagon on Vietnam was essential. And the new president felt sandbagged by the coup.

Trueheart didn't say as much, but might have, and I would: a deeper professional engagement in the looming disaster in Vietnam was something he was fortunate to have been spared. By the fall of 1964, the senior advisers remaining at the State Department, the Pentagon, and the National Security Council were more willing to consider the military escalation in Vietnam, the bombing, the surge in combat troops that Johnson felt compelled to undertake in the months and years that followed.

"Only a few voices urged caution and questioned the need for escalation: midlevel staffers in the State Department such as William Trueheart, Alan Whiting, Robert Johnson, and Carl Salans," writes Jeffrey W. Helsing in *Johnson's War*. But their influence was limited by their middling stature and their lack of coherence in the bureaucracy.

These dissenters "lacked pulling power against men of the stature of Taylor, the Bundy brothers, Rostow, or Gen. Earle Wheeler, the new chairman of the Joint Chiefs of Staff," according to a shrewd Vietnam-savvy

FSO who worked with them, Paul Kattenburg. "They were all sufficiently career oriented not to dare pit their personal futures on the single issue of stopping the slide towards bombing. . . . [G]estures such as press statements or resignations would, in the context of these early times, have proved futile in any case."[6]

A colleague from the embassy in Saigon, George Bogardus, ran into Bill Trueheart at a party in Washington that spring, where "he said he was no longer a hawk."[7] One of the officers in the Southeast Asia Bureau, Norman B. Hannah, recalled his first meeting with his new boss, when Trueheart put his cards on the table right away: "Norm, I'm a dove."[8]

Few American fathers of his generation reached this conclusion about the Vietnam War so long before their sons. Bill Trueheart was undergoing his second Vietnam conversion. But I doubt he ever considered resigning from the Foreign Service over the deepening war in Vietnam. I believe he compartmentalized it. He couldn't imagine another life. But he did strenuously discourage the early interest I had in joining the Foreign Service, an interest the Foreign Service examinations wholly extinguished ten years later.

Trueheart did say, retrospectively, that he was glad to have been freed of Vietnam, "since I was totally out of sympathy with the policies that were being followed, particularly in further U.S. military involvement." As that took place, pushing US military personnel in Vietnam into the hundreds of thousands, Trueheart became a tolerated skeptic. President Johnson and Secretary Rusk had found it useful to retain Under Secretary George Ball as the loyal opposition; Trueheart termed him "the family dissenter" on Vietnam. Ball recruited Trueheart, among others, to prepare and frame his arguments. "I did," Trueheart recalled, "although I must say that I never had any particular solutions to this problem, other than to get out. I never saw any miraculous way to produce a negotiated solution to the problem. That wasn't a solution that was acceptable to the President and, for all I know, anybody else for a long time to come."[9]

Trueheart's State Department brief until 1966, as the officer in charge of the dominoes, "was to make sure, as far as we could, that the war wasn't allowed to spill over into Cambodia and into Laos." He said he never objected to bombing the Ho Chi Minh Trail, "provided we had the kind of controls on targeting." As for Cambodia, there was no doubt that Prince Sihanouk was facilitating the Viet Cong, but "I certainly objected very strongly to any actions which would take us across the border into Cambodia."

The Noltings in Washington

Fritz and Bittie Nolting had been back in Washington since September. With the expropriation of their farm, they had bought a stone colonial on Quebec Street near American University. Nolting was assigned to the USIA promotion board, a hall-walking job. After Lyndon Johnson became president, he was appointed to a talking shop called an "intelligence study group." President Kennedy's sincere instructions to find a senior posting for a diplomat he admired had expired in Dallas.

By February 1964, to no one's surprise, Fritz Nolting had decided to quit the Foreign Service. His name circulated for various jobs, including head of his alma mater, St. Christopher's School, in Richmond. In the end he took a plum position with Morgan Guaranty Bank in Paris. Of this career upheaval, Fritz tried to be jovial. Reporting the news to a friend, he wrote, "I'm joining the War on Poverty—starting with the Noltings!"[10] (The War on Poverty was one of Lyndon Johnson's Great Society programs.)

Nolting was still nursing his wounds. Though he retired in an official letter on February 25, two weeks later he wrote Secretary of State Rusk privately and plaintively:

I have been told that you feel:
1. That I was unwilling to go along with the State Department's policy while serving as US ambassador in Vietnam;
2. That I refused your personal request to extend my tour of duty there beyond two years;
3. That I was over-zealous after my return from Saigon in urging [support of Diem and opposing efforts to weaken him].

Nolting wrote there was "not one iota of truth" to number one, and "you and I know to what extent there is anything in the other two. I am quite sure there is no misunderstanding."[11]

He gnawed on this bone for a long time. In an April 14, 1964, letter to Rusk prolonging the argument, he expressed his resentment at the implication that he had abandoned the ship in Saigon—"left when the going got tough." On September 24 he sent Rusk another missive, seven accusatory pages long: "You well know to what extent my reputation and the well-being of my family have been hazarded for political reasons. Yet you never raised a finger to counteract false interpretations. . . . It was you who finally participated in the rug-pulling job."

Nolting believed he had been "accused of leaving when the going got rough. And that really burned me up."[12] To Maggie Higgins, who sent him chapters of her new book on Vietnam that summer, he wrote: "It still makes my blood boil to relive those days."[13] To General Harkins, his old confrère, Fritz wrote that Bittie had told him, "'If we don't get off this subject we will both go nuts.' She is right. It has been the most painful and frustrating eight months I have ever been through."[14]

I feel the guilt of having had a clumsy supporting role in the Nolting-Trueheart family breach.

Despite a gap of three years in our ages—we were twelve and fifteen now—Jane Nolting and I had been friends for a long time. One day in Washington, in the spring of 1964, as the Noltings were picking up and moving again to Paris, Jane stopped by for a visit. It may have been to say goodbye. I asked her if she'd like to see my room in our new house. I was proud of my new furniture and the fact that I had my own telephone extension in the bedroom.

What I had not thought through carefully, as I escorted Jane upstairs to see it, were the things I had recently taped to a wall of my room. Jane spotted them the moment she walked in: the *Time* and the *Newsweek* covers featuring Henry Cabot Lodge in the wake of his New Hampshire primary victories. Jane looked at me, stricken. I am sure she saw a face no less stricken. She said, "I don't know why you have that up there." I said, "I don't either." We walked out of the room in silence. This remains one of the two or three most embarrassing moments of my life.

The story goes that the Noltings and the Truehearts severed their ties after the summer of 1963. Fritz and Bill "never spoke to each other again"— that's what I say now. In point of fact, according to Phoebe, Bill and Fritz once did cross paths, literally, at the Metropolitan Club in Washington in the mid-1960s. The two gentlemen former friends, unexpectedly approaching one another in the gilded spaces, apparently found greetings unavoidable. Phoebe told me they asked about each other's children and moved on.

Late in her ninety-seventh year, Bittie Nolting and I became reacquainted on visits to see her in Charlottesville, where she lives in her own apartment at a well-heeled eldercare complex. I finally wound around gingerly to the matter of the severed family ties.

Bittie Nolting at first expressed surprise that I would think such a thing. Or she tried to. I was openly skeptical.

Did you see each other in Washington after we had returned?

"Oh yes," Bittie said. She recalled that Phoebe and I had come over to the house they were vacating on Quebec Street to say goodbye. She remembered me sitting atop a rolled-up rug.

Okay, but what about the four of you, the two couples?

She had to think about that, but not long. "Maybe just Phoebe." This I can imagine. Their friendship of two decades, through their husbands, demanded as much.

When I mentioned later that the whole business had hurt both of their careers, Bittie begged to differ about Bill. "Bill was almost immediately appointed ambassador to Nigeria."[15] Six years later, I thought, but did not say.

Fritz still fought the old battles. Every year he would be sought out by anniversary-obsessed news organizations around November 1 to look back at the 1963 coup. In correspondence with his friend Cy Sulzberger at the *New York Times,* in 1966, Nolting made the only reference I have found that either he or Bill ever made to their philosophical training in Charlottesville: "The attempt to define representative government is as old as Plato, but, by any reasonable definition, the Vietnamese people had more of it under President Diem—and a far better opportunity to perfect it—than they have had since his overthrow."[16]

That summer, holidaying on Elba, Fritz wrote his brother Buford about a young cousin of theirs who had been killed in Vietnam: "How sad it is. If I had won my fight against turning a pacification program into a big war it might never have happened to Erskine and many others. But what to do now I cannot see. Restless even in this beautiful calm place."[17]

In December, Nolting wrote Sulzberger again to share his animus about the journalists and the burning bonzes: "I cannot help believing that certain American reporters in Vietnam could, on several occasions, have saved a life (and lost a story) simply by turning to the nearest Vietnamese policeman to report what they knew about the preparations for the next dreadful and pitiable self-sacrifice." On the tenth anniversary of the coup Nolting said he saw it as "a somber reminder that honorable conduct and the successful pursuit of our national goals are indivisible."[18]

Nguyen Van Thu

The Truehearts brought Vietnam home to Washington in the living form of Nguyen Van Thu. Thu had been the ranking member of our Saigon domestic staff. He was a brisk, self-effacing man of about fifty. The opportunity to live in the United States and work for us must have appealed to Thu, as it did for us to ease the trauma of Phoebe's transition from extravagant overseas help to suburban housewife drudgery. Edward, the London-born dachshund, had stayed behind in Saigon in the Nes household, and so Nes—having tried and failed to get the dog on a military plane returning to Washington with Secretary McNamara—made arrangements for the dog to fly with Thu, commercial, just in time for Thu to help unpack the shipping boxes as we moved into our new house in Spring Valley, on Tilden Street in northwest Washington.

There Thu lived in a third-floor bedroom. He did household chores well below his previous standing in Saigon—vacuuming, laundering, cooking (for Josh and me), and shopping, although he spoke no English. The language lessons we sprung for never took; in any case we were all comfortable in French. Thu was in touch with other expatriate Vietnamese in Washington (there were a few even then) and usually went off Sundays to join their regular conclave.

I remember as a seventh-grader spending afternoons in the basement on Tilden Street with Thu while he ironed—shades of hanging with Sinh in the driveway. While he worked at the ironing board, periodically Thu would strike a match and suck on a contraption consisting of a square Twinings Tea can filled with water, into which a thin bamboo stem had been inserted. He would stand back from the long inhale and spew a long stream of unfamiliar smoke into the room.

He received supplies of his special tobacco, if I am not mistaken, through the diplomatic pouch, via the US embassy in Saigon, along with other comestibles and medicines he required and that his family at home supplied. In college I recognized the device retrospectively as a bong, but still have to believe that even in those simpler days Thu wouldn't have been smoking cannabis in front of me, or in the house, let alone having it sent through official channels. But who knows?

Knowing what we know now—for example, in the famous case of Pham Xuan An, the American journalists' loyal fixer of the day who was working all along for the North Vietnamese[19]—I have to ask myself whether Nguyen Van Thu played another role, in Saigon and then with us in Washington, than household servant. If so, he deserved an Oscar. He stayed in Washington no more than two years, as he had family awaiting him.

Paris, 1969

I had some correspondence and one encounter with Fritz Nolting in the years that followed our departures from Saigon.

In 1969, as I was graduating from Exeter, I sent commencement invitations to a few adults, as was the custom, more by way of courtesy than expectation. One was to Michael Forrestal, now back practicing law at Shearman and Sterling and active as a leading Exeter alumnus; he had written a letter of recommendation for my admission. I also invited my godparents.

Writing from the Place Vendôme offices of Morgan Guaranty, in his orderly hand marked with strong ascenders and descenders, Fritz wrote back in thanks with regrets:

> I have been a far-away and neglectful God-father (or is it "guard-father"?) but I see that has done no harm—probably the reverse. Just keep up the good work and you may be President—if you want to.
>
> Do you remember the old man with the white beard you were baptized with, Mr. Mason, who, you said, looked like Santa Claus? Well, I saw him the other day—unchanged, except his beard has gotten thinner and turned yellow.
>
> Jane asked me—"Hey, am I included in the invitation?" I said, "Yes." OK? We'd all like to be there, but we can't.
>
> Best of luck. Fritz.[20]

A few weeks later I was in Paris, too, with a summer job. Naturally I returned to the American Cathedral, where I had been baptized in 1957, on many Sunday mornings. One Sunday, as I had hoped I would, I glimpsed Fritz from behind, sitting a few pews ahead. I recorded the encounter in a letter to a friend who knew the story. With the service over,

I stood out in the aisle and turned toward him, smiling. He gave me a pleasant smile and I continued to smile and he did a proverbial doubletake.

He: Is that you?

Yes, it is.

(Arm around me.) Well I'll be damned. (Thick southern accent; I had forgotten.) It's great to see you.[21]

He introduced me to a few other people and repeated the story of old Mr. Mason and the beard and Santa Claus at my baptism. Afterward on his way home he dropped me off at a Metro station. I never saw him again, although four years later, I sent the Noltings an invitation to my Amherst commencement. In a letter that doesn't survive, Fritz wrote with congratulations and said he hoped I would explain to Josh what had happened, when the time was appropriate. This narrative fulfills that obligation.

Evidently I was shamelessly hedging my bets. As my Exeter graduation approached, I also sent an invitation to Henry Cabot Lodge. "We would accept with the greatest pleasure if it were possible," he wrote back. "Remembering you so well from our days in Saigon in 1963, I shall always follow your advance through life."[22]

Lodge dictated this letter to me from Paris on June 3, 1969. After a second brief tour as ambassador in Saigon, and a year as US ambassador to West Germany, Lodge was now President Richard Nixon's chief negotiator (and Averell Harriman's successor) at the Vietnam peace talks, then groaning forward in their second year in Paris.

For Fritz Nolting the reappearance of his successor was distasteful. He had remade his life at Morgan Guaranty and become a vestryman at the American Cathedral, and here was the bitter Vietnam memory back in his midst. Like many Episcopal priests, the then dean of the Cathedral, the Very Rev. Sturgis Riddle, had a magnetic attraction to power. Once Lodge, an Episcopalian, reached Paris, Riddle immediately proposed the distinguished statesman for the vestry, the church's governing council.

Nolting wrote Riddle privately at once. He said his "convictions" about Lodge "involve more than judgments about policy, on which we have all made mistakes. They involve what I think religion is about—the behavior of a man towards his fellow-man in the light of his spiritual beliefs." After reciting to the clergyman the history of the coup, Nolting concluded: "The albatross of Diem's murder still hangs heavy around our country's neck, and especially around the necks of those who plotted his downfall. But, my dear friend, if I am faced with the duty of voting upon his nomination as a member of our vestry, I could not in good conscience vote for him . . . and I would have to make clear my reasons among our colleagues."[23] No reply from Riddle is extant. Henry Cabot Lodge never served on the Cathedral vestry. For many months the two former ambassadors from Saigon could not have avoided seeing one another in the pews or at the communion rail, almost certainly nodding politely.

Both men left Paris shortly thereafter. Lodge became US ambassador to the Holy See, which apparently did not share Nolting's ethical concerns. The Noltings moved to New York and an apartment on Fifth Avenue as Fritz joined Morgan Guaranty's home office for four more years.

Ambassador Trueheart

In an echo of his earliest years in government, Trueheart's next assignment was as number two in INR, the State Department's Bureau of Intelligence and Research. For two years Trueheart was back at his old game of interagency coordination on intelligence matters; the revelations of CIA funding of US student organizations and publications was one, the sinking of the USS *Pueblo* in 1968 another. In August 1969 President Nixon appointed Trueheart US ambassador to Nigeria. Lagos, then the capital city, was a class 1 post, one of the largest embassies in the world, and Trueheart was but fifty. He was sworn in at the State Department by Elliot Richardson, the under secretary of state, and retired Supreme Court justice Stanley Reed, a Maysville "cousin" of Phoebe. Swooning with pride, Sallie came up from Richmond for the event.

It was at that seventh-floor ceremony that Jonathan Moore, Richardson's aide and a onetime State Department colleague of Trueheart, is reported by Halberstam to have told me on the sidelines that Bill's ambassadorship was "overdue, long overdue, it should have been done a long time ago." Moore (a future boss of mine) must be Halberstam's source for this anecdote, as I don't recall it happening that day. It appears on page 261 of *The Best and the Brightest,* concluding Halberstam's section on the Nolting-Trueheart affair. My passing mention in the book briefly earned me a nickname at Amherst College after it was published: "Page 261."[24]

Even before he reached Nigeria, Trueheart's adventures in Saigon were resuscitated. "Some important people believed he was a CIA spymaster incarnate," said his DCM in Lagos, Edward Mulcahy, much later, and "others believed that he had been sent to stage a coup against the Federal Military Government."[25]

Nigeria in 1969 was, as Vietnam had been, a country divided and at war. The oil-rich southeastern region of Biafra was in the grips of an armed secession movement that had attracted sympathy in Western countries because of the ensuing humanitarian crisis. The Nixon administration was in favor of maintaining the enormous Nigerian federation, even as some of its allies (such as the French and the Israelis) were shipping arms to the rebels. Congressional Democrats in Washington also warmed to the Biafran secessionists.

"We had taken a very curious position as a government," Ambassador Trueheart recalled: "We had said we would be neutral in this matter. Of course, to the Nigerian Government, being neutral in a conflict to secede was hardly neutral in their minds. We had carried this to the point where we would not even supply spare parts for weapons which we had already provided the federal government under military assistance arrangements. So by the time I got there, our relations with the federal government were very cool."

Trueheart struggled, too, with the lack of consensus about Nigeria policy in Washington, notably divergences between the White House and the State Department, whose minds were in any case fixated on . . . Vietnam: "When you got a telegram from Washington, you had to think very hard, 'Which department did this one come from?' It really was that bad. The infighting was extreme. . . . I found it, by all odds, even much worse than Vietnam, my worst experience in trying to carry out a policy directed from a divided Washington."[26] Strong words given his experience in Saigon.

This icy relationship did not make for an enviable assignment for Trueheart. Accustomed to calling regularly on a chief of state, even as *chargé d'affaires* in Saigon, the new ambassador was stiff-armed by the Nigerian leadership, led by a sober young general named Yakubu Gowon. Trueheart waited five weeks to present his credentials in Lagos and had trouble securing appointments with leading officials thereafter.

He also had trouble with his own overlords in Washington. As one of his embassy political officers, Howard Walker, later told the story, Trueheart had orders to deliver to General Gowon a lecture about the government's approach to Biafra:

> Trueheart felt instruction was unwise. But he was a real professional. He understood that you don't just tell Washington that this is hairbrained. [In a telegram to the State Department] he argued a substantive point that demonstrated an appreciation of the bureaucratic politics back in Washington. . . . But Bill, being the erudite person he was, had a sentence in there: "All right, I will bell the cat." We learned later this just sent people bananas. [In Washington, they] hit the roof . . . The message back to Trueheart was, 'You carry out these instructions clearly or we'll get someone else.' They very quickly did. They yanked this first-class officer out of there. That was the end of his career.[27]

In his own telling for an oral history, Bill Trueheart did not mention that contretemps. He said instead that he ran afoul of the Nigerian ambassador in Washington, who sought to undercut him, including making veiled references to his southern background. Mulcahy, his DCM, remembered that the Nigerian diplomat, Joseph Iyalla, "had spread the word that Trueheart was a racist . . . and this helped poison the well too."[28] Ambassador Walker, who is both a Virginian and an African American, told me there is "not a scintilla" of truth to this judgment of Trueheart.[29]

Many years later, in Paris, I found a clue to what helped to poison the well for Bill in Lagos. It came from my *other* godfather, Benjamin Pierce, at the only occasion I had to see him in his last twenty years of life. With wicked panache, in front of others who did not know my parents, Ben volunteered the story of a letter my mother had written to her mother in Maysville, describing their new ambassadorial life in Lagos.

My grandmother, who had all of Phoebe's grasping but none of her judgment, shared the letter with her friend Martha Comer, editor of the local *Ledger-Independent* and a longtime chronicler of Phoebe's foreign exploits. Martha in turn published the letter's most amusing passages as part of a long feature about the glamorous life of the hometown girl in a far-off embassy. "She ruined his career!" Ben Pierce cackled.

I don't know on what authority Ben had this, but he obviously knew something. Even at the time Phoebe had mailed me a clipping of the Maysville article (headline: "She Copes with Staff of 12"), whose descriptions of the household staff and Nigerians in general were not exactly racist but hardly presentable, then or now. I remember Phoebe's mortification (and my own) and her fury at her mother, but the matter may have been more serious than I thought.[30] It was serious enough, according to a Trueheart family friend in Washington, that "poor Bill had to go to the [Nigerian] government and explain. That was all he needed. I think Phoebe has stopped writing letters home, except maybe, 'Having wonderful time. Wish you were here.'"[31]

Be that as it may, Bill Trueheart's only ambassadorship was a dud. I think he felt out of place. His superior in the State Department, assistant secretary David Newsom, didn't like him either. He was not, like Newsom, an Africa hand. Nor was meant to be.

After two years in Lagos, Bill Trueheart came home for the last time. He became diplomat-in-residence at the Air War College at Maxwell Air Force Base, in Montgomery, Alabama, for two years—a reliable pasture for senior FSOs who may not be heading anywhere—and then took a State Department job in Washington involving negotiations on the Law of the Sea. It was not exactly walking the halls, but it was clear his career was over. He retired from the Foreign Service in October 1974, aged fifty-five, after thirty-three years on the government payroll.

Halberstam Redux

Another person from Saigon, with whom I traded only handshakes as a little boy, came into my life when I was a senior in college: David Halberstam. I was looking for a job on a newspaper, and doubtless thanks to a prompt from Bill Trueheart, Halberstam agreed to see me one day in the spring of 1973 at his apartment in Turtle Bay. He knew from Bill that I had been a college journalist, as well as the author of a book published while I was a sophomore, but he was not acquainted with my work, such as it was.

Nonetheless we sat down over strong coffee and cigarettes at his kitchen table and—I could hardly believe this as it unfolded—one of the most famous journalists in America proceeded to telephone the editors (all of them his friends) of the *Boston Globe, Minneapolis Tribune, Newsday,* and *Philadelphia Inquirer.* Hard to imagine in this day and age, but David reached all of them just like that, chewed the fat, extolled my virtues, and said they should hire me. I was chagrined that none did, although each later made generous time for me. I did find my first job in journalism through another older reporter who thought I was worth the trouble, and my new employers were impressed that I had provided Halberstam as a reference on my thin résumé.

David Halberstam entered my life once more during those years, in that first job, as an editorial writer and book page editor of the *Greensboro (NC) Daily News.*

Halberstam, a best-selling author now, much in demand, appeared in Greensboro on the evening of Tuesday, October 14, 1975, for the city's "Town Meeting on Books" at Greensboro College, preceded by a dinner among the town swells at the Greensboro Country Club. Having had a hand in extending David the invitation, I was unnerved to discover what many years of running speaker programs has since revealed to be utterly routine: the contents of his thirty-minute address were held on the back of a folded envelope in a few illegible scrawls, perhaps no more than twenty random words. Halberstam would be ad-libbing his address, not that the well-oiled audience would care.

While the other featured author, the North Carolina novelist Doris Betts, was speaking first, David asked me to join him for a smoke in the wings, offstage in the auditorium. We were in the semi-darkness. We must have started talking about Fritz and Bill—which I don't believe we had in his apartment in New York—because at one point he turned to me and said the story would make a great novel.

He pulled out his pen and started scratching out an outline on the other side of the folded envelope. The Virginia gentlemen and their excellent adventure. The college pals in the crucible of Vietnam. The betrayal over matters of conscience and duty. I remember only this specific detail of what Halberstam said: the symbolic fact that Bill Trueheart had two *sons,* whereas Fritz Nolting had four *daughters.* A bizarre and irrelevant apposition, but David seemed to think it meant something.

Halberstam was that kind of man. Certainly tall and confident and unsubtle—and "*so* attractive," per Phoebe—but who could get carried away with the sound of his own voice, on paper and in person. But for all that, it's fair to say that the suggestion from Halberstam that night in Greensboro set me to thinking and has made its way through four decades of thinking into these pages of nonfiction.

The Business with Fritz

Since the early 1960s the Richmond papers had faithfully chronicled the two Virginians in Saigon. In 1976 they took the opportunity of Trueheart's presence in town, for his mother Sallie's funeral, to interview him. In retirement he had just completed a stint on the staff of the Senate Select Committee on Intelligence, which was looking into the CIA and the assassination plots, including the one he knew something about.

From the Vietnam experience then beginning to recede from view, Trueheart drew four lessons for the Richmond reporter. The "incorrect analysis" of a unified Sino-Soviet bloc. "Associating ourselves with elements of society that are out of touch with the historical forces." The limits of military prowess. And finally, "the idea that you can build support in this country for any policy if you put your mind to it."

The *Richmond Times-Dispatch* reporter, Ray McAllister, brought up Nolting.

"We had a long friendship which ended with this period," Trueheart said, adding somewhat surprisingly or disingenuously, "It didn't on my part, but he was certainly very unhappy with what happened." He summarized the dispute from his point of view: "I think he felt my job was to do nothing, except to hold the reins. I felt that I was in charge, and had to report and recommend . . . without regard for what he might have done."

McAllister called Nolting for comment: "'I don't want to talk about that. He was an old friend . . .' The voice trailed off."[32]

Toward others he thought had double-crossed him, Nolting was less gentlemanly. He told Averell Harriman's biographer, Rudy Abramson, that "Hilsman got the rap (which he deserved) but Harriman bears the main responsibility. . . . Nobody, in my opinion is as directly responsible for that disaster as is Averell Harriman."[33] Puzzlingly, he told Abramson not to quote him on that point.

After retiring from Morgan in New York, the Noltings moved to Charlottesville, where Fritz was diplomat in residence at the University of Virginia, then a professor of business administration, and then the first director of UVA's Miller Center, a public policy institute.

By the mid-1980s, Fritz Nolting had begun to write his Vietnam memoir. He wrestled with what he regarded as a last will and testament. To help him perfect his draft, he called on the services of a State Department historian, Suzanne Coffman. When I spoke to her in 2020, she described Fritz as "tired, but not bitter. He seemed content, on an even keel, low-key, gracious. He wanted to get the memoir done. He smoked like a chimney." Coffman said, "I admire that kind of stubbornness. You're paid not just to do the job but to give people the benefit of your experience. You have to say, 'this is wrong.'"[34]

She recalled just one sudden reference Nolting made to Trueheart in one of their meetings in Charlottesville: "The son of a bitch is my friend." Coffman was struck by Fritz's use of the present tense.

What *was* the business with Fritz? Was it nothing more than a terrible misunderstanding? A rational person or an advice columnist might say that Fritz and Bill could have straightened things out between them if only they had talked, talked as only friends can talk. Not just when Fritz was on the high seas in June 1963, but before and after, and even long after.

I'm confounded that they didn't, or wouldn't. I'm struck by Fritz's passivity when he and his beliefs were most in jeopardy. Granted, Bill among many others kept Fritz out of the picture during the dramatic days of June 1963. But why did Fritz not take the initiative on his own? He was the American ambassador to a country riveting his own government's attention, and intermittently the world's. As my brother asked, why did he assume someone else would let him know what was important? I think Fritz knew what was going on; he was too smart not to suspect it.

Mea culpa is what Bill wrote and said after he reestablished contact, in the letter Fritz tore to pieces. That is contrition in any language. But I would make a distinction between the remorse Bill felt about keeping Fritz unwitting about serious events, and Bill's conviction that he had to do what was right by his lights as *chargé*. Not just in following orders on matters of high diplomacy, as he was, but in carrying out a policy he had come to embrace.

Arthur Miller, the playwright, once said, "betrayal is the only truth that sticks." *Truth* is an interesting choice of word there. Miller seems to be saying that betrayal is not a matter of opinion; it either is betrayal or it isn't, and it never goes away. Putting it in a marital context sharpens the point.

The only salve for betrayal is forgiveness. I think the record is pretty clear that neither Fritz nor Bill ever forgave the other. They couldn't. It was a matter of principle.

There are much bigger principles here that don't have anything to do with the vagaries of friendship. Bill Trueheart, who made no bones about the American blessing and impetus for the 1963 coup, was asked later what he thought of the murder of Diem and Nhu: "I was sorry to hear it, but I certainly wasn't too surprised," he replied. All the US intelligence and analysis he had seen suggested this "would be a very likely concomitant of a coup in Vietnam."[35]

A rather bloodlessly analytical response. I have often asked myself, in trying to plumb why Bill never wanted to talk about Vietnam as it went on to dominate American life, whether he felt, among other things, that he had blood on *his* hands—and not just that of the Ngo brothers. An unconscious part of Bill's anger at Fritz after the damning efficiency report might have been fueled by his own shame at the grisly denouement of the Diem era, or even at the inevitability it gave to the tragic war. This theory is only that.

Asked about the "ethics" of taking out a foreign leader, dead or alive, Bill Trueheart expressed both his guiding principle and the exception that proved the rule. This is the way he cast his professional judgments.

"I have as many questions about the basic ethics of it as I do about the efficacy of it," he said. "Having been involved with State Department approval of covert operations in a very broad way, I'm inclined to think that over time these operations have cost this country far more than we have ever achieved from them."

Then he turned to the exception: Vietnam, 1963. "In this case and by this time, these concerns were greatly offset by the feeling that we had been *had* by these people. We felt we had a broader commitment than just to Diem. We had a commitment, in effect, to the Vietnamese people. To do anything to perpetuate this Diem regime was not in the interests of Vietnam *or* the United States."[36]

These are brave words. Yet look where that commitment led us. To put it mildly, as Bill might, overthrowing governments is not worth the candle. On that first principle, he and Fritz would have to agree.

ACKNOWLEDGMENTS

Diplomats at War is the work of scores of people who deserve recognition and gratitude far greater than these acknowledgments can suggest.

For generous hospitality on my research trips and writing binges: In Virginia, Jay Tolson and Jane Little, Haywood and Joanne Blakemore, Zachary and Donna Fleetwood, Robert and Martha Wilson, and Lincoln Perry and Ann Beattie; in Washington, Jerry Knight, and Amy Bondurant and David Dunn; in Boston, Heather and Robert Keane, and James Houghton and Connie Coburn; in Florida, Phyllis Rose and Laurent de Brunhoff, and Jeffrey Hunter and Janet Griffin; and in Santenay, France, Timothy Boggs and James Schwartz.

For the wonderful writing spaces where this book came together, other than the American Library in Paris, endless thanks to Kim and Mary Lou Bradley for the use of their *pied-à-terre* in Neuilly, and before that, to the American Center for Art and Culture in Paris, better known for years as the Mona Bismarck Foundation, and Bianca Roberts and Patricia Quevedo Henry in particular.

For conversations and correspondence about our Vietnam days, I'm grateful to have renewed acquaintance after six decades with onetime Saigon kids C. J. Bready, David Burford, Duncan Caldwell, Carl Colby, Kathy Dobronyi, Lisa Manfull Harper, Todd Layton, Towny Manfull, Priscilla Mendenhall, Alain Perry, Marie Perry, and John H. Richardson. Among the Saigon 1963 survivors who were adults at the time, those who spoke to me were Anthony Lake and, before their recent deaths, Claire Breckon, Thomas Hughes, Robert McCabe, the Honorable Robert Miller, Rufus Phillips, and Kenneth N. Rogers. Jim Nach, a retired Foreign Service Officer who served in Vietnam in the late 1960s and again in the early 2000s, is a storehouse of information about the US embassy in Saigon dating back to World War II. He was exceedingly generous with his time.

For insights, assistance, and comfort along the way, I am thankful to Alex and Hong Brassert, Suzanne Coffman, Francesca Forrestal, George Gibson, Ellen Hampton, Dong Hoa Ho, Diane Johnson, Alice Kaplan, Christopher Klein, Emily Lodge, the late Honorable James Lowenstein, the late David McGovern, Viet Thanh Nguyen, Alan Riding, George Rodrigue, Elvira Roussel, Chris Schaefer, Frances Plough Seder, Susan Sheehan, Whit Stillman, Henry Trueheart, Louise Trueheart, Matthew Trueheart, Edward L. Turner, the Honorable Howard K. Walker, and Ben Wilkinson. For the chance to write about Vietnam in their pages while I was researching this book, thanks too to Bruce Falconer at the *American Scholar* and Philip Terzian at the *Weekly Standard*.

Fredrik Logevall at Harvard has given warm encouragement to this book from its inception. Fred's work on the French in Indochina, *Embers of War*, is a revelatory cautionary tale; his monograph *Choosing War* is the indispensable exploration of the Vietnam might-have-beens of 1963—to which I would add Marc Selverstone's new work, *The Kennedy Withdrawal*. At Dartmouth College, one of the great contemporary scholars of the period and a particular expert on the Buddhist crisis, Edward Miller, received me warmly as a walk-in and shared with me his thoroughgoing analysis of the Buddhist crisis. William Rust and the late William Prochnau, who interviewed Bill Trueheart for their books on this period, were generous with their help; Rust's unpublished manuscript on the life of Lucien Conein was enlightening. Luke Nichter, author of the newest biography of Henry Cabot Lodge, also did me a favor by sharing his research.

Marc Selverstone at the University of Virginia's Miller Center opened university doors for me at the outset, offered research guidance and gentle correction throughout, and pointed me toward a fine publisher at the end: a real gift. Thanks also at the University to the unfailingly helpful and efficient people at the Albert and Shirley Small Special Collections Library, where I spent many days plumbing Fritz Nolting's papers. Stephen Marrone, a PhD candidate in philosophy at UVa, read and analyzed the Nolting and Trueheart philosophy dissertations with helpful acumen so that I wouldn't have to; his adviser, Talbot Brewer, steered me to Stephen.

At the National Archives and Research Administration, John Carland was a generous sherpa, as was Tiffany Hamlin Cabrera at the State Department's Office of the Historian. Her insightful PhD dissertation from Howard University explores the global phenomenon of self-immolation as a frame for the bonze burnings of 1963. Lindsey Krasnoff, a former State Department historian, pointed the way for me. Other research assistance for which I am grateful came from Abigail Altman and Bojan Kupirovic at the American Library in Paris, Stacey Chandler at the John F. Kennedy Library in Boston, Anna Clutterbuck-Cook at the Massachusetts Historical Society in Boston, Laura Russo at the Howard Gotlieb Archival Research Center at Boston University, and Monica Johnson at the Association for Diplomatic Studies and Training.

At the University of Virginia Press, lasting gratitude to my superb editor, Nadine Zimmerli, who handled me and this book with compassion and respect, and also to Susan Murray, for sharp copyediting, Ellen Satrom, for cheerfully managing the publication process, and to Clayton Butler, Jason Coleman, and Mary Kate Maco, for finding the best audience for the book. A tip of the hat to Rafe Sagalyn for his engagement with the Press on my behalf and to David Lindroth for his maps of Vietnam and Saigon in 1963.

The warmest gratitude of all goes to the other family in this story: to Bittie Nolting, Lindsay Nolting, Jane Nolting, and Mary Tyler Temple for their understandably cautious but somehow trusting embrace of this project. Since 2016, Lindsay, the family historian, has been unstinting in her cooperation while always sticking up for her dad, may he, too, rest in peace.

My lasting thanks finally for the kindness and acumen of Cullen Murphy and Robert Ruby for reading and improving the full manuscript, and for critical commentary on various sections as the book took shape by David Mosser Brown, Anne Swardson, and Josh Trueheart.

The aforementioned Anne Swardson was the indispensable ingredient in this enterprise, as its champion and sounding board. Thus, in the hope of repaying hers, my dedication.

CT
September 2023
Staunton, Virginia

In the prologue I describe *Diplomats at War* as a work of memory hiding inside a work of history. That's one way to put it, but only to avoid calling it a memoir outright.

There is no escaping that I lived this experience as a child old enough and curious enough, even at ten and eleven and twelve, to remember things. The narrative surfaces what I do recall, but my recall is selective, as well it might be for a preadolescent eyewitness (and an aging scribe). Of course I was aware of the troubles besetting the leaders of South Vietnam and the United States, and aware that my father was working very hard, but I took the most wrenching and violent moments of the period in stride, remarkably so. My preoccupations were my school and my friends. I had no inkling of the personal drama between Bill and Fritz while it was going on from May through September 1963. My mother filled me in a bit just afterward, and she, at least, was writing down important things for unspecified future eyes.

Remembered though it is, this account is chiefly a work of history— that is, research, rediscovery, information sought and learned, beginning with fellow witnesses. *Diplomats at War* gave me a pretext to look up old friends from Saigon days. Today the sixth-graders of 1963 are in their seventies if they are still alive. The Facebook page called "Saigon Kids" covers a cohort dating into the late 1950s and ending abruptly in early 1965, when President Johnson ordered all the families ("dependents") out of Vietnam. I am struck in every post I read by how we experienced the same things largely in the same way, and how the experience defined us as definite oddities immediately thereafter in the climate of the US war in Vietnam, and long since. Along with my contemporaries, I am grateful to my parents for keeping close track of my activities for the benefit of their families back in the United States; as a historian I am especially grateful to my paternal grandmother for saving every scrap they and I sent her during this period (and long before and after).

Former kids aside, the real loss for the late-arriving historian is that most of the adult men and women in this story, its principal actors, are no longer alive. Their response to this book would have been of profound importance to me. Several whom I was lucky enough to interview, young sprouts in Vietnam in those days, have since gone to their reward. Thus the official oral history interviews they granted are essential to this book and to understanding what it was like then and there, even if they were recorded two or three decades after the fact: The interviewees still had their wits about them; Vietnam was almost invariably (as for Bill and Fritz) the crucible of their professional lives; and they had had a long time already to think about it. Their memories were rinsed, of course, with the hindsight of a story that went terribly wrong, the shame of a generation. That's the subliminal part of this whole drama.

Happily, and provocatively, what the writer is denied from these actuarial facts is offset by the staggering scholarship and memoirship that explores this two-year period. I'd like to think I've read every book that treats it, and the reader can judge for herself whether there are serious omissions, but the list below represents homage to those who have plowed the field before me with truly serious intent. Judging by the citations, you can tell which works of history and recollection made the biggest impression on this narrative: John Mecklin's nearly contemporaneous and idiosyncratic *Mission in Torment;* Neil Sheehan's masterful macro/micro *A Bright Shining Lie;* both of David Halberstam's Vietnam books; the recorded recollections in particular of President Kennedy's young assistant Michael Forrestal and the future Foreign Service eminence William Sullivan; the memoir of John Richardson, another Saigon kid with a fixation on his father; among others. It goes without saying that I hoovered everything I could find of what Bill Trueheart and Fritz Nolting had to say about all this. Fritz had the historiographical advantage, with a slender memoir and a university archive and a more important role in history. But Bill got his story out—he was, after all, in good company as everything went awry in Vietnam—in ways more indirect and characteristic of him.

My debt to the many professional historians and archivists who assisted me in this project can be found in the acknowledgments, but this is one place to give credit to two little-known institutions which were essential to this work.

The first is the Office of the Historian at the Department of State. It's something of a miracle that it has escaped the chopping block of zealous members of Congress. Its four-volume (1961–63) Vietnam series of compendiums of *Foreign Relations of the United States* (*FRUS*) reproduce the official telegrams and other declassified correspondence of the period. These documents—White House memos to the president, dispatches from Saigon on breaking developments, CIA analyses of policy options, infighting and towel-snapping among the principals, and discerning *comptes-rendus* of conversations with the Vietnamese chief of state—are generously sampled and superbly annotated and indexed. They were my principal map for this narrative.

The other institution sounds like a covert intelligence agency in a spy novel: the Association for Diplomatic Studies and Training (ADST). The oral histories ADST has archived and in most cases conducted, using experienced retired Foreign Service Officers as interviewers, gave me the deepest insights into what Fritz and Bill and many others candidly thought, as well as what they said that was sometimes at odds with the truth—even the truth as they knew it. The historian can't ask for more than that, and seldom gets it even from personal letters. But as I read and reread dozens of these interviews, of the most junior embassy diplomats and the most powerful Washington insiders, recounting how they found their way from the unlikeliest corners to a peripatetic life as diplomats and a very specific brush with history in Vietnam, I was constantly reminded what a service ADST is providing to future historians by putting the questions that mattered to the people who had had to answer them. I know ADST has kept busy interviewing succeeding generations of American Foreign Service Officers who have had to deal with decisions from on high that do not always accord with reality or common sense. In an age when perishable email has made the historical record evanescent, such work has never been more important.

When not otherwise noted, direct quotations from Frederick Nolting and William Trueheart come chiefly from oral history interviews conducted by the John F. Kennedy and Lyndon B. Johnson Presidential Libraries and by ADST. In Nolting's case, the interviews were in 1966, 1970, and

1982; in Trueheart's, in 1982 and 1989. Nolting, among others, is also quoted extensively in chapter 9 through transcripts (and my auditions) of the White House recording system, then in its infancy, brief portions of which remain classified to this day.

Authorship of the telegrams, as distinct from other correspondence in *FRUS,* can be uncertain, as the secretary of state (or acting secretary) is the official signatory to any telegram from Washington to a US embassy, and the ambassador or *chargé d'affaires* the signatory to telegrams leaving the post. *FRUS* also provides essential information on who drafted telegrams and who approved them. When Nolting or Trueheart (or others) use the first person, however—in recounting their interactions with Vietnamese officials, for example—the authorship is clear.

Other oral histories I consulted include those of John M. Anspacher, Robert E. Barbour, Lucius Battle, George Bogardus, William G. Bradford, William P. Bundy, Thomas Conlon, Elbridge Durbrow, Frederick Flott, Michael V. Forrestal, Roswell Gilpatric, Paul A. Harkins, Averell Harriman, Theodore J. C. Heavner, Roger Hilsman, Thomas L. Hughes, Paul Kattenburg, Joseph A. Mendenhall, Robert H. Miller, James M. Montgomery, David Nes, Rufus Phillips, Kenneth N. Rogers, James D. Rosenthal, Dean Rusk, and Maxwell D. Taylor.

NOTES

Prologue

1. Halberstam, *The Best and the Brightest,* 252.
2. Richardson, *My Father the Spy,* 246.
3. W. E. Colby, *Lost Victory,* 132.
4. K. W. Thompson, *Diplomacy, Administration, and Policy,* 17.
5. Galbraith, *Ambassador's Journal,* 207.
6. For more on sourcing for this narrative, see the "Note on Sources" on page <<00>>.
7. Frederick (Fritz) Ernest Nolting (hereafter FEN) to author, 14 January 1960, Frederick (Fritz) Ernest Nolting, Jr. Papers, Special Collections, University of Virginia Library (hereafter cited as "Nolting Papers, UVA"). In the original, Nolting misspells "sleigh" as "slay."
8. Jane Nolting to author, 5 November 2009, and letter resumed 14 April 2010.

1. Legends of the Fall

1. Rostow recounted the story to A. J. Langguth (quoted in Langguth, *Our Vietnam,* 113–14).
2. Logevall, *Embers of War,* 492–94.
3. Congressional testimony, 6 April 1954, quoted in Mecklin, *Mission in Torment,* 8.
4. Kennedy quoted in Ball, *The Past Has Another Pattern,* 365n4.
5. Shaw, *Lost Mandate of Heaven,* 36.
6. Mecklin, *Mission in Torment,* 31.
7. Ibid.
8. McClintock quoted in Catton, *Diem's Final Failure,* 9.
9. *New Republic,* 16 May 1955.
10. *Life,* 13 May 1957; Logevall, *Embers of War,* 675–77; Olson, *Mansfield in Vietnam,* 64–67, 75–76.
11. Logevall, *Embers of War,* 678.
12. Robert Scheer quoted in Logevall, *Embers of War,* 682.
13. Graham quoted in Jacobs, *Cold War Mandarin,* 50–51.
14. The Dooley story is covered in Jacobs, *Cold War Mandarin,* 46–51; and Boot, *The Road Not Taken,* 223–25.

15. Boot, *The Road Not Taken,* 208.
16. Quoted in Boot, *The Road Not Taken,* 281.
17. The same could be said of *The Best and the Brightest.*
18. FEN to J. Graham Parsons, 11 February 1961, Nolting Papers, UVA.
19. Sheehan, *A Bright Shining Lie,* 75.
20. Ward and Burns, *The Vietnam War: An Intimate History,* 54.
21. Jacobs, *Cold War Mandarin,* chapter 5, covers the events of 1960 in excellent detail.
22. Elbridge Durbrow oral history, Association for Diplomatic Studies and Training (hereafter cited as ADST), 3 June 1981.
23. Most recently, the columnist David Brooks in the *New York Times* of 14 June 2018.
24. Hammer, *Death in November,* 80.
25. Sheehan, *A Bright Shining Lie,* 179.
26. Halberstam, *The Making of a Quagmire,* 205.
27. Durbrow oral history (ADST), 1981.
28. Joseph Mendenhall oral history (ADST), 11 February 1991.

2. Assignment Saigon

1. Report quoted in Boot, *The Road Not Taken,* 350.
2. Boot, *The Road Not Taken,* 355.
3. Lansdale oral history interview at JFKL, quoted in Boot, *The Road Not Taken,* 351. Lansdale told his close friend Rufus Phillips he thought the ambassadorship in Saigon was one of the "world's worst jobs" (Phillips, interview by author, 29 September 2017).
4. G. Jefferson Parsons, assistant secretary of state for Far Eastern affairs, quoted in *Foreign Relations of the United States* (hereafter cited as *FRUS*), vol. I, document 5, p. 19.
5. Nolting, *From Trust to Tragedy,* 16.
6. John Anspacher oral history (ADST), 22 March 1988.
7. Nolting, *From Trust to Tragedy,* 11.
8. William H. Sullivan oral history, John F. Kennedy Presidential Library (hereafter cited as JFKL), 16 June 1970.
9. Nolting Papers, UVA.
10. Nolting, *From Trust to Tragedy,* 17.
11. *FRUS,* vol. I, document 30, p. 72, 15 April 1961.
12. Nolting, *From Trust to Tragedy,* 12.
13. FEN to Durbrow, 25 February 1961, Nolting Papers, UVA.
14. Durbrow to FEN, 8 March 1961, Nolting Papers, UVA.
15. Durbrow to FEN, 8 March 1961, Nolting Papers, UVA.
16. Elbridge Durbrow oral history, LBJ Presidential Library (hereafter cited as LBJL), 11 December 1985. At the end of these ruminations about Diem and South Vietnam, Durbrow's interviewer, Ted Gittinger, asks him what he told Nolting when they met in Hawaii, and Durbrow replied, "I told him more or less what I am telling you now. We were very old friends."
17. FEN oral history (JFKL), 14 May 1966.
18. Ibid.
19. FEN to J. Graham Parsons, 11 February 1961, Nolting Papers, UVA.
20. Nolting, *From Trust to Tragedy,* 19.

21. Langguth, *Our Vietnam,* 131.
22. Thomas Conlon oral history (ADST), 12 August 1992.
23. Dallek, *Flawed Giant,* 14n21.
24. Mendenhall oral history (ADST), 11 February 1991.
25. Anspacher oral history (ADST), 22 March 1988.
26. Nolting, *From Trust to Tragedy,* 21.
27. Ibid.
28. Quoted in Langguth, *Our Vietnam,* 131–32.
29. *FRUS,* vol. I, document 60, pp. 154–57.
30. Nolting, *From Trust to Tragedy,* 3.
31. Ibid., 23.
32. Saigon diary of Frances Nolting (copy shared with author by her daughter).
33. Nolting, *From Trust to Tragedy,* 24.
34. *FRUS,* vol. I, document 92, p. 217.
35. *FRUS,* vol. I, document 100, pp. 234–35.
36. *FRUS,* vol. I, document 51, p. 131.
37. Trueheart to FEN, 17 June 1961, Nolting Papers, UVA.
38. Thurston to FEN, 6 July 1961, Nolting Papers, UVA.
39. William C. Trueheart (hereafter WCT) to FEN, 17 June 1961, Nolting Papers, UVA.
40. WCT to Sallie Shepherd Williams, 17 June 1961.
41. FEN to WCT, 11 June 1961, WCT personal papers.
42. WCT to Sallie Shepherd Williams, 11 July 1961.
43. Ibid.
44. WCT oral history (LBJL), 1982.
45. The meeting with Johnson is described in WCT oral history (LBJL), 2 March 1982.
46. *Richmond News Leader,* 3 September 1961.
47. Today, Ho Chi Minh City's airport goes by Tan Son Nhat, a variant spelling.
48. WCT to Sallie Shepherd Williams, 21 October 1961.
49. *FRUS,* vol. I, document 393, p. 688.
50. Boot, *The Road Not Taken,* 374.
51. *FRUS,* vol. I, document 152, pp. 335–36.
52. *FRUS,* vol. I, document 158, pp. 346–47.
53. WCT oral history (LBJL), 1982.
54. Schlesinger, *A Thousand Days,* 547.
55. *FRUS,* vol. I, document 253, p. 605.
56. *FRUS,* vol. I, document 254, pp. 607–10.
57. *FRUS,* vol. I, document 255, p. 611.
58. *FRUS,* vol. I, document 266, pp. 643–44.
59. *FRUS,* vol. I, document 278, p. 667.
60. *FRUS,* vol. I, document 292, pp. 685–86.
61. *FRUS,* vol. I, document 274, p. 662.
62. *FRUS,* vol. I, document 274, p. 662.
63. Today, East Asian and Pacific Affairs.
64. Ball, *The Past Has Another Pattern,* 366.
65. Ibid., 367.
66. My brother, who grew up a half generation later in an ambassador's residence, tells the

equivalent story on himself, newly arrived in Lagos, Nigeria, eight years old, pushing a bell and ordering "a Coke and a cookie" up to his room. "Coke and a cookie" is now a family mantra.

67. WCT to Sallie Shepherd Williams, 30 October 1961.

68. Phoebe E. Trueheart (hereafter PET) to Sallie Shepherd Williams, 5 December 1961.

69. WCT to Sallie Shepherd Williams, 4 November 1961.

70. The personal calendars of both Bill and Phoebe from these years survive.

71. Lindsay Nolting, interview by author, 19 March 2018.

72. PET to Sallie Shepherd Williams, 5 December 1961.

73. WCT to Sallie Shepherd Williams, 10 December 1961.

74. WCT to Sallie Shepherd Williams, 27 November 1961.

75. WCT to Sallie Shepherd Williams, 17 December 1961.

76. William Bundy oral history (JFKL), 25 April 1972.

77. Galbraith, *Ambassador's Journal,* 107.

78. Ibid., 154.

79. Ibid., 260.

80. Ibid., 311.

81. Averell Harriman Papers, Library of Congress, container 463.

3. Two Gentlemen of Virginia

1. Anthony Lake, interview by author, 5 February 2020.

2. Timetable courtesy of Richmond Railroad Museum.

3. WCT to Sallie Shepherd Trueheart, undated, 1933.

4. WCT oral history (LBJL), 2 March 1982.

5. *Richmond Times-Dispatch,* 15 July 1956.

6. *Richmond Times-Dispatch,* 15 May 1955.

7. WCT to Sallie Shepherd Williams, undated, 1935.

8. WCT to Sallie Shepherd Williams, undated, 1935.

9. WCT to Sallie Shepherd Williams, undated, 1935.

10. Virginia Historical Society.

11. "RVA Legends—Hobson-Nolting House," by Rocket Weeks, 29 March 2018, rvahub.com.

12. According to Lindsay Nolting, interview by author, 19 March 2018.

13. Nolting Papers, UVA; the recipient of the recommendation (19 July 1945) was Edward Stettinius, who had just resigned as secretary of state.

14. Bittie Nolting, interview by author, 27 May 2018.

15. Lindsay Nolting, interview by author, 19 March 2018.

16. Bittie Nolting, interview by author, 10 July 2016.

17. WCT oral history (ASDT), 17 March 1989.

18. R. H. Miller, *Vietnam and Beyond,* 10–11.

19. WCT oral history (ADST), 17 March 1989.

20. R. H. Miller, *Vietnam and Beyond,* 18.

21. Nolting Papers, UVA.

22. Uncannily, in later life I worked briefly at the US embassy in Paris and occupied the same suite of offices in the Talleyrand.

23. WCT to Sallie Shepherd Williams, undated, 1955.
24. For more on these years in Paris, see my essay in the Cathedral's *Trinité* magazine, spring 2019.
25. R. H. Miller, *Vietnam and Beyond*, 2.
26. WCT oral history (ADST), 17 March 1989.
27. WCT oral history (ADST), 17 March 1989.
28. WCT oral history (ADST), 17 March 1989.
29. WCT to Fletcher Warren, 9 July 1959, WCT personal papers.
30. FEN to WCT, 30 July 1959, Nolting Papers, UVA.
31. WCT to Sallie Shepherd Williams, 16 May 1960.
32. FEN to Elwood Quesada, 2 December 1957, Nolting Papers, UVA. Friendship, the only international airport serving the capital region, was then the name of what is now Baltimore/Washington International Thurgood Marshall Airport.
33. FEN to James Keith, 8 August 1958 and 18 August 1958, Nolting Papers, UVA.
34. Halberstam, *The Best and the Brightest*, 130.
35. Prochnau, *Once upon a Distant War*, 169 and 322.

4. Sink or Swim

1. Mecklin, *Mission in Torment*, 16.
2. WCT oral history (ADST), 2 March 1982.
3. Mecklin, *Mission in Torment*, 20–22.
4. The story is recounted by A. J. Langguth in *Our Vietnam*.
5. WCT's discussion of Farmgate is from oral history (ADST), 2 March 1982.
6. *FRUS*, vol. II, document 108, p. 225.
7. Langguth, *Our Vietnam*, 162.
8. Moyar, *Triumph Forsaken*, 149.
9. *FRUS*, vol. II, document 99, p. 207.
10. *FRUS*, vol. II, document 109, p. 246.
11. *FRUS*, vol. II, document 95, p. 194.
12. *New York Times*, 13 February 1962.
13. Richardson, *My Father the Spy*, 162.
14. WCT to Sallie Shepherd Williams, 28 March 1962.
15. Frances Nolting wrote this in an article for a campus publication at Wellesley (undated, Nolting Papers, UVA).
16. These and other Saigon memories were enhanced by conversations with Saigon friends cited in the acknowledgments, and from such alumni memoirs as John Richardson's *My Father the Spy*; *Saigon Kids* by Les Arbuckle; and *The Ignorance of Bliss* by Sandy Hanna. The Saigon Kids Facebook group is also a clearinghouse for memories.
17. WCT oral history (ADST), 2 March 1982.
18. Michael Forrestal oral history (JFKL), 14 August 1964.
19. *FRUS*, vol. II, document 14, p. 31; document 18, p. 37.
20. Nolting, *From Trust to Tragedy*, 81.
21. *FRUS*, vol. II, document 25, pp. 46–48 and fn 3; FEN oral history (LBJL), 11 November 1982.
22. *FRUS*, vol. II, document 25, pp. 47–48.

23. *FRUS,* vol. II, document 40, p. 70.
24. Forrestal oral history (JFKL), 1964.
25. Nolting, *From Trust to Tragedy,* 59.
26. WCT oral history (ADST), 1982.
27. *FRUS,* vol. II, document 327, p. 762.
28. *FRUS,* vol. II, document 199, pp. 409–14. Other US accounts of Diem's monologues are included in this sampling.
29. Mecklin, *Mission in Torment,* 41.
30. Nolting, *From Trust to Tragedy,* 49.
31. Moyar, *Triumph Forsaken,* 151–52.
32. Mecklin, *Mission in Torment,* 18.
33. Bittie Nolting, interview by author, 27 May 2018.
34. *FRUS,* vol. II, document 93, pp. 187–93.
35. *FRUS,* vol. II, document 120, pp. 254–55.
36. *FRUS,* vol. II, document 131, p. 276.
37. *FRUS,* vol. II, document 115, p. 247.
38. *FRUS,* vol. II, document 42, p. 81.
39. *FRUS,* vol. III, document 4, p. 8.
40. Paul Harkins oral history (LBJL), 10 November 1981.
41. Langguth, *Our Vietnam,* 162.
42. Sheehan, *A Bright Shining Lie,* 291.
43. Harkins oral history (LBJL), 10 November 1981.
44. Taylor, *Swords and Plowshares,* 237.
45. Langguth, *Our Vietnam,* 174.
46. WCT to Sallie Shepherd Williams, 13 May 1962.
47. Prochnau, *Once upon a Distant War,* 23.
48. Ibid., 195.
49. Ibid., 84.
50. Mecklin, *Mission in Torment,* 105.
51. Prochnau, *Once upon a Distant War,* 50–51.
52. Sheehan, *A Bright Shining Lie,* 316. Halberstam, in his first book on Vietnam, *The Making of Quagmire,* attributes the remark to himself (73).
53. *FRUS,* vol. II, 133, 279–81.
54. Nolting, *From Trust to Tragedy,* 88.
55. Prochnau, *Once upon a Distant War,* 81–82.
56. *Richmond Times-Dispatch,* 27 June 1962.
57. Undated but clear from the context (Trueheart family papers).
58. PET to Sallie Shepherd Williams, 10 July 1962.
59. Archibald Calhoun to FEN, 6 July 1962, Nolting Papers, UVA.
60. PET to Sallie Shepherd Williams, 10 July 1962.

5. Doubting Thomases

1. John Archibald Calhoun, the first US ambassador to Chad, to FEN, 6 July 1962, Nolting Papers, UVA.
2. Robert H. Miller oral history (ASDT), 23 May 1990.

3. R. H. Miller, *Vietnam and Beyond*, 56.

4. WCT oral history (ASDT), 2 March 1982.

5. Mecklin, *Mission in Torment*, 39.

6. WCT oral history (ASDT), 2 March 1982.

7. FEN oral history (LBJL), 11 November 1982.

8. *FRUS*, vol. II, document 268, pp. 597–98.

9. *FRUS*, vol. II, document 268, p. 601.

10. *FRUS*, vol. II, document 229, p. 477.

11. Galbraith, *Ambassador's Journal*, 312.

12. Although the subject remained alive (see chapter 10).

13. *FRUS*, vol. II, document 156, pp. 325–27.

14. Yet Nhu himself came to see their political utility in in the closing days of the regime (see chapter 10).

15. *FRUS*, vol. II, document 164, p. 336, 19 April 1962.

16. Author's personal papers.

17. *FRUS*, vol. II, document 331, p. 788n.

18. Prochnau, *Once upon a Distant War*, 167.

19. WCT to David Kaiser, 14 November 1991.

20. *FRUS*, vol. II, document 277, pp. 622–33. The eight thousand words are broken into only eight paragraphs.

21. W. Colby, *Lost Victory*, 264.

22. *FRUS*, vol. II, document 227, p. 470.

23. Roger Hilsman was the visiting official (*FRUS*, vol. II, document 114, p. 245).

24. Nolting, *From Trust to Tragedy*, 82.

25. Ibid., 83–84.

26. Ibid., 128–29.

27. *FRUS*, vol. II, document 234, p. 498.

28. *FRUS*, vol. II, document 239, p. 514.

29. *FRUS*, vol. II, document 304, p. 707.

30. *FRUS*, vol. II, document 306, p. 717.

31. *FRUS*, vol. II, document 307, p. 717. In the end, Diem and the Americans were able to finesse the stalemate: the North Vietnamese mission was not downgraded, but it was headed by a *charge d'affaires,* not an ambassador. Diem reluctantly signed the agreement.

32. WCT to Sallie Shepherd Williams, 30 October 1962.

33. *FRUS*, vol. II, 327, 762.

34. Francois Sully's expulsion is covered by Halberstam, Sheehan, Langguth, Prochnau, and Nolting in their books. Sully was pronounced the French way, not the way the Noltings pronounced their former Virginia farm.

35. Halberstam, *The Best and The Brightest,* 252.

36. WCT oral history (ADST), 2 March 1982.

37. Mecklin, *Mission in Torment,* 136.

38. Prochnau, *Once upon a Distant War,* 133.

39. Halberstam, *Making of a Quagmire,* 26.

40. Ibid., 73–74.

41. Prochnau, *Once upon a Distant War,* 172.

42. Nolting, *From Trust to Tragedy,* 90.

43. FEN oral history (JFKL), 7 May 1970.

44. Prochnau, *Once upon a Distant War,* 59.

45. Nolting, *From Trust to Tragedy,* 93.

46. FEN oral history (JFKL), 14 May 1966.

47. WCT oral history (ASDT), 1982.

48. Paul Harkins oral history (LBJL), 1981.

49. Halberstam, *Quagmire,* 169.

50. Prochnau, *Once upon a Distant War,* 184.

51. *FRUS,* vol. II, 322, p. 746.

52. Prochnau, *Once upon a Distant War,* 171.

53. Mecklin, *Mission in Torment,* 258.

54. PET to Sallie Shepherd Williams, undated.

55. At lunch in San Francisco in 2015, C. J. said she still wasn't sure whether her father's Pan Am job was CIA cover or not.

56. WCT to Sallie Shepherd Williams, 18 November 1962.

57. *FRUS,* vol. II, document 327, pp. 760–62.

58. Nolting, *From Trust to Tragedy,* 34.

59. *FRUS,* vol. III, document 20, p. 63.

60. Nolting, *From Trust to Tragedy,* 85–86.

61. WCT oral history (LBJL) 1982.

62. Prochnau is the source of the purported wincing. He interviewed WCT for his book but was unable to recover the transcript of their conversation before his own death in 2018.

63. Prochnau, *Once upon a Distant War,* 209–10.

64. Meloy, as ambassador to Lebanon in the 1980s, was kidnapped and murdered by Hezbollah.

65. WCT oral history (LBJL), 1982.

66. Quoted in Olson, *Mansfield in Vietnam,* 108. Olson's book covers the visit in detail.

67. All report citations are from *FRUS,* vol. II, document 330, pp. 779–87.

68. Nolting, *From Trust to Tragedy,* 98.

69. WCT to Sallie Shepherd Williams, 29 December 1962.

6. Burning Arrow

1. Nolting Papers, UVA.

2. Abramson, *Spanning the Century,* 612.

3. Nolting, *From Trust to Tragedy,* 105.

4. Though it was a secret at the time, Forrestal was also the most senior White House official in the Kennedy administration who was gay.

5. Ibid., 96.

6. *FRUS,* vol. III, document 2, p. 4.

7. Hilsman, *To Move a Nation,* 456.

8. Michael V. Forrestal oral history (JFKL), 1964.

9. Prochnau, *Once upon a Distant War,* 239.

10. *FRUS,* vol. III, document 6, p. 13.

11. Hilsman, *To Move a Nation,* 461.
12. Ibid.
13. *FRUS,* vol. III, document 8, p. 16.
14. Author's personal papers.
15. Sheehan, *A Bright Shining Lie,* 204–5.
16. Ibid., 262–63. The early reports of four dead that Phoebe heard were incorrect.
17. Ibid., 228.
18. Ibid., 231.
19. This is Sheehan's rendition of Madame Nhu's comments (*A Bright Shining Lie,* 278).
20. Prochnau, *Once upon a Distant War,* 225.
21. Halberstam, *Quagmire,* 157.
22. Sheehan interviewed on C-SPAN, 5 December 1988.
23. Halberstam, *Quagmire,* 156.
24. Sheehan, *A Bright Shining Lie,* 276.
25. Halberstam, *Quagmire,* 156.
26. Max Hastings, *Vietnam: An Epic Tragedy,* 167.
27. Halberstam, *Quagmire,* 160.
28. Sheehan, *A Bright Shining Lie,* 271.
29. Ibid., 315.
30. Sheehan, interview on C-SPAN.
31. Sheehan on *Vietnam: A Television History,* 1983.
32. Chalmers B. Wood to FEN, 11 February 1963, Nolting Papers, UVA.
33. 6 April 1963, Nolting Papers, UVA.
34. Forrestal oral history (JFKL), 1964.
35. *FRUS,* vol. III, document 30, pp. 98–102.
36. *FRUS,* vol. III, document 29, pp. 67–69n.
37. *FRUS,* vol. III, document 33, p. 106.
38. FEN to Averell Harriman 27 Feburary 1963, Nolting Papers, UVA.
39. FEN to Averell Harriman 27 Feburary 1963, Nolting Papers, UVA.
40. FEN to Averell Harriman 27 Feburary 1963, Nolting Papers, UVA.
41. *FRUS,* vol. III, document 50, pp. 132–33.
42. *FRUS,* vol. III, document 52, pp. 136–40.
43. Forrestal oral history (JFKL), 1964.
44. *FRUS,* vol. III, document 62, p. 162.
45. Nolting, *From Trust to Tragedy,* 98.
46. *FRUS,* vol. III, document 60, pp. 152–56.
47. *FRUS,* vol. III, document 78, pp. 201–2.
48. *FRUS,* vol. III, document 81, pp. 208–13.
49. *FRUS,* vol. III, document 81, pp. 208–13.
50. *FRUS,* vol. III, document 89, pp. 225–26.
51. Winters, *Year of the Hare,* 28.
52. *FRUS,* vol. III, document 127, pp. 307–8.
53. *FRUS,* vol. III, document 123, pp. 296–300.
54. *FRUS,* vol. III, document 126, pp. 306–7.
55. Russell quoted in *Time,* 12 April 1963, 34.

7. Out of Nowhere

1. This account is drawn from *FRUS*, vol. III, documents 112, 116, 117, 118, and from Edward Miller's definitive "Religious Revival and the Politics of Nation Building," *Modern Asian Studies,* August 2014.
2. Halberstam, *The Best and the Brightest,* 250.
3. Michael Forrestal oral history (JFKL), 1964.
4. Halberstam, *Quagmire,* 196.
5. Hammer, *Death in November,* 139; Moyar, *Triumph Forsaken,* 215 and 457n46.
6. Winters, *Year of the Hare,* 25.
7. E. Miller, "Religious Revival and the Politics of Nation Building," 29.
8. FRUS, vol. III, document 116, p. 285.
9. FEN oral history (JFKL), 7 May 1970.
10. *FRUS*, vol. III, document 122, pp. 294–96 and notes.
11. Hammer, *Death in November,* 124.
12. *FRUS*, vol. III, document 133, pp. 317–24.
13. Quoted in Mecklin, *Mission in Torment,* 50.
14. *FRUS*, vol. III, document 131, 314.
15. Phillips, *Why Vietnam Matters,* 155.
16. PET to Sallie Shepherd Williams, June 1963, undated.
17. *FRUS*, vol. III, document 140, p. 338.
18. *FRUS*, vol. III, document 142, pp. 340–41.
19. Jones, *Death of a Generation,* 249.
20. *FRUS*, vol. III, document 149, pp. 350–51.
21. *FRUS*, vol. III, document 157, pp. 362–63.
22. *FRUS*, vol. III, document 160, pp. 366–69.
23. Halberstam, *Best and the Brightest,* 259.
24. Halberstam, *Quagmire,* 59.
25. Correspondence with historian David Kaiser, 14 November 1991, WCT personal papers.
26. Prochnau, *Once upon a Distant War,* 307–8.
27. Browne, *Muddy Boots and Red Socks,* 11.
28. *FRUS*, vol. III, document 165, pp. 377–78.
29. *FRUS*, vol. III, document 165, p. 377n3; *FRUS,* vol. III, document 181, p. 402 The official palace rendition of the statement was "Buddhism in Vietnam finds its fundamental safeguard in the Constitution, of which I personally am the guardian" (*FRUS*, vol. III, document 185, p. 411n3).
30. Hammer, *Death in November,* 145.
31. Langguth, *Our Vietnam,* 216.
32. Winters, *Year of the Hare,* 34.
33. Frances Nolting kept a diary of her years in Vietnam, which her daughter shared with me. When she typed it up in early 1964, according to the diary that survives, she decided to omit all the entries covering the Aegean cruise because they sounded too much like a "travel-log." A copy of the original family vacation itinerary is in the Nolting papers at UVA.

34. Nolting, *From Trust to Tragedy,* 111.
35. *FRUS,* vol. III, document 167, p. 381.
36. *FRUS,* vol. III, document 169, pp. 385–86.
37. *FRUS,* vol. III, document 169, pp. 386–87n.
38. *FRUS,* vol. III, document 175, p. 394.
39. *FRUS,* vol. III, document 179, pp. 398–99.
40. Halberstam, *Best and the Brightest,* 252.
41. Joshua Trueheart, interview by author, 10 November 2017.
42. Higgins, *Our Vietnam Nightmare,* 60.
43. William Sullivan oral history (JFKL), 16 June 1970.
44. Robert H. Miller oral history (ADST), 23 May 1990.
45. Mecklin, *Mission in Torment,* 169.
46. In his oral history, Michael Forrestal said that ambassador Elbridge Durbrow would "bang his fists on the table and shout" at Diem.
47. FEN oral history (LBJL), 1982.
48. Mecklin, *Mission in Torment,* 171.
49. Phillips, interview by author, 29 September 2017. Phillips died in December 2021.
50. Winters, *Year of the Hare,* 34, 35, 214, 217.
51. Ibid., 48.
52. Nolting Papers, UVA.
53. This subtopic is of interest to almost every oral historian interviewing American diplomats and generals about Saigon in 1963.
54. FEN oral history (JFKL), 14 May 1966.
55. The phrase is proffered by Barbour's interviewer, Charles Stuart Kennedy, a Vietnam aficionado.
56. Robert E. Barbour oral history (ADST), 30 November 1992.
57. WCT oral history (ADST), 1982, for all the preceding quotes in this section.
58. Robert H. Miller oral history (ADST), 23 May 1990.
59. *FRUS,* vol. III, document 185, pp. 411–13.
60. Halberstam, *Quagmire,* 212–13.
61. Blair, *Lodge in Vietnam,* 13.
62. Michael Forrestal oral history (JFKL), 1964.
63. *FRUS,* vol. III, document 187, p. 415.
64. *FRUS,* vol. III, document 186, p. 414.
65. Lindsay Nolting, interview by author, 19 March 2018.
66. PET to Sallie Shepherd Williams.
67. *FRUS,* vol. III, document 192, pp. 427–28.
68. Nolting, *From Trust to Tragedy,* 113.
69. Also see FEN oral history, 1982.
70. Joshua Trueheart, interview by author, 10 November 2017.
71. Lindsay Nolting, interview by author, 19 March 2018.
72. FEN oral history (JFKL), 1970.
73. FEN oral history (JFKL), 1970.
74. FEN quoted in Winters, *Year of the Hare,* 47.
75. 10 July 1963.

76. *FRUS*, vol. III, document 205, p. 453.
77. FEN to Dean Rusk, September 24, 1964, part of a long complaint to the Secretary of State about his treatment in Vietnam. Nolting Papers, UVA.
78. *FRUS*, vol. III, document 196, pp. 433–34.
79. *FRUS*, vol. III, document 200, pp. 445–46.
80. *FRUS*, vol. III, document 203, p. 449.
81. *FRUS*, vol. III, document 202, p. 448.

8. Malice in Wonderland

1. *FRUS*, vol. III, document 203, pp. 449–50.
2. *FRUS*, vol. III, document 204, p. 451n4.
3. *Liste des personnalités 1963*, official Republic of Vietnam directory of the federal bureaucracy including the diplomatic corps (Trueheart Papers).
4. Sheehan, *Bright Shining Lie,* 350.
5. Ibid., 351.
6. Rust, "No Boy Scout" (manuscript). Rust interviewed Conein, before his death in 1988, for the biography, which is to date unpublished.
7. Hammer, *Death in November,* 157.
8. *FRUS*, vol. III, document 213, p. 478.
9. Sheehan, *A Bright Shining Lie,* 352.
10. *FRUS*, vol. III, document 211, pp. 472–73.
11. *FRUS*, vol. III, document 211, pp. 472–73n.
12. *FRUS*, vol. III, document 214, pp. 479–80n5.
13. *FRUS*, vol. III, document 215, pp. 481–82.
14. Halberstam, *Best and the Brightest,* 261.
15. Hammer, *Death in November,* 158.
16. Herken, *The Georgetown Set,* 286.
17. FEN to Bittie Nolting, 16 July 1963, Nolting Papers, UVA.
18. Bittie Nolting, interview by author, 19 March 2018.
19. *FRUS*, vol. III, document 239, pp. 531–43, for this and all that follows from Manning.
20. *FRUS*, vol. III, document 239, pp. 533–34.
21. *FRUS*, vol. III, document 243, p. 550.
22. Halberstam, *Making of a Quagmire,* 218.
23. Ibid.
24. Nolting, *From Trust to Tragedy,* 117.
25. The readout is in the Halberstam Papers archive at Boston University.
26. *FRUS*, vol. III, document 247, pp. 556–57.
27. *FRUS*, vol. III, document 248, pp. 557–58.
28. *FRUS*, vol. III, document 250, pp. 560–61.
29. *FRUS*, vol. III, document 251, pp. 562–63.
30. Halberstam, *Best and the Brightest,* 260.
31. Halberstam, *Making of a Quagmire,* 217.
32. Prochnau, *Once upon a Distant War,* 350; Sheehan, *Bright Shining Lie,* 347.
33. Sheehan, *Bright Shining Lie,* 349.
34. Winters, *Year of the Hare,* 49.

35. *New York Herald Tribune,* 9 August 1963.
36. *Herald Tribune,* 15 August 1963.
37. *Herald Tribune,* 19 August 1963.
38. Prochnau, *One upon a Distant War,* 257.
39. Nolting Papers, UVA.
40. Halberstam, *Making of a Quagmire,* 219.
41. Bittie Nolting, interview by author, 10 July 2016.
42. *FRUS,* vol. III, document 253, pp. 565–66.
43. *FRUS,* vol. III, document 254, p. 567n4b.
44. The conversations can be heard on line through the John F. Kennedy Presidential Librart website. As of 2023, transcripts of the recordings are available from the Presidential Recordings Program at the Miller Center at the University of Virginia.
45. Foregoing drawn from JFK Tape 104/A40.

9. The Guns of August

1. Michael Forrestal oral history (JFKL), 14 August 1964.
2. PET to Thelma Everett, 20 August 1963, Trueheart family papers.
3. Sheehan, *A Bright Shining Lie,* 355.
4. *FRUS,* vol. III, document 263, pp. 598–99.
5. Sheehan, *A Bright Shining Lie,* 356.
6. PET to Thelma Everett, 20–25 August 1963. This letter was written and updated over a span of several days.
7. *FRUS,* vol. III, document 261, p. 596.
8. Phillips, *Why Vietnam Matters,* 164.
9. *FRUS,* vol. III, document 261, p. 596.
10. *FRUS,* vol. III, document 266, p. 603.
11. *FRUS,* vol. III, document 270, pp. 607–10.
12. *FRUS,* vol. III, document 263, pp. 598–99.
13. UPI dispatch, 27 August 1963. Mau later was rehabilitated and served as an ambassador and senator. In 1975, he became the last prime minister of South Vietnam—for two days—before the government collapsed.
14. Sheehan, *A Bright Shining Lie,* 355.
15. Frederick Flott oral history (LBJL), 22 July 1984.
16. Bittie Nolting, interview by author, 27 May 2018.
17. H. C. Lodge, *The Storm Has Many Eyes,* 206.
18. From the same letter begun on August 20.
19. Flott oral history (LBJL), 22 July 1984.
20. Sheehan, *A Bright Shining Lie,* 360.
21. Blair, *Lodge in Vietnam,* 37–38.
22. Luke Nichter's new biography of Lodge, *The Last Brahmin,* stresses Lodge's experience with Catholic voters in Massachusetts.
23. Blair, *Lodge in Vietnam,* 38. In the final diplomatic posting of his career (1970–77), Lodge served as ambassador to the Holy See.
24. WCT oral history (LBJL), 2 March 1982.
25. PET to Sallie Shepherd Williams, 23 August 1963.

26. Abramson, *Spanning the Century*, 620.
27. *FRUS*, vol. III, document 281, pp. 628–29.
28. Forrestal oral history (JFKL), 14 August 1964, here and in foregoing sentence fragments.
29. Forrestal oral history (JFKL), 14 August 1964.
30. Thomas Hughes, interview by author, 13 March 2018. William Trueheart became Hughes's deputy at INR four years later. Hughes died in 2023.
31. *FRUS*, vol. III, document 278, p. 625.
32. Powers, *The Man Who Kept the Secrets*, 164.
33. Thomas Hughes, interview by author.
34. This abbreviated narrative of the drafting of the August 24 Telegram draws on multiple reconstructions by, and does not attempt to reconcile differences among participants and historians cited in the source notes.
35. Forrestal oral history (JFKL), 1964.
36. Abramson, *Spanning the Century*, 622.
37. Rust and Editors of US News Books, *Kennedy in Vietnam*, 119. Forrestal was interviewed by Rust.
38. Abramson, *Spanning the Century*, 623n37, from *Robert Kennedy in His Own Words*, ed. Guthman and Schulman.
39. Ball, *The Past Has Another Pattern*, 373–74.
40. *FRUS*, vol. IV, document 12, p. 21.
41. *FRUS*, vol. IV, document 18, pp. 35–36.
42. Abramson, *Spanning the Century*, 622n37.
43. Schlesinger, *Robert Kennedy and His Times*, 770.
44. Rust and Editors of US News Books, *Kennedy in Vietnam*, 122.
45. Quoted ibid.
46. Nolting, *From Trust to Tragedy*, 124.
47. Nolting recalled this incident in an interview of uncertain origin whose transcript is in the Nolting Papers at UVA.
48. The White House conversations that week were recorded and are also available from the Miller Center Presidential Recordings Program at the University of Virginia.
49. Abramson, *Spanning the Century*, 622.
50. Roswell Gilpatric oral history (JFKL), 5 May 1970.
51. Kattenburg, *The Vietnam Trauma*, 119–20.

10. Silent Treatment

1. *FRUS*, vol. IV, document 70, p. 129n5.
2. This and subsequent quotes are all from *FRUS*, vol. IV, document 77, pp. 141–44.
3. *FRUS*, vol. IV, document 97, p. 195.
4. *FRUS*, vol. IV, document 102, p. 203.
5. *FRUS*, vol. IV, document 130, p. 262.
6. Mecklin, *Mission in Torment*, 228.
7. Halberstam, *The Best and the Brightest*, 288.
8. Mecklin, *Mission in Torment*, 168.
9. Winters, *Year of the Hare*, 44.

10. Jones, *Death of a Generation,* 312.

11. Maneli, *War of the Vanquished,* 140–41.

12. Jones, *Death of a Generation,* 312.

13. Maneli, *War of the Vanquished,* 144.

14. *FRUS,* vol. IV, document 69, p. 126.

15. Maneli, *War of the Vanquished,* 148.

16. Hughes quoted in Hersh, *The Dark Side of Camelot,* 423.

17. Robert Miller oral history (ADST), 23 May 1990.

18. FEN oral history (JFKL), 6 May 1970.

19. WCT oral history (LBJL), 1982.

20. Conein interview by Zalin Grant, in Grant, *Facing the Phoenix,* 202.

21. From Conein's 1975 US Senate testimony.

22. CIA telegram at JFKL.

23. All preceding quotes are from PET to Sallie Shepherd Williams, 23 September 1963.

24. Jane Nolting to the author, undated (around late August to early September 1963), author's personal papers.

25. In the FEN Papers at UVA, there are handwritten drafts of some of this language on TWA stationery.

26. WCT personal papers.

27. All from Anthony Lake, interview by author, 5 February 2020.

28. Copy of Harriman letter, 13 September 1963, WCT personal papers.

29. Averell Harriman oral history (JFKL), 6 June 1965.

30. Copy of Hilsman letter, 5 September 1963, WCT personal papers.

31. *FRUS,* vol. IV, document 116, p. 235.

32. *FRUS,* vol. IV, document 83, pp. 162–63n5.

33. Phillips, *Why Vietnam Matters,* 185–86.

34. Ibid., 190.

35. Nolting, *From Trust to Tragedy,* 130.

36. *FRUS,* vol. IV, document 86, pp. 171–74.

37. *FRUS,* vol. IV, document 101, p. 202.

38. *FRUS,* vol. IV, document 96, pp. 194–95.

39. WCT oral history (LBJL), 1982.

40. *FRUS,* vol. IV, document 126, p. 255.

41. *FRUS,* vol. IV, document 128, p. 257.

42. W. Colby, *Lost Victory,* 144.

43. *FRUS,* vol. IV, document 86, p. 171.

44. Michael Forrestal oral history (JFKL), 1964.

45. Jones, *Death of a Generation,* 372.

46. Taylor quoted in Rust and the Editors of US News Books, *Kennedy in Vietnam,* 143.

47. *FRUS,* vol. IV, document 159, p. 322.

48. *FRUS,* vol. IV, 162, p. 326n.

49. *FRUS,* vol. IV, document 173, p. 357.

50. All the foregoing: PET to Bennett and Shirley Boskey, Oscar and Lee Tyree, and Roger and Bessie Nelson, 23 September 1963. One of the friends saved the letter and returned it to Phoebe (Trueheart family papers).

11. Waiting for the Generals

1. Art Buchwald to WCT, 1 October 1963, Trueheart family papers.
2. The foregoing account was enhanced by the research of Monique Brinson Demery for her *Finding the Dragon Lady: The Mystery of Vietnam's Madame Nhu.*
3. Ibid., 175.
4. *FRUS,* vol. IV, document 186, p. 386.
5. Demery, *Finding the Dragon Lady,* 190. In a macabre coda to this scene, long after, in 1986, Madame Nhu's brother, the Chuongs' only son, Tran Van Khiem, strangled his parents to death in that house on Western Avenue.
6. *Los Angeles Times,* 26 July 1986.
7. Phillips, *Why Vietnam Matters,* 199.
8. Richardson, *My Father the Spy,* 198.
9. Ibid., 180.
10. WCT oral history (LBJL), 1982.
11. Richardson, *My Father the Spy,* 146. The house had once been used by the French Deuxieme Bureau, during World War II, to torture prisoners, whose ghosts remained on in the minds of the Richardsons' household staff. "We hired a team of Buddhist bonzes," Richardson said, "to chant and burn incense and hang mirrors over all the doors. Supposedly the ghosts would see themselves in the mirrors and run away."
12. Lodge quoted by Blair, *Lodge in Vietnam,* 40.
13. *FRUS,* vol. IV, document 182, p. 379.
14. *FRUS,* vol. IV, document 192, p. 393.
15. Colby. interview by Zalin Grant in his *Facing the Phoenix,* 205.
16. *FRUS,* vol. IV, document 177, p. 366.
17. Conein's 1975 Senate testimony is quoted in Hersh, *The Dark Side of Camelot,* 416.
18. Langguth, *Our Vietnam,* 245.
19. Quoted in Mecklin, *Mission in Torment,* 120.
20. Ibid.
21. All quotes from *FRUS,* vol. IV, document 183, pp. 380–82.
22. Clippings of the syndicated column and the Maysville play are in Trueheart family papers.
23. Here and below: *FRUS,* vol. IV, document 193, pp. 394–95 and 394–95n3; and transcript of White House meeting recording, 25 October 1963 at JFKL.
24. Meeting tape 117 a/53, October 25, 1963, Miller Center UVA; original tapes at JFKL.
25. *FRUS,* vol. IV, document 207, pp. 423–24n.
26. *FRUS,* vol. IV, document 215, p. 434.
27. *FRUS,* vol. IV, document 217, p. 437.
28. *The Man Nobody Knew: In Search of My Father,* documentary film by Carl Colby, 2011.
29. Lodge's account of his last encounter with Diem is from *FRUS,* vol. IV, document 221, pp. 442–46.
30. *FRUS,* vol. IV, document 225, p. 450.
31. *FRUS,* vol. IV, document 231, p. 464.
32. *FRUS,* vol. IV, document 234, pp. 468–69.
33. *FRUS,* vol. IV, document 236, p. 474.
34. *FRUS,* vol. IV, document 240, pp. 479–82.

35. *FRUS*, vol. IV, document 242, p. 486.
36. *FRUS*, vol. IV, document 249, p. 500.
37. Phillips, *Why Vietnam Matters*, 201.

12. All Saints' Day

1. *FRUS*, vol. IV, document 262, pp. 516–17.
2. Anthony Lake, interview by author, 5 February 2020.
3. *Newsweek*, 11 November 1963.
4. *Time*, 8 November 1963.
5. WCT oral history (LBJL), 1982.
6. Michael Forrestal oral history (JFKL), 1964.
7. Mecklin, *Mission in Torment*, 263.
8. Ibid., 265. Mecklin does not use Trueheart's name in this 1965 book, but I recall the passage being shown to me then by Phoebe, who knew it was Bill. Nguyen Dinh Thuan escaped with his family to Paris, where he lived out his years. He died in 2014.
9. *FRUS*, vol. IV, document 267, p. 523.
10. There is no authoritative account of the sequence of events that ended in the brothers' death. This is an amalgam of the most reliable versions. Don, in his memoir (p. 111), was told by Minh, "Why does it matter that they are dead?" Luke Nichter, in his thorough biography of Lodge, also offers a sampling of scenarios sourced to various people involved.
11. *FRUS*, vol. IV, document 269, pp. 525–26.
12. *FRUS*, vol. IV, document 270, p. 526.
13. *Newsweek*, 11 November 1963.
14. Demery, *Finding the Dragon Lady*, 205.
15. Frederick Flott oral history (ADST), 22 July 1984.
16. Demery, *Finding the Dragon Lady*, 206.
17. Rufus Phillips oral history (ADST), 19 July 1995.
18. Herring, *America's Longest War*, 127.
19. *The Man Nobody Knew: In Search of My Father*, documentary film by Carl Colby, 2011.
20. W. Colby, *Lost Victory*, 158.
21. Richardson, *My Father the Spy*, 205.
22. Nolting, *From Trust to Tragedy*, 133.
23. *Time*, 15 November 1963.
24. Demery, *Finding the Dragon Lady*, 207.
25. *FRUS*, vol. IV, document 291, pp. 560–61.
26. PET to Sallie Shepherd Williams 18 November 1963. Phoebe added: "The bitch hasn't had the grace to thank the American Embassy for their troubles. She would hate it if she knew Bill had gotten her children out, she hates Bill so."
27. Lodge, *The Storm Has Many Eyes*, 210.
28. Flott oral history (ADST), 1984.
29. Ambassador Lodge and the Papal Nuncio in Saigon had had a hand in making this happen.
30. *FRUS*, vol. IV, document 284, p. 546.
31. Sheehan, *A Bright Shining Lie*, 371.

32. Hughes oral history (ADST), 7 July 1999.
33. James Rosenthal oral history (ADST), 1996.
34. *FRUS*, vol. IV, document 291, p. 562.
35. *FRUS*, vol. IV, document 284, p. 549.
36. *FRUS, vol.* IV, document 291, p. 562.
37. *Time,* 8 November 1963.
38. *FRUS*, vol. IV, document 321, p. 608n.
39. Forrestal oral history (JFKL), 1964.
40. Hammer, *Death in November*, p. 170.
41. *FRUS*, vol. IV, document 322, 625.
42. From Reuters world roundup, 25 November 1963.
43. Caro, *The Passage of Power*, 585.
44. Reedy, interview by Steve Atlas for *LBJ's War* (PBS).
45. *FRUS*, vol. IV, document 330, p. 635.
46. Lodge, *The Storm Has Many Eyes,* 209.
47. *FRUS*, vol. IV, document 324, p. 628.
48. WCT oral history (LBJL), 1982.
49. WCT interview in *Richmond Times-Dispatch*, 25 April 1976.

Endings

1. WCT to Henry Cabot Lodge, Trueheart family papers. This may be a Foreign Service trope. In their fine book about their father, Ambassador Llewellyn Thompson, and their Foreign Service childhood years in Moscow, Jenny Thompson and Sherry Thompson record the identical phrase about Bulgarian rail travel being used by their father, although he said "fifth-class" (*The Kremlinologist*, 83).
2. Carbon copy of the letter in Trueheart family papers.
3. Winters, *Year of the Hare*, 42.
4. WCT oral history (LBJL), 1982. Trueheart's new boss was McGeorge Bundy's older brother William, who moved over to State from a senior role at the Pentagon. Bill Trueheart and Bill Bundy had been classmates at Yale.
5. WCT oral history (LBJL), 1982.
6. Kattenburg, *The Vietnam Trauma*, 129–30. Kattenburg himself, in a footnote to this passage, says he regrets not doing so himself, "however little fuss my resignation would have made."
7. George Bogardus oral history (ADST), 10 April 1996.
8. Norman Hannah, *The Key to Failure: Laos and the Vietnam War* (Madison Books, 1987), 92.
9. WCT oral history (ADST), 1989.
10. FEN to Amory Houghton 2 April 1964, Nolting Papers, UVA.
11. FEN to Dean Rusk 18 March 1964 and 24 September 1964, Nolting Papers, UVA.
12. FEN oral history (JFKL), 7 May 1970.
13. FEN to Marguerite Higgins 13 May 1965, Nolting Papers, UVA.
14. FEN to Paul D. Harkins, (undated 1964), Nolting Papers UVA.
15. Bittie Nolting, interview by author, 27 May 2018.
16. FEN to Cyrus Sulzberger 12 July 1966, Nolting Papers, UVA.

17. Lindsay Nolting read me this letter from her files during a conversation on 2 July 2020.
18. Nolting Papers, UVA.
19. Pham Xuan An's story is told by Larry Berman in *Perfect Spy*.
20. FEN to the author, 29 May 1969, Trueheart family papers.
21. Charles Trueheart, *Kyrie: Letters to a Friend* (Boston: Houghton Mifflin, 1971), 199.
22. Henry Cabot Lodge to the author, 3 June 1969, Trueheart family papers.
23. FEN to the Very Rev. Sturgis Riddle, 22 January 1969, Nolting Papers, UVA. .
24. Subsequent editions of the book, as editors strained for compression, omitted this passage.
25. Edward Mulcahy oral history (ASDT), 23 March 1989.
26. WCT oral history (ADST), 1989.
27. Howard Walker oral history (ADST), 14 November 2001.
28. Edward Mulcahy oral history (ADST), 1989.
29. Howard Walker, interview by author, 17 September 2020.
30. Mulcahy oral history (ADST), 1989; *Maysville Ledger Independent* clipping in Trueheart family papers.
31. Shirley Boskey to unknown, Trueheart family papers.
32. *Richmond Times-Dispatch,* 25 April 1976.
33. FEN to Rudy Abramson 25 January 1984, Nolting Papers, UVA.
34. Suzanne Coffman, interview by author, 27 August 2020.
35. WCT oral history (LBJL), 1982.
36. All quotes from WCT oral history (LBJL).

SELECTED BIBLIOGRAPHY

The following books, articles, films, and broadcasts were consulted in reconstructing events covered in this narrative:

Abramson, Rudy. *Spanning the Century: The Life of W. Averell Harriman, 1891–1986*. New York: William Morrow, 1992.

Ahern, Thomas L., Jr. *Vietnam Declassified: The CIA and Counterinsurgency*. Lexington: University Press of Kentucky, 2009.

Anderson, Scott. *The Quiet Americans: Four CIA Spies at the Dawn of the Cold War*. New York: Doubleday, 2020.

Arbuckle, Les. *Saigon Kids: An American Military Brat Comes of Age in 1960s Vietnam*. Coral Gables, FL: Mango Publishing Group, 2017.

Atlas, Steve. *LBJ's War*. Episode 1: "The Churchill of Asia." PBS, 2017.

Ball, George W. *The Past Has Another Pattern: Memoirs*. New York: Norton, 1982

Bass, Gary J. *The Blood Telegram: Nixon, Kissinger, and a Forgotten Genocide*. New York: Vintage, 2014.

Berman, Larry. *No Peace, No Honor: Nixon, Kissinger, and Betrayal in Vietnam*. New York: Free Press, 2009.

———. *Perfect Spy: The Incredible Double Life of Pham Xuan An*. New York: HarperCollins, 2007.

Blair, Anne. *Lodge in Vietnam: A Patriot Abroad*. New Haven, CT: Yale University Press, 1995.

Boot, Max. *The Road Not Taken: Edward Lansdale and the American Tragedy in Vietnam*. New York: Liveright, 2018.

Bowles, Chester. *Promises to Keep: My Years in Public Life, 1941–1963*. New York: Harper and Row, 1971.

Branch, Taylor. *Pillar of Fire: America in the King Years*. Vol. 2: *1963–65*. New York: Simon and Schuster, 2007.

Browne, Malcolm. *Muddy Boots and Red Socks: A Reporter's Life*. New York: Times Books, 1993.

Buttinger, Joseph. *Vietnam: A Dragon Embattled*. New York: Praeger, 1997.

Caro, Robert A. *The Years of Lyndon Johnson*. Vol. 4: *The Passage of Power*. New York: Knopf, 2012.

Cabrera, Tiffany Hamelin, "Dying for Peace: Self-Immolation during the Vietnam War 1963–1972." PhD diss., Howard University, 2014.

Carver, George A. "The Real Revolution in South Vietnam." *Foreign Affairs,* April 1975.

Catton, Philip E. *Diem's Final Failure: Prelude to America's War in Vietnam.* Lawrence: University Press of Kansas, 2002.

Charlton, Michael, and Anthony Moncrieff. *Many Reasons Why: The American Involvement in Vietnam.* New York: Hill and Wang, 1978.

Colby, Carl. *The Man Nobody Knew.* Documentary film. 2011.

Colby, William. *Honorable Men: My Life in the CIA.* New York: Simon and Schuster, 1978

———. *Lost Victory: A Firsthand Account of America's Sixteen-Year Involvement in Vietnam.* Chicago: Contemporary Books, 1989.

Cooper, Chester. *The Lost Crusade: America in Vietnam.* New York: Dodd, Mead, 1970.

Dallek, Robert. *Flawed Giant: Lyndon Johnson and His Times, 1961–1973.* New York: Oxford University Press, 1998.

Demery, Monique Brinson. *Finding the Dragon Lady: The Mystery of Vietnam's Madame Nhu.* New York: Public Affairs, 2013.

Di Leo, David L. *George Ball, Vietnam, and the Rethinking of Containment.* Chapel Hill: University of North Carolina Press, 1991.

Diem, Bui. *In the Jaws of History.* Bloomington: Indiana University Press, 1999.

Don, Tran Van. *Our Endless War: Inside Vietnam.* San Rafael, CA: Presidio, 1978.

Fall, Bernard B. *Street without Joy.* Mechanicsburg, Pa.: Stackpole, 1961

———. *Vietnam Witness: 1953–66.* New York: Praeger, 1966.

FitzGerald, Frances. *Fire in the Lake: The Vietnamese and the Americans in Vietnam.* Boston: Little, Brown, 1972.

Frankum, Ronald Bruce, Jr. *Vietnam's Year of the Rat: Elbridge Durbrow, Ngo Dinh Diem, and the Turn in U.S. Relations, 1959–1961.* Jefferson, NC: McFarland, 2014.

Galbraith, John Kenneth. *Ambassador's Journal.* Boston: Houghton Mifflin, 1969.

———. *A Life in Our Times.* Boston: Houghton Mifflin, 1981.

Gibbons, William Conrad. *The US Government and the Vietnam War: Executive and Legislative Roles and Relationships.* Part II: 1961–1964. Princeton, NJ: Princeton University Press, 1986.

Goldstein, Gordon M. *Lessons in Disaster: McGeorge Bundy and the Path to War in Vietnam.* New York: Times Books, 2008.

Grant, Zalin. *Facing the Phoenix: The CIA and the Political Defeat of the United States in Vietnam.* New York: Norton, 1991.

Greene, Graham. *The Quiet American.* London: William Heinemann, 1955.

Halberstam, David. *The Best and the Brightest.* New York: Random House, 1972

———. *The Making of a Quagmire.* New York: Random House, 1965

———. "Return to Vietnam." *Harper's,* December 1967.

Hammer, Ellen J. *A Death in November: America in Vietnam, 1963.* New York: Dutton, 1987.

Hanna, Sandy. *The Ignorance of Bliss: An American Kid in Saigon.* New York: Post Hill, 2019.

Hannah, Norman B. *The Key to Failure: Laos and the Vietnam War.* Madison Books, 1987.

Hastings, Max. *Vietnam: An Epic Tragedy 1945–1975.* New York: Harper, 2018.

Helsing, Jeffrey W. *Johnson's War/Johnson's Great Society: The Guns and Butter Trap.* Santa Barbara, CA: Praeger, 2000.

Herken, Gregg. *The Georgetown Set: Friends and Rivals in Cold War Washington.* New York: Vintage, 2015.

Herring, George C. *America's Longest War: The United States and Vietnam, 1950–1975.* New York: McGraw-Hill, 2002.

Hersh, Seymour M. *The Dark Side of Camelot.* Boston: Little, Brown, 1997.

Higgins, Marguerite. *Our Vietnam Nightmare.* New York: Harper & Row, 1965.

Hilsman, Roger. *To Move a Nation: The Politics of Foreign Policy in the Administration of John F. Kennedy.* Garden City, NY: Doubleday, 1967.

Holbrooke, Richard. "Carpe Diem." *New Republic,* December 1987.

Hovis, Bobbi. *Station Hospital Saigon: A Navy Nurse in Vietnam, 1963–1964.* Annapolis, MD: Naval Institute Press, 1992.

Jacobs, Seth. *Cold War Mandarin: Ngo Dinh Diem and the Origins of America's War in Vietnam, 1950–1963.* Lanham, MD: Rowman & Littlefield, 2006.

Jones, Howard. *Death of a Generation: How the Assassinations of Diem and JFK Prolonged the Vietnam War.* New York: Oxford University Press, 2003.

Kahin, George McT. *Intervention: How America Became Involved in Vietnam.* New York: Anchor, 1986.

Kaiser, David. *American Tragedy: Kennedy, Johnson, and the Origins of the Vietnam War.* Cambridge, MA: Belknap Press at Harvard University Press, 2000.

Karnow, Stanley. *Vietnam: A History.* New York: Viking, 1983.

Kattenburg, Paul M. *The Vietnam Trauma in American Foreign Policy, 1945–75.* New Brunswick, NJ: Transaction, 1980.

Keever, Beverly Deepe. *Death Zones and Darling Spies: Seven Years of Vietnam War Reporting.* Lincoln: University Press of Nebraska, 2013.

Kinzer, Steven. *All the Shah's Men: An American Coup and the Roots of Middle East Terror.* Hoboken, NJ: Wiley, 2008,

Langguth, A. J. *Our Vietnam: The War 1954–1975.* New York: Simon and Schuster, 2000.

Lederer, William J., and Eugene Burdick. *The Ugly American.* New York: Norton, 1958.

Lodge, Emily. *The Lodge Women, Their Men and Their Times.* Privately published, 2013.

Lodge, Henry Cabot. *As It Was: An Inside View of Politics and Power in the '50s and '60s.* New York: Norton, 1976.

———. *The Storm Has Many Eyes: A Personal Narrative.* New York: Norton, 1973.

Logevall, Fredrik. *Choosing War: The Lost Chance for Peace and the Escalation of War in Vietnam.* Berkeley: University of California Press, 1999.

———. *Embers of War: The Fall of an Empire and the Making of America's Vietnam.* New York: Random House, 2012.

———. *JFK.* Vol. 1: *Coming of Age in the American Century, 1917–1956.* New York: Random House, 2020.

Maneli, Mieczysław. *War of the Vanquished.* New York: Harper & Row, 1971.

Mann, Robert. *A Grand Delusion: America's Descent into Vietnam.* New York: Basic, 2001.

McCarry, Charles. *The Tears of Autumn.* Woodstock, NY: Overlook, 1974.

McLaughlin, Sean. *JFK and de Gaulle: How America and France Failed in Vietnam, 1961–1963.* Lexington: University Press of Kentucky, 2019.

McMaster, H. R. *Dereliction of Duty: Lyndon Johnson, Robert McNamara, the Joint Chiefs of Staff, and the Lies That Led to Vietnam.* New York: Harper Perennial, 1997.

McNamara, Robert S. *In Retrospect: The Tragedy and Lessons of Vietnam*. New York: Times Books, 1995.

Mecklin, John. *Mission in Torment: An Intimate Account of the US Role in Vietnam*. Garden City, NY: Doubleday, 1965.

Miller, Edward. *Misalliance: Ngo Dinh Diem, the United States, and the Fate of South Vietnam*. Cambridge, MA: Harvard University Press, 2013.

———. "Religious Revival and the Politics of Nation Building: Reinterpreting the 1963 'Buddhist Crisis' in South Vietnam." *Modern Asian Studies* 49, no. 6 (August 2014): 1–60.

Miller, Robert Hopkins. *The United States and Vietnam 1787–1941*. Washington, DC: National Defense University Press, 1990.

———. *Vietnam and Beyond: A Diplomat's Cold War Education*. Lubbock: Texas Tech University Press, 2002.

Miller, William J. *Henry Cabot Lodge: A Biography*. New York: Heineman, 1967.

Milne, David. *America's Rasputin: Walt Rostow and the Vietnam War*. New York: Hill and Wang, 2008.

Morgan, Ted. *Valley of Death: The Tragedy at Dien Bien Phu That Led into the Vietnam War*. New York: Random House, 2010.

Moyar, Mark. *Triumph Forsaken: The Vietnam War, 1954–1965*. New York: Cambridge University Press, 2006.

Nach, James. "A History of the US Consulate Saigon 1889–1950." Unpublished manuscript.

Newman, John M. *JFK in Vietnam: Deception, Intrigue, and the Struggle for Power*. New York: Warner Books, 1992.

Nguyen, Viet Thanh. *Nothing Ever Dies: Vietnam and the Memory of War*. Cambridge, MA: Harvard University Press, 2016.

Nichter, Luke A. *The Last Brahmin: Henry Cabot Lodge Jr. and the Making of the Cold War*. New Haven, CT: Yale University Press, 2020.

Nolting, Frederick. *From Trust to Tragedy: The Political Memoirs of Frederick Nolting, Kennedy's Ambassador to Diem's Vietnam*. New York: Praeger, 1988.

Olson, Gregory. *Mansfield in Vietnam: A Study in Rhetorical Adaptation*. East Lansing: Michigan State University Press, 1995.

Packer, George. *Our Man: Richard Holbrooke and the End of the American Century*. New York: Knopf, 2019.

Phillips, Rufus. *Why Vietnam Matters: An Eyewitness Account of Lessons Not Learned*. Annapolis, MD: Naval Institute Press, 2008.

Powers, Thomas. *The Man Who Kept the Secrets: Richard Helms and the CIA*. New York: Knopf, 1979.

Prochnau, William. *Once upon a Distant War: David Halberstam, Neil Sheehan, Peter Arnett—Young War Correspondents and Their Early Vietnam Battles*. New York: Vintage, 1995.

Reeves, Richard. *President Kennedy: Profile of Power*. New York: Simon and Schuster, 1993.

Reeves, Thomas C. *A Question of Character: A Life of John F. Kennedy*. New York: Free Press, 1991.

Richardson, John H. *My Father the Spy: An Investigative Memoir*. New York: Harper Perennial, 2005.

Rust, William J. "No Boy Scout: Lucien Conein and Intelligence Agencies." Unpublished manuscript.

Rust, William J., and the Editors of US News Books. *Kennedy in Vietnam.* New York: Charles Scribner's Sons, 1985.

Schlesinger, Arthur M., Jr. *Robert Kennedy and His Times.* New York: Knopf, 1978.

———. *A Thousand Days: John F. Kennedy in the White House.* Boston: Houghton Mifflin, 1965.

———. *The Bitter Heritage: Vietnam and American Democracy 1941–1966.* Boston: Houghton Mifflin, 1967.

Schulzinger, Robert D. *A Time for War.* New York: Oxford University Press, 1997.

Selverstone, Marc J. *The Kennedy Withdrawal: Camelot and the American Commitment to Vietnam.* Cambridge, MA: Harvard University Press, 2022.

Shaw, Geoffrey. *Lost Mandate of Heaven: The American Betrayal of Ngo Dinh Diem, President of Vietnam.* San Francisco: Ignatius, 2015.

Sheehan, Neil. *A Bright Shining Lie: John Paul Vann and America in Vietnam.* New York: Random House, 1988.

———. CSPAN interview. 17 October 1988.

Sorensen, Theodore. *Kennedy.* New York: Harper & Row, 1975.

Taylor, Maxwell. *Swords and Plowshares.* New York: Norton, 1972.

Thomas, Evan. *Robert Kennedy: His Life.* New York: Simon and Schuster, 1992.

———. *The Very Best Men: Four Who Dared: The Early Years of the CIA.* New York: Simon and Schuster, 1995.

Thomas, Evan, and Walter Isaacson. *The Wise Men: Six Friends and the World They Made.* New York: Simon and Schuster, 1986.

Thompson, Jenny, and Sherry Thompson. *The Kremlinologist: Llewellyn E. Thompson, America's Man in Cold War Moscow.* Baltimore, MD: Johns Hopkins University Press, 2018.

Thompson, Kenneth W., ed. *Diplomacy, Administration, and Policy: The Ideas and Careers of Frederick E. Nolting, Jr., Frederick C. Mosher, and Paul T. David.* Lanham, MD: University Press of America, 1995.

Thompson, (Sir) Robert. *Make for the Hills: Memories of Far Eastern Wars.* London: Leo Cooper, 1989.

Thomson, James C. Jr. "The Effectiveness Trap." *Atlantic,* April 1968.

———. "Getting Out and Speaking Out." *Foreign Policy,* Winter 1973–74.

Tuchman, Barbara. *The March of Folly: From Troy to Vietnam.* New York: Random House, 1995.

VanDeMark, Brian. *Road to Disaster: A New History of America's Descent into Vietnam.* New York: Custom House, 2018.

Ward, Geoffrey C., and Ken Burns. *The Vietnam War: An Intimate History.* New York: Vintage, 2017.

Warner, Denis. *The Last Confucian.* New York: Penguin, 1964.

Weiner, Tim. *Legacy of Ashes: The History of the CIA.* New York: Anchor, 2008.

West, Morris L. *The Ambassador.* New York: Bantam, 1965.

Winters, Francis X. *The Year of the Hare: America in Vietnam, January 25, 1963–February 15, 1964.* Athens: University of Georgia Press, 1999.

INDEX

Miller Center Studies on the Presidency

Year Zero: The Five-Year Presidency
CHRISTOPHER P. LIDDELL

*The Presidency and the American State: Leadership and Decision Making
in the Adams, Grant, and Taft Administrations*
STEPHEN J. ROCKWELL

Mourning the Presidents: Loss and Legacy in American Culture
LINDSAY M. CHERVINSKY AND MATTHEW R. COSTELLO, EDITORS

The Peaceful Transfer of Power: An Oral History of America's Presidential Transitions
DAVID MARCHICK AND ALEXANDER TIPPETT, WITH A. J. WILSON

Averting Doomsday: Arms Control during the Nixon Presidency
PATRICK J. GARRITY AND ERIN R. MAHAN

The Presidency: Facing Constitutional Crossroads
MICHAEL NELSON AND BARBARA A. PERRY, EDITORS

Trump: The First Two Years
MICHAEL NELSON

Broken Government: Bridging the Partisan Divide
WILLIAM J. ANTHOLIS AND LARRY J. SABATO, EDITORS

Race: The American Cauldron
DOUGLAS A. BLACKMON, EDITOR

Communication: Getting the Message Across
NICOLE HEMMER, EDITOR

American Dreams: Opportunity and Upward Mobility
GUIAN MCKEE AND CRISTINA LOPEZ-GOTTARDI CHAO, EDITORS

Immigration: Struggling over Borders
SIDNEY M. MILKIS AND DAVID LEBLANG, EDITORS